THEORETICAL FOUNDATIONS OF LAW AND ECONOMICS

The economic approach to law, or "law and economics," is by far the most successful application of basic economic principles to another scholarly field, but most of the critical appraisal of the field has been scattered among law reviews and economics journals. *Theoretical Foundations of Law and Economics* is the first original, book-length examination of the methodology and philosophy of law and economics, featuring new essays written by leading legal scholars, philosophers, and economists. The contributors take issue with many of the key tenets of the economic approach to law, such as its assumption of rational behavior, its reliance on market analogies, and its adoption of efficiency as the primary goal of legal decision making. They discuss the relevance of economics to the law in general, as well as to substantive areas of the law, such as contracts, torts, and crime.

Mark D. White is an associate professor in the Department of Political Science, Economics, and Philosophy at the College of Staten Island/City University of New York (CUNY), where he teaches courses in the intersections of economics, philosophy, and law. He is also on the economics faculty of the CUNY Graduate Center. Previously, he taught at Miami University Hamilton and the University of Cincinnati.

His other edited books include *Economics and the Mind* (with Barbara Montero, 2007), *The Thief of Time: Philosophical Perspectives on Procrastination* (with Chrisoula Andreou, forthcoming), *Batman and Philosophy* (with Robert Arp, 2008), and *Watchmen and Philosophy* (2009). He is associate editor of the *Forum for Social Economics*, serves on the editorial board of *Ethique et Economique/Ethics and Economics*, and is editing a special issue of the *Review of Social Economy* on ethics and economics (due 2009).

He has published articles in *Southern Economic Journal, Eastern Economic Journal, Economics Letters, Economics Bulletin, Journal of Economic Behavior and Organization, European Journal of Political Economy, International Economic Journal, Journal of Economic Methodology, Review of Social Economy, Review of Political Economy, Forum for Social Economics, Journal of Socio-Economics,* and *Journal of Private Enterprise*. He also has published book chapters in volumes devoted to law and economics, ethics and economics, and social economics, as well as numerous volumes in the Blackwell Philosophy and Pop Culture series.

White is active in organizing conference sessions for such organizations as the Eastern Economic Association, the Association for Social Economics, the International Network for Economic Method, the History of Economics Society, and the Society for the Development of Austrian Economics. He has been a member of the organizing committee for the Eastern Economic Association annual meetings since 2003 and was a founding member of the program committee for the Eastern Study Group of the North American Kant Society (on which he served from 2004 to 2008). He also regularly presents papers at scholarly conferences.

Theoretical Foundations of Law and Economics

Edited by

Mark D. White

College of Staten Island/City University of New York

CAMBRIDGE UNIVERSITY PRESS

CAMBRIDGE UNIVERSITY PRESS
Cambridge, New York, Melbourne, Madrid, Cape Town, Singapore,
São Paulo, Delhi, Dubai, Tokyo, Mexico City

Cambridge University Press
The Edinburgh Building, Cambridge CB2 8RU, UK

Published in the United States of America by
Cambridge University Press, New York

www.cambridge.org
Information on this title: www.cambridge.org/9780521889551

First published 2009

A catalogue record for this publication is available from the British Library

Library of Congress Cataloguing in Publication Data

Theoretical foundations of law and economics / Mark D.White.
    p.   cm.
Includes bibliographical references and index.
ISBN 978-0-521-88955-1 (hardback)
1. Law and economics.   I.White, Mark D., 1971–
K487.E3T454   2009
340'.11   dc22   2008027711

ISBN 978-0-521-88955-1 Hardback

To the memory of Anne White, beloved grandmother and friend.

Contents

Foreword

RICHARD A. EPSTEIN

THE TWO SIDES OF SOCIAL SCIENTISTS

Social scientists of all stripes – and for these purposes I award lawyers their hard-earned stripes – face a peculiar personal challenge. How do they reconcile the way they think with the way they live? On the one hand, everyday observation suggests that in the course of a given day, people from all walks of life, social scientists included, make thousands of decisions both large and small, and routinely seem to experience little anxiety before and no regret after the process. Indeed, a moment's reflection indicates how hard it would be to live a happy and productive life if faced with constant torment over these nonstop routine matters. The results of these commonplace actions are, of course, not uniform. For small repetitive events, most people do pretty well, most of the time.

The basic picture is not always so cheery. When the choices become larger and the need for fresh and full information more insistent, two things happen. Most ordinary people will reflexively invest more to get information before making decisions, only to discover in retrospect that the decisions they make frequently turn out less well than they had hoped. But these reversals, as the expression goes, "have to be taken in stride," because there is no decision protocol or magic potion that relieves people from the burdens of risk and uncertainty, either on an individual or on the collective level. People try to learn from their mistakes, and they sometimes do. But often they make other mistakes in the future precisely because they spend too much time fighting the last war. And too much caution can lead to paralysis. The best anyone can do is to minimize the severity of any erroneous decision conditional on the level of uncertainty and decision-making costs. No one, acting in either a private or a public capacity, is able to eliminate decision errors, and no one should devote excessive energy to what can turn out to be a futile or even counterproductive quest.

And yet ordinary people must be doing something right "to last two hundred years," as was said in Robert Altman's *Nashville*. Look back even one hundred years, and things are unambiguously better today than they were then, both in the level of resources at our disposal and in the moral attitudes (at least in most western-style democracies). Whatever mishaps take place in decision making at the individual and collective levels cannot negate the powerful, if simple-minded, conclusion that in the grand scheme of things the negative consequences of wrong decisions are outweighed by the positive consequences of correct ones. The former decisions may receive most of the attention, as failures typically do, but that large base of success builds the material and moral capital that allows progress to take place. There is, as it were, in academic work a kind of selection bias that lays much stress on the failures and far less on the successes.

By and large social scientists – lawyers still included – do not find themselves paralyzed by the full range of theoretical difficulties that beset decision making by rational (a loaded word) agents. But notwithstanding their comparative success (as judged by income and achievement), they are drawn as moths to flames to examine the obstacles that block the path of sound decisions in all walks of life. And this set of essays is directed to various ways of addressing the major theoretical and practical problems that have to be faced in dealing with decision making. The stakes in the issues addressed in this work are enormous.

We can make with confidence two general statements about our public, business, and personal institutions. The first is wonderment at how they manage to function at all. The second is the evident truth that in spite of their disabilities they do manage to function. We can think of society as a piston engine, which produces a lot of energy, most of which is dissipated in heat, with just enough useful output to propel the vehicle forward. On this model, social output can double by increasing the efficiency of the engine from 20 to 40 percent, even though in both states of the world we waste more than we use. Knowing this, our collective ability to point out systemic errors may look to generate only smallish gains. But if we can wring, collectively and individually, another 5-percentage-point improvement that takes us from, say, 20 to 25 percent, then we can increase social output by 25 percent. The further we move up the cycle, the smaller the percentage increase from any new increment of gain.

For the foreseeable future, this form of invisible social leverage may promise major gains. But, as in all systems, leverage works in both directions. Let the wrong set of procedures be adopted, and a 5-percentage-point loss in overall output could reduce the efficiency of our social piston engine from 20 to 15 percent, for a perceived 25-percent loss in efficiency. The stakes then are enormous.

THE PROGRAM OF THIS BOOK: SOCIAL DECISION FROM THEORY TO PRACTICE

In one way or another each of these chapters seeks to address some of the fundamental questions that stand in the path of sound decisions. Many of the chapters in this volume start with the most fundamental of questions: what social criterion or criteria should be used to judge the success or failure of any decision? The choice of the singular "criterion" versus the plural "criteria" opens up a can of worms, which is thoughtfully addressed by William A. Edmundson in his chapter, "Pluralism, Intransitivity, Incoherence," which grapples with this dilemma. A monist criterion gives a unique metric for making a decision, but it excludes the richness and diversity that plural criteria can supply at the cost, of course, of some incoherence. Which are we to choose? We are left to ponder.

Asking this question leads to others, such as to what extent within a plural world we rely on slimmed-down conceptions of utility to resolve all questions within an economic framework, as has been powerfully argued by Louis Kaplow and Steven Shavell in their controversial book, *Fairness versus Welfare* (2002). In this volume, this question is tackled in at least two different ways. The first asks whether there is sufficient internal coherence in the economic tests themselves. In his chapter, "Bounded Rationality and Legal Scholarship," Matthew D. Adler examines the difficulties in figuring out within this tradition the correct form of rational decision making by individuals who have rational expectations but not the capability to implement confidently the kind of welfarist criterion proposed by Kaplow and Shavell.

Sometimes the theoretical attacks on welfarist models cut deeper. David Ellerman's "Numeraire Illusion: The Final Demise of the Kaldor–Hicks Principle" takes the strong position that the measurement errors within standard economics render largely unintelligible the Kaldor–Hicks principle, which holds, of course, that a change in social rules counts as a social improvement if the winner under the changes can fully compensate the losers and still be left better off in the bargain.

In addition to those examinations of decision-making theory that operate within the economic tradition, other critiques seek to limit what might be termed their imperial ambitions. Mark Tunick, in his chapter "Efficiency, Practices, and the Moral Point of View: Limits of Economic Interpretations of Law," raises some general objections to the constraints that a given notion of fairness should properly place on any efficiency notion of social welfare. Writing in a similar vein, Sarah Holtman, in her chapter "Justice, Mercy, and Efficiency," asks the further questions of how institutions of mercy and forgiveness can exist side by side with justice and how this combination bears on the efficient operation of our other social institutions. The relationship between the normative and positive accounts is further explored by Horacio Spector in his chapter "Legal Fictionalism and the Economics of Normativity," which pushes hard on the distinction between simple coercion by a powerful force and legitimate coercion used within the framework of a sound set of political institutions. In their chapter, "Functional Law and Economics," Jonathan Klick and Francesco Parisi further pursue the effort to integrate the normative with the positive from a public choice perspective that examines how legislation, adjudication, and private markets can promote sound institutional structures that facilitate individual decision making. Lewis A. Kornhauser picks up a similar theme in his chapter on "Modeling Courts," by asking what count as sound models of judicial behavior, taking into account the complex interplay between large policy judgments on the one hand and particular case decisions on the other.

The question of understanding the complexities of decision making must also be addressed in a somewhat narrower context that looks at the operation of legal rules and legal analysis in particular contexts. Michael B. Dorff and Kimberly Kessler Ferzan take a broad look at several areas of law – baby-selling, racial discrimination, and insider trading – whose thesis is well summarized in their title: "Is There a Method to the Madness? Why Creative and Counterintuitive Proposals Are Counterproductive." Peter H. Huang tackles the perceptions of economic analysis on the part of noneconomic lawyers and laypersons, based on visceral affect and varying mathematical expertise, in his chapter, "Emotional Reactions to Law and Economics, Market Metaphors, and Rationality Rhetoric."

The influence of cost–benefit arguments also weaves its way through the other chapters in this volume that concentrate on particular areas of substantive law. Guido Pincione, in his chapter "Welfare, Autonomy, and Contractual Freedom," strikes a strong libertarian chord in stressing the intimate connection among these three venerable conceptions. Brian H. Bix writes on a similar theme in "Law and Economics and Explanation in Contract Law," about the extent to which the approach that law and economics brings to ordinary conceptions of contractual justice can be squared with economic conceptions of efficiency. Mark A. Geistfeld also examines, in his chapter, "Efficiency, Fairness, and the Economic Analysis of Tort Law," the possibility of a strong reconciliation of traditional norms of fairness with the economic analysis of law. Finally, Mark D. White, the energetic organizer of this volume, poses a strong challenge to the criminal-law theories of deterrence and retribution in a world of limited resources by asking in his chapter, "Retributivism in a World of Scarcity," the simple but disarming question: is there only a right, or also a duty, of the state to punish those who have broken the law?

ONE PERSON'S BRIEF WORLDVIEW

Faced with these detailed expositions, it would be presumptuous of me in a short introduction to give my views on the many methodological and practical issues considered in such detail in this volume. But I cannot altogether resist the temptation to say a few words on behalf of my own views. The entire topic of cost–benefit analysis is driven by a sense of fatalism: however much we criticize various forms of cost–benefit analysis, we cannot live without such determinations. There is a real question how these calculations are to be made, but absent any real presentation of a comprehensive worldview that does without them, it seems best to figure out how these are best done, rather than to abandon their use in favor of political caprice or arbitrary power.

How then might this task be discharged? In this regard, it is critical to distinguish between two types of inquiries. The first is that which is appropriate in a state-of-nature setting, which seeks to set out some view of individual rights and duties in some hypothetical original condition. The second asks how to do cost–benefit analysis in the here and now.

On the initial question, it is necessary to paint with a very broad brush in order to design human institutions to take into account one imperative from which no one can escape: the power of individual (and familial) self-interest in a world of scarcity. I have little doubt that in working on this large canvas there is much to be said for making the judgments that have long animated the defenders of limited government (Locke, Hume, Smith, Madison, Mill, Hayek, and Friedman, to name a few) that see these essential elements in the overall system. A strong sense of individual autonomy that resists the collective ownership of individual talents and abilities; the creation of easy rules that allow for the creation of private ownership in otherwise unowned land and objects, which is usually done through a system of first possession; the protection of these entitlements against force and fraud, but not against competition; and a recognition of the limitations inherent in this system because of several consistent problems of market failure – the premature exhaustion of common goods resources, the need to create social infrastructure funded by tax revenues, and some legal rules to address monopolization and cartelization. The risks of excessive government power, however, argue for the creation of separate powers that are able to check the operation of each other. The exact details of these systems are beyond the scope of this foreword, but their simple enumeration explains why such fields as property, contract, tort, and restitution dominate the private law, and matters of government structure and the protection of individual rights dominate our constitutional thinking. The goal here is to pick a few tasks to be done well, and to avoid more ambitious schemes that end in failure. A global cost–benefit analysis shows how each of these departures from a state of nature is likely to improve human welfare.

There is, of course, a profound sense in which these large questions have already been put to rest one way or the other, so that cost–benefit analysis in the modern setting has to do with the design of public highway systems that must address at the micro level such mundane questions as where roads should be located and how traffic should be governed by line markers, traffic lights, and stop signs. Similarly, countless judgments have to be made as to what drugs or chemicals should be allowed on the market, with what kinds of warnings, and subject to what kinds of liability. These questions are manifestly not amenable to the big-think approach that dominates state-of-nature theory. But for them two kinds of general guideposts seem appropriate. The first of these is to try to privatize as many of the cost–benefit decisions as possible. A tort law (like a sporting contest) that judges individuals by the outcomes of their behavior will do better than one that seeks to make a collective, and retrospective, cost–benefit analysis of their choice. That is why we ask only whether the ball was hit fair or foul, ignoring all questions of inputs. And in those cases where collective choices have to be made, as with the location of an airport, the proper approach is to ask individuals to compare alternative proposals *at the margin*, in the effort to see what kinds of trade-offs are likely to produce positive or negative social effects. The more focused the inquiry, the better the outcome is likely to be. In general, a sensible system of collective cost–benefit analyses should steer us away from ambitious and utopian objectives, most of which will fail. Regimes of positive rights (good against the state and funded by tax revenues) are likely to come up short whether we deal with agriculture, housing, or health care. Our collective tools are limited, and so too should be our collective ambitions. After reading these chapters, the reader has to decide whether this brief philosophical outlook is welcome realism – or unwarranted pessimism.

Preface

MARK D. WHITE

It has long been my opinion that advocates of the economic approach to law – with the notable exception of Richard Posner – have been almost entirely unreflective on the methodological foundations of their field and the philosophical commitments implied thereby. (To be fair, this is true of most economists overall, but I think they ought to be especially careful when playing in someone else's sandbox.) This shortcoming was all too well evidenced by the critical drumming taken by Louis Kaplow and Steven Shavell's 2002 book, *Fairness versus Welfare*, which was the subject of dozens of published essays by legal scholars, including almost all of the contributors to this book, many of whom address it in their chapters as well. While law-and-economics scholars continue to employ the same tools, rusty and outdated though some of them may be – the tools, not the scholars! – it seems to fall to legal, moral, and political philosophers (and a few vagabond economists) to recommend improvements, refinements, and occasionally abandonment of the toolbox. The chapters in this volume offer a contribution to this effort, and if they inspire others to take up the cause, so much the better.

I would like to express my appreciation for the support and encouragement of John Berger and Cambridge University Press, who helped immeasurably in making this collection a reality. I also want to thank Roger Backhouse (International Network for Economic Methodology) and Mary Lesser (Eastern Economic Association), who graciously hosted conference sessions in which several of the contributors presented their work. Finally, my most heartfelt gratitude is owed to all of the fine scholars involved in this book, who made my job as editor a most rewarding and painless one.

Notes on Contributors

Matthew D. Adler is Leon Meltzer Professor of Law at the University of Pennsylvania Law School. His work lies at the intersection of law-and-economics and law-and-philosophy, and focuses on constitutional law, administrative law, regulation, and policy analysis. Since his appointment to the Penn faculty in 1995, Adler has published almost fifty articles or shorter scholarly works, including publications in the *Harvard, Yale, Duke, Michigan, Minnesota, Northwestern, NYU, Virginia,* and *University of Pennsylvania Law Reviews; Supreme Court Review; Journal of Legal Studies;* and *Legal Theory,* as well as his recent book coauthored with Eric Posner, *New Foundations of Cost–Benefit Analysis* (2006). He is the author of the forthcoming *Social Welfare, Lifetime Well-Being, and Equity: A Framework for Policy Analysis* (2010) and coeditor of *The Rule of Recognition and the U.S. Constitution* (2009).

Brian H. Bix is the Frederick W. Thomas Professor of Law and Philosophy at the University of Minnesota. He holds a J.D. degree from Harvard University and a doctorate from Balliol College, Oxford University. His publications include *Jurisprudence: Theory and Context* (4th ed., 2006); *A Dictionary of Legal Theory* (2004); and *Law, Language, and Legal Determinacy* (1993). He writes and teaches in the areas of jurisprudence, contract law, and family law.

Michael B. Dorff is the associate dean for research and a professor of law at Southwestern Law School. He has also taught at UCLA School of Law and Rutgers Law School. He earned his A.B. from Harvard College and his J.D. from Harvard Law School (*magna cum laude*). He writes primarily in corporate law, behavioral economics, and the philosophy of law and economics, and his publications in those areas include "The Group Dynamics Theory of Executive Compensation" (*Cardozo Law Review,* 2007), "Does One Hand Wash the Other: Testing the Managerial Power and Optimal Contracting Theories of Executive Compensation" (*Journal of Corporation Law,* 2005), and "Why Welfare Depends on Fairness: A Reply to Kaplow and Shavell" (*Southern California Law Review,* 2002). He has taught contracts, business associations, corporate mergers and acquisitions, and securities regulation.

William A. Edmundson, professor of law and of philosophy at Georgia State University, is the author of *Three Anarchical Fallacies* (Cambridge, 1998) and a general editor of *Cambridge Introductions to Philosophy and Law.*

David Ellerman has retired from academic teaching and work in the World Bank and is now a visiting scholar at the University of California in Riverside. His research is largely in the theory of property rights, democratic theory, development theory, and the foundations of mathematics. Recent articles in these fields include "The Market Mechanism of Appropriation" (*Journal des Economistes et des Etudes Humaines*, 2004), "*Translatio* versus *Concessio*: Retrieving the Debate about Contracts of Alienation with an Application to Today's Employment Contract" (*Politics and Society*, 2005), "Helping Self-Help: The Fundamental Conundrum of Development Assistance" (*Journal of Socio-Economics*, 2007), and "Counting Distinctions: On the Conceptual Foundations of Shannon's Information Theory" (*Synthese*, 2008). His most recent books are *Property and Contract in Economics* (1992); *Intellectual Trespassing as a Way of Life: Essays in Philosophy, Economics, and Mathematics* (1995); and *Helping People Help Themselves: From the World Bank to an Alternative Philosophy of Development Assistance* (2005).

Richard A. Epstein is the James Parker Hall Distinguished Service Professor of Law at the University of Chicago, where he has taught since 1972. He has also been the Peter and Kirstin Senior Fellow at the Hoover Institution since 2000 and a visiting law professor at New York University Law School since 2007. Prior to joining the University of Chicago Law School faculty, he taught law at the University of Southern California from 1968 to 1972. He served as editor of the *Journal of Legal Studies* from 1981 to 1991 and of the *Journal of Law and Economics* from 1991 to 2001. At present he is a director of the John M. Olin Program in Law and Economics. His recent books include *Cases and Materials on Torts* (9th ed., 2008); *Supreme Neglect: How to Revive Constitutional Protection for Private Property* (2008); *Antitrust Consent Decrees in Theory and Practice: Why Less Is More* (2007); *Overdose: How Excessive Government Regulation Stifles Pharmaceutical Innovation* (2006); *How Progressives Rewrote the Constitution* (2006); and *Skepticism and Freedom: A Modern Case for Classical Liberalism* (2003). He has also written numerous articles on a wide range of legal and interdisciplinary subjects.

Kimberly Kessler Ferzan is the associate dean for faculty affairs, a professor of law, and the codirector of the Institute for Law and Philosophy at Rutgers University School of Law, Camden. Dean Ferzan is a criminal-law theorist, whose book *Criminal Law: A Culpability-Based Account* (with Larry Alexander and Stephen Morse) will be published by Cambridge. She is also a coeditor of the Criminal Law Conversations project (with Paul Robinson and Stephen Garvey), which has introduced a new Web-based peer-engaged process for the creation of a book, the content of which is enduring criminal-law issues.

Mark A. Geistfeld is the Crystal Eastman Professor of Law at New York University School of Law. Trained as both a lawyer and an economist, he has published extensively on tort law and products liability. His most recent book, *Tort Law: The Essentials* (2008), develops a rights-based understanding of tort law that critically depends on economic analysis.

Sarah Holtman is an associate professor of philosophy at the University of Minnesota, Twin Cities. She holds a J.D. from the University of Virginia and a Ph.D. in philosophy from the University of North Carolina at Chapel Hill. Holtman works mainly on issues of justice in the realms of moral, political, and legal philosophy, from a distinctly Kantian perspective. Her publications include "Kant, Ideal Theory, and the Justice of Exclusionary Zoning" (*Ethics*, 1999); "Kantian Justice and Poverty Relief" (*Kant-Studien*, 2004); and "Autonomy and the Kingdom of Ends" (*Blackwell Companion to Kant's Ethics*, forthcoming).

Peter H. Huang is the inaugural Harold E. Kohn Chair Professor of Law at Temple University's James Beasley Law School. He was a member of the School of Social Science at the Institute for Advanced Study during its psychology and economics theme during academic year 2005–06. His research specializes in emotions and law; law, happiness, and subjective well-being; behavioral law and economics; legal real options; and securities regulation. He received an A.B. from Princeton University, S.M. and Ph.D. in applied mathematics from Harvard University, and J.D. from Stanford University. His recent publications include "Diverse Conceptions of Emotions in Risk Regulation" (*University of Pennsylvania Law Review PEN-Numbra*, 2008); "Authentic Happiness and Meaning at Law Firms" (with Rick Swedloff, *Syracuse Law Review*, 2008); and "How Do Securities Laws Influence Affect, Happiness, and Trust?" (*Journal of Business and Technology Law*, 2008).

Jonathan Klick is a professor of law, business, and policy at the University of Pennsylvania. Prior to his current position, he was the Jeffrey A. Stoops Professor of Law and Economics at Florida State University, and he held visiting appointments at Northwestern University, the University of Southern California, Columbia University, and the University of Hamburg. He has published empirical and theoretical work in the *Journal of Law and Economics*; the *Journal of Law Economics and Organization*; the *Journal of Legal Studies*; and the *Journal of Economic Perspectives*, in addition to numerous other law, economics, and medical journals.

Lewis A. Kornhauser is Alfred B. Engelberg Professor of Law at New York University.

Francesco Parisi is the 2007–08 Vance K. Opperman Research Scholar and Professor of Law at the University of Minnesota Law School and a professor of economics at the University of Bologna, Department of Economics. Professor Parisi is the author of 10 books and more than 150 papers in the field of law and economics. He previously taught at George Mason University, where he served as a professor of law and the director of the Law and Economics Program and as an associate director of the J. M. Buchanan Center for Political Economy, and at the University of Milan (Statale), where he held a chair in private law from 2002 to

2006 as Professore Ordinario per Chiara Fama. Professor Parisi received his D.Jur. degree from the University of Rome "La Sapienza"; an LL.M., a J.S.D., and an M.A. degree in economics from the University of California at Berkeley; and a Ph.D. in economics from George Mason University. Professor Parisi is currently serving as editor-in-chief of the *Review of Law and Economics*, and he served as editor of the *Supreme Court Economic Review* from 2002 to 2008. He is a member of the board of editors of the *International Review of Law and Economics*, the *Journal of Public Choice*, and the *American Journal of Comparative Law*, and he serves on the board of advisers of the *Social Sciences Research Network*.

Guido Pincione is a professor of law and philosophy at the Universidad Torcuato Di Tella, Buenos Aires, and in spring 2008 was a visiting scholar at the Social Philosophy and Policy Center, Bowling Green State University. He specializes in moral and political philosophy. His most recent publication is "The Trolley Problem as a Problem for Libertarians" (*Utilitas*, 2007). He coauthored, with Fernando R. Tesón, *Rational Choice and Democratic Deliberation: A Theory of Discourse Failure* (Cambridge, 2006).

Horacio Spector earned his law degree and doctor of jurisprudence degree from the Universidad de Buenos Aires. He is professor of law and philosophy and the founding dean of the School of Law of Universidad Torcuato Di Tella, Buenos Aires. A 1992 Research Fellow with the John Simon Guggenheim Memorial Foundation, and twice Fellow of the Alexander von Humboldt Foundation, he has visited at Oxford University's Balliol College, the University of Mannheim, the University of Heidelberg, the Paul M. Hebert Law Center of Louisiana State University, the University of Toronto, the University of San Diego, and the Universidad de Alicante in Spain. Dean Spector has published two books: *Autonomy and Rights: The Moral Foundations of Liberalism* (1992/2008) and *Analytische und Postanalytische Ethik: Untersuchungen zur Theorie moralischer Urteile* (1993).

Mark Tunick teaches political theory and constitutional law at the Wilkes Honors College of Florida Atlantic University, where he is a professor of political science and an associate dean. His publications include *Practices and Principles: Approaches to Ethical and Legal Judgment* (1998) as well as articles on privacy, property rights, culture and the law, the moral obligation to obey law, and the political thought of Kant, Hegel, and Mill.

Mark D. White is an associate professor in the Department of Political Science, Economics, and Philosophy at the College of Staten Island/CUNY, and in the economics program at the CUNY Graduate Center. He teaches and writes in the intersection of economics, philosophy, and law and has authored several dozen journal articles and book chapters in these areas. His other edited books include *Economics and the Mind* (2007) with Barbara Montero and *The Thief of Time: Philosophical Essays on Procrastination* (forthcoming) with Chrisoula Andreou.

1 Modeling Courts

LEWIS A. KORNHAUSER

Models constitute a central element in the methodology of economic analysis of law. John Brown's model of accident law[1] and others' models of settlement and litigation,[2] for instance, have provided numerous insights into tort law and to civil procedure respectively. Other models have been less successful. Despite their ubiquity, however, the role of models in economic analysis of law has been little discussed. How do models explain? How, or what, do we learn from them? What explains the differential success of models? What makes a model a good one? Under what circumstances ought policymakers rely on the results of a model?

These questions are notoriously difficult, in part because the concept of a model is itself unclear. I shall address the question of what makes a "good" model by discussing in detail two narrow classes of models of adjudication that have often been understood as competitive. These classes – which I shall call, in the context of courts, *case space* (but in the more general context of administrative agencies and legislatures *fact space*) and *policy space* models – seek to explain the behavior of individual judges.

[1] John P. Brown, 1972, "Towards an Economic Theory of Liability," *Journal of Legal Studies*, 2, pp. 323–349. The intellectual history of the economic analysis of accident law would provide an alternative domain for illuminating the use of models. Two papers by Peter Diamond (1974, "Single-Activity Accidents," *Journal of Legal Studies*, 3, pp. 107–164; 1974, "Accident Law and Resource Allocation," *Bell Journal of Economics and Management Science*, 5, pp. 366–405) appeared roughly simultaneously with Brown's article. Though in many ways economically more sophisticated, Diamond's papers are less cited. A short time later, Diamond and James Mirrlees developed an alternative model of accident law (1975, "On the Assignment of Liability: The Uniform Case," *Bell Journal of Economics and Management Science*, 6, pp. 487–516).

[2] For a survey of the vast literature on settlement and litigation see Andrew Daughety, "Settlement," in Boudewijn Bouckert and Gerrit DeGeest, eds., *Encyclopedia of Law and Economics* (http://encyclo.findlaw.com/7400book.pdf), and Kathryn Spier, 2007, "Litigation," in A. Mitchell Polinsky and Steven Shavell, eds., *The Handbook of Law and Economics*, New York: Elsevier, pp. 259–342.

This research was supported by a grant from the NYU School of Law Filomen D'Agostino and Max E. Greenberg Research Fund. I thank participants in the NYU Colloquium on Law, Economics, and Politics for helpful comments. Jeffrey Lax provided comments on an earlier draft, and I have benefited from many conversations with Charles Cameron who, nonetheless, is not responsible for the views expressed here.

Models grounded in policy space abstract from the specific cases that, in actual adjudication, trigger judicial intervention and are the occasion for whatever policy-making courts do. Policy space models treat policies as fundamental and cases as nonexistent. Models grounded in case space, by contrast, take cases as fundamental; policies are described in terms of case dispositions. Policy space and case space models differ in other respects as well. First, the two classes of models identify the domain over which judges have fundamental preferences slightly differently. In policy space models, judges care exclusively about policies; policy space is the domain of preference. Some case space models adopt a similar domain of preference, but case space models are sufficiently flexible to allow a richer domain of preference that includes both policies and case dispositions. Second, in policy space models, each judge chooses a policy, but in case space, each judge also (or exclusively) endorses a disposition of the case. Finally, and particularly important for models of collegial courts, the court in policy space models again announces a policy, but in case space models the court first renders judgment in the case and may also, incidentally, announce a policy.

Policy space models dominate the literature in political science and economic analysis of law. Moreover, I shall argue that all models of collegial courts, whether starting in case space or not, rely on a common set of formal results. They offer different, but complementary, interpretations of that formal structure. Nevertheless, I shall argue that, for several reasons, case space models have a certain priority over policy space models. First, case space provides microfoundations for policy space. Second, it provides a common framework within which to analyze and differentiate courts from legislatures and administrative agencies. Each of these institutions has policy effects, but they differ in who sets the agenda and what the agents within them choose or do. Models that begin in case space illuminate these similarities and differences.

The discussion proceeds as follows. Section I begins with a brief taxonomy of models. It then defines case space and policy space as well as identifying their relation to each other and to three other potential domains relevant to the study of courts. Section II argues that the appropriate domain of fundamental judicial preference includes policy space but may also reflect concerns for case dispositions. The remaining sections discuss several examples to argue that case space is prior to policy space as a foundation for models of courts.

I. FORMAL MODELS OF ADJUDICATION AND THEIR INTERPRETATIONS

A. A Variety of Court Models

Models of courts have several distinct purposes and ambitions. For instance, they may be normative or positive. Normative models prescribe either the structure of adjudication or the behavior of judges, whereas positive models describe these phenomena. Much legal writing about adjudication is normative; much of the literature on adjudication in the economic analysis of law, by contrast, is positive. Here I shall restrict attention to the positive purposes of explanation and prediction.

Within this limited range, however, models might still have distinct purposes and structures. Consider purpose first, with respect to which these models fall generally into two broad categories: systemic and behavioral. Systemic models seek to explain various features of adjudicatory systems such as hierarchy, division of labor, and various internal practices of the court. When will a court system exhibit hierarchy? If it is hierarchical, how many tiers will it have? The model might seek to explain when and what division of labor we might expect to observe in adjudicatory systems. Will some courts specialize in fact-finding, others in error correction, and still others in law creation? When will we observe judges sitting collegially, and when alone? What use will the court make of precedent, the body of previously decided cases? Will they adhere to a rule of horizontal *stare decisis*? To a rule of vertical *stare decisis*?

Behavioral models, by contrast, take the structure of adjudication as fixed and seek to explain the conduct of judges and the development of the law within the given institution. How will a court decide a given case? How will a judge vote on a given case? If the court issues opinions, who will write the opinion? Will a dissent occur (if dissents are permitted)? What will the content of these opinions be? Models may address these questions differently in distinct adjudicatory contexts. How are common law cases decided? How are cases of statutory interpretation decided? How are cases of constitutional interpretation decided? Adjudication in civil-law systems presents similar questions.

Finally, positive models might adopt different explanatory strategies. One might contrast structural and individualist models. Structural models of adjudication explain the behavior of judges or systemic features of courts in terms of systemic features of adjudication or aggregate features of the society. Individualist models explain the systemic features and individual behavior individualistically. Individualist models, of course, may rely on rational choice explanations or on other psychological models.

No one model is apt to be best for each of these purposes. A likely answer, therefore, to the question "are models of type A better models of adjudication than models of type B?" is thus likely to be no. Sometimes type A models will be the appropriate ones, and sometimes type B models will be. We must evaluate models in terms of their fitness for their intended use.

In this chapter, I restrict attention to individualist, behavioral models of judicial decision.[3] An individualist, behavioral model derives the decisions of a court from the actions of the individual judges.[4] A great many models fall within this broad class, and they too vary in purpose. A complete behavioral theory of adjudication in

---

[3] Not all models of courts in economic analysis of law are individualist. Examples of structural models of judicial hierarchy include Steven Shavell, 1995, "The Appeals Process as a Means of Error Correction," *Journal of Legal Studies*, 24, pp. 575–612, and the first half of Charles Cameron and Lewis A. Kornhauser, 2006, "Appeals Mechanisms, Litigant Selection, and the Structure of Judicial Hierarchies," in Jon Bond, Roy Flemming, and James Rogers, eds., *Institutional Games and the Supreme Court*, Charlottesville: University of Virginia Press.

[4] In fact, one might address the behavioral questions noted with models that are structural rather than individualistic in nature. Evolutionary models of the common law, for example, study forces that shape the law regardless of the decisions of judges.

the United States would ideally explain why the court ruled for or against a plaintiff and the content of any rule the court announced, and, on a collegial court, identify which judge announced the majority rule (if any) as well as which judges dissented and the alternative rules they advocated in dissent. Most models, of course, are less ambitious and less comprehensive.

B. Formal Models and Their Interpretations

A model has two parts: a formal theory and an interpretation. The formal theory may be interpreted in a number of different ways. It is these differing interpretations that distinguish case space and policy space models.

I address the formal theory and its interpretations in two stages. In the first stage, interpretation applies to the formal theory necessary for even the simplest model of adjudication, one in which there is a single, immortal judge on a single court that decides all cases in the jurisdiction. This context presents the contrast between case space and policy space most starkly, so that in it the priority of case space over policy space and the complementarity of the two interpretations appear most clearly.

In the second stage, interpretation applies to the formal theory that underlies the most common models of adjudication; these models generally consider collegial courts. At this second stage, models of courts share a core formal theory that reflects the fact that collegial courts decide by majority rule. Thus, all models of collegiality rely on simple theories of voting, and the basic results establishing stability (or instability) of court decisions rest on the same theorems. Differences across the models, then, largely lie in the different interpretations given to the core elements of the theory. These different interpretations suggest different ways to elaborate the core theory. I argue that case space models permit the analyst to address a broader set of questions.

To begin, consider the basic formal elements of an individualistic, behavioral model. For each agent, we must specify a domain of preference, the set of entities over which the agent has basic or fundamental preferences, and a domain of choice or action that identifies the set of actions available to each agent. Finally, we must specify the relation between the action undertaken by each agent and the actions of all other agents (and any influence of "nature"). I shall call the "output" of the court – the sum of the actions of each judge and the other agents in the model – the *legal consequence*, the *legal outcome*, or the *legal disposition*.

In most studies of adjudication, the model specifies the domain of preference **D** as some subset of R^n, often an interval on the real line, and the domain of choice **A** as a subset of **D**. Moreover, the space O of legal outcomes that result from judicial actions lies generally in **A**, but certainly in **D**. Thus, each judge chooses actions from the domain over which he has preferences, and his actions yield a (legal) outcome in the same domain. Usually, this domain of preference choice and legal outcome is designated as *policy space*. This name suggests an obvious interpretation: judges have preferences over, choose among, and finally announce policies, with the term "policy" understood more or less in its ordinary language sense as a complex statute or set of rules regulating some broad area of conduct.

This standard approach faces two difficulties. The first is formal: for many purposes, it is inappropriate to equate **D**, **A**, and **O**. Judges, in many models, choose actions from a space significantly different from the domain over which they have preferences, and legal outcomes may lie in a third domain. Models that *begin* in case space make more explicit the need to specify these domains individually.

The second difficulty is interpretive. I shall suggest that this suggestive interpretation of "policy" as equivalent to a complex statute is inapt. The best interpretation of "policy space" in standard political science models of adjudication (and legislation) is not as policy in the ordinary language sense of the term. Indeed, I shall suggest that the best interpretation of "policy space" in standard political science models of *legislation* is similarly not a policy in ordinary language; rather we best interpret the domains of preference, choice, and legal outcome in these legislative models more abstractly as (what I call in the following) a policy evaluation space. On this interpretation, models based in "policy space" are too far removed from the details of adjudicatory practice to explain much of judicial activity.

C. Interpretations of the Domains of Preference, Choice, and Outcome

Models of adjudication consider a number of settings: a single court that consists of a sequence of judges deciding cases, collegial courts in which multiple judges render a single decision, and courts in a hierarchical relation to each other. To catalog interpretations of the domains of preference, choice, and outcome that play a role in each of these settings, consider the simplest judicial system: a single, immortal judge who sits on a single court and hears all cases in the jurisdiction.[5]

We might interpret each domain in one of at least five different ways. (Of course, any specific model, as I shall argue, need not interpret each of the domains of preference, choice, and outcome identically.) For expository convenience, however, I speak initially in terms of the domain of (fundamental) preference.[6] Judges may have preferences over *social consequences*, over *policy evaluations*, over *policies*, over *doctrine*, or over *case dispositions* (or *legal outcomes*). The specification of a domain of preference does not include a specification of the grounds of the preference; it thus does not distinguish between "legal" and "political" models of adjudication.[7]

---

[5] To complete this taxonomy of models of adjudication set out in section I.A, one must identify the number of, and relation among, the judges in the model. Thus, the analyst may introduce additional judges, either on the same court, deciding collegially, or on inferior courts or on subsequent courts. In this context, models must specify the degree of heterogeneity in the preferences of the judges. In *team* models, judges have identical preferences. In *political* (sometimes called *principal–agent*) models, judges have heterogeneous preferences.

[6] When the domain of fundamental preference differs from the domain of choice or the domain of outcomes, the judge may nevertheless have *induced* preferences over her choices or over adjudicatory outcomes. That is, her fundamental preferences over X (say, policies) allow her to rank, say, her actions. But the existence of induced preferences over these domains is a contingent matter; it depends on the structure of her preferences over this basic domain. See the following for an example in which a judge with fundamental preferences over policies does not have well-defined preferences over case dispositions.

[7] Political models generally assume that judges decide cases on the basis of their personal, ideological preferences and beliefs. Legal models, by contrast, generally assume that judges decide cases on the basis of the "law," which many lawyers and most political scientists assume is independent

Case dispositions are the most straightforward domain over which an agent may have preferences. We might understand the case disposition in either of two ways. The most basic simply considers the *judgment* in the case: whether the court rules for plaintiff or for defendant. More complexly, we might understand the case disposition as the court's ruling on each of the underlying issues that it must decide in order to render judgment. Most cases involve multiple legal issues; in an accident case, for example, the court may have to determine, first, whether the defendant's action caused the plaintiff's injury and, second, whether the defendant acted negligently. In this example, there are four possible issue-by-issue case dispositions: (defendant caused the accident, defendant was negligent), (defendant did not cause the accident, defendant was negligent), (defendant caused the accident, defendant was negligent), and (defendant did not cause the accident, defendant was negligent). The analyst might begin with preferences over the space defined by these issue-by-issue dispositions.

To characterize the other four domains of preference, a definition of a *case space* will be helpful. Simply put, the case space consists of all possible cases that a court might decide.[8] A case *c* here is simply a complete description of the dispute before the court. It includes all decision-relevant facts and all *identifying facts*, that is, facts that identify who the parties are and the nature of the case. Many of the elements of a case vector *c* are thus discrete (and often binary) but some may be continuous.

As an example consider a simple accident case in which there is a single actor – the injurer – and a passive victim. A point in this case space consists of the names of the parties, the location of the accident (or alleged accident), the state of the world (denoted by θ) in which the accident occurred (e.g., foggy and rainy or clear and dry), and the sequence of events leading up to and following the accident. The description of these events must include the set of alternatives available to the injurer at each moment in time. To simplify, consider this accident from an economic perspective. To keep the example simple, let the choice x of the injurer by a nonnegative number that we shall call *care*. Then, a point in case space may be usefully described by the identities of the parties; the cost function $c(x; \theta)$ that determines the cost of injurer's care (conditional on the state of the world); a

---

of the personal ideology of the judge (but see Ronald Dworkin, 1987, *Law's Empire*, Cambridge, MA: Harvard University Press, for a normative legal model in which the ideology of the judge plays a prominent role in the conception of law). In each instance, one might impute preferences over policies to judges. The considerations that give rise to these preferences, however, differ. The "ground" of decision in political models is thus ideology and the "ground" of decision in legal models is "law," but both models might nonetheless take preferences over policies as basic. (The formalism of preference is neutral concerning the grounds of decision because the concept of preference is a formal one; the content of the preference might have either ground.)

The team model, mentioned in a previous note, has one element that might characterize a legal model of adjudication. Legal models commonly assume that legal questions have determinate answers (or at least right answers); homogeneity of preference is consistent with this characterization, as all judges within a legal model would seek the "correct" legal answer. Preferences, however, might be homogeneous without being legal.

[8] The idea of a case space was introduced in Lewis A. Kornhauser, 1992, "Modeling Collegial Courts I. Path Dependence," *International Review of Law and Economics*, 12, pp. 169–185, and 1992, "Modeling Collegial Courts II. Legal Doctrine," *Journal of Legal Studies*, 8, pp. 441–470.

technology $p(x;\theta)$ of accidents that describes how care (again conditional on the state of the world) influences the probability of an accident; a damage function $D(x;\theta)$ that expresses the level of harm suffered by the passive victim as a function of the injurer's care level; and the level of care x that the injurer actually adopted in the event.[9]

We may now define policies in terms of the case space. Define a policy simply as a mapping from the case space into a set O that may often be taken to be the two-element set $(0,1)$.[10] When $O = \{0,1\}$, we have a standard legal outcome set; when O is more complex, we must interpret legal outcomes more broadly. Policy space thus consists of all possible mappings from case space into the legal outcome space. On this account, when we say that legislators choose a policy, we mean that they choose a bill from the set of possible bills, with each possible bill simply a mapping from the entire case space C into O. A court, by contrast, decides a case; that is, it decides the outcome of that case by assigning an element of O to the case c before it. This case disposition, in a judicial system that honors precedent, specifies *part* of a policy. Over time, a court that observes precedential practices such as *stare decisis* will arrive at a legal rule that maps C into the outcome space O; the court will have made law, or, more precisely, *announced* a policy.[11] Of course, a court might decide a case by announcing a policy and then applying the policy to the case before it. Whether the judicial announcement of a policy actually *institutes* or *implements* that policy, however, depends on practices within the judicial system and the executive. If future courts are not bound by the policy announcements in prior decisions and we have no reason to believe that a future court will adhere to the previously announced policy, then the announcement does not institute the policy. This procedure of judicial policy announcement describes a process somewhat at odds with standard legal understandings of the common-law process.

In the simple accident example, then, a policy is an assignment of liability for the harm caused by the accident to either the plaintiff–victim or the defendant–injurer. Obviously, there are many such possible policies. Fix the technology – that is, fix the functions $c(x;\theta)$, $p(x;\theta)$, and $D(x;\theta)$ – and assume that there is only one state of the world (so we may suppress θ in the functional expressions). Then any anonymous policy space[12] is a partition of the interval $[0,\infty)$. Normally, we consider only *regular* partitions of this interval, ones in which both the set of x such that injurer bears the liability and the set of x such that the victim bears the cost of the accident are connected. That is, we consider the class of *negligence* rules

---

[9] Of course, the actual case space is much more complex because care is not a scalar. In an auto accident, care includes the speed chosen by the driver and the attention he gives to the task. Also, note that this description of case space is really a projection of the full case space onto the subspace that ignores the identity of the parties and other (irrelevant) features of the situation.

[10] Binary outcome sets are typical in judicial settings but less typical in legislative settings. Consider the tax code. One way to model the policy space is as a function from the characteristics of individuals into the amount of tax owed.

[11] Notice that there will be some constraints on the set of possible bills that renders the effective policy space, the set of all possible bills, smaller than the set of all possible functions from C into O. For instance, bills presumably should be anonymous; the name of an individual should be irrelevant.

[12] Anonymity here means that liability does not depend on the names of the parties – only on the values of x, $c(x)$, $p(x)$, and $D(x)$.

in which the injurer is liable if $x < X$ for some X in $[0, \infty)$ and the victim is liable otherwise. (Strict liability sets $X = \infty$.) Of course, even in this simple context where both sets in the partition are connected, a completely specified policy would set the standard of care for every possible triple of cost function, technology, and damage function $(c(x; \theta), p(x; \theta), D(x; \theta))$ in every state of the world θ. Obviously, a policy is a complex object, and actual policy spaces are immense. A preference over this policy space will be equally formidable.

As a second example, consider a legislatively created policy such as a tax on personal income. To describe the space of tax policies over which a legislator has preferences, we must first define the "case space," though, in the legislative context, it might more appropriately be called the *fact space*. A reasonable definition of the fact space would include the labor-market opportunities and outcomes of each individual subject to the tax, her past income (including gains) from capital, details of her consumption, and information about her family and physical status. A tax policy is then a map from this space of individual characteristics into the real numbers; for each taxpayer, the map assigns the tax (or subsidy in the event of earned income credits) owed by the individual. The relevant policy space is the set of all possible partitions of this fact space into equivalence classes defined by the legal outcome space, here the amount of tax owed. Again, the policy space is vast; normally, of course, the analyst considers only some subset of policy space that consists of "morally reasonable," "politically feasible," or "administratively acceptable" policies.

Consider now the social consequence space. Every policy has consequences when it is implemented. Imagine, in our simple accident example, a population of injurers and victims. There will be some distribution of care taken by the population of injurers and then a distribution of injuries to victims. Again, for simplicity, assume a fixed technology, fixed cost and damage functions, and a single state of the world. Suppose that injurers face different costs of care but the announced standard of care is not conditional on the injurer's cost of care. Then, for most standards of care, some injurers will choose to be negligent and others will not. Different standards thus induce different distributions of care levels adopted by agents. Moreover, the judge or legislator will be uncertain about the distribution of costs of care in the injurer population.

Consider now a policy evaluation. A policy evaluation is an assessment of the policy on one or more dimensions. Assessment of a policy, however, is complex. We might proceed in a number of distinct ways. We might consider, or predict, the consequences of the policy and evaluate the predicted consequences. Alternatively, we might assess the policy more naively; we might assume its success in the sense that the actual social outcomes correspond to the legal outcomes dictated by the policy and evaluate it in terms of these "successful" consequences. A third route would be more complex than a direct evaluation of the predicted consequences of a policy. This assessment would depend not only on the predicted consequences of a policy but also on the *out-of-equilibrium* implications of the policy, that is, on the dictates of the policy when unanticipated events or behaviors arise. In any of these cases, a policy evaluation is a function from policy space into an evaluation space (usually R^n).

Again, consider our simplest accident example (with a single state of the world and fixed technology, costs, and damages). Define the policy evaluation space as a two-dimensional assessment of the policy: the total number of accidents that occur under the policy and the percentage of accident expenditures borne by injurers. In the following, I will argue that the assessment of policy requires that we consider out-of-equilibrium consequences.

Finally, consider doctrinal space. As defined thus far, a policy is simply a long list of outcomes associated with facts. Doctrine provides a structure to policy, an organized way for the judge to assess responsibility. Doctrine organizes this list into a manageable tool by organizing case space into a logically related set of simpler questions that depend on only the facts of a subspace of case space. Doctrine identifies the factors that are relevant to decisions and indicates how these factors should be weighed.

Judges make two types of doctrinal decisions: They choose *among* doctrines; and they choose *within* doctrines. Define a doctrinal frame as some class of functions from subsets of case space into (legal) outcome space (with each subset and function defining an issue) and then a second class of functions from the product of these (legal) outcome spaces into a final (legal) outcome space.[13] At least intuitively, we might think of this frame as *indexing* the possible policies. A policy consists of a choice of a function from each subset and a choice of the final function. Of course, the index might be quite complex, involving multiple dimensions. On this account, we might consider doctrinal space as the set of all possible doctrinal frames; this specification would facilitate the analysis of choices among doctrines.[14] Doctrinal space might alternatively be defined as a specific doctrinal frame; in this context, judges choose a specific doctrine within this subset of indexed doctrines.

An extension of our simple example illustrates doctrinal space. Again, fix the technology and cost and damage functions and assume there is only one state of the world. Let the fact/case space include not only the levels of care that an injurer might adopt, but also the (more or less complex) causal chains that might connect the injurer's behavior to the victim's injury. Consider four possible doctrinal frames. In the most complex, there are two issues: cause and care. A specific doctrine partitions each issue into two sets, one in which plaintiff prevails on the issue and one in which defendant prevails. These two partitions then yield a partition of case space; to prevail in the case, plaintiff must prevail on both issues. Another doctrinal frame, called the causal frame, might have a single issue that depends on only the realized causal chain. A third frame would rely on the single issue of care. A fourth would be absolute: either plaintiff always prevails or she always loses. The judge then has a preference over the structuring of doctrine; she believes that doctrine ordered around standards of care – choosing policies from the class of negligence rule policies – is better than some no-fault doctrinal structure that, say,

---

[13] This definition coincides with the definition of doctrine offered in Kornhauser, "Modeling Collegial Courts II." The discussion there is more complete and includes the concept of a cause of action as well as that of an issue.

[14] Doctrinal space understood this way is not identical to policy space, because a specific policy may be realizable through many different doctrinal frames.

divides the loss between the parties without regard to the actions of the defendant. We might consider several different classes of legal rules. I previously described the class of partitions that consist only of two connected subsets of the half line. We might also consider the class of partitions that consist of an interior line segment in which plaintiff bears the cost and two surrounding sets in which defendant bears the liability. We might consider other, more complex classes of partitions.

Alternatively, if we make the doctrinal choice that the law has in fact made and limit the admissible partitions, as the common law does to those partitions in which all subsets are connected, then the judge chooses a specific doctrine within that frame. The judge then might have preferences over the policies within a given doctrinal frame. On this account, doctrinal space is simply a subset of policy space that has a convenient interpretation. If we understand the doctrinal frame as an indexed set of policies, then the judge has preferences over these indices. When the index set is multidimensional, this formulation yields a rich way of understanding judicial preference and choice.

As a simple illustration consider a judge developing doctrine within the context of a modified version of the simple accident situation described previously, again with the technology fixed and a single state of the world. Now, however, let the victim also have a choice of care available to him. Designate the injurer's choice of care as x and the victim's as y. A policy is now a partition of (x,y) space into two subsets, one in which the victim bears the costs of accidents and one in which the injurer does. Consider the doctrinal frame of negligence with contributory negligence that is indexed by the pair (X,Y) such that the injurer is liable if and only if $x < X$ and $y \geq Y$. We interpret X as the injurer's standard of care and Y as the victim's standard of care. The judge has preferences over the set of doctrines – that is, pairs (X,Y) – within this doctrinal frame. Normally, however, in any given case, her domain of choice is, at best, restricted to the choice of *one* standard.[15]

Notice that this discussion of domains of preference applies equally to legislators and judges with the exception of case dispositions. As legislators consider and enact policies *ex ante* rather than *ex post*, without particular cases in front of them, they could not have primitive preferences over case dispositions. But they might have fundamental preferences over consequences, policy evaluations, policies, or doctrines. In most practical contexts, the choice of the domain of preference may be driven by the aim of the model and analytic tractability.

Consider now the judge's domain of choice and the outcome domain. Any of the five domains mentioned previously, or subsets of them, might serve as these domains. Judges may render judgments, resolve issues, announce doctrine, make policy, articulate policy evaluations, or determine social outcomes. Indeed, ordinary discourse generally attributes the first four of these six types of actions to common-law judges. They do render judgment, resolve issues, announce doctrine and, to some extent, make policy in the same case. It is, however, illuminating to consider how various theoretical frameworks model adjudication. Similarly, judicial choices, once aggregated, might yield an outcome in one or more of these domains.

---

[15] On many understandings of common-law adjudication, the judge simply decides the case.

II. CHOOSING THE DOMAIN OF PREFERENCE

How should an analyst choose the domain over which judges have fundamental preferences? The prior section identified five different possible domains: case dispositions (or legal outcomes), policies, policy evaluations, doctrine, and social consequences. I shall argue that, in the simplest model of a single, immortal judge on a single court, policy, understood as a mapping from case space into outcome space, is the appropriate domain for basic preferences.[16] In more complex judicial environments, the analyst must ascribe fundamental preferences over a more complex domain.

One may easily dismiss both conceptions of case dispositions as the relevant domain of fundamental preference. Case disposition as possible judgments is an austere domain over which to have fundamental preferences. The judge may care whether plaintiff wins or loses, but her concern is likely derivative of some other concern. After all, the judge is supposed to be impartial between the parties, and a bare preference for the triumph of one party over the other seems to violate this neutrality on its face. Moreover, in many instances a judge's preferences over judgments in case A will depend on the resolution of case B; the judge may prefer ruling for plaintiff in A should B be resolved for plaintiff, but for defendant in A should B be resolved for defendant. In this instance, the judge would not have well-defined preferences over single case dispositions, but she might have well-defined preferences over a more complex entity such as legal rules – or, as I have defined them, policies.[17]

The second conception of case disposition as the resolution of all legal issues in the case is, of course, infused with legal content; it presumes a doctrinal structure that governs the disposition of a case. The analyst, however, seeks to explain, among other phenomena, the emergence of doctrine and the role, if any, that it plays in structuring and constraining judicial decisions. Defining fundamental preferences over a domain already infused with doctrine threatens this project with circularity.

This discussion applies equally to one of the two understandings of doctrinal space. In the more restricted interpretation, doctrinal space is simply an indexed

---

[16] Of course, in many instances, the analyst may choose the domain of preference for analytic convenience. She has a particular problem in mind – say, predicting the dispositions of cases by a court – and, for that immediate purpose, the domain of case dispositions seems reasonable. She has no need to build microfoundations (so to speak) for her model; not every model must begin at the bottom and derive all necessary intermediate concepts. But theory *should* aspire to such microfoundations. Moreover, without them, the analyst may be led into error. Empirically, it seems plausible that judges do not have well-defined preferences over case dispositions.

[17] For example, in an accident situation in which both injurer and victim face a standard of care and victim and injurer care are substitutes, the judge might think, when the injurer's standard of care is set at the level X^* that minimizes total social costs, that the victim's standard of care y should also be set at the level Y^* that minimizes total social costs. If, however, the injurer's standard of care x is set at $x' > X^*$ (that is, above the cost-minimizing level), the judge might think that the victim's standard should be set at $y' < Y^*$ (below the cost-minimizing level). Thus, if the victim chooses a level of care y such that $y' < y < Y^*$, she will be held contributorily negligent if $x = X^*$, but nonnegligent if x' is the injurer's standard.

subset of policy space. The index set implies a given doctrinal structure within which the court is already working. The court then chooses a policy by specifying a particular doctrine indexed by the frame. If judges begin with preferences over doctrinal space understood in this way, it will be difficult to provide a noncircular explanation of the emergence of doctrine and its role in shaping the law. The second understanding of doctrinal space regards it as the set of all (indexed) subsets of policy space. This space consists of all possible doctrinal frames on policy space; it is extremely complex and difficult to imagine.

Consider next policy evaluation space. Many models implicitly interpret the domain of judicial preference in this manner. The attitudinal model, which arose in the late 1950s and early 1960s with its roots not in economics and rational choice theory but in psychology, may be understood as choosing this domain as the basic one.[18] In its initial formulation, the facts of a case serve as a stimulus, and the judicial response is determined by a judicial *attitude*, or value. In practice, this simple story means that both cases and judicial attitudes are scaled in what corresponds to a policy evaluation space, generally one-dimensional. On this account, then, judges have preferences over a policy evaluation space, and they choose case dispositions in the sense of judgments for or against plaintiff.

Similarly, when students of Congress note that virtually all votes by all senators and representatives may be explained by the official's location in a one-dimensional "policy" space, they seem implicitly to interpret "policy" as "policy evaluation" or "ideology." Each elected official has an "ideological" position measured on a "liberal–conservative" axis, and she assesses policies (in the sense of this paper) in terms of this evaluative position. After all, policies are complex and do not easily reduce, if at all, to a one-dimensional (or even low-dimensional) space.

Policy evaluation space, however, is too abstract to serve as the domain of fundamental preference. In general many different policies will yield the same policy evaluation. As a consequence, preferences over policy evaluations will not explain which *policy* the courts (or Congress) adopt; it will explain only the evaluative or ideological valence that the adopted or enacted policy has.[19] Consider, once more, the simple tort example. Many different policies will induce the same behavior among injurers and victims; on some accounts, this single set of behaviors will induce the same policy evaluations. How are we to explain the choice of actual policy? Which of these equivalent policies is implemented? If the judge is indifferent among all policies that receive the same policy evaluations, then she should be content to choose the announced policy randomly. But judges and legislators do distinguish among such evaluatively equivalent policies.[20] In the context of Congress at least, officials expend much time and other resources drafting, debating, and negotiating the fine detail of statutes.

[18] See, for example, Glendon Schubert, 1965, *The Judicial Mind: Attitudes and Ideologies of Supreme Court Justices 1946–1963*, Evanston, IL: Northwestern University Press.
[19] Steven Collander, "A Theory of Policy Expertise" (mimeo, October 5, 2006), raises essentially this objection to current models of Congress.
[20] Of course, one might contend that if judges do distinguish among evaluatively equivalent policies, then perhaps the policy evaluation space is not properly defined.

From a consequentialist perspective, the space of social consequences, rather than the space of policies, is the "natural" domain of preference. After all, a policy has no intrinsic value; it is only valuable instrumentally, because of the consequences it has in the real world. Unfortunately, when agents either are irrational, act under uncertainty, or periodically make errors, preferences over social consequences are an insufficient domain for fundamental preferences. Three interrelated arguments support this conclusion. First, many policies yield the same social consequences. Second, evaluation of policy does not depend only on realized or expected consequences; it may depend also on counterfactual consequences. Third, policy space facilitates the simultaneous analysis of the broad set of decisions rendered by courts.

Policies do not map one-to-one onto consequences.[21] Many different policies may yield the same distribution of consequences. Consider once more the simple accident example. As before, fix the technology and the cost and damage functions, and assume only one state of the world. Suppose the court seeks to minimize total social costs, the sum of the cost of taking care and the costs created by accidents. Then many legal rules induce this outcome: for example, strict liability, a negligence rule with the standard of care set at the total cost-minimizing level of care, and negligence rules with sufficiently high standards of care (so that it is cheaper for the injurer to be negligent and bear the costs of accidents than to meet the standard). These policies have identical (equilibrium) social consequences, but a policymaker might still differentiate among them in terms of out-of-equilibrium behavior. The same problem identified in the prior discussion of policy evaluation space recurs in outcome space; preferences over outcomes are insufficient to identify which policy will be enacted or announced.

Second, social consequences depend on the policy but also, and importantly, on decisions of agents in light of the policy (as well as on chance). Social consequences are thus generally a prediction of equilibrium behavior in light of the policy. This procedure is quite reasonable in many contexts, but not obviously in a judicial context. Courts in general, and high appellate courts in particular, often confront strange (out-of-equilibrium) behaviors. Moreover, we often assess policies in terms of their treatment of out-of-equilibrium behavior cases. Our evaluation of the fairness of a policy often relies on how the policy would treat someone with given characteristics and in specific circumstances even if the circumstances do not arise or if no individual, in the relevant circumstances, acts in the manner specified.

Finally, adjudication is complex. As already noted, judges render judgment, make doctrine, announce policy, and assess policy. Policies stand at the center of these decisions. Cases are resolved in light of the policies announced. Similarly, doctrine structures policy in a particular way that allows us to evaluate it reasonably. Taking policy space as the fundamental domain of preference permits the analysis of all these decisions.

---

[21] This statement requires qualification. If one uses a suitably naive mapping from policies to consequences, the map is one-to-one. Suppose for example that one believes that citizens simply do what is required by the policy; then the policy describes the social consequences and the map is one-to-one.

III. AN ILLUSTRATIVE EXAMPLE

An important recent article by Gennaioli and Shleifer helps to illustrate the concepts set out in the preceding section.[22] They use a simple "dog bites man" example to motivate their model, a slightly more complicated version of the simplest example of the accident model already discussed. In their example, technology is not fixed, though there is only one state of the world.

Let us begin with their initial case space. It includes an action x chosen from the two-element set {"put dog on leash" (L), "do not put dog on leash" (NL)}. The cost C of putting the dog on the leash constitutes a second dimension of case space. The probability $p(x)$, the probability that the dog bites a man as a function of the action taken, constitutes a third dimension. The fourth dimension, the harm done, is normalized to one. Finally, there are two other dimensions of case space: an index a in the interval $[0,1]$ representing the aggressiveness of the dog, and an index d, also in the interval $[0,1]$, corresponding to the density of the population in which the owner walks the dog. (The victim is passive and cannot influence the likelihood or severity of an accident.) The indices a and d determine the technology of the accident; that is, we should write the probability of a bite as conditional not only on the owner's action but also on the aggressiveness of the dog and the density of the population: $p(x;a,d)$.

In their model, a policy is simply a partition of this space into two sets: the set in which the owner bears the costs of dog bites and the set in which the victim bears those costs. They however work in "doctrinal space," not the policy space. Indeed, the point of their model is to study the development of doctrine. To do this, they restrict the class of legal rules in two important respects. First, they consider only negligence rules with "finite" standards of care; that is, they permit a no-liability rule and a standard of care of "putting on the leash," but exclude a strict owner liability rule – a restriction, as we shall see, of some importance. They investigate when the law will select the standard of care that minimizes total social costs, $c(x) + p(x;a,d)$. This objective function entails that the standard is to be set at "put on a leash" if and only if $p(L;a,d) - p(NL;a,d) > C$.

The second, assumed restriction on policy space involves the ability of the court to adjust the standard of care to the technology of accidents; that is, in Gennaioli and Shleifer's model, as a and d change, the court is not allowed to make trade-offs between the two. Note that, because they assume that a standard of care of "put on a leash" minimizes total social costs if and only if $a + d > 1$, the ideal partition of case space would set the owner liable when and only when $a + d > 1$ and she had not put a leash on the dog.

Courts, however, cannot choose this policy. They are restricted to doctrinal frames of the form $(A,(D_{>A}, D_{<A}))$ in which the owner is liable if and only if either $a < A$, $d > D_{<A}$, and the owner does not use a leash, or $a > A$, $d > D_{>A}$, and the owner does not use a leash. In terms of doctrine, then, Gennaioli and Shleifer assume that the court chooses between two classes of doctrinal frames. In

---

[22] Nicola Gennaioli and Andrei Shleifer, 2007, "The Evolution of the Common Law," *Journal of Political Economy*, 115, pp. 43–73.

the first, there is a single issue, the aggressiveness of the dog (and the court must choose the standard of aggressiveness that triggers a standard of care of L); the second doctrinal frame has two issues, aggressiveness and population density, with population density chosen second. The nature of common-law reasoning, they argue, justifies this structure. In their view, common-law judges choose doctrine and these choices proceed in a sequential fashion. So, by assumption, the first case raises the question of the role of aggressiveness in the determination of the standard of care. The first judge announces a rule of the form: "The standard of care is 'put on a leash' if and only if $a > A$." The next case presents the question of the role of dangerousness in the determination of the standard of care. The second judge chooses *both* $D_{>A}$ and $D_{<A}$ to arrive at the final partition of the entire case space.[23] This sequential structure is meant to capture the practice of "distinguishing cases," and it does so in an illuminating way. Notice however that, by assumption, the model excludes a doctrinal frame with a single issue, "dangerousness," that weighs aggressiveness and density to reach a judgment of the threat posed by the dog in the circumstances and on which the court could condition liability; this doctrinal frame, of course, would include the ideal, social-cost-minimizing policy.

Given this choice set Δ of "doctrines," equal to the set of all partitions of the form $(A, D_{>A}, D_{<A})$ – with standard-of-care set as described – the policy that minimizes total social cost over the entire case space is not achievable. Judges thus seek a second-best outcome, and their preferences over the set Δ depend on the relative weights that each judge places on type I and type II error, that is, the error of setting the standard at "no leash necessary" when the standard should be "put on a leash" (call this *owner-biased error*) and the error of setting the standard at "put on a leash" when the standard should be "no leash necessary" (call this *victim-biased error*). Judges dislike making mistakes, but they differ in how they weight these mistakes. Owner-biased judges would rather reduce victim-biased error, whereas victim-biased judges would rather reduce owner-biased error. Judicial preferences can then be characterized by two parameters: b_O and b_V, the weights that the judge places on victim-biased and owner-biased error, respectively.[24]

Gennaioli and Shleifer thus choose the domain of preference as a two-dimensional policy evaluation space defined by the extent of owner-biased error and by the extent of victim-biased error. Each type of judge has an unique, ideal policy and elliptical preference curves around that point with the major and minor axes given by b_V and b_O. A policy-space analysis would thus represent the choices made by each judge in terms of this policy evaluation space. The policy evaluation space, however, is in many respects unilluminating. Which actual partition is chosen – which $(A, D_{>A}, D_{<A})$ is actually adopted – is much more informative. Were the constrained and unconstrained choices of doctrine not unique, the problem with the policy evaluation space would be more evident; we would not know *which* policy with the desired policy evaluation was actually chosen.

---

[23] I shall challenge this characterization of legal reasoning in the following, but for now I pursue the logic of their argument.

[24] The notation here is a bit intricate. The subscript on b indicates the party that the judge favors, but favoring a particular party means reducing errors in the other party's favor.

The domain of choice is in doctrinal space. Courts use cases to announce rules, but there is no strong connection between the choice of doctrine and the decision of the case before the court. As I suggest in the next section, grounding models of adjudication in case space facilitates the simultaneous study of the interlocking case resolution and policy formulation aspects of judicial decision making.

Gennaioli and Shleifer's model tells us something about the evolution of legal doctrine, but at the same time it raises many questions. Note first that, as in virtually any model in doctrinal space, the class of policies available to the courts has been severely limited in several respects. Doctrine must be of the form $(A, D_{>A}, D_{<A})$ with A chosen first and $D_{>A}$ and $D_{<A}$ chosen simultaneously. Second, courts are restricted to negligence rules; moreover, an infinite standard of care is not available. This last restriction is particularly limiting in that the single-set partition "owner liable everywhere" induces the first-best outcome, for the owner bears all the social costs of the accidents and hence makes the optimal decision for every level of aggression and density possible. (Moreover, she will adjust the level and location of her activity – how often and where the dog is walked – optimally.) One might accept this restriction because it promotes the virtue of simplicity; permitting strict liability would require consideration of a much more complex model to address the effects of distinguishing on the development of the law.

More seriously, the judges are constrained to develop the law in an issue-by-issue fashion. First, the court resolves the aggression issue, and then it resolves the density issue. Why should this be? The court knows the way the technology varies with a and d; it needs to know this relationship to calculate the extent of owner-biased and victim-biased error. Why should it not deploy this knowledge in its structuring of doctrine?

The initial description of the problem in case space, and the observation that courts decide cases, suggest a different judicial process, one closer to the motivation behind the model developed by Cooter, Kornhauser, and Lane[25] in which the courts learn from their cases.[26] When the court hears case 1, it observes the level of aggressiveness a_1 of the dog involved and the population density d_1 at the site at which the injury occurred. It thus observes the actual probability of an accident under the condition "no leash" (assuming no leash was used) and can estimate the probability of an accident under the condition of "leash." It will then choose the correct standard of care for this case c_1. Moreover, if it does not know the complete relationship among technology, aggressiveness, and density, but simply that the probability of an accident is increasing in both aggressiveness and density, the decision in c_1 also determines the standard of care in many other cases. Suppose that c_1 lies to the southwest of the border of the optimal rule – that is,

[25] Robert Cooter, Lewis A. Kornhauser, and David Lane, 1979, "Liability Rules, Limited Information, and the Role of Precedent," *Bell Journal of Economics*, 10, pp. 366–373.

[26] Even within Gennaioli and Shleifer's framework, the judicial process is a bit strange. Why must the second judge choose both $D_{>A}$ and $D_{<A}$? The case before him presents one situation or the other. Either the level of aggressiveness of the dog involved in the case is greater than A, in which case the judge must choose $D_{<A}$ to resolve the case, or it is less than A, in which case the judge must choose $D_{>A}$. Why must they be chosen at the same time? Notice that sequential choice of the two D's implies that, possibly, the two standards will be chosen by judges with different biases.

of the diagonal from $(0,1)$ to $(1,0)$. Then the optimal standard of care in case c_1 is "no leash necessary." Knowledge of the sign of the partial derivatives allows the inference that the appropriate standard of care in any case (a,d) with $a < a_1$ and $d < d_1$ is also "no leash necessary."[27] Over time, the court will fill in the entire case space and approach the optimal partition.

One might imagine that, with this judicial process, in which judges respect the dispositions of the case but not necessarily any rule announced in it, judges might nonetheless try to articulate a general rule – that is, a complete partition of case space (or of doctrinal space). They might do so by trying to estimate the function that divides doctrinal space from the results in the observed cases. On average, how many observations would be necessary to get a reasonable estimate of the actual rule?

IV. THE COMPLEXITY OF ADJUDICATION

As noted in the prior section, taking policy space as the domain of fundamental preference permits a more complex analysis of adjudication because it permits us to see the relation between case dispositions and policy choice in a revealing light. This insight, however, requires the analyst to interpret policy in the complex way suggested here, as a mapping from case space to outcome space, rather than considering policy as an abstract idea.

To understand this logic more clearly, consider a recent model of opinion assignment by Lax and Cameron, which seeks to explain the assignment of opinions on the Supreme Court.[28] They are thus concerned with decision making on a collegial court. An opinion for them is a policy – or, perhaps more accurately, a set of policies, as it is costly to specify a policy precisely. Each judge has preferences over policies (and leisure), and the outcome space is a policy (or set of policies).

How is opinion assignment and the Court's announcement of policy tied to case disposition? Their model permits an analysis of this question, though they do not pursue it. To motivate their model they consider a simple, one-dimensional case space. The agent chooses some action in an interval $[0,1]$, and a policy is simply a partition of the unit interval into two sets, in one of which plaintiff prevails and in the other she loses. They restrict attention to a one-dimensional subspace of policy space; in their subspace, each set in the partition is connected and a policy is identified with a point in the unit interval.[29]

---

[27] Of course, if c_1 lies above the diagonal, then the same assumption about the sign of the partial derivatives permits the inference that the appropriate standard of care in any case (a,d) with $a > a_1$ and $d > d_1$ is also "put on a leash."

[28] See Jeffrey Lax and Charles Cameron, 2007, "Bargaining and Opinion Assignment on the U.S. Supreme Court," *Journal of Law Economics and Organization*, 23, pp. 276–302.

[29] They assert that "in the special case of one-dimensional case spaces and one-dimensional policy spaces, the legally oriented case space framework and the legislatively oriented spatial framework are virtually isomorphic for many analytic questions" (ibid., p. 280, n. 5). The point of this section is to show that this claim is false. It is also worth noting that, in the one-dimensional case space posited, a two-dimensional policy space is plausible. Consider judicial regulation of driving on a limited access highway. The standard of care might generally be phrased as "take a reasonable speed." The case space consists of the speed at which the defendant travels. Reasonableness, however has two

In their model, the cost of drafting opinions implies that a justice will endorse an opinion that announces a policy that deviates from her most preferred policy. In this setting they prove a number of theorems about the optimal opinion assignment policy of the Chief Justice. They do not note, however, that, in their model, a justice might endorse a policy that dictates a case disposition that differs from the case disposition required by the Justice's most preferred policy. These situations present an interesting conflict between doing justice in the case before the court and making good law.

Moreover, this conflict in their model is not hypothetical. Their model implies, though again they do not note this, that the Chief Justice should always vote in the majority even when he disagrees with the case disposition. In this model, then, the Chief Justice would often endorse a legal rule that, on his view, wrongly decided the case before him.

A model that takes the policy space as primitive – as does, for example, the model of opinion assignment devised by Hammond, Bonneau, and Sheehan – cannot address this question.[30] Their model ignores case space. It assumes that judges have preferences over a one-dimensional policy space and that each judge chooses a policy; the outcome of the court is also a policy. Cases and judgments in cases have no formal existence in the model, and consequently, it is not possible for a justice to face a conflict between her view of the correct decision in the case and what second-best policy she can announce.

V. MORE COMPLEX COURTS

The same formal theory underlies much of the manipulation of case space as multidimensional policy space itself. After all, we construct policy space from case space; policy space is a partition of case space. Basic *stability* results thus arise from the common formal structure.

Consider, for example, the results in Lax's recent article showing that a median rule exists on a collegial court even when there is no median judge.[31] He proves this result in a case space formulation with each judge having preferences over cases. This ascription of preferences over cases, however, is equivalent to an assumption that policy preferences are separable in cases.[32] Thus, a median rule exists if policy space is separable over cases.

This result, however, parallels a well-known result about multidimensional policy space. The latter states that, when preferences over policies are separable, the

---

dimensions: a minimum and a maximum speed. It may be unreasonable to go too slowly just as it may be unreasonable to go too quickly.

[30] Thomas H. Hammond, Chris W. Bonneau, and Reginald S. Sheehan, 2005, *Strategic Behavior and Policy Choice on the U.S. Supreme Court*, Palo Alto, CA: Stanford University Press.

[31] Jeffrey Lax, 2007, "Constructing Legal Rules on Appellate Courts," *American Political Science Review*, 101, pp. 591–604.

[32] A policy is a map from case space into outcome space. So we may write a policy as a sequence of zeros and ones or of Y's and N's; in such cases a policy is simply a long string. Let S and S' be two distinct strings of results in all cases except case c. That is, S and S' are partial policies that will be completed by the resolution of case c (as either Y or N). Preference over policy space is separable in cases if and only if the judge prefers the policy YS to NS when and only when the judge prefers YS' to NS' for all possible S and S'.

issue-by-issue median is a stable, majority-rule outcome of the legislature.[33] (In adjudication, courts might reach stable outcomes when judges have nonseparable preferences over policies if they adhere to a practice of *stare decisis*.[34])

Case space, however, is not equivalent to policy space. We may see this most directly with a one-dimensional case space. There is no simple isomorphism to one-dimensional policy space unless we restrict the class of policies that might govern the one-dimensional case space. Consider a specific interpretation of our simple accident example in which the states of the world and the technology are fixed. The (effective) case space is now one-dimensional, and we interpret "care" as the speed s at which the agent travels on a limited-access highway. Naively, we might think that the relevant policy space is the one-dimensional family of partitions defined by a cut point S that divides the case space into two sets: $NL = \{s | s \leq S\}$, where the driver is not responsible for costs created by any accident, and $L = \{s | s > S\}$, where the driver bears the costs of any accident.

On reflection, however, a "reasonable" driver would also not drive too slowly, so that an appropriate policy space is actually two-dimensional with a policy P given by a pair (S_{min}, S_{max}). The partition is now given by the two sets $NL = \{s | S_{min} \leq s \leq S_{max}\}$ and $L = \{s | s < S_{min} \text{ or } s > S_{max}\}$. The set of all *possible* policies, of course, is much larger.

CONCLUDING REMARKS

"Policy space" and "case space" are sometimes cast as competing models of adjudication.[35] A closer examination suggests a more complex picture. I have argued first that "policy space" is an ambiguous designation for a model. A number of different interpretations are consistent with the common deployment of policy space models. More importantly, I have argued that case space provides microfoundations for policy space; policies in the ordinary-language sense are defined in terms of case space, and all the other interpretations of "policy space" build on this basic, naive understanding of policy.

Case space and policy space are thus complementary rather than competing models for adjudication. Nonetheless, the previous discussion has provided some insight into the question "What makes a good model?" Several reasons justify treating case space as prior to policy space and models grounded in case space as more fundamental.

First, as already noted, case space provides microfoundations for policy space models. Starting in case space, moreover, facilitates the analysis of the interlocking set of decisions that courts render. Understanding the relation between the court's

---

[33] Theorem 6.1 in Peter Ordeshook, 1986, *Game Theory and Political Theory*, Cambridge: Cambridge University Press, p. 250. A recent paper by Robert Anderson and Alexander Tahk, "Structure and Equilibrium in the United States Supreme Court" (presented at the annual meeting of the Midwest Political Science Association, 2006, http://www.allacademic.com/meta/p139287_index.html) replicates this result. Lax's result is stronger than Theorem 6.1 in Ordeshook, as the latter assumes dimension-by-dimension voting, whereas stability is more robust in Lax's case space formulation.

[34] Kornhauser, "Modeling Collegial Courts I."

[35] See, for example, Lax, "Constructing Legal Rules," and Lax and Cameron, "Bargaining and Opinion Assignment."

judgment in the case before it, whatever rule it announces, and its development of doctrine requires that one begin with case space; only there can one provide a thorough analysis of adjudication.

Second, case space provides a common framework in which to compare and evaluate courts as well as legislatures and administrative agencies. Policy space models assimilate adjudication to legislation. Yet courts differ dramatically from legislatures. The nature of the institutional agendas, who sets the agenda, and the actions available to the officials all differ across institutions.

2 Is There a Method to the Madness? Why Creative and Counterintuitive Proposals Are Counterproductive

MICHAEL B. DORFF AND KIMBERLY KESSLER FERZAN

Baby-selling.[1] Racial discrimination.[2] Insider trading.[3] These are just a few of the legions of contrarian proposals advanced by legal economists as efficient.[4] Such proposals are at least counterintuitive, and perhaps even shocking. In fact, from a careerist perspective, their startling quality may be their primary virtue. But in pursuing the attention that comes with novelty, the authors of these works have overlooked the negative externalities that also accompany avant-garde positions. Legal rules that strike most people as unjust may upset community expectations and undermine the efficiency of the very rules proposed. In short, such rules may not prove wealth-maximizing at all.

Counterintuitive rules are even less likely to prove *welfare*-maximizing. The proclaimed goal of economics is to find welfare-maximizing policies. Because of the difficulties associated with measuring welfare, many economists – and the vast majority of legal economists – focus instead on wealth maximization. The generally implicit (but flawed) assumption is that social welfare rises monotonically with social wealth. In fact, people often express a willingness to trade some material wealth in exchange for intangible values such as justice, fairness, or even predictability. Rules that seem unjust, then, are even less likely to maximize social welfare than they are to enhance social wealth.

[1] Elisabeth M. Landes and Richard A. Posner, 1978, "The Economics of the Baby Shortage," *The Journal of Legal Studies*, 7, pp. 323–348.
[2] Richard Epstein, 1992, *Forbidden Grounds: The Case against Employment Discrimination Laws*, Cambridge, MA: Harvard University Press.
[3] Dennis W. Carlton and Daniel R. Fischel, 1983, "The Regulation of Insider Trading," *Stanford Law Review*, 35, pp. 857–896.
[4] See also Thomas J. Miceli and Kathleen Segerson, 2007, "Punishing the Innocent along with the Guilty: The Economics of Individual versus Group Punishment," *The Journal of Legal Studies*, 36, pp. 81–106 (group punishment); James D. Miller, 1997, "Using Lotteries to Expand the Range of Litigation Settlements," *The Journal of Legal Studies*, 26, pp. 69–94 (settling disputes by lottery); Moin A. Yahya, 2006, "Deterring Roper's Juveniles: Using a Law and Economics Approach to Show that the Logic of Roper Implies that Juveniles Require the Death Penalty More than Adults," *Penn State Law Review*, 111, pp. 53–106 (executing minors).

For comments on this chapter, we thank Mark White.

In this chapter, we argue that legal economists' failure to include people's preferences for fairness undermines their policy prescriptions. Section I discusses three prominent counterintuitive proposals from legal economists. Section II argues that the proper focus of law and economics is welfare and not wealth, and legal economists should not assume welfare is enhanced whenever wealth is maximized. Section II then turns to people's preferences for fair rules. Here, we discuss the empirical evidence of people's preferences for fair rules, and argue that given this evidence, it is methodologically unacceptable for legal economists to fail to include (and to give sufficient weight to) these preferences within their calculations. Section III discusses the likely costs of actually adopting rules that are broadly perceived as surprising and unfair. Such rules are likely to defeat reasonable expectations, instigate resistance, and undermine the overall legitimacy of the legal system. As a result, these proposals fail even on their own wealth- and welfare-maximizing terms.

I. A FEW SALIENT EXAMPLES

The law-and-economics literature is rife with examples of proposals that would strike most noneconomists as unfair, immoral, or at least unexpected. In this section, we highlight a few prominent examples to concretize the phenomena and ground our subsequent discussion.

A. Baby-Selling

Richard Posner is generally considered the most prominent legal economist alive today. In 1978 he and coauthor Elisabeth Landes proposed that "baby-selling" (their term, not ours) be legalized.[5] Employing sophisticated mathematical modeling and statistical analysis, the authors claimed that creating an open legal market for paying a natural mother for the right to adopt her child would have numerous positive effects. They argued that paying mothers for their children would reduce the number of abortions, eliminate the shortage of babies available for adoption, and decrease the number of unadopted children kept in foster care.

Posner and Landes acknowledged that many people would consider a market in children "undesirable," and they cited commentators who referred to such a market as "dealings in human flesh" and a "taint on civilized society."[6] They also admitted that permitting natural parents to sell their children might "smack of slavery" and produce "moral outrage."[7] But they argued that these objections were not well founded. Unlike slaves, children sold through their system would retain the protections of legal prohibitions on child abuse and neglect, though these protections might admittedly prove inadequate. Also, although a market system would not screen parents for suitability the way the current system does, they doubted the value of such screening and proposed requiring some "minimal background investigation" for buyers in the baby market, a sort of driver's license

[5] Landes and Posner, "Baby Shortage," pp. 323–348.
[6] Ibid., p. 339.
[7] Ibid., pp. 344–345.

for baby purchasers.[8] Landes and Posner took comfort in their faith that people do not generally buy expensive items in order to damage them, analogizing adoption of a child to the purchase of a television set.[9]

Perhaps their most telling point is their analysis of the likely costs of babies in the newly legalized market. Although the black market for babies results in high prices, they argued that in a legal market babies would be relatively affordable.[10] Among their arguments, Landes and Posner contended that the *net* cost would be quite low because the costs to the natural mother would be substantially identical to those saved by the adoptive mother in not bearing a child herself. Although this theory might have some validity when applied to medical costs,[11] we think most mothers would find quite surprising the proposition that the amount they would demand to give up their children consists mostly of the medical costs they incurred during pregnancy and birth.

B. Racial Discrimination

In his landmark 1992 book *Forbidden Grounds*, Richard Epstein relied on economic arguments to explain why the laws prohibiting racial discrimination in employment should be repealed.[12] Epstein's arguments are no more premised on malice toward racial minorities than Landes and Posner's were based on hatred of babies. To the contrary, Epstein believes that laws prohibiting racial discrimination actually harm racial minorities (along with everyone else) and that repealing these laws would benefit everyone.

Epstein premised his case on the notion that discrimination may sometimes reduce agency costs and therefore prove efficient.[13] Governance costs rise as the tastes of the firm's members and employees diverge. One way to reduce agency costs and promote harmony within the firm, then, is to hire employees with similar tastes. Employees who share the same tastes in music, Epstein illustrated, will not quarrel over what type of music to play in a common workspace. Finding workers with similar tastes will often result in hiring a disproportionate number of some particular racial minority, whose members may be more likely to share some tastes than the components of a more diverse group.

Another way to reduce agency costs is to recruit through a third-party referrer who implicitly bonds the workers' performance.[14] For an example, Epstein drew on the case of the Daniel Lamp Company, which established relationships with two Hispanic groups, the Spanish Coalition and the Latino Youth Organization, each of which recommended unskilled workers for employment. The organizations then

---

[8] Ibid., p. 343.

[9] Ibid.

[10] Ibid., pp. 339–341.

[11] Even when applied to medical costs, we actually doubt the theory's validity. Presumably, mothers giving up their children would tend to be of much lower economic status than adopting mothers, and therefore much less likely to have adequate medical insurance.

[12] Epstein also argued against laws prohibiting gender, age, and disability discrimination (*Forbidden Grounds*, p. 9).

[13] Ibid., pp. 57–65

[14] Ibid., pp. 70–71.

had a vested interest in ensuring that the workers they recommended were of high quality, because otherwise the company would stop trusting them for referrals and they would lose a valuable opportunity for their members. This system resulted in cheap bonding for the workers and an inexpensive source of reliable labor, helping to maximize the company's earnings. The system also resulted in the company hiring mostly Hispanic workers and commensurate liability under the antidiscrimination laws.

Finally, Epstein pointed out that if bigots concentrated themselves in firms that discriminated against racial minorities, firms that did not discriminate would end up relatively bigot-free. Without the interference of antidiscrimination laws, this would be likely to occur. Bigots would likely seek out firms that discriminated, because they strongly preferred to avoid contact with racial minorities. By means of the bigots' self-selection, firms that did not discriminate would have few bigots, even if the companies themselves were indifferent as to whether their employees were bigots. Firms without bigots should be easier to manage and therefore face lower governance costs.[15]

Epstein fully understood that his proposal was alarming. On the very first page of his book he stated, "There is little question that a broad antidiscrimination principle lies at the core of American political and intellectual understandings of a just and proper society, not only in employment but also in housing and public accommodations, medical care, education, indeed in all areas of public and private life."[16] He reiterated this point several times in different ways, stating that the antidiscrimination statutes command "enormous support" from U.S. elites, quoting President George Herbert Walker Bush vilifying discrimination as a "'fundamental evil that tears at the fabric of our society,'"[17] and claiming that even as strong and independent an institution as the U.S. Supreme Court could not "withstand the pounding that would result if it undertook a frontal assault on the basic antidiscrimination norm."[18] Nevertheless, he concluded that the antidiscrimination statutes should be repealed.[19] Discrimination should be legal because it was often rational and wealth-maximizing.[20]

C. Insider Trading

In the *Stanford Law Review*, renowned legal economists Dennis Carlton and Daniel Fischel argued that insider trading should be permitted.[21] They acknowledged that

---

[15] Ibid., pp. 74–75.

[16] Ibid., p. 1.

[17] Ibid., p. 3.

[18] Ibid., p. 6.

[19] Ibid., p. 9 (advocating the repeal of Title VII as it applies to private employers operating in competitive markets without legal protections against new entries).

[20] Ibid., pp. 68–69.

[21] Carlton and Fischel, "Insider Trading." They are certainly not alone. See, for example, Edmund W. Kitch, 1980, "The Law and Economics of Rights in Valuable Information," *The Journal of Legal Studies*, 9, pp. 683–724 (permitting insider trading would result in more accurate securities prices); Henry G. Manne, 1970, "Insider Trading and the Law Professors," *Vanderbilt Law Review*, 23, pp. 547–590 (same).

many consider insider trading unfair,[22] but concluded that the practice was efficient nonetheless. They argued that insider trading would at least in some cases promote more accurate securities prices.[23] Insider trading provides an alternative avenue of communication from the firm to investors. When the market detects trading by insiders, it adjusts the company's stock price accordingly, bidding the price up higher if insiders are buying and reducing the price if insiders are selling. The end result under ideal conditions may approach the effect of actually disclosing the inside information. Companies may prefer to disclose through insider trading for a number of reasons, such as when disclosure would destroy the value of the information (such as the presence of oil under land the company is considering buying) or when the information is uncertain and the company wishes to avoid liability for a misdisclosure if the information turns out to be false. Accurate pricing is wealth-maximizing for a number of reasons, but chiefly because correct prices permit investors to reduce their investments on discovering improperly valued securities.

Carlton and Fischel also contended that insider trading would constitute a more efficient way to compensate and hire managers.[24] Shareholders desire compensation schemes that will induce managers to seek out and implement high-expected-value opportunities. Legalizing insider trading may produce the correct incentives. Insider trading rewards managers who discover good opportunities and put them into effect by permitting them to trade in advance of public knowledge of the company's imminent success. Insider trading may prove a cheaper method of incentivizing managers than renegotiating each time a corporate opportunity arises or structuring complicated incentives contracts *ex ante*. In addition, insider trading may turn out to be a valuable screening tool in selecting managers who will work hard and will take efficient levels of risk.[25] Because insider trading rewards hard-working managers who create profitable opportunities for the corporation, only such managers should be willing to accept insider trading as a substantial component of their compensation. These are precisely the managers corporations generally want to hire.

Carlton and Fischel acknowledged that insider trading might not always be efficient for every corporation.[26] They discussed numerous concerns that might render insider trading disadvantageous for some companies in some circumstances, such as the moral hazard problem and issues concerning disclosure timing.[27] The inherent unfairness of insider trading to noninsider market participants, however,

---

[22] See *In re Cady Roberts & Co.*, 40 SEC 907, 912 (1961) (concern that uninformed may be exploited); Donald C. Langevoort, 1982, "Insider Trading and the Fiduciary Principle: A Post-Chiarella Assessment," *California Law Review*, 70, pp. 1–53 (rule's acceptance rests in intuition that insider trading is unfair); Donald C. Langevoort, 1999, "Rereading Cady, Roberts: The Ideology and Practice of Insider Trading Regulation," *Columbia Law Review*, 99, pp. 1319–1343 (rationale is that insiders should not be permitted to take advantage of shareholders); Saul Levmore, 1982, "Securities and Secrets: Insider Trading and the Law of Contracts," *Virginia Law Review*, 68, pp. 117–160 (insider trading violates fairness goals).

[23] Carlton and Fischel, "Insider Trading," pp. 865–868.

[24] Ibid., pp. 869–872.

[25] Ibid., pp. 871–872.

[26] Ibid., pp. 861–866.

[27] Ibid., pp. 872–882.

received short shrift. In a few short paragraphs, the authors argued that if insider trading is efficient, and therefore increases the total resources to be divided, then it benefits both insiders and outsiders as a class.[28] In other words, because insider trading makes even outsiders wealthier than they would be without insider trading, the practice cannot be unfair.

II. WEALTH, WELFARE, AND FAIRNESS

These three examples – baby-selling, employment discrimination, and insider trading – highlight the tendency of legal economists to treat fairness concerns as largely irrelevant to their policy recommendations. Legal rules that produce greater wealth should be chosen even if – perhaps *especially* if – they contradict commonly held notions of justice and fair play. In section III, we argue that this strategy is misguided under both wealth- and welfare-maximization frameworks.

The purpose of the present section is to introduce two methodological difficulties. First, legal economists often focus on maximizing wealth as a proxy for maximizing welfare. However, it is social *welfare* that economists seek to enhance, and wealth is often a poor approximation of welfare. Second, legal economists discount or completely ignore people's preferences for fairness, at most mentioning that their proposals run contrary to these tastes. In this section, we argue that there is robust empirical evidence of people's preference for fairness and that this preference cannot be ignored in legal economists' welfare calculations.

A. Wealth versus Welfare

More than twenty-five years ago, in a famous pair of articles, Richard Posner argued that the goal of legal economists should be to divine the policies that would promote wealth maximization, rather than welfare maximization.[29] Although the extreme version of this view of wealth maximization as moral theory has been energetically criticized (and Posner himself has disavowed this view), economists often defend wealth maximization models as a useful simplification that tracks social welfare.[30] More importantly, in practice legal economists overwhelmingly use wealth-maximization models, rather than welfare maximization.[31]

This tendency courts frequent and substantial analytical errors. Wealth does not equate with welfare. To the contrary, under many circumstances people will willingly trade material goods for other values, such as distributional fairness or

[28] Ibid., pp. 880–882.
[29] Richard Posner, 1979, "Utilitarianism, Economics, and Legal Theory," *The Journal of Legal Studies*, 8, pp. 103–140; and 1980, "The Ethical and Political Basis of the Efficiency Norm in Common Law Adjudication," *Hofstra Law Review*, 8, pp. 487–508.
[30] See Louis Kaplow and Steven Shavell, 2002, *Fairness versus Welfare*, Cambridge, MA: Harvard University Press, p. 37 (criticizing wealth maximization); Richard Posner, 1995, "Wealth Maximization and Tort Law: A Philosophical Inquiry," in David G. Owen, ed., *Philosophical Foundations of Tort Law*, Oxford: Oxford University Press, pp. 99–111 (disavowing wealth maximization as a moral theory but defending the use of wealth-maximization models in choosing legal rules).
[31] See, for example, Kaplow and Shavell, *Fairness versus Welfare*, pp. 100–103, 124–133, 174–203, 232–241, 254–272 (using wealth-maximization models).

justice. Experience provides numerous examples of such choices, such as blood donations, charitable gifts, and wealthy people supporting a sharply progressive taxation system. Considerable ingenuity has been devoted to developing strategic explanations for some of these behaviors,[32] and experiments such as the ultimatum game verify the widely held intuition that wealth often yields to other values.[33] The growing research on happiness also calls into question the extent to which increases in wealth correlate with overall increases in well-being.[34]

B. Fairness

1. **Fairness as a preference.** Within welfare economics, an actor's concern for fairness is simply one preference among others. Hence, to the extent that citizens express a preference for fairness, this preference – like preferences for money or happiness – must be taken into account. Some welfare economists label this preference for fairness a "taste for fairness."[35]

For our purposes here, we will use the term "fairness" as a rough proxy for other-regarding preferences that deviate from the presumption that individuals prefer those things in their rational self-interest. That is, individuals may have fairness preferences in equality and proportionality, but they may also be motivated by altruism or envy.[36]

Because this chapter is an internal critique of law and economics, we will take seriously the claim that fairness concerns are simply preferences. But before doing so, we wish to note two ways in which fairness may be more than simply a preference.

First, welfare economists must make initial determinations about how to aggregate preferences. Does everyone count? Does everyone count equally? These questions cannot be answered without making value judgments. Moreover, a selection among distributive approaches will have an effect on the outcome of the social welfare function. For example, a decision to count everyone's preferences equally yields a very different result than counting only the preferences of white males. Crucially, the decision between these possibilities must be made by a criterion outside of the welfare counting mechanism itself.[37]

---

[32] See Eric A. Posner, 2000, *Law and Social Norms*, Cambridge, MA: Harvard University Press.

[33] For example, Ruben Durante and Louis Putterman recently conducted a fascinating experiment that found that a large majority of subjects were willing to give up a significant portion of the game's payoff in "taxes" in exchange for a more equal distribution of profits. See Durante and Putterman, "Preferences for Redistribution and Perception of Fairness: An Experimental Study" (http://ssrn.com/abstract=1004573, accessed July 27, 2007). For further discussion of the ultimatum game, see text accompanying notes 45 and 46.

[34] See generally Ed Diener and Martin E. P. Seligman, 2004, "Beyond Money: Toward an Economy of Well-Being," *Psychological Science in the Public Interest*, 5, pp. 1–31.

[35] As described by Kaplow and Shavell, individuals may have "a taste for a notion of fairness, just as they may have a taste for art, nature, or fine wine" (*Fairness versus Welfare*, p. 21).

[36] For an empirical attempt to distinguish among these preferences, see Jeremy Clark, 1998, "Fairness in Public Good Provision: An Investigation of Preferences for Equality and Proportionality," *Canadian Journal of Economics*, 31, pp. 708–729.

[37] On these points, see generally Michael B. Dorff, 2002, "Why Welfare Depends on Fairness: A Reply to Kaplow and Shavell," *Southern California Law Review*, 75, pp. 847–900.

Second, many theorists believe that fairness concerns may trump otherwise welfare-maximizing rules. In the hypothetical case "Surgeon," a surgeon seeks to cut up one healthy individual and distribute his organs to five sick individuals.[38] Theorists argue that even if this rule were welfare-maximizing,[39] cutting up one individual would be impermissible because doing so would be appropriating him.[40]

At this point, however, we would like to put these two (substantial) concerns to the side. For the remainder of this chapter, we will try to assess the strength of the "taste for fairness," and argue that, even when fairness is viewed as a taste, economists are paying too little attention to how this taste may undermine not only the legal rule that they are proposing but also the legal regime as a whole.

2. Evidence of the preference for fairness. A thorough empirical calculation must include all factors that could influence the result. Of course, some factors may not be statistically significant, and depending upon one's discipline and the need for exact calculations, some factors may be ignored. However, the mere lip service that is given to the taste for fairness within the legal economist's typical empirical conclusions is utterly unacceptable. The taste for fairness is pervasive, and the preference for fairness is strong.

At the outset, we note that we do not need to rely on empirical studies to make this claim. The taste for fairness is patent within our society. Children complain if a rule is "unfair" but not if it is inefficient. We teach our children what it means to deserve praise and blame. And we teach our children not to discriminate against people of different sexes, races, or religions; to believe that humans may not be bought or sold; and to value fair play.

However, we can make our case beyond even these obvious observations. The taste for fairness runs deep. Consider first the capuchin monkey: scientists conducted tests in which they gave capuchins food in exchange for rocks.[41] Capuchins like cucumbers and happily exchange rocks for them. However, capuchins prefer grapes to cucumbers. During the test, the scientists gave some monkeys grapes for rocks and others cucumbers for rocks. After seeing that other monkeys were receiving grapes, the cucumber-receiving monkeys stopped exchanging the rocks for food or refused to eat the cucumbers – "a directly accessible food that they readily accept and consume under almost any other set of circumstances."[42] From this, the researchers concluded that capuchins "measure reward in relative terms, comparing their own rewards with those available, and their own efforts with those

---

[38] See Judith Jarvis Thomson, 1986, "The Trolley Problem," in William Parent, ed., *Rights, Restitution, and Risk: Essays in Moral Theory*, Cambridge, MA: Harvard University Press, pp. 95–116. For the argument that such a rule would not be Pareto-superior, see Kimberly Kessler Ferzan, 2004, "Some Sound and Fury from Kaplow and Shavell," *Law and Philosophy*, 23, pp. 73–102.

[39] That is, assuming that this would not lead to great social instability and so forth (the very repercussions we discuss in the following).

[40] Larry Alexander, 2005, "Lesser Evils: A Closer Look at the Paradigmatic Justification," *Law and Philosophy*, 24, pp. 611–643.

[41] Sarah F. Brosnan and Frans B. M. de Waal, 2003, "Monkeys Reject Unequal Pay," *Nature*, 425, pp. 297–299.

[42] Ibid., p. 298.

of others."[43] Thus, to a monkey, it is not simply how many rewards one may receive that matters, but how well off one is compared to others.

Even among human beings, the scientific documentation of the taste for fairness is robust. Individuals have tastes for fairness that run contrary to rational-actor assumptions. One study asked individuals how tickets should be distributed in a case in which demand exceeded supply.[44] The subjects' clear order of preferences was standing in line, then a lottery, then an auction. Of course, economic predictions run in the exact opposite order – favoring auctions (he who values the ticket most will pay most) and disfavoring lines (which are wasteful).

Perhaps the most famous endorsement of fairness is the ultimatum game.[45] In the ultimatum game, two subjects are told that they will split a sum of money. One subject proposes how the two will split the money. The second subject then either accepts or rejects the offer. If the offer is accepted, the money is split according to the offered terms. If the offer is rejected, neither subject receives anything. Purely rational actors in the proposing role would offer a split in which the offeror receives nearly all the money and the offeree receives next to nothing. Purely rational offerees would accept these offers because even a little money is better than nothing. Each subject plays the game only once, so there are no incentives to cooperate stemming from a repeated-play strategy. In a result surprising only to economists, across many cultures offerors often propose a roughly even split (around 40 percent on average), and offerees faced with drastically unfair proposals frequently reject the offer.[46] In other words, the ultimatum game demonstrates robustly that people willingly sacrifice their pecuniary self-interest to promote other values such as fairness.

These are but a few of the empirical studies that clearly demonstrate that individuals have a strong preference for fairness. Indeed, this preference is sometimes stronger than any preference individuals have to act in their rational self-interest. Because individuals weight fairness so heavily, any policy that seeks to enhance their welfare must take account of their fairness preferences.

3. Responses to fairness. Given the empirical evidence of the taste for fairness, one should expect that fairness significantly figures into social welfare calculations made by legal economists. This, however, is not the case. Rather, legal economists

---

[43] Ibid., p. 299.

[44] Daniel Kahneman, Jack L. Knetsch, and Richard H. Thaler, 1986, "Fairness and the Assumptions of Economics," *The Journal of Business*, 59, pp. S285–S300.

[45] See Joseph Neil Bearden, "Ultimatum Bargaining Experiments: The State of the Art" (http://ssrn.com/abstract=626183, November 2001); Werner Guth et al., 1982, "An Experimental Analysis of Ultimatum Bargaining," *Journal of Economic Behaviour and Organization*, 75, pp. 367–388.

[46] Bearden, "Ultimatum Bargaining," pp. 5–7; Alvin E. Roth et al., 1991, "Bargaining and Market Behavior in Jerusalem, Ljubljana, Pittsburgh, and Tokyo: An Experimental Study," *American Economic Review*, 81, pp. 1068–1095; Joseph Henrich et al., 2001, "In Search of Homo Economicus: Behavioral Experiments in 15 Small-Scale Societies," *American Economic Review*, 91, pp. 73–78; Hessel Oosterbeek et al., 2004, "Differences in Ultimatum Game Experiments: Evidence from a Meta-analysis," *Experimental Economics*, 7, pp. 171–188 (although exact percentages vary quite a bit, the average of the means of the offered shares is approximately 40 percent).

seem to adopt one of two strategies: some have simply ignored fairness, whereas others have attempted to explain it away.

More often than not, fairness is simply ignored. As Kahneman, Knetsch, and Thaler have noted,

> The economic agent is assumed to be law-abiding but not "fair" – if fairness implies that some legal opportunities for gain are not exploited. This nonfairness assumption expresses a resistance to explanations of economic actions in moral terms that has deep roots in the history of the discipline. The central insight that gave rise to modern economics is that the common good is well served by the free actions of self-interested agents in a market.[47]

As Kahneman, Knetsch, and Thaler note, there are two possible reasons for this neglect – one substantive and one methodological.[48] The substantive claim is that one may believe that there is no real substantive content to fairness. If fairness concerns are really just charades for self-interest, then there is no need to account for fairness. The methodological claim is simply this – things just get too complicated when theorists must take into account fairness calculations. If the benefit of economic modeling is answers, then the more factors, the more complicated the model, and the harder those answers are to come by.

Taking the methodological rationale first, we simply believe that this factor cannot be ignored. *Legal* economists are presumably making policy recommendations that they believe *should become the law*. The calculations may be complicated. However, if a theorist is going to advocate a particular position as the welfare-maximizing one, then that policy should truly – all things considered – maximize welfare. As for the substantive claim, it seems to us that the burden is on legal economists to *show* – through empirical data – that fairness in effect is simply self-interest in disguise. However, given the current data that exist, the taste for fairness runs deep and must be accounted for, not ignored.

Some legal economists attempt to undermine the role of fairness by explaining our attachment to it. For instance, Harvard legal economists Louis Kaplow and Steven Shavell present a two-step argument against fairness.[49] First, they link fairness theories to social norms. Here, they assert a causal thesis to explain why the reader is attracted to fairness, arguing that the attachment to fairness theories comes from their similarity to social norms that are inborn (via evolution) or inculcated. Second, Kaplow and Shavell argue that social norms themselves should not provide an independent basis for making legal policy decisions. They claim that social norms serve as rules of thumb for advancing social welfare and have evolved or were indoctrinated for this purpose; hence, because welfare economics can calculate social welfare directly, reliance on these social norm proxies is unnecessary.[50]

There are two problems with this argument. First, as Jules Coleman comments, "the view that the existence of a causal explanation of the facts that someone holds or asserts a particular claim undermines the truth of the claim asserted simply

[47] Kahneman et al., "Fairness and Assumptions," p. S286.
[48] Ibid.
[49] Kaplow and Shavell, *Fairness versus Welfare*, pp. 63, 136–139, 357–359.
[50] Ibid., pp. 68, 71.

cannot be sustained."[51] Indeed, as Coleman notes, even if evolution selected for beliefs, why would it select for false beliefs over true ones?[52] Second, Kaplow and Shavell's move from the observation that social norms enhance welfare to the claim that they were inculcated for this purpose is a *non sequitur*.[53] There are other explanations for why fairness beliefs may often be welfare-enhancing. Fairness beliefs and social norms may be linked by a common morality, and, even if not aimed at maximizing welfare, it would be a short-lived morality that did not somehow enhance it.

III. THE PERILS OF IGNORING FAIRNESS

In this section, we argue that when theorists fail to take fairness into account, their proposals may maximize neither wealth nor welfare, because they defeat reasonable expectations or even instigate resistance. Additionally, the legal rule may have significant negative externalities – it may undermine the legal system as a whole.

A. Getting the Calculation Wrong: The Failure of the Legal Rule to Maximize

1. Defeating reasonable expectations. In a democracy, people should and generally do expect the country's laws to be fair and to make sound intuitive sense. For small-scale transactions, those whose value does not justify paying for sophisticated legal assistance, the participants are likely to rely primarily on their intuitions as to the content of the governing background rules. These expectations are reasonable and, in the aggregate, will be heavily relied upon. Legal rules that go against the grain of expectations will be ignored in such transactions, rendering even the most interesting and potentially efficient rules useless in instilling appropriate incentives. A large part of any rule's value lies not in the results it produces in litigation but in the shadow it casts on behavior outside of litigation. These motivating effects are severely diluted to the extent they fall below the radar of their targets and run counter to intuition.

Worse, litigation over such small-scale transactions will likely unwind the parties' precautions and produce unjust windfalls. At the time they enter into their transaction, both parties likely think the governing rule is the intuitive rule. That rule allocates rights to the parties in a way they both understand and consider to be fair. They build the transaction around the rule as they think it to be, and price the deal accordingly. They also take whatever steps they think prudent to ensure performance and to insure against risk according to their understanding of how the law will allocate each party's rights and duties. If the parties later have a dispute arising from the transaction, the court will declare victory for one party over the other on the basis of the actual legal rule in effect. When the legal rule produces a different result from the rule the parties thought applied, their preparations are

---

[51] Jules L. Coleman, 2003, "The Grounds of Welfare," *Yale Law Journal*, 112, pp. 1511–1544.
[52] Ibid., p. 1534.
[53] See generally Ferzan, "Sound and Fury," p. 93.

likely to go awry. Plus, the surprised victor will gain a windfall at the expense of the dismayed loser. The parties agree to the contract price with a common understanding that they are allocating certain entitlements to each. When the court reverses the parties' distribution, it essentially forces the losing party to pay for the entitlement twice: once as part of the contract price and a second time as damages from the litigation.

Although high-value transactions guided by expensive counsel seem less vulnerable to this phenomenon, rules governing obscure or rare aspects of the transaction may suffer from a similar dynamic. Even experienced lawyers are unlikely to be aware of rules that cover relatively rare situations. A lawyer uncertain about the law could expend resources in research to discover the truth, but that search will occur only when the lawyer is aware of his or her ignorance. In the more likely situation in which a lawyer is unaware that a special exception exists, that exception may be ignored until it is too late, again defeating expectations.

To understand this dynamic more concretely, imagine that a state adopted a law reinstating the doctrine of *caveat emptor* ("buyer beware") for a narrow class of contracts only – say, contracts dealing with the sale of used cars by used car dealers. Ignoring the expectation problems described in this section, such a rule might be efficient. In such sales, both parties can easily be placed on roughly equal footing. Although the seller possesses more information about the car's history, that advantage can easily be eliminated by the buyer's hiring a mechanic to inspect the car or making the sale contingent on a complete disclosure of the car's maintenance records. In this context, then, there may not be any great need to overcome legal economists' usual presumption, illustrated by all three of our introductory examples, that freedom of contract should triumph over any regulatory impulses to protect one side or the other in a transaction. Our claim is not that such a rule would *actually* be efficient – we can certainly see some arguments that alternative rules might be better, such as the advantages of imposing liability on the party with more information *ex ante* – but only that there are sufficiently strong arguments in its favor that it is reasonable to suppose it *might be* efficient.

Once we consider the rule's effects on settled expectations, however, its efficiency becomes much more doubtful. In the last few generations, American consumers have increasingly come to expect a certain level of fairness protection in their transactions, especially in their transactions with relatively sophisticated counterparties. In fact, this *caveat emptor* proposal would represent a significant change in the existing law of most states. The sale of a car is regulated by Article 2 of the Uniform Commercial Code, because cars are movable goods.[54] Article 2 applies certain implied warranties in the absence of express disclaimers.[55] One of these is the *implied warranty of merchantability*, that provides that, unless excluded, a warranty is implied in the sale of goods by a merchant (such as a used car dealer)

---

[54] Uniform Commercial Code § 2-102 (Article 2 applies to contracts for the sale of goods) and § 2-105 (goods are all things that are movable, with certain exceptions not relevant here).

[55] See, for example, Uniform Commercial Code § 2-314 (Merchantability) and § 2-315 (Fitness for a Particular Purpose).

that the goods will be merchantable, meaning essentially that they are fit for the ordinary purposes for which such goods are used.[56] Many states provide even more protection in the form of *lemon laws*, which provide enhanced remedies when dealers sell consumers cars that are in particularly poor shape and cannot be adequately repaired.[57] The proposed *caveat emptor* rule, by contrast, would not imply any warranties at all. Instead, the background default rule would provide that buyers of used cars took them on a strictly "as is" basis, even if they turned out not to run.

The *caveat emptor* rule, then, would represent a sharp diversion from consumers' current expectations. Consumers buying used cars from dealers expect a certain level of basic protection. Although at one time this may not have been true – witness the still lingering reputation of used car dealers as untrustworthy – we suspect Article 2 and the passage of lemon laws in many states have largely changed consumers' expectations. Consumers now are much less likely to take precautions when buying a used car from a dealer, such as having the car inspected by a mechanic or insisting on a written warranty. Should the law change to a regime of *caveat emptor*, these consumers would go unprotected and often end up with a lemon without recourse against the dealer. Over time, consumer groups might manage to educate the public about the new need to take greater care, but until then (and for many consumers, even after then), consumers as a group would likely suffer a substantial loss from the adoption of the new rule. This loss detracts greatly from the proposal's efficiency, perhaps enough to outweigh whatever gains might be made from the increased freedom of contract. At a minimum, legal economists have paid insufficient attention to the effect on settled expectations, an important factor in measuring a proposal's efficiency.

2. **Instigating resistance.** Whereas the last section discussed a fairly technical problem that is often overlooked by economists, in this section we focus on an issue further afield from the rational-actor model legal economists favor. Legal economists tend to think of people's attitudes towards rules as reflective of their underlying pecuniary interests. Corporations care about maximizing their profits; individuals care about maximizing their income. Both corporations and individuals will support policies that enhance their financial prospects and oppose policies that will likely cause them economic harm. But actual human beings often care most about concerns that are entirely nonpecuniary and will sometimes willingly suffer financial losses in order to further other interests. Although it would be trite to state this in any noneconomic context, human beings often care deeply about justice, equality, freedom, fairness, and religion, to name but a few of humanity's core nonpecuniary concerns.

Nonpecuniary interests are often the most powerful motivators of human behavior, and social engineers such as legal economists ignore them at their peril. In

---

[56] Uniform Commercial Code § 2-314.

[57] See, for example, 8 Ala. Code § 8-20A-2 (dealer must refund purchase price and pay any damages for car that cannot be brought into conformity with express warranties); Cal. Civil Code §§ 1793.22–1793.25 (same); Fl. St. Ann. §§ 681.10–681.118 (same); NY Gen. Bus. Law § 198-a (same).

particular, individuals who find a particular law offensive may actively attempt to circumvent it and undermine its enforcement even when such opposition is costly. This behavior may impair the efficiency benefits that would come from broad compliance.

As an example of this problem, let us imagine that Congress adopted Richard Epstein's proposal to eliminate the antidiscrimination statutes. What would actually happen to a company that adopted an expressly discriminatory hiring policy? Antidiscrimination norms have taken deep root in the past two generations. Under these conditions, who would do business with a company that blatantly discriminated in hiring? Even a company that adopted its discrimination policy quietly would risk exposure every time an applicant of a disfavored race was rejected despite excellent qualifications. In fact, it would be difficult for a company to reap the benefits Epstein identified without making some public statement of its policy, so that members of the privileged race would know to apply in greater numbers (not to mention the bigots). Once a company's discrimination policy was revealed to the public, it would no doubt face immediate public condemnation and boycotts organized by groups representing the excluded races. Indeed, the boycotts would likely be joined by groups representing every race and religious group, because no race (and no representative group) would want to be seen as condoning racial discrimination. It is difficult to imagine that any company that stuck to an express discriminatory hiring policy could long survive, regardless of the policy's legality. The apparent efficiencies that Epstein argued could be gained by eliminating the legal restrictions on racial discrimination evaporate once we take into account people's likely resistance to laws they strongly oppose.[58]

Epstein's proposal represents perhaps an extreme, in that nearly everyone at least publicly expresses opposition to racial discrimination. Other proposals might be less universally condemned and therefore receive less effusive opposition. But our point holds true for any policy that a sizable group passionately opposes on principled grounds. A sufficiently outraged opposition will take steps to undermine the law it opposes, even when such opposition's expense far outweighs any anticipated material benefits from a policy change. The resulting costs should be taken into account when determining if a proposed law is truly wealth-maximizing.

B. The Hidden Externalities of Unfair Rules: Undermining Moral Norms and Legitimacy

1. Why citizens obey the law. Why do people obey the law? The economist's answer focuses on deterrence: the law induces obedience by establishing appropriate incentives. We obey the law because the law ensures that it is in our interests

---

[58] Epstein might contend that our analysis proves his point, that laws forbidding racial discrimination are unnecessary, because the same result – nondiscriminatory hiring – can be achieved without them. But this is not how he justified his argument in *Forbidden Grounds*. Instead, there he relied on the efficiencies that would result from permitting discrimination. More importantly, our purpose is not to argue the merits of any particular policy proposal, but to demonstrate that legal economists frequently overlook the important consequences that result from individuals' strong opposition to some legal rules.

to do so.[59] The law can create these incentives either by promising rewards for compliance or by threatening punishment for disobedience.

The law's success in coaxing obedience depends on the credibility of the threatened punishment, which in turn hinges on both the likelihood of detection and the magnitude of punishment.[60] If we believe we are almost certain to be caught and punished, we are much less likely to steal than if we believe we are likely to escape with the stolen goods. Deterrence, however, is costly. To make the threat of punishment credible, a government must invest heavily in police, courts, and prisons, both to increase the perceived risk of capture and to imprison those who are caught and convicted. For this reason, economists' vision of the law's goal is not necessarily to achieve perfect deterrence – and therefore perfect obedience – but rather to find the point at which the next dollar spent on deterring crime yields less than one dollar's worth of crime prevention. The goal, in other words, is an efficient level of crime.[61]

Although economists believe that citizens obey the law because they are threatened into obedience, other scholars who have studied this question take a broader view of the possible causes of obedience.[62] Sociologists, social psychologists, and political scientists argue that important factors in addition to deterrence include peer attitudes toward crime, internal moral norms, and the legitimacy of the government institutions that create, administer, and enforce the law.[63] Deterrence and peer attitudes are both externally imposed methods of achieving obedience, whereas internal moral norms and legitimacy are internally motivated sources of compliance.[64] These four sources of obedience are interrelated, so that a change in one may have a greater or lesser impact through resulting changes in the others.

In some cases, deterrence is a factor. Material incentives are an important determinant of human behavior. Not surprisingly, because this is the element economists favor, incentives are the factor least likely to be directly affected by the choice of counterintuitive or apparently unfair rules. As long as the incentives are clear and well known, they should tend to make the desired behavior more likely (and the undesired behavior less likely). But the results frequently will be less straightforward than economists predict, depending on the remaining three factors.

---

[59] See generally Gary S. Becker, 1968, "Crime and Punishment: An Economic Approach," *Journal of Political Economy*, 76, pp. 169–217.

[60] Ibid., p. 176.

[61] Ibid., p. 170; see also Keith N. Hylton, 2005, "The Theory of Penalties and the Economics of Criminal Law," *Review of Law and Economics*, 1, pp. 175–201 (reconciling Becker's optimal-level-of-crime approach with Posner's full-deterrence approach). However, this goal has proven elusive. See Paul H. Robinson and John Darley, 2004, "Does Criminal Law Deter? A Behavioural Science Investigation," *Oxford Journal of Legal Studies*, 24, pp. 173–205.

[62] See Tom Tyler, 1990, *Why People Obey the Law*, New Haven: Yale University Press.

[63] See generally ibid.; Mark D. White, 2005, "A Social Economics of Crime (Based on Kantian Ethics)," in Margaret Oppenheimer and Nicholas Mercuro, eds., *Law and Economics: Alternative Economic Approaches to Legal and Regulatory Issues*, Armonk, NY: M.E. Sharpe, pp. 351–373; Paul H. Robinson and John M. Darley, 1997, "The Utility of Desert," *Northwestern University Law Review*, 91, pp. 453–499.

[64] See Tyler, *Why People Obey the Law*, pp. 23–26.

Peer attitudes toward compliance with the law, in contrast, may tend to undermine obedience to rules that are surprising or seem unfair. Tom Tyler's seminal Chicago study of legal adherence demonstrated that people distinguish among different laws when asked whether their peers would disapprove if they were arrested for committing one of a series of crimes. Whereas only about half of respondents felt that their peers would disapprove if they were arrested for making too much noise, littering, speeding, or parking illegally, the vast majority of respondents predicted their peers would disapprove if they were arrested for drunk driving (86 percent) or shoplifting (89 percent).[65] Tyler's study demonstrated that anticipated peer attitudes vary with the seriousness or moral blameworthiness of the crime. Crimes that appear less blameworthy, either because they cause less harm or do not violate a core moral precept, garner less peer censure than those that are likely to cause great harm (such as drunk driving) or those that do violate fundamental moral principles (such as the prohibition against theft). Violations of laws that outlaw conduct that appears harmless or innocent are unlikely to provoke much peer criticism. Such laws are consequently less likely to be obeyed. Economists who focus solely on material incentives in predicting compliance will therefore greatly overstate the likelihood of observance of counterintuitive or seemingly unfair rules.

Like peer attitudes, internal moral norms may limit compliance with odd or immoral laws. Tyler's Chicago study demonstrated that most people feel that breaking the law is morally wrong, and that this is one of the major reasons why people tend to obey the law.[66] To the extent people do not feel a particular law parallels their personal morality, then, their internal moral norms are far less likely to help to induce compliance.[67] This effect should prove particularly powerful when people believe a law opposes their morality. We see a dramatic example of this effect in abortion foes who bomb clinics. Although they know that destruction of property is illegal, they proceed because they believe their actions serve a higher moral purpose, that of preventing what they perceive to be legally sanctioned murder. They choose to violate laws they presumably agree with (those banning destruction of others' property) in order to prevent enforcement of a law they virulently oppose (legalization of abortion). Although this is an extreme example, it does illustrate the guiding principle: people are less likely to obey a law that is not reinforced by their internal moral norms.

The fourth and final source of obedience comes from a law's legitimacy. "Legitimacy" refers to the perceived obligation to obey.[68] Citizens may feel an obligation to obey a law or a legal authority (such as a leader, judge, or police officer) when that law or authority stems from a process or institution that they feel creates an adequate justification for obedience.[69] For example, Americans who believe

---

[65] Ibid., p. 44.

[66] Ibid., p. 56.

[67] The Chicago study also found that the vast majority of respondents said that people should obey a law even if goes against what they think is right (ibid., p. 46). This finding, however, must be read in conjunction with the studies that demonstrate that this measure of legitimacy declines among people who disagree with the government's substantive policy choices.

[68] See ibid., pp. 27–28; Max Weber, 1947, *The Theory of Social and Economic Organization* (trans. A. M. Henderson and Talcott Parsons), London: Free Press of Glencoe.

[69] See Tyler, *Why People Obey the Law*, p. 28.

in representational democracy may feel that a statute passed by both the House and the Senate and signed by the president should be obeyed even if they disagree with the statute's substance. The institutions that promulgated the law are rooted in a principle – representational democracy – that most Americans feel rightly demands their obedience. As a result, those institutions have a great deal of legitimacy in American political culture and can often induce compliance even from those who dissent from particular policy decisions.

Legitimacy, however, is a variable sociological characteristic, not a physical constant. The legitimacy of sources of law and those who enforce it may decline if the laws seem wrong or bizarre. As a result, people may stop obeying even laws that do not seem strange, because the overall legitimacy of the system is undermined. Sociological studies support this notion that those who oppose the decisions of legal institutions also feel those institutions are less legitimate.[70] Legitimacy thus provides some maneuvering room for governmental agents to advance policies that may not be popular, but legitimacy is ultimately linked to a government's ability to fulfill its people's desires.[71] A government that advances laws that appear immoral or strange may find its legitimacy undermined. Legal economists should consider these risks when arguing for such proposals, because the harmful effects on the government's legitimacy may far outweigh any marginal efficiency gained by adopting counterintuitive rules. Counterintuitive and/or unfair rules may sometimes prove wealth-maximizing, but that calculation is far more complex than most legal economists have heretofore acknowledged. Such rules may have nuanced effects on social wealth through their effect on expectations, their conflict with nonpecuniary interests, and their deleterious impact on citizens' tendency to obey the law.

These insights imply that the best way to prevent crime may not be to focus on deterrence directly. Applying the findings of Tyler and others, Paul Robinson and John Darley contend that the criminal law is best served by conforming to citizens' perceptions of just desert.[72] As they argue, criminal law serves an essential function in both shaping and enforcing moral norms. When citizens perceive a law to be unfair, this may undermine the criminal law's legitimacy and the willingness of citizens to defer to the law in unclear cases. As Robinson and Darley forcefully argue, legal economists' prescriptions to deviate from desert are far from costless, but rather, may significantly undermine crime control.[73]

2. The flouting thesis. Very little has been done to test the empirical assumption that unfair rules will undermine overall faith in the justice system. Still, it seems that any theorist who argues that his counterintuitive rule is efficient is implicitly (albeit unwittingly) making the claim that, even taking into account the extent

---

[70] See ibid., p. 30; see also Anke Grosskopf and Jeffery J. Mondak, 1968, "Do Attitudes toward Specific Supreme Court Decisions Matter? The Impact of Webster and Texas v. Johnson on Public Confidence in the Supreme Court," *Political Research Quarterly*, 51, pp. 633–654; Valerie J. Hoekstra, 2000, "The Supreme Court and Local Public Opinion," *The American Political Science Review*, 94, pp. 89–100; Walter F. Murphy and Joseph Tanenhaus, 1968, "Public Opinion and the United States Supreme Court: Mapping of Some Prerequisites for Court Legitimation of Regime Change," *Law and Society Review*, 2, pp. 357–384.

[71] See Tyler, *Why People Obey the Law*, p. 30.

[72] Robinson and Darley, "Utility of Desert."

[73] Ibid., p. 478.

to which this rule undermines citizen respect for the law, it is still the best rule. And, because the legal economist is making such a claim, the burden lies on the economist to address and to refute any arguments that this rule will be more detrimental than beneficial.

Preliminary research does confirm that the legal economist should take these concerns seriously. One theorist who has attempted to understand the extent to which an unfair rule will undermine overall faith in the system is Janice Nadler.[74] Nadler recently examined the assumed but unproven *flouting thesis*: "When a person evaluates particular legal rules, decisions or practices as unjust, the diminished respect for the legal system that follows can destabilize otherwise law-abiding behavior."[75] In the course of three experiments, Nadler first exposed subjects to a story depicting a just or an unjust outcome. Then, in a seemingly unrelated experiment, Nadler tested whether subjects would commit "borderline" crimes or engage in jury nullification. In two of the three experiments, those subjects exposed to an unjust story were then later willing to break an unrelated law. There is certainly more empirical work to be done, but Nadler's research confirms that the flouting thesis is not just a matter of theoretical concern. Unfair rules may ultimately undermine the law itself.

With the flouting thesis in mind, let us return to the proposals with which we began. Imagine that laws were enacted that allowed for baby-selling, discrimination, and insider trading. We now see that these sorts of laws may undermine the law's overall legitimacy. If most people believe that discrimination is profoundly wrongful, then they will view the law as making a profound moral mistake in allowing for discrimination. As already mentioned, it is entirely possible that they would then be less willing to defer to the law as a source of moral advice when they are unsure of what to do. Thus, even if these laws are wealth- or welfare-maximizing in the individual case, they may ultimately have significant external costs that do not render them wealth- or welfare-maximizing when considering the legal system as a whole.

3. Undermining the value of rules. There is one final way in which the law may lose its power. The legal rule may undermine the social norm and the fairness belief itself. That is, even assuming that Kaplow and Shavell are correct and fairness rules are but imperfect proxies for complex social welfare standards, the economist cannot ignore the value of having rules. When legal economists urge that we look beyond fairness beliefs to see whether in any particular case a rule is maximizing, they are choosing between the value of rules and the value of standards. This trade-off must also be taken into account in their calculations.

The rule-versus-standards debate is perhaps most famously embodied in the debate between Oliver Wendell Holmes and Benjamin Cardozo. To Holmes, the "featureless generality" of negligence would ultimately give way to specific *per se* rules, such as "stop, look, and listen."[76] But Cardozo had the last word, holding

---

[74] Janice Nadler, 2005, "Flouting the Law," *Texas Law Review*, 83, pp. 1399–1442.
[75] Ibid., p. 1401.
[76] See *Baltimore & O.R. Co. v. Goodman*, 275 U.S. 66, 70 (1927); Oliver Wendell Holmes, 1881, *The Common Law*, New York: Dover.

that such *per se* rules could not take into account all the circumstances so as to adjudicate correctly negligence liability in future cases.[77]

There are values to having rules as opposed to standards.[78] First, rules can solve physical coordination problems. In situations in which there are several different (and incompatible ways) to resolve a problem (for example, which side of the street to drive on), a rule can offer a solution.[79] Rules can also solve social coordination problems. To the extent that the morally right thing to do turns in part of what others are likely to do (for instance, a prisoner's dilemma), rules provide a basis for prediction.[80]

But rules have other values as well. The rule promulgator may have greater moral or factual knowledge than a citizen.[81] Additionally, rules help avert errors. When a complex decision must be made, actors who must decide under a standard – analyzing a multitude of factors – may simply get the calculations wrong.[82] And, by having a rule, decision-making costs are reduced.[83] As Larry Alexander and Emily Sherwin have explained, "The quality that identifies a rule and distinguishes it from a standard is the quality of determinateness.... [A] rule is a posited norm that fulfills the function of posited norms, that is, that settles the question of what ought to be done."[84]

Despite the values of rules, there is the problem is that they may be overinclusive. This is, of course, Kaplow and Shavell's complaint. If the standard is welfare maximization, and a fairness rule is but a rough proxy, the rule may sometimes be wrong.[85] Interestingly, however, oftentimes rules are effective only because citizens do not frequently question whether they should follow a rule in any particular case.[86]

For our purposes, what is essential to note is that *even if fairness rules only serve a proxy function*, undermining that function may have devastating effects in cases in which we want citizens to follow the rule. Ultimately, the value of legal rules is consequentialist. Thus, even if the underlying consequentialist standard (assuming this is what underlies the rule, of course) dictates that discrimination, or cheating, or baby-selling is the appropriate course in one specific set of circumstances, this sort of deviation from the norms of fairness and equality may undermine the value of the rules themselves. A legal economist cannot afford to ignore such consequences.

---

[77] *Pokora v. Wabash Ry. Co.*, 292 U.S. 98, 104 (1934).

[78] See generally Larry Alexander and Emily Sherwin, 2001, *The Rule of Rules: Morality, Rules, and the Dilemmas of Law*, Durham, NC: Duke University Press; Frederick Schauer, 1991, *Playing by the Rules: A Philosophical Examination of Rule-Based Decision-Making in Law and in Life*, Oxford: Clarendon Press.

[79] See Alexander and Sherwin, *Rule of Rules*, p. 56; Schauer, *Playing by the Rules*, § 7.7.

[80] See Alexander and Sherwin, *Rule of Rules*, pp. 57–58.

[81] Schauer, *Playing by the Rules*, p. 55.

[82] Ibid., p. 150.

[83] Ibid., p. 137.

[84] Alexander and Sherwin, *Rule of Rules*, p. 30.

[85] Ibid., pp. 32, 35.

[86] See generally Larry Alexander and Emily Sherwin, 1994, "The Deceptive Nature of Rules," *University of Pennsylvania Law Review*, 142, pp. 1191–1226.

CONCLUSION

In this chapter, we have sought to urge legal economists to take fairness concerns seriously. There is robust evidence that individuals have a preference for fair rules. Without taking these strong preferences into account, a legal economist cannot be sure that his proposal is actually welfare-maximizing. Moreover, even if a proposal is discretely maximizing, an unfair rule may do significant damage to the value of the rule of law itself. In the face of this empirical evidence, legal economists who fail to take fairness preference into account are ignoring a variable essential to their calculations.

Perhaps the failure to include fairness concerns reflects the legal economists' fear that to do so would be to abdicate their calculators for armchairs. The economist, who seeks empirical data, may find the prospect of navel gazing about fairness to be the antithesis of his discipline. But the legal economist need not fear. Rather, just as the legal economist may wish to empirically discover the best legal rule, he may also empirically test the strength of individuals' tastes for fairness. Indeed, some studies have found that the citizenry's taste for fairness (or lack thereof) may not coincide with initial expectations.[87] Of course, fairness theorists may be unwilling to concede that preference for fairness is just a taste, but legal economists' acknowledging that fairness is valued will lead to better proposals and more productive scholarship.

---

[87] Kahneman et al., "Fairness and Assumptions," p. S295.

3   Functional Law and Economics

JONATHAN KLICK AND FRANCESCO PARISI

During its relatively short history, the law-and-economics movement has developed a wide spectrum of methodological approaches, distinguishable for their respective emphasis on positive, normative, or functional economic analysis. Ronald Coase's "The Problem of Social Cost" is generally considered to provide the foundations of the first identifiable school of thought – the Chicago school of positive law and economics.[1] Proponents of the Chicago school argue that market forces cause the common law to develop efficient, or wealth-maximizing, legal rules. As suggested by the Coase theorem, only transaction costs will impede first-best efficiency. An important premise of law and economics is that the common law is the result of an effort, conscious or not, to induce efficient outcomes. This premise, first intimated by Coase, and known as the hypothesis of efficiency of the common law, suggests that common-law rules enjoy a comparative advantage over legislation in fulfilling this task because of the evolutionary selection of common-law rules through adjudication and the gradual accretion of precedent.[2] Much of the early work of the positive school of law and economics aims at explaining how common-law rules provide individuals with proper incentives such that society's wealth is maximized. To the extent that positive law-and-economics scholars formulate any prescriptive corollaries, they tend to focus on the reduction of transaction costs that stand in the way of wealth maximization.

Although the positive arguments apply less well to statutory law, adherents of the Chicago school often also believe in the efficiency of political markets, and argue that market forces in the political arena will also tend to generate wealth-maximizing outcomes, subject to the transaction-cost proviso.[3] In the choice between having politicians and having courts govern individual behavior, the positive school favors the institution facing lower transaction costs. Following Coase,

---

[1] Ronald H. Coase, 1960, "The Problem of Social Cost," *Journal of Law and Economics*, 3, pp. 1–44.

[2] This hypothesis is developed more fully in Richard A. Posner, 2007, *Economic Analysis of Law*, 6th ed., New York: Aspen Publishing, and Paul Rubin, 1977, "Why Is the Common Law Efficient?," *Journal of Legal Studies*, 6, pp. 51–63.

[3] For the clearest expositions of this position, see Gary Becker, 1983, "A Theory of Competition among Pressure Groups for Political Influence," *Quarterly Journal of Economics*, 98, pp. 371–400, and Donald Wittman, 1995, *The Myth of Democratic Failure: Why Political Institutions Are Efficient*, Chicago: University of Chicago Press.

Richard Posner has played a key role in shaping the methodological approach of the Chicago school. Posner believes that positive economic analysis is immune to most abuse and misuse, because it is merely used to explain or predict incentives that guide individuals and institutions under alternative legal rules. The primary hypothesis is the notion that efficiency is the predominant factor shaping the rules, procedures, and institutions of the common law. Posner contends that efficiency is a defensible criterion in the context of judicial decision making because "justice" considerations, for which there are no academic or political consensus, introduce unacceptable ambiguity into the judicial process. In arguing for positive use of economics, Posner does not deny the existence of valuable normative law-and-economics applications. In fact, law and economics often have many insights into normative analysis of policy.

The second school of law and economics emerges around the Yale school. Due to its methodological emphasis, the Yale school is generally described as the normative school of law and economics. Unlike the Chicago school, the Yale school is much more skeptical of the natural development of the common law, in view of the presence of market failures, which impede the achievement of efficiency. Further, proponents of the normative school suggest that efficiency is only one of many normative goals that can and should be pursued through the law. The Yale school of law and economics believes that there is a larger need for legal intervention in order to correct for pervasive forms of market failure. Distributional concerns are often regarded as an integral part of efficiency considerations by the scholars who adhere to this school. The overall philosophy of this school is often criticized by the Chicago school for being value-tainted and excessively prone to policy intervention.

The Yale school considers market failures to be more pervasive than Chicago scholars are willing to admit.[4] Employing similar tools to the positive school, normative law and economics pushes the analysis to formulate propositions on what the law ought to be like. Legal intervention becomes a critical policy instrument for correcting market failures. Given the overriding need to pursue justice and fairness in distribution through the legal system, most Yale-style scholars would suggest that efficiency, as defined by the Chicago school, could never be the ultimate end of a legal system.[5] Chicago scholars, on the other hand, acknowledge that although normative corollaries are in principle useful and desirable, in assessing the costs and benefits of a proposed rule the weighting of noneconomic factors renders the analysis highly vulnerable to subjective ideology.

Some degree of controversy still surrounds several of the methodological, normative, and philosophical underpinnings of the economic approach to law, although most of the ideological differences tend to lose significance because they

---

[4] Ejan Mackaay, 2000, "History of Law and Economics," in Boudewijn Bouckaert and Gerrit de Geest, eds., *Encyclopedia of Law and Economics*, vol. 1, Cheltenham: Edward Elgar Publishing, pp. 65–117.

[5] Put another way, whereas both schools largely adopt forms of utilitarian social welfare functions in their implicit optimization problems, Yale school adherents are more likely to adopt nonuniform weights on the individual utility arguments because of their normative positions on the importance of distributional concerns.

lead to analogous results when applied to real cases. Some scholars perceive that the current state of law and economics is comparable to the state of economics prior to the advent of public choice theory, insofar as an understanding of "political failures" was missing from the study of market failures.[6] Public choice may indeed inject a skeptical, and at times disruptive, perspective into the more elegant and simple framework of neoclassical economics, but this added element may well be necessary to understand a complex reality.

As the domain of law and economics has expanded, a new generation of literature, developed at the intersection of law, economics, and public choice theory, has pushed the boundaries of the economic analysis of law, studying the origins and formative mechanisms of legal rules. The resulting approach, the *functional* approach to legal analysis, is quite skeptical of both the normative and the positive alternatives.[7] The functional approach is wary of the generalized efficiency hypothesis espoused by the positive school. In this respect, the functionalists share some of the skepticism of the normative school. There is little empirical support for a generalized trust in the efficiency of the law in any individual area of the law, much less a universal efficiency. The functional school of law and economics is even more vocally skeptical of a general efficiency hypothesis when applied to sources of the law other than common law (e.g., legislation or administrative regulations). The functional approach is also critical of the normative extensions and *ad hoc* corrective policies that are often advocated by the normative schools. Because economic models are merely a simplified depiction of reality, functionalists think it is generally dangerous to use such tools to design corrective or interventionist policies. In this respect, the functionalists are aligned with the positive school in their criticism of the normative approach. According to both the positivists and the functionalists, normative economic analysis often risks overlooking the many unintended consequences of legal intervention.[8]

Individuals subscribing to the functional school of law and economics are less sanguine about both the efficiency tendencies of the common law and the ability of legal and political elites to micromanage decisions to achieve nonefficiency goals. Although functional law-and-economics scholars recognize the potential for market failures to inhibit the common law from naturally achieving wealth maximization, they also draw from the field of public choice economics to highlight the dangers of giving political or judicial policymakers substantial discretion.

---

[6] See James M. Buchanan, 1974, "Good Economics – Bad Law," *Virginia Law Review*, 60, pp. 483–492, and Charles K. Rowley, 1981, "Social Sciences and the Law: The Relevance of Economic Theories," *Oxford Journal Legal Studies*, 1, pp. 391–405.

[7] For the earliest comprehensive formulation of this position, see Gordon Tullock, 1971, *The Logic of the Law*, New York: Basic Books.

[8] For a more extensive intellectual history, see Francesco Parisi, 2005, "Methodological Debates in Law and Economics: The Changing Contours of a Discipline," in Francesco Parisi and Charles K. Rowley, eds., *The Origins of Law and Economics: Essays by the Founding Fathers*, Cheltenham: Edward Elgar, pp. 33–52. For a recent articulation of this position in the face of one of the modern branches of the normative school, the behavioral law-and-economics movement, see Jonathan Klick and Gregory Mitchell, 2006, "Government Regulation of Irrationality: Moral and Cognitive Hazards," *Minnesota Law Review*, 90, pp. 1620–1663.

I. CONSTITUTIONAL DESIGN AND METARULES

Public choice theory and constitutional political economy provide the methodological foundations for the functional school of law and economics. The findings
of public choice theory, though supporting much of the traditional wisdom, pose
several challenges to neoclassical law and economics. In spite of the advances
of economic analysis, judges and policymakers in many situations still lack the
expertise and methods for evaluating the efficiency of alternative legal rules. The
functional approach to law and economics is informed by an explicit recognition
that whatever social reality we seek to explain at the aggregate level ought to be
understood as the result of the choices and actions of individual human beings
who pursue their goals with an independently formed understanding of the reality
that surrounds them,[9] and will be conditioned on the incentive structure in which
they operate.[10] Courts and policymakers should therefore first inquire into the
incentives and the social structure underlying a legal problem, rather than directly
attempting to weigh the costs and benefits of individual rules.[11]

In this way, the functionalist approach to law and economics can extend the
domain of the traditional law-and-economics inquiry to include both the study
of the influence of market and nonmarket institutions (other than politics) on
legal regimes, and the study of the comparative advantages of alternative sources
of centralized or decentralized lawmaking in supplying efficient rules. With this
focus on the underlying legal and social structure, micromanaging individual legal
and policy decisions becomes less attractive. Such micromanagement is likely to
suffer from the rent-seeking activities of interested parties. Much of the intellectual
foundation for this structural focus can be found in the seminal writings of James
Buchanan.[12] Buchanan eloquently describes the constitutional political economy
research program in his Nobel Prize address: "I sought to make economic sense
out of the relationship between the individual and the state before proceeding to
advance policy nostrums."[13]

Drawing on the method of constitutional political economy, the functional law-
and-economics school focuses on the creation of incentive-compatible metarules

---

[9] Viktor J. Vanberg, 1994, *Rules and Choice in Economics*, London: Routledge.

[10] For empirical illustrations of this general point, see Eric Helland and Alexander Tabarrok, 2002,
"The Effect of Electoral Institutions on Tort Awards," *American Law and Economics Review*, 4,
pp. 341–370; Eric Helland and Jonathan Klick, 2007, "The Effect of Judicial Expedience on Attorney
Fees in Class Actions," *Journal of Legal Studies*, 36, pp. 171–188; and Nuno Garoupa, Eric Helland,
and Jonathan Klick, 2008, "The Effect of Attorney Compensation on the Timing on Settlements"
(unpublished manuscript, regarding how judges make decisions in specific institutional settings,
leading to a fairly clear divergence from efficiency or even the kinds of goals generally espoused by
those in the normative school).

[11] On this point, see Robert Cooter, 1994, "Structural Adjudication and the New Law Merchant:
A Model of Decentralized Law," *International Review of Law and Economics*, 14, pp. 215–231
(introducing the similar idea of structural adjudication of norms).

[12] A good summary of Buchanan's structural vision of government and society can be found in Geoffrey
Brennan and James M. Buchanan, 1985, *The Reason of Rules: Constitutional Political Economy*, New
York: Cambridge University Press.

[13] James M. Buchanan, 1987, "The Constitution of Economic Policy," *American Economic Review*, 77,
p. 243.

to which rational individuals would consent at the constitutional stage of decision making while they are uncertain as to how those rules will directly affect their own self-interest. This constitutional perspective was first used in economics by James Buchanan and Gordon Tullock[14] and bears a good deal of resemblance to the "veil of ignorance" mechanism introduced by John Rawls[15] around the same time.[16] The *ex ante* perspective avoids the temptation to engage in micro-level social engineering because it depends on committing to rules that will be optimal in expectation, while recognizing that those rules will likely generate undesirable outcomes from time to time.

The constitutional design element of functional law and economics deviates from the Chicago school to the extent that efficient institutions are not assumed simply to evolve over time. Instead, functionalists take as their primary function the design of institutions in which individual incentives are harnessed to reach the social goals agreed upon at the constitutional stage. Recognizing that market failures limit the natural evolution of efficient legal rules, functionalists attempt to design institutions that internalize the external costs and benefits created by individual behavior in order to achieve the social goals chosen at the constitutional stage. However, also recognizing the existence of government failure, functionalists are not willing to allow political and legal elites or majorities to align individual actions with social goals on an issue-by-issue basis. Eschewing any romantic visions of government or the courts, functionalists assume that public figures are self-interested and will pursue their own interest, often to the detriment of the social interests that would be acceptable to all at the constitutional stage.

To mediate between distrusting the natural evolution of law and being suspicious of government or legal interference in social interactions, functionalists examine both formal and informal institutions to determine the underlying processes that give rise to the institutions and whether the institutions would be acceptable to a rational individual at the constitutional stage. The benchmark against which the value of any institution is to be judged is an individual's *ex ante* decision to submit to the institution or the proposed change to the institution. This benchmark implies a modified unanimity rule in which adoption or modification of a social institution requires effective unanimity among those affected by the institution. Although true unanimity is the ideal, functionalists recognize that, at the constitutional stage, individuals would voluntarily agree to a sub-unanimity rule due to the transaction costs generated by requiring unanimous agreement.[17] In practice, the inquiry advocated by functional law-and-economics scholars requires an investigation into the origins of the social institution, the incentives created by the social institution,

---

[14] James M. Buchanan and Gordon Tullock, 1962, *The Calculus of Consent: Logical Foundations of Constitutional Democracy*, Ann Arbor: University of Michigan Press.

[15] John Rawls, 1971, *A Theory of Justice*, Cambridge, MA: Belknap Press.

[16] Whereas both sources seem to have been influenced by John Harsanyi (1953, "Cardinal Utility in Welfare Economics and in the Theory of Risk-Taking," *Journal of Political Economics*, 61, pp. 434–435), Rawls departs from Harsanyi (and Buchanan and Tullock) by implicitly imposing a condition of severe risk aversion, which generates his maximin criterion for just social rules.

[17] See Jonathan Klick and Francesco Parisi, 2003, "The Disunity of Unanimity," *Constitutional Political Economy*, 14, pp. 83–94.

and an articulation of the conditions that have changed, making the original consent to the institution no longer tenable from the *ex ante* perspective. This kind of principled inquiry reduces the scope for legal and political entrepreneurs to implement extractive rules that exploit diffuse interests in favor of concentrated ones.[18]

II. FUNCTIONAL PRINCIPLES OF LAWMAKING: SOME EXAMPLES

Functionalists examine decentralized, voluntary exchanges as a mechanism for welfare maximization. The school challenges the positivist belief that rules must come from an institutionalized authority such as a legislative or judicial body to constitute proper law. In the absence of market failures, voluntary social arrangements offer a rebuttable presumption of efficiency, even in those areas where notions of market failure and high transaction costs have justified formal legislation. In the following we will illustrate the methodology of functional law and economics by reference to two examples: choice of law and the principle of reciprocity.

A. The Metaphor of the Market for Legal Rules

The Coase theorem suggests that when the contractual surplus exceeds transaction costs, parties will enter into welfare-enhancing contractual arrangements. Similarly, parties will select the most efficient legal regime whenever the benefits drawn from choosing a foreign body of law exceed the attendant transaction costs. Liberal rules for the enforcement of choice-of-law provisions are therefore instrumental in reducing the transaction costs of the bargain. The normative corollary calls for a clear and unambiguous enforcement of such agreements.[19]

Despite this efficiency rationale, whether and to what extent parties should be free to choose the law that regulates their actions and relationships is an age-old quandary.[20] According to its advocates, choice of law provides the basis for interjurisdictional competition. Any restriction on the contractual freedom of choice of law, like any constraint on market competition, should be utilized only when

[18] For a systematic and exhaustive discussion of this point, see James M. Buchanan and Roger D. Congleton, 1998, *Politics by Principle, Not Interest: Toward Nondiscriminatory Democracy*, Cambridge: Cambridge University Press.

[19] For an empirical examination of the potential efficiency loss generated when legal institutions create an impediment to this contractual choice of legal regime, see Jonathan Klick, Bruce Kobayashi, and Larry Ribstein, 2008, "The Effect of Contract Regulation: The Case of Franchising" (unpublished manuscript).

[20] Historically, the parties' autonomy in choosing the applicable law originated from international commercial law. For example, medieval Europe featured autonomous systems of law (e.g., mercantile law and maritime law) whose applicability turned on the express or implied choice of the parties. Sixteenth- and seventeenth-century legal scholars in England and continental Europe referred to the parties' intentions as the primary criterion for the resolution of conflicting contract clauses. The same characterized the French approach at the time of the 1804 codification and nineteenth-century German scholarship, though there is some disagreement on the matter (for a historical analysis, see Ole Lando, 1976, "Contracts," in R. David et al., *International Encyclopedia of Comparative Law*, Tübingen: JCB Mohr, pp. 17–23). Later, both in Europe and in the United States, legislative and jurisprudential solutions limited the parties' autonomy in their choice of governing law.

there is systematic institutional or market failure. Scholars have considered the desirability of a constitutional constraint on the state's ability to impose unilateral restrictions on choice of law.[21]

The modern rules for enforcing choice-of-law agreements limit the freedom of parties in various ways. Even the most liberal choice-of-law regimes (e.g., France) condition the enforcement of choice-of-law agreements on preserving the integrity of essential interests of the domestic legal system. Other systems allow it only if the agreement does not circumvent mandatory provisions of the domestic legal system (e.g., Austria). Yet other jurisdictions tend to regulate choice of law with a complex mixture of standard- and rule-based criteria (e.g., the United States) that are often complemented by an intricate combination of exceptions that are rarely linked by a common rationale.[22]

There are various practical reasons for parties to choose a law different from their forum law, not all of which are immediately consistent with the efficiency hypothesis. Several functionalist arguments have been put forward to identify the proper limits of freedom of contract vis-à-vis state and third-party interests.[23] As previously discussed by Parisi and Ribstein,[24] these arguments include those that are (1) externality-based, (2) information-based, and (3) market-based.

1. Individual autonomy and externality-based limitations. One of the most frequently addressed issues in the choice-of-law debate relates to the tension between the private interests of contracting parties and the interests held by the state and third parties. For example, the unconstrained freedom of private parties may circumvent state policy and infringe upon the interests of parties not in privity with the contract. The Coasian presumption of the social desirability of transactions

---

[21] A similar analysis should be extended to the role of public international law in constraining states' assertions of superior interest in limiting free choice of law. See, for example, Arthur von Mehren and Donald T. Trautman, 1981, "Constitutional Control of Choice of Law: Some Reflections on the Hague," *Hofstra Law Review*, 10, pp. 35–57, and Frederic L. Kirgis, Jr., 1976, "The Roles of Due Process and Full Faith and Credit in Choice of Law," *Cornell Law Review*, 62, pp. 94–150.

[22] The U.S. Restatement (First) of Conflict of Laws of 1934 did not contain any provision for contractual choice of law. Courts tended to enforce choice-of-law clauses where the parties' express choice resolved an otherwise present conflict-of-law problem. See Larry Ribstein, 1993, "Choosing Law by Contract," *Journal of Corporation Law*, 18, pp. 245–300. The Restatement (Second) of Conflicts established the enforceability of express choice of law as a primary factor for conflict of law analysis in contracts. A standard-based criterion was introduced in the United States by the Uniform Commercial Code, which adds a "reasonable relation" requirement for the enforcement of contractual choice of law. For a discussion of the modern choice of law, see Francesco Parisi and Erin O'Hara, 1998, "Conflict of Laws," in Peter Newman, ed., *New Palgrave Dictionary of Economics and the Law*, New York: Palgrave Macmillan, pp. 491–492.

[23] In transnational contracts, parties select a neutral law different from their individual domestic legal systems, according to how future disputes will be resolved per the neutral law. In other instances, the parties select a foreign body of law because of its relationship to the purpose of their contract, to avoid the simultaneous application of different legal systems to the same relationship, to homogenize the governing law when a party enters a contract with several different parties of different nationalities, to reduce bargaining costs, to opt out of some undesirable provisions of the otherwise applicable legal system, or to take advantage of greater familiarity with the chosen law than with the otherwise applicable forum law.

[24] Francesco Parisi and Larry Ribstein, 1998, "Choice of Law," in Peter Newman, ed., *New Palgrave Dictionary of Economics and the Law*, New York: Palgrave Macmillan, pp. 238–240.

is relaxed in the presence of Pareto-relevant externalities, which are often found when the analysis incorporates third-party expectations.[25] In other instances, the externality turns on state interests. This may refer simply to the interests of the residents or citizens of the forum state, or to a claim of infringement of a direct state interest. Most often, such claims are made in conjunction with the forum state's coordination policies.[26] Alternatively, the state may assert a need to maintain coherent and uniform case law within forum courts.[27] A third issue raised in the choice-of-law debate involves administrative and judicial costs. When choice of law is not accompanied by a choice-of-forum clause, courts are forced to apply a system of rules with which they may be grossly unfamiliar, having no record of past decisions on the point. This may lead to substantial information costs and unpredictability in the decision-making process.[28]

According to the functionalist paradigm, the externality-based arguments to justify legal limits on freedom of choice are often ill informed. Restrictions on choice of law aimed at containing the judicial or administrative costs are generally inappropriate. Rather than limiting the autonomy of the parties, forum courts should restrict parties' choice of law, inducing them to take full account of the increased costs due to their decision to use foreign laws. An individualized evaluation of the private surplus and external costs would impose a formidable burden on the courts, resulting in prejudice to reliability and predictability. A rule-based approach, though possessing greater transparency, would unnecessarily limit the freedom of the parties, curtailing possible Pareto-superior arrangements. A sound economic analysis should focus more attentively on the endogenous and price-based institutional correctives of the externalities, perhaps leading to differential tax rates applied to transactions or parties deviating from forum law to internalize these external costs.

2. Information-based rationales for restrictions on choice of law. Another set of functional arguments for limiting the parties' autonomy rests on asymmetric information.[29] Several legal systems distinguish between bargained-for contracts

---

[25] From an economic perspective, most of the arguments based on third-party protection are logically vitiated. For instance, if externalities were to be conceived as a result of the parties' choice of law, a social welfare analysis should consider the trade-off between the benefit to the contracting parties and the potential external cost imposed on the third parties. The resulting case-by-case analysis would impose a formidable judicial burden on courts and generate much uncertainty. Furthermore, a contract that affects third parties does not create relevant externalities if the third parties have a low-transaction-cost opportunity to protect themselves via relevant contractual terms (Parisi and Ribstein, "Choice of Law," p. 238). This too is a simple application of the Coase theorem.

[26] Modern legal systems often distinguish between the choice of law governing the validity of the agreement and the choice of law governing its content. States will more rigorously scrutinize choice of law affecting the validity of contracts to preserve their interest in this area.

[27] Ole Lando, "Contracts," pp. 33–34.

[28] In order to correct this problem, some legal systems create an exception to the *ius novit curia* rule, according to which foreign law is treated as a fact and subjected to the burden of pleading and proof of the parties.

[29] For example, in the case of contractual choice of law, limits are imposed in order to protect uninformed parties who may agree to a choice-of-law clause without being aware of the substantive content of the invoked rules. Similarly, the Restatement (Second) of Conflict of Laws § 568 contemplates rules designed to protect a person from the oppressive use of superior bargaining power.

and standard-form agreements. The protection of uninformed parties is more rigorous in the case of standard-form agreements, given the asymmetric incentives to acquire information regarding the governing law and the less visible elements of the agreement. A contractual choice of law allegedly gives the drafter an advantage in selecting a more favorable set of terms without expressly bargaining with the other contracting party.

Recent functionalist scholarship has suggested that most of the information-based rationales for limiting choice of law do not survive close scrutiny. Quite frequently, parties are ill informed on the applicable forum law but are not exempted from its application. This result should not change in the choice-of-law context, because parties have no better knowledge of the forum law than the law they expressly choose in their contract. If anything, the express choice of the parties should signal their informed preference for the chosen law. Any limitation of the parties' freedom on the basis of an imputed lack of information is therefore likely to be purely paternalistic, but there is generally no reason to assume that the state is in a better position to know what is in the parties' best interests.

3. The market for rules. Yet another functional approach is to conclude that the optimal restriction on choice of law is none at all. Choice-of-law provisions tend to increase efficiency by allowing parties to contract away inefficient forum laws that could not be modified through express contractual terms. Individuals and firms can select away from inefficient mandatory rules by choosing an alternative legal system without bearing the cost of relocation or acquiring a particular status in the chosen jurisdiction. The scholarship hypothesizes that liberal choice-of-law regimes give states an incentive to compete by providing efficient legal rules.[30] Choice of law, in other words, behaves similarly to the product marketplace.[31] Furthermore, the competitive supply of laws constrains rent-seeking legislation. Redistributive policies will not be possible under an unrestricted choice-of-law regime, given the adverse selection that would be generated.

The analogy of law as a product[32] provides the basis for a general theory of competitive supply of laws. Freedom of choice of law is an essential prerequisite for any process of effective competition. The application of the theory of market failures to the efficiency hypothesis discloses some issues of potential relevance.[33] Any limitation on the enforcement of contractual choice of law should only be used when the less disruptive cost-based alternatives appear to fail.

Choice-of-law advocates claim that competitive supply may improve the selection and quality of laws. In general, there is no clear public choice model that

---

[30] Larry Ribstein, "Choosing Law," pp. 249–250.

[31] Roberta Romano, 1985, "Law as a Product: Some Pieces of the Incorporation Puzzle," *Journal of Law, Economics and Organization*, 1, pp. 225–283.

[32] Ibid.

[33] Some demand-side constraints may be readily discarded for their paternalistic nature and for failing to consider the transaction-specific knowledge that parties use to determine their choice of governing law, which will be largely unavailable to the jurisdiction's lawmakers and will generally doom the "one size fits all" nature of most paternalistic interventions. The analysis should also consider the reach of endogenous market and institutional devices in the correction of possible spillover effects of the parties' choice of law.

supports the hypothesis that legislators maximize the popularity of their legislation outside their jurisdiction. Lawmakers do not have a residual claim on the supplied legislation, such as the ability to charge a hypothetical price for the adoption of the supplied law by foreign parties. Likewise, there is no revenue effect of the parties' choice of law (e.g., increased tax revenues from companies incorporated in the territory). Good law is a public good because legislators do not capture the entire benefit created by the law that they supply. As such, law may remain chronically undersupplied. Choice of law allows parties to pick the best available law, mitigating the effects of the undersupply of good law, but it does not remedy that undersupply problem. If lawmakers cannot benefit from making better law, then the fact that parties can select better laws from different jurisdictions does not entirely remedy that incentive problem.

B. Reciprocity as a Metarule in the Design of Law

Another example of functional legal analysis is given by the principle of reciprocity. This rests on the observation that individuals choose among rules of behavior by employing the same optimization logic they use for all economic choices. True preferences are unlikely to be revealed when individual interests are not aligned. Strategic preference revelation has traditionally been viewed as a hindrance to the spontaneous emergence of cooperation. Such a problem is likely to be minimized in situations of role reversibility or stochastic symmetry,[34] which induce each member to agree to rules that benefit the entire group, thus maximizing the individual's expected share of the wealth.[35]

There is always the possibility of subsequent opportunistic deviation when roles are later reversed.[36] Where rules are breached following role reversal, norms play a collateral yet crucial role in sanctioning case-by-case opportunism. A merchant who invokes a particular rule when buying but refuses to abide by the same

---

[34] See Francesco Parisi, 1995, "Toward a Theory of Spontaneous Law," *Constitutional Political Economy*, 6, pp. 211–231, and Vincy Fon and Francesco Parisi, 2008, "Role-Reversibility, Stochastic Ignorance, and Social Cooperation," *Journal of Socio-Economics*, 37, pp. 1061–1075.

[35] These conditions occurred during the formative period of the medieval law merchant when traveling merchants acted in the dual capacity of buyer and seller. The law merchant illustrates a successful system of spontaneous and decentralized law (see Bruce L. Benson, 1989, "The Spontaneous Evolution of Commercial Law," *Southern Economic Journal*, 55, pp. 644–661; Bruce L. Benson, 1990, *The Enterprise of Law without the State*, San Francisco: Pacific Research Institute; and Avner Greif, 1989, "Reputation and Coalitions in Medieval Trade: Evidence on the Maghribi Traders," *Journal of Economic History*, 49, pp. 857–882). In *The Morality of Law* (1969, New Haven: Yale University Press), Lon L. Fuller observes that frequent role changes foster the emergence of mutually recognized and accepted duties "in a society of economic traders" (p. 24).

[36] The general acceptance of (or acquiescence in) a custom depends primarily on its anticipated effect on the group. Those strategies that maximize the expected payoff for each participant if reciprocally undertaken evolve into norms; see Max L. Stearns, 1994, "The Misguided Renaissance of Social Choice," *Yale Law Journal*, 103, pp. 1243–1244. Stearns observes that courts and legislatures might have a comparative advantage in devising market-facilitating rules if participants were unable to devise rules governing future interactions, and if unforeseen circumstances placed them in a forced market relationship requiring postcontractual negotiations. Unlike market participants, courts and legislatures choose from among alternatives *ex ante* without attempting to strategically maximize the advantage caused by unforeseen circumstances. (See also Martin Shubik, 1987, *Game Theory in the Social Sciences: Concepts and Solutions*, Cambridge, MA: MIT Press.)

when selling would be regarded as violating a basic norm of business conduct. Consequently, he would suffer reputational costs within the business community. Therefore, conditions of role reversibility, coupled with norms that generate disincentives to adopt opportunistic double standards, are likely to generate optimal rules via spontaneous processes.[37]

1. Reciprocity and the prisoners' dilemma. When unilateral defection promises higher payoffs and there is no contract enforcement mechanism, players are tempted to depart from optimal strategies, often generating outcomes that are Pareto-inferior for all. This type of opportunistic behavior is well known as the prisoners' dilemma game.[38]

Reciprocity may prevent the suboptimal outcome. The players, for example, can bind their strategic choices to those of their opponents, changing the equilibrium of the game by eliminating the reward for unilateral defection.[39] Mechanisms for automatic reciprocity tend to populate environments where custom is recognized as a primary source of law, such as international treaty negotiations.[40] In the absence of an established legal system or commonly recognized rule of law, reciprocity implies that parties can do unto others what has been done to them, subject to the limits of their reciprocal strengths.[41] Positions taken by one state generate a standard that may be used against that state on future occasions.[42] Reciprocity therefore deters noncooperative, Pareto-suboptimal equilibria among nations.[43]

---

[37] The group's ability to impose a sanction depends on an individual's accountability for her past behavior. Bruce L. Benson (1992, "Customary Law as a Social Contract: International Commercial Law," *Constitutional Political Economy*, 3, pp. 1–27) explores the role of reputation in situations of repeated market interaction, observing that reputation serves as a source of collective knowledge regarding past actions.

[38] See Andrew Schotter, 1981, *Economic Theory of Social Institutions*, Cambridge, MA: Harvard University Press; David Lewis, 1969, *Convention: A Philosophical Study*, Cambridge, MA: Harvard University Press; and Harvey Leibenstein, 1982, "The Prisoner's Dilemma in the Invisible Hand: An Analysis of Intrafirm Productivity," *American Economic Review*, 72, pp. 92–97. All analyze the role of conventions in correcting prisoners' dilemma situations.

[39] See Vincy Fon and Francesco Parisi, 2003, "Reciprocity-Induced Cooperation," *Journal of Institutional and Theoretical Economics*, pp. 76–92, and Vincy Fon and Francesco Parisi, 2007, "Matching Rules," *Managerial and Decision Economics*, 28, pp. 1–14. For a similar argument relying on tit-for-tat strategies, see Robert Axelrod, 1984, *The Evolution of Cooperation*, New York: Basic Books.

[40] Francesco Parisi and Nita Ghei, 2003, "The Role of Reciprocity in International Law," *Cornell International Law Journal*, 36, pp. 93–123.

[41] The international law formation process provides states with numerous occasions for opportunistic behavior, including holdout strategies and free riding. These strategies occur less frequently than expected, because states then follow basic norms of reciprocity.

[42] Consider Art. 21(1)b of the 1969 Vienna Convention, which creates a mirror-image mechanism for unilateral reservations. Art. 21(1)b states, "[a] reservation established with regard to another party... modifies those provisions to the same extent for that other party in its relations with the reserving state." As shown by Parisi ("Spontaneous Law," pp. 211–231), by imposing a symmetry constraint on the parties' choices, this rule offers a possible solution to prisoners' dilemma problems.

[43] Reciprocity does not solve all strategic problems. For example, when a conflict occurs along the diagonal possibilities of the game so that the obtainable equilibria are already characterized by symmetric strategies, a reciprocity constraint will not eliminate the divergence of interests between the players and will not affect the results of the game. This occurs in the battle-of-the-sexes game and in pure conflict (i.e., zero-sum) situations.

2. Other forms of stochastic reciprocity. Evolutionary models further examine the role of long-term relationships in fostering desirable outcomes. The impact of long-term human relationships in encouraging cooperation is twofold. First, relationships strengthen human bonds and render others' well-being relevant to one's own decision making. Individual welfare maximization turns on both payoffs from future interactions and the well-being of close members within the group.[44]

Repeated social interactions in a close-knit group also allow the development of an institutional memory of parties' past behavior. Consequently, there is a possible role for reputation and the social sentiments of approbation and disapprobation. If models of cooperation allow the intensity of those sentiments to vary with the relative frequencies of the two strategies in the population, the degree of spontaneous norm enforcement is likely to increase with a reduction in the proportion of defectors in society. Likewise, norms that are followed by a large majority of the population are more likely to be internalized by marginal individuals in the absence of coercion.[45] The various models formulated in the functionalist literature suggest that iterated interactions with role reversibility, reciprocity constraints, and structural integration facilitate the emergence and recognition of customary law. The dynamic of the norm formation may unveil the existence of a "tilt point" beyond which emerging beliefs become stable and self-sustaining. Individuals who frequently exchange roles in their social interactions have incentives to constrain their behavior to conform to socially optimal norms of conduct.[46]

3. Reciprocity and generality constraints in legislation. A third role for reciprocity is its use as a constraint on centralized lawmaking. Constitutional rules of equality under the law and nondiscrimination can be viewed as a reciprocity constraint on legislation. Public choice theory reveals the fundamental importance of such a constraint on limiting special interest legislation. According to such principles, rules imposing sanctions or exemptions should apply to all individuals within their logical scope. The legitimacy of any apparent over- or underinclusion should be subject to the strictest constitutional scrutiny. The role of such a generality constraint is twofold. First, it prevents arbitrary use of special interest legislation as

---

[44] Such a theoretical framework allows for a more optimistic prediction of spontaneous order. This insight is consistent with the predictions of evolutionary models of social interaction, where low discount rates for future payoffs and close-knittedness are found to be positively correlated with the emergence of optimal social norms. However, see Jonathan Klick and Francesco Parisi, 2008, "Social Networks, Self-Denial, and Median Preferences: Conformity as an Evolutionary Strategy," *Journal of Socio-Economics*, 137, pp. 1319–1327, for a model suggesting that this process might actually change preferences of individuals, generating some problems for a standard welfare analysis. Models based on interdependent utility and close-knittedness generate results that are qualitatively similar to those discussed in the case of role reversibility.

[45] Along with the adjustments taking place in the initial time period, an additional "internalization effect" will occasion a dynamic adjustment. An initial change in the players' level of norm internalization reproduces the conditions of instability occasioned by the initial emergence of the norm, allowing it to become self-reinforcing.

[46] James Buchanan (1975, *The Limits of Liberty: Between Anarchy and Leviathan*, Chicago: University of Chicago Press) insightfully anticipated this result. He suggested that even stronger logic explained the emergence of cooperation in situations of induced reciprocity. In both cases, the nonidealistic and self-interested behavior of human actors would generate optimal norms.

a redistributive tool. Second, by linking the effects and benefits of legislation to a large class of potential beneficiaries, it creates a collective-action problem in rent-seeking and lobbying efforts. As a result, generality constraints have a profound economic effect, because the dissipation of economic rent is considerably reduced in such a system.[47]

Because the civil code's tendency toward generality has endured over the long run, it is useful to examine whether the economic effect of this environment has contributed to its resilience. In this regard, game theory offers a particularly appropriate vehicle for analysis. If a legal regime can enforce rules that create an effective reciprocity constraint, optimal outcomes of wealth creation can occur.[48] The contrary is also true. If a legal regime fails to implement such rules, suboptimal outcomes will prevail. The question then becomes how to sustain the rules that promote reciprocity.[49]

SUGGESTIONS FOR FUTURE RESEARCH

To highlight the promise of the functional law-and-economics perspective, we suggest two distinct areas where its insights may be particularly valuable. The first is in the field of behavioral law and economics, which posits that individuals exhibit systematic departures from the rational choice model of human behavior. These biases and heuristics, it is argued, leave room for policymakers to intervene in market decisions to counteract individual irrationality in the hope of improving welfare. Although the functional school would not necessarily rule out the possibility of systematic mistake-making on the part of individuals, it would generally view these interventions with suspicion.

First, these interventions will not generally be guided by completely rational and self-sacrificing automatons, but rather by self-interested politicians and bureaucrats, who, in addition to exhibiting behavioral biases themselves, will also be influenced by the rent seeking that is endemic to the public policymaking process. Second, scholars from the functional school stress that individual decision-making needs to viewed in its institutional context. Whereas individuals may exhibit large departures from the rational choice model in the contrived atmosphere of a lab, there may be strong institutional and social forces that limit the practical significance of these departures. For example, individuals especially prone to behavioral biases may self-select into domains where the costs of these biases

[47] The generality constraint in legislation has created high thresholds of political and social consensus to implement changes to a code. Consider, for example, the fact that the French Civil Code of 1804 remains essentially unchanged to the present time.

[48] The end result of this popular antagonism toward special interests is that the legislative role tends to be restricted to general legislation that is welfare-enhancing. The powerful constraint on *ad hoc* decision making resulting from deductive jurisprudence and general legislation produces a legal environment centered around universally applicable legal principles.

[49] Popular resistance to the code's alteration restrains special interest legislation. This can be formalized in such requirements as supermajority or executive approval for constitutional changes or executive approval. Additionally, the code should contain provisions encouraging its expansive and analogical interpretation, while adopting restrictive interpretations of rules serving a special interest. This will discourage rent seeking through the courts or the legislature.

are small.[50] Also, the structure of the market itself may provide a natural limit on the costs of these biases.[51]

A second extension involves replacing the positive and normative schools' approaches to analyzing the merits of legal rules by looking at them in isolation. That is, whereas the positive school tends to fit models to existing legal rules with the goal of describing how those rules are, in fact, efficient, and the normative school focuses on why market failures undermine those results, the functional school suggests that one needs to focus on the sources of a rule and how it is embedded in a specific institutional context. If the process generating the legal rule satisfies certain conditions that are widely accepted by those affected by the ultimate legal rule, then the rule itself is presumed to be acceptable. This structural adjudication approach, highlighted by Cooter, suggests a reorientation of theoretical law and economics in which scholars focus on the sources of law, adopting a decidedly institutionalist perspective.[52]

Functional law and economics revisits the institutional design of lawmaking through a structural analysis that evaluates alternative sources of law by their abilities to produce beneficial legal rules. Functional law and economics rejects both the efficiency claims of the positive school and the normative school's willingness to allow judicial and political elites to micromanage social interactions. Informed by public choice theory, functionalists are hesitant to trade market failures for government failures. Instead, they focus their attention on constitutional design issues and favor metarules that give prominence to individual choice and consent *ex ante*. This approach exploits the comparative advantage of different legal and social institutions in the production of legal rules by considering agency problems, rule-making costs, and preference-revelation mechanisms that induce individuals to select socially efficient arrangements. The functionalist literature offers insights into how iterated interactions, role reversibility, and reciprocity constraints can shape customary law and legislation. It also provides a framework for analyzing the externality, information, and market-based rationales for defining the limits of choice of law.[53]

[50] See, for example, John A. List, 2004, "Neoclassical Theory versus Prospect Theory: Evidence from the Marketplace," *Econometrica*, 72, pp. 615–625.
[51] See, Alan Schwartz, 2008, "How Much Irrationality Does the Market Permit?" *Journal of Legal Studies*, 37, pp. 131–159.
[52] Cooter, "Structural Adjudication."
[53] For further insights, the authors suggest Robert Cooter, 2002, *The Strategic Constitution*, Princeton, NJ: Princeton University Press; Jonathan Klick and Francesco Parisi, 2005, "Wealth, Utility, and the Human Dimension," *NYU Journal of Law and Liberty*, 1, pp. 590–608; and Francesco Parisi and Jonathan Klick, 2004, "Functional Law and Economics: The Search for Value-Neutral Principles of Lawmaking," *Chicago-Kent Law Review*, 79, pp. 431–450.

4   Legal Fictionalism and the Economics of Normativity

HORACIO SPECTOR

It is a classic tenet of jurisprudence that there is a deep difference between legal directives and the commands of a band of robbers. For instance, Cicero declared: "What of the fact that many harmful and pernicious measures are passed in human communities – measures which come no closer to the name of laws than if a gang of criminals agreed to make some rules?"[1] And Augustine said: "Justice being taken away, then, what are kingdoms but great robberies? For what are robberies themselves, but little kingdoms? The band itself is made up of men; it is ruled by the authority of a prince; it is knit together by the pact of the confederacy; the booty is divided by the law agreed on."[2] Ever since Cicero and Augustine resorted to justice to mark law off from other coercive practices, natural lawyers have availed themselves of various normative notions for interpreting governmental coercion as lawful.

Law is essentially associated with the idea of normativity. Though there are different conceptions of legal normativity, most of them pertain to two kinds: *justified normativity* and *social normativity*.[3] Natural lawyers, such as Cicero, Augustine, and Aquinas, defended justified normativity. On this view agents must rationally accept legal norms or standards that derive from absolute moral principles and act in accordance with them. Normative practices therefore rely on true moral beliefs. In contrast, H. L. A. Hart embraced social normativity in proposing the practice theory of social rules, according to which rules have two aspects: an *external aspect* and an *internal aspect*. Whereas regularity of behavior constitutes the external aspect of rules, the ability of rules to guide and justify decision making is its internal aspect. Hart applies this framework to the rule of recognition, by which public officials and judges identify legal rules to resolve cases. Though Hart

---

[1] Cicero, 1998, *The Republic [and] The Laws*, trans. Niall Rudd, Oxford: Oxford University Press, "The Laws," Book 2, Section 13.

[2] Saint Augustine, 1950, *The City of God*, trans. Marcus Dods, New York: The Modern Library, Book IV, 4.

[3] The distinction between "social normativity" and "justified normativity" was introduced by Joseph Raz (1979, *The Authority of Law*, Oxford: Clarendon Press, p. 134).

I am grateful for helpful comments to Larry Alexander, Lewis Kornhauser, Larry Laudan, Guido Pincione, Ezequiel Spector, Mark D. White, and Matt Zwolinski. I revised this chapter while holding a visiting professorship at the School of Law of the University of San Diego.

does not require judges to accept the moral validity of the law, they must accept the rule of recognition, which means that they must recognize legal commands identified by the rule of recognition as peremptory (i.e., excluding deliberation) and content-independent reasons for action.[4]

Unlike Hart, Joseph Raz gives an account of legal normativity that rests on the concept of justified normativity. In fact, Raz holds that law includes a claim to moral legitimacy, and defines normativity in terms of *exclusionary reasons*. For Raz, an exclusionary reason R to do A is a second-order reason that preempts the consideration of other relevant reasons in favor or against A. A *protected reason R* to do A conjoins a first-order reason to do A and a second-order reason that excludes consideration of potential reasons against doing A. Raz holds that legal obligations are protected reasons in this sense. In fact, he says: "The law's claim to legitimate authority is not merely a claim that legal rules are reasons. It includes the claim that they are exclusionary reasons for disregarding reasons for nonconformity."[5] The exclusionary quality of legal reasons tends to secure conformity: "It is the essential exclusionary *character* of a rule that it resists permanent revision. It is immune from the claim that it should be re-examined with a view to possible revision on every occasion to which it applies."[6] In brief, on Raz's account, users of legal discourse claim law's validity, but this does not mean that law *is* valid. Raz emphasizes: "A legal system may lack legitimate authority. If it lacks the moral attributes required to endow it with legitimate authority then it has none. But it must possess all the other features of authority, or else it would be odd to say that it claims authority."[7] Among those other features there stands out law's nondependence on morality, without which law could not function as a system of purported exclusionary reasons.

There is widespread skepticism about the ability of rational choice theory to explain justified normativity in its own right.[8] The contemporary literature has opted either for reducing normativity to factual concepts (*legal reductionism*) or for substituting social normativity for justified normativity (*legal conventionalism*). In this chapter I will explore a different route; I will reject both legal reductionism and legal conventionalism. Instead, I will propose a rational choice explanation of legal normativity that takes account of its reason-giving, duty-imposing features. In order to do this, I will submit a fictionalist account of justified normativity.[9]

[4] H. L. A. Hart, 1994, *The Concept of Law*, 2nd ed., Oxford: Clarendon Press, pp. 88–90; H. L. A. Hart, 1982, *Essays on Bentham*, Oxford: Clarendon Press, pp. 253–262.
[5] Raz, *The Authority of Law*, p. 30.
[6] Ibid., p. 33.
[7] Joseph Raz, 1985, "Authority, Law, and Morality," *The Monist*, 68, p. 300.
[8] See, for instance: Lewis Kornhauser, 1999, "The Normativity of Law," *American Law and Economics Review*, 1, pp. 13–14; Gerald F. Gaus, "The Limits of *Homo Economicus*," in Gerald F. Gaus, Julian Lamont, and Christi Favor, eds., *Values, Justice, and Economics*, Amsterdam: Rodopi (forthcoming).
[9] Fictionalism was originated by Jeremy Bentham (see C. K. Ogden, 1959, *Bentham's Theory of Fictions*, Paterson, NJ: Littlefield, Adams & Co.). However, the German philosopher Hans Veihinger made the first modern exposition of fictionalism; see Hans Veihinger, 1924, *The Philosophy of "As If*," trans. C. K. Ogden, London: Kegan Paul. For recent works, see Anthony Everett and Thomas Hofweber, eds., 2000, *Empty Names, Fiction, and the Puzzles of Existence*, Stanford: CSLI Publications; Richard Joyce, 2001, *The Myth of Morality*, Cambridge: Cambridge University Press; Mark Eli Kalderon,

Legal fictionalism includes a semantic as well as an epistemological claim. It (a) asserts that legal statements represent normative propositions, but (b) denies that competent users of legal language should rationally believe those normative propositions.[10] Thus, propositions represented by legal statements are systematically false because political enactments are not truth-makers of normative, reason-giving propositions. I will also argue that law's justified normativity is a fiction created by the state's ideological apparatus as a mechanism for the reduction of policing and enforcement costs. Therefore, legal fictionalism makes it possible to understand justified normativity within the framework of rational choice theory.

I. LEGAL REDUCTIONISM

Legal reductionists face the problem of normativity by throwing the baby out with the bathwater. In fact, reductionists analyze obligations in terms of sanctions, and deny that obligations create reasons of any kind other than prudential reasons or expected costs associated with penalties. Because the reduction ends up with expected costs rather than reasons, reductionism solves the normativity puzzle.[11] John Austin, for instance, defines law as the sovereign's general threat-backed commands. Austin defines the sovereign as the person whom the populace habitually obeys but who does not obey (or habitually obey) anyone else. In *The Concept of Law* Hart criticized Austin's suggestion to use the "gunman's situation" as "the key to the science of jurisprudence." Hart characterizes this situation in these terms: "The gunman [A] orders his victim [B] to hand over this purse and threatens to shoot if he refuses; if the victim complies we refer to the way in which he was forced to do so by saying that he was *obliged* to do so."[12] Hart comments on this example: "It is, however, equally certain that we should misdescribe the situation if we said, on these facts, that B 'had an obligation' or a 'duty' to hand over the money. So from the start it is clear that we need something else for an understanding of the idea of obligation."[13] However, we must notice that Hart had said a few lines earlier that for the theory of law as coercive orders (i.e., Austin's theory) "legal obligation is to be found" in a situation where "A must be the sovereign habitually obeyed and the orders must be general, prescribing courses of conduct, not single actions."[14] Hart's claim that the gunman's orders oblige the victim but do not create a duty or an obligation of his is consistent with claiming that an Austinian sovereign's general commands do create duties or obligations befalling on the population. When Hart says, "[s]o from the start it is clear that we need something else for an

---

2005, *Moral Fictionalism*, Oxford: Clarendon Press; and Mark Eli Kalderon, ed., 2005, *Fictionalism in Metaphysics*, Oxford: Clarendon Press.

[10] Under this broad characterization, "fictionalism" amounts to what Mark Eli Kalderon calls "non-factualism." See Kalderon, *Moral Fictionalism*, pp. 97–114.

[11] Similarly, Kornhauser says that a sanction theory of obligation, in contending that the "individual obeys the law in order to avoid a sanction," "is obviously congenial to an economist who also grounds motivation in self-interest" ("The Normativity of Law," p. 6).

[12] Hart, *The Concept of Law*, p. 6.

[13] Ibid., p. 82.

[14] Ibid.

understanding of the idea of obligation," Austin might have replied that he had offered something else, that is, the notion of a "general habit of obedience."

Reductionism might take economics-minded forms today. Like Austin, positive economists must avoid normative terms to define law. However, unlike Austin, they could avail themselves of incentive-based notions to differentiate law from the commands of robbers. Thus, Mancur Olson draws a distinction between a "roving bandit" and a "stationary bandit." A roving bandit depredates a group in a territory and then moves to another area for further depredation. By contrast, a stationary bandit (i.e., an autocrat) stays in a territory and extracts wealth from the group through tax collections on a durable basis. Because an autocrat has an encompassing interest in the group, he will limit the extent of his tax collections. Starting from this basic model, Olson studies the incentive structures of majorities in democratic regimes. The interesting point here is that an economic jurisprudential theory might assimilate law to the general commands issued by a tax collector who has a sufficiently encompassing interest in society (v.gr., an Austinian sovereign).[15] Although the gunman's (roving bandit's) orders seem quite different from legal rules, general commands issued by Olsonian tax collectors might provide a model for the understanding of law.

Now, even if reductionist analyses cannot be dismissed without further ado, simply by noting that there is a difference between "being obliged" and "having an obligation," it is certainly true that reductionism cannot explain the link between obligations and justificatory reasons. If an agent ought to do M, he is justified in doing M.[16] Obligations provide reasons in a way in which "being obliged" does not. So the challenge is to explain the emergence of justified normativity as a conceptual scheme that links the sovereign's commands to justificatory reasons.

II. LEGAL CONVENTIONALISM

For social normativity theorists, law's normativity is not related to normative truth. Rather, it is a kind of social fact, however complex it might be. Hart explains the role of the rule of recognition as a reason-giving social fact in terms of the acceptance by the political and judicial bureaucracy of certain criteria for identifying legal rules – that is, the *internal point of view*. However, as Jules Coleman argues, there are two features of the rule of recognition as a duty-imposing norm that cannot be accounted for by the internal point of view, that is, by the fact that judges take the rule as providing reasons:

> First, a duty-imposing rule cannot normally be extinguished unilaterally, whereas rules that are reasons solely in virtue of one's commitment to them can, in the typical case, be unilaterally extinguished. Second, the particular kind of duty one has under a rule of recognition is to act in a coordinative way with others to achieve certain ends, and in doing so to be responsive to the interests, intentions, preferences, and actions of others.[17]

---

[15] Mancur Olson, 2000, *Power and Prosperity*, New York: Basic Books, ch. 1.

[16] Aleksander Peczenik and Horacio Spector, 1987, "A Theory of Moral Ought-Sentences," *Archiv für Rechts und Sozialphilosophie*, 73, pp. 441–475.

[17] Jules Coleman, 2001, *The Practice of Principle*, Oxford: Oxford University Press, pp. 95–96.

Instead of the unilateral endorsement of the rule of recognition, Hartian scholars have appealed to notions of collective agency to account for the two normative aspects mentioned by Coleman. In a pioneering essay Gerald Postema proposed a reconstruction of the rule of recognition in terms of coordination equilibrium.[18] For Postema the rule of recognition plays the dual role of coordinating the strategic interaction of citizens and law-applying officials, and that of officials among themselves. Postema's is a sort of Hobbesian approach to the rule of recognition, not in the sense that legal rules can solve a conflict game (e.g., prisoners' dilemma) implicit in the state of nature, but in the quite different sense that authority can make law possible, whatever its role is thought to be. In fact, Hobbes's social contract can be explained in terms of an *impure coordination* game in which players have differential gains from accepting different kings, but all of them have disproportionately greater losses from remaining in a state of anarchy.[19] Just as the social contract can be seen as a solution to the impure coordination game of choosing the sovereign, the rule of recognition can be understood as a solution to the impure coordination game of choosing the membership conditions of rules within a legal system. The two ideas have a great deal of overlap, because to choose the sovereign *is* to establish whose commands will count as legal norms.

Now, in coordination games participants have a self-interested reason to abide by the coordination equilibrium, however it has been reached. This is a mere tautology, because the coordination equilibrium is defined by strategies that maximize each participant's payoff. Therefore, if the rule of recognition establishes an equilibrium in the specified sense, law-applying officials have a self-interested reason to follow the rule of recognition. This, however, does not imply that officials are *duty-bound* by the rule of recognition. Postema is aware of this, and therefore he invokes moral principles that can generate judicial obligations from expectations induced by the courts. Thus, he claims that "the court *induces* expectations (and reliance on them) on the part of citizens," and he argues that the principle of reliance on induced expectations grounds judges' obligation to respect those expectations.[20] Yet, in resorting to independent moral principles, Postema reintroduces the notion of justified normativity, thus acknowledging that social normativity alone is unable to ground obligations.

Coleman claims that the coordination account is defective in that certain legal systems might depend on coordinative structures other than those depicted in impure coordination games. Though Coleman fails to give an example, it is arguable that the establishment of government in some constitutional settings, and therefore the multilateral endorsement of the rule of recognition by judges and public officials, respond sometimes to what Russell Hardin calls "constitutional coordination." Instead of an impure coordination game, constitutional coordination is a prisoners' dilemma game in which a pair of outcomes (viz., the unilateral depredation outcomes) are in conflict, whereas the other two outcomes represent

---

[18] Gerald J. Postema, 1982, "Coordination and Convention at the Foundations of Law," *Journal of Legal Studies*, 11, p. 165.

[19] Gregory S. Kavka, 1986, *Hobbesian Moral and Political Theory*, Princeton: Princeton University Press, p. 185. The battle-of-the-sexes game is the textbook example of an impure coordination game.

[20] Postema, "Coordination and Convention," p. 197.

a potential for mutual gain because one of them (bilateral depredation) is the unproductive state of nature and the other (the setting of government) allows the dynamic creation of wealth.[21] In other words, a different coordinative structure (i.e., one closer to Hobbes's state-of-nature game) could sometimes be appropriate to understand the rule of recognition.

Coleman does not employ a constitutional coordination approach to the rule of recognition, but rather tries to maintain the social interpretation of collective agency. He renders the idea of mutual obligation of the judiciary in terms of Bratman's concept of a shared cooperative activity (SCA) and a shared intention.[22] Examples of the former are "you and I sing a duet together," or "you and I paint the house together." Bratman defines a SCA in terms of three conditions: (i) mutual responsiveness, (ii) commitment to the joint activity, and (iii) commitment to mutual support.[23] Now, the explanation of the rule of recognition's normativity in terms of the concept of SCA risks circularity, because the notion of commitment is central to the definition, and commitment is a normative notion. The notion of shared intention seems more appropriate because it only involves intentions and beliefs, rather than commitments. Thus, Bratman says: "We intend to J if and only if (i) I intend that we J and you intend that we J, (ii) our intentions are interrelated, and (iii) we have common knowledge of (i) and (ii)." Bratman's example of a shared intention is: "You and I have a shared intention to paint the house together." Bratman distinguishes two senses of a shared intention: a weaker sense, defined by conditions (i) through (iii), and a stronger sense, which includes a further condition, "that there be a binding agreement."[24] However, Bratman remarks that a shared intention "is typically but not necessarily accompanied by relevant conditional obligations."[25]

In a later essay, Bratman clarified his position by saying that "the normal etiology of a shared intention does bring with it relevant obligations and entitlements when the shared activity is itself permissible."[26] Bratman also claimed that a principle of fidelity "captures what is at the heart of the idea that there is a close connection between shared intention and mutual obligation."[27] This means that it is not shared intention by itself that explains mutual obligations, but rather an underlying moral principle that requires performing the expectations that one has voluntarily created in other people. Once again we must notice that appealing to the fidelity principle amounts to reintroducing justified normativity by the back door. It seems then that the concept of shared intention, just like that of coordination equilibrium, cannot ground a social account of the rule of recognition as a duty-imposing norm.

---

[21] Russell Hardin, 1992, *Liberalism, Constitutionalism, and Democracy*, Oxford: Oxford University Press, pp. 97–98.

[22] Coleman, *The Practice of Principle*, pp. 96–99; Michael E. Bratman, 1999, *Faces of Intention: Selected Essays on Intention and Agency*, Cambridge: Cambridge University Press, pp. 98–99.

[23] Bratman, *Faces of Intention*, pp. 94–95.

[24] Ibid., p. 127.

[25] Ibid., p. 128.

[26] Ibid., p. 132.

[27] Ibid., p. 137. Here Bratman refers to Scanlon's principle of fidelity ("principle F"), for which see T. M. Scanlon, 1998, *What We Owe to Each Other*, Cambridge, MA: Harvard University Press, pp. 302–309.

III. HUME'S LEGAL FICTIONALISM

As stated in the introduction, my purpose is to explore a fictionalist account of law's normativity. It is generally believed that legal fictionalism was adumbrated by Jeremy Bentham; in fact, as Hart says, "the demystification motif colours [Bentham's] general theory of law."[28] In Hart's illuminating exposition, Bentham thought that "laws are at bottom nothing but commands, prohibitions or permissions, artefacts of the human will," though law's real nature is concealed by the conventional formulation of laws in nonimperative language.[29] Without denying the Benthamite pedigree of legal fictionalism, in my opinion it was David Hume who provided the most fruitful analysis of the role of deception in the maintenance of legal conventions. For Hume justice is an *artificial* virtue arising from the conventions of justice – stability of possessions, transfer of property by consent, and promises. Hume extended this conventionalist approach to political allegiance. Therefore, the normativity of political conventions can also be explained in terms of the fictionalist approach developed for the conventions of justice. Though Hume's account could certainly be considered a form of legal conventionalism, it should be distinguished from contemporary forms of legal conventionalism by its fictionalist analysis of normativity.

A. The Artifice of Fictional Motives

Hume's theory of the conventions of justice has given rise to deep controversies. To start with, we must notice that Hume analyzes moral concepts in sentimentalist terms. For Hume moral terms *denote* (as opposed to *express*) the speaker's *natural moral sentiments*. Indeed, Hume says that "when you pronounce any action or character to be vicious, you mean nothing but that from the constitution of your nature you have a feeling or sentiment of blame from the contemplation of it."[30] He also states that "when any action, or quality of the mind, pleases us *after a certain manner*, we say it is virtuous; and when the neglect, or nonperformance of it, displeases us after a like manner, we say that we lie *under an obligation* to perform it."[31] Hume applies this sentimentalist scheme of analysis to what he calls the "natural virtues," such as beneficence, clemency, generosity, and charity. However, Hume claims that justice is an "artificial virtue." In stressing the artificiality of justice, Hume parts company with a long classical tradition that proclaims that justice is established by natural law and apprehended by practical reason.

For Hume justice derives from conventions arising from self-interest. In effect, Hume rejects the proposition that keeping promises is a natural virtue. He says that the obligation to keep promises is conventional, and the acts discharging this obligation reveal an artificial virtue. It is worthwhile quoting one of his statements:

---

[28] Hart, *Essays on Bentham*, p. 23.

[29] Ibid. For Bentham's criticism of common law, see especially Gerald J. Postema, 1986, *Bentham and the Common Law Tradition*, Oxford: Clarendon Press, pp. 286–301. Postema argues that Bentham's philosophical theory of fictions was irrelevant in his demystification of common law.

[30] David Hume, 1978, *A Treatise of Human Nature*, 2nd ed., Oxford: Clarendon Press, p. 469.

[31] Hume, *Treatise*, p. 517; italics added.

"But as there is naturally no inclination to observe promises, distinct from a sense of their obligation; it follows, that fidelity is no natural virtue, and that promises have no force, antecedent to human conventions."[32] How does Hume explain the fact that the obligation to keep promises is usually regarded as a moral obligation, not just a conventional one? He resorts to his well-known view that "mankind is an inventive species."[33] Man invents conventions and artificial virtues, and whereas promising is among the former, the virtue of keeping promises is among the latter.

Hume shows the artificiality of the virtue of justice by means of a proof, premised on the proposition that the virtue of an act resides in the virtuous motive or motivational state that moved the act rather than in the external performance of it:

(1) Any act X is virtuous if X is done from a virtuous motive.

The performance of a virtuous act is usually a sign that the corresponding virtuous motive is present and is therefore a reasonable basis for approving the act and praising the agent. But the performance is not per se virtuous. Hume goes on to assert that the virtuous motive must be identified independently. In effect, suppose we define a virtuous motive by reference to a virtuous act:

(2) A virtuous motive is "regard to the fact that an act is virtuous."

If the virtuous motive were identified by reference to the external act, (1) and (2) would generate circular reasoning, because the term "virtuous" recurs in the *definiens* in (2). Hume's proof requires that, if justice is a virtue, there be a noncircular motive behind all just acts. Hume discusses three possible motives: self-love, general benevolence or public benefit, and private benevolence or goodwill; and he finds out that none of these motives lies – can possibly lie – behind all just acts. (Because we are here interested in Hume's account of legal normativity, we will avoid his discussion at this point.) Hume concludes that the only possible motive that can dictate just acts is regard for the justice of just acts, that is, a "sense of duty." Now the problem is that a sense of duty so understood cannot count as a noncircular virtuous motive, and so when (1) and (2) are applied to the virtue of justice, we are caught in "evident sophistry and reasoning in a circle." Therefore, unless "nature has establish'd a sophistry," we are led to conclude that justice is not a natural virtue.

Commentators have shown two ways out of this vicious circularity. One of these ways out, suggested by Mackie and followed by Rawls, is to differentiate between two questions: (a) what makes just behavior virtuous, and (b) what ensures that a just action is really virtuous, as opposed to only apparently virtuous? If proposition (1) is an answer to question (a), the circularity is unavoidable, as we have seen. In contrast, if (1) is only a form of answering question (b), the circularity does not arise, because virtue does not reside in the motive, but rather

---

[32] Ibid., p. 519.
[33] Ibid., p. 484.

in the external performance of just actions.[34] On this view, justice would be a *rule-based* virtue, rather than a *motive-based* one. When justice is equated with the external performance of acts that comply with the rules of justice, the sense of duty might be identified in a noncircular way, because justice is to be found in the external performance, not in an internal motivational state. For instance, the sense of duty could be the sentiment that just acts are obligatory. This internal sentiment would only become relevant to ensure that the act is really (i.e., "subjectively") just, as opposed to only apparently (i.e., "objectively") just.

This way out of the "sophistry" problem is to relax proposition (1) so that it only applies to natural virtues, not to artificial ones. For artificial virtues, like justice, Hume could only accept proposition (1) construed in the innocuous way in which it is only an answer to question (b). This maneuver is hardly consistent with Hume's virtue ethics.[35] It means, among other things, rejecting Hume's clear statement that "*all* virtuous actions derive their merit only from virtuous motives, and are consider'd merely as signs of these motives."[36] Hume does not distinguish here between natural and artificial virtues, and of course it is a central thesis of his that justice is an artificial virtue.

The second route away from the vicious circularity is to appeal to a sort of legal conventionalism. Thus, Stephen Darwall proposes to understand the motive lying behind just acts in terms of *rule acceptance*.[37] Darwall points out that it is crucial for Hume that the rules of justice have for each participant what Hart called an "internal aspect" – that each regard the rules prescriptively. Darwall says:

> What this says is that just persons regard the rules of justice as normative, conditional on others' doing so. They conditionally treat these rules . . . as authoritative, as in themselves giving reasons – indeed, conclusive reasons – not to take the property of others, to keep their promises, and so on. In one sense of the word, therefore, just persons would appear to regard the fact that something belongs to another, or that the rule of property requires forbearance, as a motive – i.e., a ground or a reason – for not taking it.[38]

Darwall's strategy is related to Mackie's, because Darwall must also assume that justice is for Hume a rule-based virtue. Unlike Darwall, however, I believe that it is more illuminating to use Hume's theory of conventions to discuss the notion of legal normativity than to proceed in the opposite direction. As we have seen, Hume defines "obligation" in a sentimentalist, "internalist" way, but he also says that the idea of obligation is "altogether unintelligible" before the "convention, concerning abstinence from the possessions of others, is enter'd into."[39] The only way to reconcile these two claims is to take Hume in the latter

[34] J. L. Mackie, 1980, *Hume's Moral Theory*, London: Routledge, p. 80; John Rawls, 2000, *Lectures on the History of Moral Philosophy*, Cambridge, MA: Harvard University Press, p. 53n2.
[35] Stephen Darwall, 1995, *The British Moralists and the Internal "Ought": 1640–1740*, Cambridge: Cambridge University Press, pp. 301–306.
[36] Hume, *Treatise*, p. 478 (italics added).
[37] Darwall, *British Moralists*, pp. 292–293; pp. 309–315.
[38] Ibid., p. 293.
[39] Hume, *Treatise*, pp. 490–491.

quotation as referring to an *artificial obligation*, that is, an obligation "invented" by the conventions of justice. Yet intelligibility does not rule out sophistry. The problem is that artificial obligations – unlike natural obligations – can only be related to a motive in a bootstrapping way. But is it really necessary to run away from "sophistry and reasoning in a circle" as long as one realizes that this sophistry is artificial rather than natural? Answering this question in the negative squares well with Mackie's insinuation that "perhaps [Hume] did merely think that what is artificial can involve a sophistry whereas what is natural cannot."[40] And Knud Haakonssen comes to a similar conclusion by reflecting on Hume's thesis that we feign the motive to fulfill promises. Haakonssen quotes Hume when he says: "Here, therefore, we *feign* a new act of the mind, which we call the *willing* an obligation; and on this we suppose the morality to depend."[41] On the strength of this quotation, Haakonssen argues that, according to Hume, conventions lead participants to *imagine* that they have motives to comply with the rules of the conventions.[42]

So the upshot of the preceding discussion is that the conventions of justice create fictional motives, which in turn ground fictional obligations. This outcome can clarify the problem of the normativity of law. A naturally virtuous action is virtuous because it springs from a natural virtuous motive in a noncircular way. An artificially virtuous action is obligatory because it flows from a fictitious, artificial sense of morality that emerges once interest in the observance of those conventions is "observ'd to be common to all mankind, and men receive a pleasure from the view of such actions as tend to the peace of society, and an uneasiness from such as are contrary to it."[43] Conventions create fictional obligations because this is instrumental to their maintenance. Hume says that this sense of morality "is also augmented by a new artifice, and that the public instructions of politicians, and the private education of parents, contribute to the giving us a sense of honour and duty in the strict regulation of our actions with regard to the properties of others."[44] Hume reproduces this argument to explain the sense of morality that emerges after we enter into the convention of promises to pursue our common benefit:

> Afterwards a sentiment of morals concurs with interest, and becomes a *new obligation* upon mankind. This sentiment of morality, in the performance of promises, arises from the same principles as that in the abstinence from the property of others. *Public interest, education,* and *the artifices of politicians,* have the same effect in both cases.[45]

It seems then that the sense of morality is a sort of fiction because it appears to be a natural motive, antecedent to the rules of justice, but is in fact a logical ghost

---

[40] Mackie, *Hume's Moral Theory*, p. 80.

[41] Hume, *Treatise*, p. 523.

[42] Knud Haakonssen, 1981, *The Science of a Legislator: The Natural Jurisprudence of David Hume and Adam Smith*, Cambridge: Cambridge University Press, pp. 34–35.

[43] Hume, *Treatise*, p. 533.

[44] Ibid., pp. 533–534.

[45] Ibid., p. 523; first italics added.

hanging from the rules of justice, for it cannot be defined independently from those rules. Mutually advantageous conventions create the sense of morality that grounds the duty-imposing capacity of their composing rules. Basically, conventions yield their own justification. In the following section I will show how the self-validation of new duties takes place within the conventions through a process of objectification backed by inference rules.

B. The Is–Ought "Fallacy"

As is well known, Hume endorses two views on the relation between facts and values that are apparently contradictory. On the one hand, as we saw in the last section, Hume adopts a sentimentalist analysis of moral terms, among them ("natural") "obligation." Thus, for Hume the judgment "we lie under an obligation to perform X" is synonymous with "the nonperformance of X displeases us from the constitution of our nature." On the other hand, Hume is famous for having denounced the "is–ought fallacy," that is, the presumed fallacy of deducing moral conclusions for premises that are merely factual.[46] Ever since G. E. Moore introduced the label "naturalistic fallacy," it has been common to think that Hume rejects the derivation of prescriptive judgments from merely descriptive statements. However, it is plain that Hume does not at all share Moore's thesis that naturalism commits any "fallacy," because he himself provides, as we have just seen, a sentimentalist analysis of moral predicates such as "virtuous," "vicious," and "obligation." This being so, it is obvious that Hume thinks that a speaker can deduce the moral judgment "X is virtuous" from the first-person naturalist statement "from the constitution of my nature I have a feeling of praise from the contemplation of X." This is no fallacy, but just the exposition of Hume's naturalist outlook. And, of course, as Frankena has shown, it would beg the question to claim that this reasoning is fallacious just because one assumes that naturalism is false.[47]

So how can we render Hume's two claims coherent? There are two keys to finding the correct interpretation. First, we must notice that Hume does not say in the famous passage that the derivation of "ought" from "is" is a fallacy. He just warns that "'tis necessary that it shou'd be observ'd and explain'd; and at the same time that a reason should be given, for what seems altogether inconceivable."[48] The puzzling derivation is not logically impossible, but requires an adequate explanation. Indeed, he says that the deduction *seems* inconceivable, and yet he does not assert that it *is* inconceivable. Second, we must observe that Hume's naturalistic analysis of moral predicates makes it unnecessary to explain how statements about our natural moral sentiments can entail moral judgments. In fact, for Hume it is a plain fact that an "ought" can be deduced from an "is" when the latter refers to the moral feelings that shape our natural constitution. Therefore, what requires an explanation is not the inference of an "ought" from *any* "is." What demands an explanation is rather the derivation of "ought" judgments from statements that denote "external"

---

[46] Hume, *Treatise*, p. 469.
[47] William K. Frankena, 1939, "The Naturalistic Fallacy," *Mind*, 48, pp. 464–477.
[48] Hume, *Treatise*, p. 469.

facts, that is, facts unrelated to our natural psychological makeup, such as facts concerning God or human affairs.

For Hume it *seems* inconceivable that facts other than those concerning our natural moral sentiments can generate obligations. Because under the sentimentalist analysis the "creation of a new obligation supposes some new sentiment to arise," it is mysterious how a promise, for example, can create a new obligation. Accordingly, Hume's is–ought problem is really that of explaining how "external" facts can entail new obligations. Indeed, as against the standard interpretation, I contend that Hume certainly allows an "ought" to be derived from an "is." This can happen in two different cases: first, when the "is" refers to the constitution of our own nature, that is, to our natural moral feelings (this is the clearest case); and second, when the "is" denotes "external" facts that are relevant within certain institutions (v.gr., the conventions of justice). In the latter cases, he does not regard the inference as impossible, but rather as puzzling, that is, as demanding an explanation. And a mysterious reasoning is not necessarily fallacious.

The best interpretation of the is–ought passage does not see it as the denunciation of a fallacy, but as the preamble to an explanation of *artificial* "ought"s. Such "ought"s can be deduced from "is"s, even if the inference is not warranted by the meaning of moral obligation. This is why Hume demands an explanation. When Hume discusses justice, in Part II, he says:

> Those, therefore, who make use of the word property, or right, or *obligation*, before they have explain'd the origin of justice, or even make use of it in that explication, are guilty of a *very gross fallacy*, and can never reason upon any solid foundation.[49]

It seems then that the "very gross fallacy" is not just in deducing "ought" from "is," but in trying to infer "ought" statements from externalist factual statements in the absence of an explanation of the origin of justice. When such an explanation is delivered, the derivation is possible, and no fallacy is involved. Now the explanation of artificial "ought"s, which Hume demands in the is–ought passage, is really the explanation of the origin of justice.

Curiously, in a classic essay John Searle sought to show that *institutional* "ought"s can be derived from institutional "is"s, but believed that this was a way of refuting Hume's is–ought doctrine. Searle claims that an "ought" can be deduced from an "is" within the context of institutionalized forms of obligation. In this way he intends "to demonstrate a counterexample" to Hume's thesis that "no set of statements of fact by themselves entails any statement of value."[50] As we have seen, this thesis cannot be Hume's when the statement of value is a judgment about the goodness of an action. But it is clear that Searle is concerned with "ought" judgments. His purported "counterexample" is related to the convention of promises:

1. Jones uttered the words "I hereby promise to pay you, Smith, five dollars."
2. Jones promised to pay Smith five dollars.

[49] Ibid., p. 491 (italics added).
[50] John R. Searle, 1964, "How to Derive 'Ought' from 'Is,'" *The Philosophical Review*, 73, pp. 43–58.

3. Jones placed himself under (undertook) an obligation to pay Smith five dollars.
4. Jones is under an obligation to pay Smith five dollars.
5. Jones ought to pay Smith five dollars.

Searle contends that "ought" judgments can be inferred from statements referring to institutional facts, that is, facts existing within systems of constitutive rules.[51] Of course, the explanation of these derivations is that "institutional facts" are inherently normative, because they are picked out in certain institutions as grounds for conventional obligation. Searle misread Hume, because his "counterexample" is really a helpful way of articulating Hume's view about artificial "ought"s. Instead, what baffles Hume is that external facts can create new obligations when they are obviously unable to modify our natural moral constitution:

> I shall farther observe, that since every new promise imposes a new obligation of morality on the person who promises, and since this new obligation arises from his will; 'tis one of the most mysterious and incomprehensible operations that can possibly be imagin'd, and may even be compar'd to *transubstantiation*, or *holy orders*, where a certain form of words, along with a certain intention, changes entirely the nature of an external object, and even of a human creature.[52]

Hume goes on to argue that the derivation of an obligation from a promising act can be explained if we understand that the obligation of promises is "merely a human invention for the convenience of society." When this explanation is given, the derivation ceases to be "one of the most mysterious and incomprehensible operations," as Searle's "counterexample," or rather example, shows.

It is important to note that Hume thinks that the convention of political authority creates legal obligations, just as the convention of promises creates moral obligations. In this respect, the convention of political authority is similar to the conventions of justice:

> 'Tis the same principle, which causes us to disapprove of all kinds of private injustice, and in particular of the breach of promises.... We blame all disloyalty to magistrates; because we perceive, that the execution of justice, in the stability of possession, its translation by consent, and the performance of promises, is impossible, without submission to government.[53]

The convention of political authority also reduces uncertainty by indicating which commands are authoritative, that is, which political pronouncements are sources of legal obligations:

> Government, therefore, arises from the voluntary convention of men; and 'tis evident, that the same convention, which establishes government, will also determine the persons who are to govern, and will remove all doubt and ambiguity in this particular.[54]

---

[51] John Rawls, 1955, "Two Concepts of Rules," *The Philosophical Review*, 64, pp. 3–32.
[52] Hume, *Treatise*, p. 524.
[53] Ibid., pp. 545–546.
[54] Ibid., p. 554.

The similarity between Hume's convention of political authority and Hart's rule of recognition is startling. Just as the conventions of justice do, the political convention includes *rules of inference* that allow the derivation of institutional "ought"s from external "is"s. Just as a promisor can bind himself by uttering certain words within the institution of promise, a king can create a new obligation by uttering certain words within the convention of monarchy. All modern legal and political systems have political conventions or rules of recognition that establish the authoritative sources of legal norms.

According to my rendition of Hume's theory of political conventions, the fundamental rules of such conventions are rules of inference that close the is–ought gap. Therefore, the normativity can be clearly defined in this way: within the context of political conventions (i.e., rules of recognition), legal "ought"s can be inferred from factual statements asserting that, for instance, the king has issued a certain command. These derivations can be explained by resorting to the artificial character of political conventions. Instead of "counterexamples," they illustrate how a sort of "transubstantiation" takes place when legal normativity arises out of legal enactments and other institutional facts. Just as promises can create new obligations on the promisor, official enactments can create new obligations on subjects or citizens. The derivation of a legal "ought" from an institutional "is" follows the same pattern as Searle's famous derivation:

1. Jones, the King, uttered the words "Subjects, pay the Crown five pounds!"
2. Jones ordered subjects to pay the Crown five pounds.
3. Jones placed subjects under an obligation to pay the Crown five pounds.
4. Subjects are under an obligation to pay the Crown five pounds.
5. Subjects ought to pay the Crown five pounds.

Law generates new obligations because it relies on a political convention, and the problem of explaining how this convention fictionally creates new duties is similar to that of explaining the fictional normativity of the conventions of justice. This "sophistry" is made by rules of inference that objectify subjective acts, such as promising or commanding. Although promising and commanding per se cannot give rise to obligations according to the sentimentalist analysis of moral terms, the rules of inference contained in the convention of promises and in the political convention can turn external "is"s into moral "ought"s. This is not a fallacy, but is a kind of "sophistry" nonetheless.

IV. IDEOLOGY AND LEGAL NORMATIVITY

Some conventions, such as the convention of promises, clearly work to everyone's advantage, and so the sense of morality naturally emerges from the perception that those conventions serve the public interest. A sense of morality cannot arise so easily when the common benefit of a convention is not clearly perceived. For instance, a political convention can differentially promote the interests of some groups at the expense of others'. Though it is a contingent matter whether a political convention serves the common benefit or rather the interests of some groups, and it is likely that all political conventions promote a mix of both, the bootstrapping justification of political and legal obligations is more difficult than that of promissory duties, which are obviously beneficial for the people at large. We can therefore predict that the "artifices of educators and politicians" will be of critical importance when it comes to the validation of political commands.

The preceding remark can also be stated by appeal to the notion of "ideology." When a convention is exploitative in that it furthers the interests of some people instead of furthering the common good alone, the emergence of a sense of morality critically depends on the working of a political ideology. By "ideology" I mean any system of concepts, meanings, or beliefs that objectify relations of political domination or coercion. Objectification can take various forms. Sometimes it conceals the rulers' orders by presenting them as features of a static, objective, and natural or supernatural reality. Natural law doctrines often fulfill this function by claiming that some political commands mirror an immutable natural law. Other times some political commands are regarded as steps in a historical progression toward an ideal society. Like traditional, static natural law, this sort of dynamic natural law doctrine, often called "historicism," also seeks to legitimize the exercise of political power.[55] Enlightenment political theories often assert that some forms of political power rely on the exercise of individual reason through the making of a covenant or contract, or on the exercise of collective or general reason.[56] Rationalistic ideologies also seek to legitimize state power by turning the imperatives of a subjective will into objective practical claims.

Ideological objectification protects political domination from rational criticism and intellectual resistance. The German philosopher Hans Albert clearly says in this connection: "anyone who accepts the classical methodology that has its origins in the principle of sufficient justification cannot possibly *distinguish ideology from knowledge* in a convincing way; for the only solution to the problem of validity considered practicable by this methodology ... is recourse to a more or less camouflaged dogma – the route, in other words, typically attributed to ideological thinking."[57] Because the whole point of legal normativity is to validate subjective imperatives as objective norms, it embraces the foundationalist model of rationality and, therefore, a dogmatic approach to legal commands. Instead of an ideological, dogmatic stance toward state power and its pronouncements, Albert proposes a model of critical rationality that emphasizes permanent rational criticism of legal norms in terms of their ability to achieve valuable social outcomes.[58] Law and economics is for Albert a form of social technology that endorses critical

---

[55] For the relation between historicism and natural law, see Karl R. Popper, 1971, *The Open Society and Its Enemies*, Princeton: Princeton University Press, Vol. I, pp. 73–84, and Vol. II, pp. 81–88; Hans Kelsen, 1949, "The Natural-Law Doctrine before the Tribunal of Science," reprinted in Hans Kelsen, 1957, *What Is Justice? Justice, Law, and Politics in the Mirror of Science: Collected Essays by Hans Kelsen*, Berkeley and Los Angeles: University of California Press, pp. 137–173.

[56] Bentham mentions the social contract as an example of fiction (C. K. Ogden, *Bentham's Theory of Fictions*, pp. 122–125).

[57] Hans Albert, 1985, *Treatise on Critical Reason*, trans. Mary Varney Rorty, Princeton: Princeton University Press, p. 111.

[58] Hans Albert, 1988, "Critical Rationalism: The Problem of Method in Social Sciences and Law," *Ratio Juris*, 1, pp. 1–19.

rationality, whereas jurisprudential theorizing about legal normativity would be a residue of the classic style of ideological thinking in the social sciences.

Dominant groups typically benefit from the compliance with legal obligations, and they will therefore rationally invest in ideological advertising. This advertising often takes the form of mythical or fictional representation. Legal normativity is one of those myths or fictions. In fact, government's commands are not naturally seen as objectively obligatory, because they express the ruler's subjective will. The function of legal normativity is to create a *sense of legality* that validates those commands. The most efficacious way of concealing the artificial quality of this sense of legality is to objectify the political convention by regarding it as justified on natural or rational bases. Once this objectification is achieved, the emerging sense of legality hides the subjective quality of the ruler's commands, which now are regarded as objective norms.

There is no doubt that legal ideologies, including myths, have invariably accompanied Western law since Greek philosophy and literature. One excellent illustration is Aeschylus' *Eumenides*, which provides a mythical validation of the jury system of criminal justice as a creation of Athena to appease the Furies. However, whether legal normativity is an essential or necessary feature of law is a different issue. Matthew Kramer poses the time-honored question whether an organized-crime syndicate that controls a certain region (i.e., a stationary bandit in Olson's jargon) could be denied the label "legal regime" just because it is a system of imperatives that do not claim moral legitimacy. Kramer answers this question in the negative:

> . . . a claim to moral legitimacy or authoritativeness is not a decisive factor; instead, the key factors are the generality and durability of the Mafia's norms, and the institutional regularity of the application of those norms. If the Mafia's system of exerting far-reaching control over people's lives does indeed very substantially partake of the key qualities just listed, and if it also meets some relevant test for efficacy (whatever that test might be), then it ought to be classified as a legal system.[59]

I am inclined to think that Kramer is wrong. "Law" is an ideological term that cloaks the practice of power in large politically centralized societies where the division of labor has led to the emergence of a professional group of full-time bureaucrats (e.g., judges, attorneys, and lawyers).[60] At this point in the evolution of human societies, a writing system also becomes available for conveying commands in writing, allowing those commands to have effect in distant times and places.[61] Aquinas noticed this feature of law when he quoted Isidore saying: "*lex* (law) *is derived from legere* (to read) *because it is written.*"[62] Legal scribes developed a specialized objectifying linguistic framework to express orders and to argue about them before courts. Political advertising intertwined with legalistic language

---

[59] Matthew H. Kramer, 1999, *In Defense of Legal Positivism*, Oxford: Oxford University Press, pp. 96–97.

[60] Jared Diamond, 1999, *Guns, Germs, and Steel: The Fates of Human Societies*, New York: W. W. Norton, pp. 89–90.

[61] Ibid., p. 216.

[62] St. Thomas Aquinas, 1956, *Treatise on Law*, Washington, DC: Regnery, p. 11 (italics in original).

to produce the idea of legal validity. The resulting ideological fiction not only facilitated the administration and enforcement of law, but actually created law as we have come to know it. Thus, we are reluctant to call a Mafia system "law" because Mafia systems are not typically camouflaged by powerful legalistic ideologies that appeal to objectifying, validating fictions. Though ideological camouflaging and objective validation are not among the Austinian–Kramerian features, they seem an essential element of law.

The German legal sociologist Theodor Geiger stressed the fictional character of normative discourse as early as the 1940s. Geiger offers an articulate view of the ideological character of objective value language.[63] He observes that value judgments have the grammatical form of factual cognitive statements: *A is B*. This form notwithstanding, value judgments are pseudo-objective statements: they objectify a subjective relationship between the speaker and an object. For Geiger the person who utters the judgment "lying is wrong" *pretends* to utter a cognitive proposition about lying, but since the reality to which the pretended proposition refers is illusory, the judgment cannot be true. But value judgments cannot be false in the usual sense either, because they denote an illusory reality. Geiger concludes that value judgments are "paratheoretical."[64]

John Mackie's "error theory" is very similar to Geiger's "paratheoretical analysis." Mackie adopts a Humean, noncognitivist position as regards moral judgments, but he argues that moral judgments have a claim to objectivity:

> I conclude, then, that ordinary moral judgments include a claim to objectivity, an assumption that there are objective values in just the sense in which I am concerned to deny this. And I do not think it is going too far to say that this assumption has been incorporated in the basic, conventional, meanings of moral terms. Any analysis of the meanings of moral terms which omits this claim to objective, intrinsic, prescriptivity is to that extent incomplete; and this is true of any non-cognitive analysis, any naturalist one, and any combination of the two.[65]

According to Mackie, objectification generally takes place by instilling the error that there are nonempirical facts that are inherently prescriptive. Applying Geiger's and Mackie's analyses to the problem of justified normativity implies regarding judges, jurists, and legal philosophers who utter judgments about legal obligations as engaged in fictionalist discourse as long as they pretend to speak about the objective validity of law.

Hans Kelsen's "pure theory of law" allows a fictionalist reinterpretation too. Kelsen contends that law performs an ideological function in interpreting unlawful private coercion as a crime and lawful public coercion as a sanction (e.g., the death penalty).[66] For legal norms to serve as schemes of interpretation, the jurist must *presuppose* that the original constitution directly or indirectly validating all the

---

[63] Theodor Geiger, 1968, *Ideologie und Wahrheit: Eine soziologische Kritik des Denkens*, Neuwied and Berlin: Luchterhand.

[64] Ibid., pp. 47–50; 58–61.

[65] J. L. Mackie, 1977, *Ethics: Inventing Right and Wrong*, London: Penguin Books.

[66] Hans Kelsen, 1992, *Introduction to the Problems of Legal Theory*, trans. Bonnie Litschewski Paulson and Stanley L. Paulson, Oxford: Clarendon Press, pp. 9–12.

other lower norms is itself a justified norm. This presupposition is the famous *basic norm*. Unlike natural lawyers' notion of committed justified normativity, Kelsen's is a notion of uncommitted or detached justified normativity.[67] The existence of law does not require that the first historical constitution be justified, or that it be recognized as justified by jurists. Law's existence only needs an epistemological presupposition. Now notice that Kelsen is a noncognitivist; for him all value judgments are subjective. If Kelsen had reached the final conclusions of his position, he might well have supported a form of "legal nihilism":

1. It is necessary that law is objectively valid.
2. For any social coercive system L to be objectively valid, L's first historical norm must be objectively valid.
3. No norm can be objectively valid (because there are no objective values).
4. Therefore, no social coercive system L is law (there is no law).

Consider now Kelsen's actual argument, which incorporates the basic norm:

1. It is necessary that law is objectively valid.
2. For any social coercive system L to be objectively valid, L's first historical norm must be objectively valid.
3. There are objective values.
4. L's first historical norm is objectively valid (basic norm).[68]
5. Therefore, L is law.

Notice that the basic norm 4 presupposes in turn what we could call the "meta-basic norm" 3, in the absence of which the whole arguments wrecks havoc. Now Kelsen must consider point 3 in this context as a fictional proposition, because, as we said, he was a noncognitivist as regards moral language. This means that for Kelsen the jurist either mistakenly believes that law could possibly be valid, or pretends to believe that law could possibly be valid. If there are no objective values, law could not be objectively valid, and therefore the epistemological presupposition contained in the basic norm would necessarily be false. In any case, Kelsen must adopt a fictionalist stance toward legal discourse, because he endorses a noncognitivist theory of value judgments. Therefore, according to Kelsen legal sentences must be construed as fictional statements. In this sense, Kelsen can be considered a defender of legal fictionalism.[69]

Unlike Kelsen, Raz appears to exclude the possibility that judges could take a fictionalist stance toward legal validity by falsely presupposing that there are

---

[67] Joseph Raz, *The Authority of Law*, pp. 145, 155–157.

[68] For Kelsen this proposition presupposes that L is in force, as legal science attributes objective validity only to the first historical norms of coercive systems that are generally obeyed.

[69] In fact, Kelsen himself declared that his theory was fictionalist, though for a different reason. He said that jurists "*presuppose* the basic norm as the meaning of an act of will." He went on to argue: "Since, however, an act of will does not exist in reality, but only in the juristic thinking of men who interpret the coercive order as an objective valid legal order, the presupposition of the basic norm is the typical case of a *fiction* in the sense of Vaihinger's *Philosophie des Als-Ob*." Hans Kelsen, 1966, "On the Pure Theory of Law," *Israel Law Review*, 1, p. 6 (italics in original).

objective reasons or values. Curiously, he asserts that "since the law claims to have authority it is capable of having it." And he goes on to assert: "Since the claim is made by legal officials wherever a legal system is in force the possibility that it is normally insincere or *based on a conceptual mistake* is ruled out."[70] Raz's example of a mistaken proposition uttered by judges on someone's authority is "trees have authority over people." In fact, it is difficult to conceive a judge sincerely asserting that trees have authority over people. Raz also says: "There are two kinds of reasons for not having authority. One is that the moral or normative conditions for one's directives being authoritative are absent. The second kind of reason for not having authority is that one lacks some of the other, non-moral or non-normative prerequisites of authority, for example, that one cannot communicate with others."[71] Raz claims that judges cannot sincerely claim that law is authoritative if law lacks the nonnormative conditions of authority, but the claim might be wrong because the normative conditions are absent. What about the metaethical conditions? In sincerely claiming law's authority, could judges be mistakenly presupposing that there are objective moral reasons? This question does not have an easy answer, because Raz generally eschews moral ontological commitments. I think, however, that Raz's claim that legal officials cannot be mistaken about the nonnormative prerequisites of law's claim to validity is at odds with a fictionalist account of legal normativity.[72]

If law rests on the fiction of its justified normativity, the only conceivable problem for rational choice theory is to explain the supply and demand of the fiction of legal normativity. As Hume envisaged, the supply is made by politicians and educators, and, specifically in the case of law, by judges and law professors.

V. LEGAL NORMATIVITY AND IDEOLOGICAL ADVERTISING

I have argued that legal normativity, which turns subjective commands into objective norms, is a fiction created by politicians and educators to validate state power. In this section I will discuss legal normativity as a form of ideological advertising developed by state power in order to increase the demand for law-abiding. Ideological advertising can perform various distorting or mystifying functions. One of these is to conceal the fact that legal and political conventions are self-validating, as Hume showed. But mystification seems to be a typical feature of all ideological

---

[70] Joseph Raz, "Authority, Law, and Morality," p. 302 (italics added).
[71] Ibid.
[72] Among contemporary legal theorists, Larry Alexander and Emily Sherwin are the ones who show the greatest affinity to legal fictionalism. Alexander and Sherwin (2001, *The Rule of Rules*, Durham: Duke University Press) say that "the only way to maintain a system of rules is by one or more forms of deception." They add that "the primary form of deception . . . is deception of rule-subjects about the nature of rules and the relationship of rules to correct moral conduct" (p. 87). However, this kind of deception hinders the correct understanding of rules as social instruments to implement moral principles under conditions of imperfect moral and/or factual knowledge. Instead, legal fictionalism focuses on the attribution of validity to political enactments and on the semantics of legal statements.

advertising. In a famous book on the sociology of religion, Peter Berger contends that the basic recipe of social legitimation is as follows:

> Let the institutional order be so interpreted as to hide, as much as possible, its constructed character. Let that which has been stamped out of the ground *ex nihilo* appear as the manifestation of something that has been existent from the beginning of time, or at least from the beginning of this group. Let the people forget that this order was established by men and continues to be dependent upon the consent of men.[73]

Though religion is the most powerful strategy of social legitimation, secularized political ideologies can also serve to maintain socially constructed realities. The usual riposte at this juncture is that Marxist theorists of ideology today reject "false consciousness" as an essential component of ideological beliefs by arguing that these beliefs are real because they are part and parcel of social life. This is a confusing view, because "false" is a predicate of propositions, not of social facts. Terry Eagleton persuasively suggests that "ideological discourse typically displays a certain ratio between empirical propositions and what we might roughly term a 'world view,' in which the latter has the edge over the former." Eagleton also says:

> The closest analogy to this is perhaps a literary work. Most literary works contain empirical propositions . . . But part of what is meant by "fictionality" is that these statements are not usually present for their own sake; they act, rather, as "supports" for the overall world view of the text itself.[74]

Similarly, the ideology of legal normativity is built on the fiction that coercive orders can generate valid obligations. This is an ideological fiction because the assumption that political enactments generate inherently prescriptive *entities* (i.e., "obligations" or "reasons"), as something different from the assumption that agents believe or pretend to believe that commands give rise to such entities, is unnecessary for the explanation of social behavior; and because the assumption's chief role is to justify the exercise of political power, rather than to subject it to rational criticism. This contention about legal normativity is consistent with claiming that sometimes political ideologies include true cognitive contents.

How can we explain the supply of ideological advertising? Under monopolistic competition consumers have imperfect information and so firms can be able to differentiate their products from other similar products through advertising. But the state has a *de iure* monopoly power over "political goods," that is, over public and private goods it provides through coercive regulation, and thus the fundamental question is why the state would rationally invest in ideological advertising addressed to objectify its pronouncements and commands. What gains could the state reap from advertising the objective interpretation of its commands if *by hypothesis* there is no other competitor in the market of political goods?

There are three fundamental reasons why it might be profitable for the state to invest in ideological advertising. First, the state's monopoly power is never perfect.

[73] Peter L. Berger, 1990, *The Sacred Canopy*, New York: Anchor Books, p. 33.
[74] Terry Eagleton, 2007, *Ideology: An Introduction*, London and New York: Verso, p. 22.

On the one hand, even after nationalization of protective services, there often are available private ways of achieving the same results (black markets, informal norms, private protective agencies, private arbitrators, etc.), or foreign suppliers of public goods (e.g., neighboring countries that offer favorable legal conditions to attract investments). The ideology of legal normativity increases the demand for formal domestic law and the formal methods of adjudication. On the other hand, there is usually extrasystemic political competition from various groups who try to obtain the constitutional power. The incumbent groups or coalitions might gain from investing in advertising if they need popular support to arrest revolutionary tendencies. In a monarchy, for instance, there might be revolutionary competitors who want to establish a republic. In this example, ideological advertising (v.gr., the doctrine of the divine origin of kings) increases the demand for the monarchical form of government.

Second, advertising can be helpful for the internalization of legal norms. As James Coleman rightly remarks, "internalization of a norm will mean that an individual comes to have an internal sanctioning system which provides punishment when he carries out an action proscribed by the norm or fails to carry out an action prescribed by the norm."[75] In fact, advertising can shift agents' preferences in ways conducive to social efficiency, or to the welfare of the ruling groups, as the case may be. This is precisely Hume's great insight. In turn, internalization of legal norms can decrease monitoring and enforcements costs. Coleman's contention is worth quoting:

> ... if internalization can be brought about at a sufficiently low cost, it is a more efficient means of social control than is external policing of actions. The question then becomes, just what are the conditions under which creation of an internal sanctioning system is likely to be more efficient than maintaining external policing of actions? [...] Deciding whether internalization of a norm in another actor is rational must involve balancing the cost of bringing about the internalization to a given degree of effectiveness against the discounted future cost of policing to bring about the same degree of compliance, where the degree of compliance is selected by balancing the costs of noncompliance against the costs of sanctioning by the most efficient means (internal or external).[76]

Thus, the point is that the delusion of objective validity is a powerful weapon to achieve the effective internalization of political commands, which in turn is conducive to reducing policing and enforcement costs. Reduction of policing and enforcement costs can take place in two different ways. On the one hand, potential lawbreakers must incorporate into their cost–benefit analysis the psychological and reputation costs derived from breaking the law. This is so because lawbreakers' internal sanctioning systems (conscience or superego) can yield high psychological costs, and because other people's own internal systems lead them to blame lawbreakers, which in turn inflicts upon them reputation losses. In addition, reputation losses produce further costs in self-esteem. Therefore, even if the penalty

---

[75] James S. Coleman, 1990, *Foundations of Social Theory*, Cambridge, MA: Harvard University Press, p. 293.
[76] Ibid., p. 294.

and the probability of apprehension are held constant, the ideology of legal norma-tivity and its increased capacity for norm internalization can increase law-abiding. On the other hand, legal normativity advertising can diminish the costs of whistle blowing and thus reduce detection costs. In fact, although denunciation of the breach of orders is not particularly praiseworthy, denunciation of the breach of objective duties certainly is.

Finally, even if the state is a monopolist supplier of political goods, it is rarely a monopsonist demander of professional or political labor. The ideological legit-imization of law allows the state to hire officials and judges at lower salaries while deterring defections promoted by private individuals and groups willing to invest resources in violating or eluding legal constraints. Legal ideologies make state per-sonnel cherish their public missions and responsibilities and consequently dimin-ish the risk of public corruption and other forms of free-riding within government. In this way, the ideology of legal normativity can diminish the administration costs of enforcement and adjudicative agencies.

CONCLUDING REMARKS

Classic conceptions of legal normativity in terms of moral validity are hardly con-sistent with rational choice theory. For this reason the rational choice analysis of legal normativity is often associated with legal reductionism or legal convention-alism. In this paper I have explored a different approach to legal normativity that was originated by David Hume. Thus I have sought to uncover in the *Treatise* a fictionalist account of legal discourse. This account explains how legal "ought"s can be inferred from political "is"s: the constitutive rules of political conventions create fictional obligations through rules of inference. No fallacy is involved in this process as long as we adopt a fictionalist interpretation of objective obligation judgments. Rules of inference that allow the derivation of obligation judgments perform an ideological function: they conceal the fact that political conventions are self-validating. The ideological advertising of such self-validation is supplied by state apparatuses in order to reduce in various ways policing and enforcement costs. Unlike the rule of recognition, which Hart conceives as a solution to the problem of uncertainty in the identification of primary rules,[77] the fundamen-tal point of self-validating political conventions and their sustaining ideological advertising is to implement social control in cost-effective ways.

[77] Hart, *The Concept of Law*, p. 92.

5 Efficiency, Practices, and the Moral Point of View: Limits of Economic Interpretations of Law

MARK TUNICK

Law-and-economics theories treat legal issues as economic problems. Because society has limited resources to devote to its legal institutions, it is important to consider their economic costs in deciding how these institutions are best operated. I shall argue, however, that for a theory to be persuasive in either explaining or prescribing legal rules, it needs to recognize moral ideals apart from economic efficiency, such as justice and fairness, that may account for why we have legal institutions in the first place and that may be essential to our finding them acceptable.

I. LAW AND ECONOMICS AS EXPLANATIVE AND NORMATIVE THEORY

Economic approaches to law generally assume that human behavior can be understood as the result of people's rational choices to maximize their utility or satisfy their preferences. Some law-and-economics proponents use this assumption to explain why practices emerge or predict how people will respond to rewards or punishments.[1] Some use this together with another assumption, that social and legal policy *ought* to be driven by the goal of promoting or maximizing social utility or welfare, to generate prescriptive or normative theories.[2] For example, on the law-and-economics approach, the purpose of punishment is to deter undesirable conduct that diminishes social utility. A sanction deters by imposing a cost on potential criminals; the harsher the sanction, the higher the price of committing

---

[1] For example, Gary Becker, 1974, "A Theory of Marriage: Part II," *Journal of Political Economy*, 82, pp. S11–S26; Thomas Ulen, 2005, "Human Fallibility and the Forms of Law," in Francesco Parisi and Vernon L. Smith, eds., *The Law and Economics of Irrational Behavior* (Stanford, CA: Stanford University Press), pp. 397–424; Steven Shavell, 1985, "Criminal Law and the Optimal Use of Nonmonetary Sanctions as a Deterrent," *Columbia Law Review*, 85, pp. 1232–1262; Frank Easterbrook, 1983, "Criminal Procedure as a Market System," *Journal of Legal Studies*, 12, pp. 289–332; Kenneth Dau–Schmidt, 1990, "An Economic Analysis of the Criminal Law as Preference-Shaping Policy," *Duke Law Journal*, 1, pp. 1–38; Robert Cooter, 2006, "The Intrinsic Value of Obeying Law," *Fordham Law Review*, 75, pp. 1275–1285.

[2] I shall focus herein on Louis Kaplow and Steven Shavell, 2002, *Fairness versus Welfare*, Cambridge, MA: Harvard University Press. See also, for example, Easterbrook, "Criminal Procedure"; Gary Becker, 1968, "Crime and Punishment: An Economic Approach," *Journal of Political Economy*, 76, pp. 169–217; Ronald Coase, 1960, "The Problem of Social Cost," *Journal of Law and Economics*, 3, pp. 1–44.

crime. Imposing sanctions has a social cost that must be weighed against the utility of deterring crime. Criminals, as rational actors, will decide whether to commit a crime according to the expected utility of doing so, which is a function of both the severity of the sanction and the probability of apprehension.[3] Depending on the rate at which potential criminals discount the disutility of punishment, and the rate at which taxpayers discount enforcement costs, it may be optimal to threaten severe sanctions that will only be imposed rarely, so long as the expected utility of committing a crime is negative.[4] If a fine of $10 would deter illegal parking, it may be efficient to impose a $10,000 fine with a probability of enforcement of 1/1,000: the expected disutility of illegally parking would be $10, but enforcement costs might be substantially reduced.[5] High fines may upset many people, and be regarded as unjust (because they are disproportionate to the offense), and unfair to the 1 in 1,000 violators who are caught.[6] But if maximizing utility is our only goal, justice and fairness are beside the point (though one might convince oneself that getting caught is like losing a gamble, and losing a gamble is not unfair).[7]

In the ways just described, law-and-economics proponents follow the path of Jeremy Bentham, who also explained human behavior as utility-maximizing, and who also believed the principle of utility offers the only rational guide for determining what the law ought to be. Though conceding that it is not susceptible of any direct proof, "for that which is used to prove everything else, cannot itself be proved," Bentham had no question that the principle of utility – "that principle which approves or disapproves of every action whatsoever, according to the tendency which it appears to have to augment or diminish the happiness of the party whose interest is in question" – is our only rational guide: "Systems which attempt to question it, deal in sounds instead of sense, in caprice instead of reason, in darkness instead of light."[8] Some proponents of law and economics share Bentham's obstinate commitment to a single principle. They take what I call a *totalizing* viewpoint, by which I mean the view that a single standard – utility, or efficiency, or welfare – provides correct policy prescriptions as well as explanations and understandings of practices, and that considerations such as justice and fairness have no independent weight. I believe that insofar as law-and-economics proponents obstinately take a totalizing point of view, they fail to provide a persuasive

---

[3] Becker, "Crime and Punishment."

[4] A. Mitchell Polinsky and Steven Shavell, 1999, "On the Disutility and Discounting of Imprisonment and the Theory of Deterrence," *Journal of Legal Studies*, 28, pp. 1–16.

[5] A. Mitchell Polinsky, 1989, *An Introduction to Law and Economics*, 2nd ed., Boston: Little Brown, pp. 77–78. People may not assess expected utility as the example suggests. Studies in behavioral economics on optimism bias, availability bias, and prospect theory suggest this high-penalty, low-enforcement-level strategy may fail. See Christine Jolls, 2005, "On Law Enforcement with Boundedly Rational Actors," in Parisi and Smith, *The Law and Economics of Irrational Behavior*, pp. 268–286.

[6] Ian Urbina, "High Fines for Speeding Anger Virginians," *New York Times*, July 19, 2007 (noting 100,000 Virginians signed a petition against $2,500 fines for driving 20 mph or more above the speed limit, but that some people acknowledge they are more careful when driving).

[7] Kaplow and Shavell, *Fairness versus Welfare*, p. 67 (a sanction dictated by welfare economics is superior to a fair sanction); Richard Posner, 1992, *Economic Analysis of Law*, 4th ed., Boston: Little Brown, p. 230 (lotteries are not unfair).

[8] Jeremy Bentham, 1781/1988, *The Principles of Morals and Legislation*, New York: Prometheus Books, ch. 1, §§11, 2, 1.

general explanative or normative theory, just as Bentham failed to do so, as is evident from his rebuked efforts to institute governments of nations on his principle of utility.

A. Law and Economics and the Moral Point of View

Not all law-and-economics proponents bluntly reject considerations apart from utility, efficiency, or welfare. Other considerations are often briefly acknowledged and put to one side.[9] But some of the most visible proponents explicitly dismiss the contribution that nonutilitarians can make to our understanding of the law; or they reduce the concern for justice, fairness, or retribution to a "taste" that utilitarians enter into their calculations but do not otherwise weigh in policy deliberations.[10] They are sharply critical of a moral point of view that is not controlled by economic analysis and, like Bentham, seem incredulous that anything other than augmenting social utility can count as a good reason for deciding upon a law or policy. Richard Posner criticizes those who do moral philosophy, which he denigrates with the label "academic moralism," for their inability to solve any modern social problems: "We can get along without doing or even thinking about moral theory."[11] Moral philosophy does not provide the needed economic tools for policy analysis, and is "insipid."[12] Kaplow and Shavell, though perhaps less overtly hostile to moral philosophy than is Posner, similarly express an inability to comprehend any ground for law and social policy other than welfare or social utility.[13] They oppose appeals to fairness, retribution, or a conception of right that is independent of welfare, because doing what is fair, just, or right may make everyone worse off from the standpoint of social utility.[14]

---

[9] Coase, "Social Cost," p. 19 ("questions of equity apart"); Easterbrook, "Criminal Procedure," p. 291 (puts to one side goals of punishment other than deterrence); Ulen, "Human Fallibility," p. 399; Shavell, "Criminal Law," p. 1232, n. 1 (recognizing other goals of punishment besides deterrence); Richard Posner, 2006, "Common-Law Economic Torts: An Economic and Legal Analysis," *Arizona Law Review*, 48, p. 736 (conditionally defends economic analysis of tort law "if the only normative issue" is the law's efficiency); Posner, *Economic Analysis of Law*, pp. 13–14 (recognizing limits of efficiency as an ethical criterion), 27 ("there is more to justice than economics"); Guido Calabresi and A. Douglas Melamud, 1972, "Property Rules, Liability Rules, and Inalienability," *Harvard Law Review*, 85, p. 1128 (efficiency is but "one view of the cathedral"); Lynn Stout, 1992, "Strict Scrutiny and Social Choice," *Georgetown Law Journal*, 80, p. 1834 (acknowledging that moral theory "may better explain many aspects of constitutional law").

[10] For treatments of fairness or equality as a taste, see Kaplow and Shavell, *Fairness versus Welfare*, p. 448; Ulen, "Human Fallibility," p. 405 (same); and Steven Shavell, 2004, *Foundations of Economic Analysis of Law*, Cambridge, MA: Harvard University Press, pp. 537–539, 608. For treatments of retribution as a preference or taste, see Dan M. Kahan, 1998, "Social Meaning and the Economic Analysis of Crime," *Journal of Legal Studies*, 27, pp. 616–620; and Edward Glaeser and Bruce Sacerdote, 2003, "Sentencing in Homicide Cases and the Role of Vengeance," *Journal of Legal Studies*, 32, pp. 363–381.

[11] Richard Posner, 1998, "The Problematics of Moral and Legal Theory," *Harvard Law Review*, 111, pp. 1671, 1638.

[12] Ibid., pp. 1670–1671, 1639–1640.

[13] Kaplow and Shavell, *Fairness versus Welfare*, pp. 299–300 (the retributive conception is "difficult to identify"); compare pp. 96, 163–165 (inability to understand a normative justification for adhering to promises).

[14] Ibid., discussed in the following; and Shavell, *Foundations*, p. 608 ("no deontological importance should be accorded [to moral notions]" – for doing so would reduce social welfare).

Many law-and-economics proponents conflate justifying a policy with *demonstrating* that it promotes welfare or utility. They identify their enterprise as scientific, though we must be careful to distinguish those who appropriately adopt a scientific method when investigating empirical questions, such as whether there is a statistically significant difference in the rate of certain crimes depending on whether discretionary gun laws are present or absent, from those who refer generally to law and economics as a science without distinguishing questions for which a scientific method is and is not appropriate.[15] In harmony with their self-identification as scientists, they believe their research goal is correct answers, discoverable by experts.[16] Because moral philosophy seems to them unable to produce correct answers, having failed to resolve centuries-old moral dilemmas, they regard questions of moral judgment as nonscientific matters of sentiment, preference, or taste, about which little can be intelligibly said.[17]

This reduction of appeals to justice and fairness to mere expressions of sentiment is deeply problematic. Although moral (and aesthetic) judgments differ from many claims in the natural sciences, they also differ from expressions of taste. When I express a taste, such as "Canary wine is pleasant," and someone challenges me, there is nothing more I can say; when I express a moral or aesthetic judgment, such as "Mahler's Ninth Symphony is a great work," or "bank robbers deserve to be punished," and someone challenges me, if I were to back up my judgment simply by saying "that is just my preference," I would prove myself an incompetent judge. A competent judge in these contexts points to reasons beyond merely having a preference or liking.[18]

B. Act versus Rule Utilitarianism and the Role of Social Practices

Reducing moral arguments for justice and fairness to expressions of taste is one way some law-and-economics proponents reveal an insufficient understanding of the reasons available when we justify our actions. Another way is failing to recognize the important role social practices play in providing reasons for acting. Because utilitarianism is a moral theory telling us how we ought to act, law-and-economics critics of a moral point of view are critical of, specifically, moral points of view that are not utilitarian. To be even more precise, they are critical of moral points of view that are not act-utilitarian.

---

[15] Those regarding law and economics as a science, generally, include Charles Rowley, 1981, "Social Sciences and Law: The Relevance of Economic Theories," *Oxford Journal of Legal Studies*, 1, pp. 391–392, 394; Thomas Ulen, 2004, "The Unexpected Guest: Law and Economics, Law and Other Cognate Disciplines, and the Future of Legal Scholarship," *Chicago-Kent Law Review*, 79, pp. 405, 408; Posner, *Economic Analysis of Law*, p. 16; Posner, "Problematics," pp. 1646–1648; Richard Posner, 1998, "Social Norms, Social Meaning, and Economic Analysis of Law," *Journal of Legal Studies*, 27, p. 565; and Robert Ellickson, 1998, "Law and Economics Discovers Social Norms," *Journal of Legal Studies*, 27, pp. 537–552.

[16] Kaplow and Shavell, *Fairness versus Welfare*, pp. 397–399 (contrasting "experts" with citizens with limited capacities to comprehend policy analysis and who "mistakenly" approve policies that are not welfare-optimal).

[17] Posner, "Problematics," pp. 1666, 1680; Shavell, *Foundations*, pp. 600–602 (moral notions are a type of "sentiment").

[18] Hanna Pitkin, 1972, *Wittgenstein and Justice*, Berkeley: University of California Press, ch.10.

Act utilitarians regard an act as justified if doing the act leads to greater utility than not doing it. Rule utilitarians, in contrast, hold that an act is justified if there is greater utility in adhering to a rule requiring we do the act than in not adhering to that rule. Rule utilitarians have us determine what practices we should adopt based on the principle of utility, but, they argue, having adopted the practice and participating in it, we are bound by its rules and do not decide what to do by considering the utility of the act.[19] The baseball batter must return to the dugout when he gets his third strike, not because doing so is "best on the whole," but because he has struck out.[20]

Deference to social practice can seem irrational to the act utilitarian, and does seem irrational to a number of law-and-economics proponents. Kaplow and Shavell argue that "if [the reason for having] social norms is to promote individuals' well-being, it would be a non sequitur to elevate social norms into independent evaluative principles that are to be given weight at the expense of individuals' well-being."[21] To them, that a practice requires that we keep our promises, or punish the guilty in proportion to their culpability, is not a good reason to do so. We should do so only if individuals are made better off – in each instance – according to a utility calculation. Law-and-economics proponents tend to understand social practices as mere behavioral regularities and not as exogenous forces, and rules of practice as summary rules, rules that merely summarize regularities and provide no reason for acting with weight independent of their utility.[22] To give independent weight to the rules of social practices in deciding what to do violates their assumption that social evaluation is to be based only on individual well-being.[23] We should value laws and practices not because of anything intrinsic to them, but only insofar as they enable individuals to obtain positive future returns, or "personal (nonaltruistic) economic gains."[24] One of the central points in John Rawls's "Two Concepts of Rules," in which he articulates a theory of rule utilitarianism, is that rules of practices are not summary rules; they are rules that give meaning to our actions. The rules define the practice and are logically prior to the performance of an action within the practice, so that to explain or defend one's actions within a practice one must appeal to the rules and not to some other principle, such as utility.[25] This is not to say that we should never reevaluate our practices or their rules using the principle of utility, but it is to recognize a distinction between justifying practices, which is a legislative function, and justifying actions within practices.[26]

Rawls is attentive to the nature of justification in a way that many law-and-economics proponents are not. He notes that a justification "is an argument

[19] John Rawls, 1955, "Two Concepts of Rules," *Philosophical Review*, 64, pp. 3–32.

[20] Compare ibid., pp. 25–27.

[21] Kaplow and Shavell, *Fairness versus Welfare*, p. 71; compare pp. 76–77, 390–391, 771. Compare Shavell, *Foundations*, p. 607 (moral notions are useful guides but "inevitably fail" in some circumstances, being simple and general so they can be easily learned and applied).

[22] Eric Posner, 2000, *Law and Social Norms*, Cambridge, MA: Harvard University Press, p. 26 (social norms are not exogenous forces but "behavioral regularities").

[23] Shavell, *Foundations*, p. 597 and n. 4; cf. Kaplow and Shavell, *Fairness versus Welfare*, 16.

[24] E. Posner, *Law and Social Norms*, p. 53.

[25] Rawls, "Rules," p. 25.

[26] Ibid., pp. 32 (not inferring that one should accept existing practices), 27–30 (on the distinction of offices).

addressed to [and seeking to convince] those who disagree with us."[27] What counts as an appropriate and persuasive argument will depend on our point of disagreement. Justifying a convict's punishment to the convict who believes he was innocent differs from justifying his punishment to a philosopher who does not think we should have the practice of punishment: their concerns are different, and different responses are appropriate. In the former case a judge could point to the criteria established in the law for determining guilt; in the latter case, one could point to the (utilitarian or nonutilitarian) reasons why we punish rather than do nothing or respond in other ways to acts we call crimes. Justification is contextual.

When we justify social policies, we seek to persuade, and an effective strategy for doing this, employed at least since Socrates practiced the elenchus, is to arrive at a position that fits with other judgments that we hold so that we are comfortable with the position. When lawmakers (be they legislators or judges) decide what sanctions to establish for a crime, whether the insane should be punished, whether illegally obtained evidence should be excluded from trial, or whether there should be restrictions against carrying concealed weapons, they confront substantial moral issues that are also matters of social policy. The question is "what is to be done" and is answered by evaluating various considerations. My criticism of law and economics is limited to those proponents who take a totalizing point of view that excludes considerations that are not act-utilitarian. It must be distinguished from the criticism some have made that economic analysis is inappropriate in explaining or deciding upon policy concerning the personal sphere of nonmarket activity (such as marriage, rape, or noncommercial promises).[28] Economic considerations are often important in the personal sphere and are undeniably important in deciding how government should allocate its scarce resources. Obviously we should not provide costly corrective justice for a trivial harm.[29] Whenever we must use institutions to promote our ideals, we are forced to take costs into account. But we should not lose sight of the ideals – both utilitarian and nonutilitarian – the institutions and its rules are intended to promote. Government would not be economically viable if every unjust action by an individual that causes harm or disappoints were remedied or punished using legal mechanisms. But it is a mistake to infer from this that the question of what is to be done is a purely economic problem to be decided by a utilitarian calculation.

II. LIMITATIONS OF LAW AND ECONOMICS AS AN EXPLANATIVE THEORY

My primary objective is to point to the limitations of law and economics as a normative theory insofar as it excludes moral points of view that are not act-utilitarian, but I also want to indicate why that approach may be limited as an explanative theory. Practices such as punishment, or promising, create reasons for

---

[27] John Rawls, 1971, *A Theory of Justice*, Cambridge, MA: Harvard University Press, p. 580.
[28] Claire Hill, 2004, "Law and Economics in the Personal Sphere," *Law and Social Inquiry*, 29, p. 219 ("the personal sphere is simply outside the ambit of what law and economics can describe").
[29] Kaplow and Shavell, *Fairness versus Welfare*, p. 97.

acting. It is possible to explain actions without appealing to the reasons held by the actors – doing so is fundamental to the theories of Marx, Freud, evolutionary psychologists, and cultural materialists such as Marvin Harris, all of whom claim that human behavior is shaped by forces of which the actors are unaware. Harris argues that although Jews and Muslims explain why they do not eat pork by appealing to religious doctrine, the true cause of their behavior is materialist: their ancestors lived in hot, arid regions, pigs do not sweat, and so expending resources to domesticate pigs in an environment hostile to pigs was inefficient. The religious taboo arose as a reason for the proscription on eating pork, but the cause is ecological.[30] Law-and-economics proponents similarly claim to uncover the true ground or cause of behavior – the pursuit of economic efficiency or welfare – even though judges and other actors who produce legal policy may be unaware of that ground and may themselves appeal to noneconomic reasons such as justice or fairness.[31] It does not matter to these proponents if people do not actually calculate like act utilitarians (and some studies suggest that people do not or are unable to calculate expected utilities,[32] and that emotions are central to how people with normal brain functioning form moral judgments[33]). All that matters is that we can understand their behavior "as if" they did.[34]

There are sometimes good reasons for seeking causal rather than reason-based explanations. People may not understand or appreciate why they act as they do. Marx and Freud looked for underlying causes of behavior precisely because they believed people had a false or incomplete self-consciousness. It makes no sense even to speak of reason-based explanations where the objects of study lack self-consciousness and intentionality, as is generally the case in the natural sciences. The power of a causal as opposed to a reason-based explanation may be its ability to predict. If, for example, we can predict that by instituting a certain enforcement level and high sanctions, crime would decrease along with government expenditures on law enforcement, this could be an important consideration for legislators, to be evaluated along with other considerations. The case for dismissing reasons for action when explaining human behavior is weaker, however, when those reasons have been articulated following deliberation and defended against objections; or when the reasons make reference to rules of practices that constitute the meaning of actions within practices.

One reason to be skeptical of "as if" explanations of human behavior is that they may be wrong. A paradigmatic causal explanation in law and economics

---

[30] Marvin Harris, 1989, *Cows, Pigs, Wars, and Witches*, New York: Vintage, pp. 35–45.

[31] Posner, *Economic Analysis of Law*, p. 23 ("the true grounds of legal decisions are concealed rather than illuminated by the characteristic rhetoric of opinions").

[32] Cass Sunstein, 2005, "On the Psychology of Punishment," in Parisi and Smith, *The Law and Economics of Irrational Behavior*, pp. 342, 353.

[33] Michael Koenigs, Liane Young, et al., 2007, "Damage to the Prefrontal Cortex Increases Utilitarian Moral Judgments," *Nature*, 446, pp. 908–911 (patients with ventromedial prefrontal cortex lesions are more likely to endorse utilitarian solutions to a moral dilemma and less likely than normal subjects to exhibit emotional responsivity such as shame, guilt, and compassion).

[34] Milton Friedman, 1953, "The Methodology of Positive Economics," in *Essays in Positive Economics*, Chicago: University of Chicago Press, pp. 3–43; Posner, *Economic Analysis of Law*, p. 4; Becker, "Crime and Punishment"; and Easterbrook, "Criminal Procedure," pp. 330–331.

is deterrence theory, which explains features of the criminal law by understanding punishment as a price for offenses, and predicts outcomes by assuming that effective deterrence is achieved by setting the expected utility of crime to be negative.[35] Empirical evidence indicates there are sentencing disparities for vehicular homicide based on the gender and race of the victim that deterrence theory cannot explain and would not predict.[36] Some criminologists argue that contrary to what deterrence theory predicts, sanctions sometimes lead to an increase in crime when offenders experience sanctions as illegitimate or unfair, are marginalized, and become defiant.[37] And some have argued that some people are not deterred, because they either conform to social norms and therefore obey law without threats of a sanction, or have a self-perceived invincibility that makes them undeterrable.[38]

Law-and-economics proponents can make *internal* criticisms of the standard model of deterrence to account for anomalies that result when punishment is treated as a price, while still working within an economics framework. For example, Cooter acknowledges that when we treat punishment as a price, we tax rather than forbid crime, and at times we want to forbid by using a sanction. But rather than appeal to a nonutilitarian explanation of the use of sanctions as opposed to prices, such as that certain behaviors such as rape and murder deserve condemnation and are not to be regarded as permissible so long as one pays the price, Cooter invokes efficiency criteria to account for when we use prices as opposed to sanctions: we choose sanctions only where, if crimes were priced, error in price-setting would yield disutilities and the information costs we would have to pay to effectively price crimes are prohibitive. Where legislators observe community standards or social norms of behavior but not costs and benefits of the behavior, it is efficient to use sanctions.[39]

What at first glance look like noneconomic determinants of behavior, such as adherence to social norms and moral ideals, are also accounted for within the law-and-economics framework by internal critics of the standard economic model, sometimes by incorporating preferences for moral condemnation into a utility

---

[35] In addition to the works cited in note 1, see Richard Posner, 1985, "An Economic Theory of the Criminal Law," *Columbia Law Review*, 85, p. 1193; Shavell, "Criminal Law"; Easterbrook, "Criminal Procedure," p. 292; and Kaplow and Shavell, *Fairness versus Welfare*, pp. 317–318.

[36] Glaeser and Sacerdote, "Sentencing in Homicide Cases" (arguing that vehicular homicides with female victims yield 59 percent longer sentences, and with black victims 60 percent shorter sentences, and because the act is random and not deterrable, only a "taste for vengeance" explains the disparities).

[37] Lawrence Sherman, 1993, "Defiance, Deterrence, and Irrelevance: A Theory of the Criminal Sanction," *Journal of Research in Crime and Delinquency*, 30, pp. 445–473.

[38] E. Posner, *Law and Social Norms*, pp. 3–5 (on nonlegal mechanisms of cooperation); David Anderson, 2002, "The Deterrence Hypothesis and Picking Pockets at the Pickpocket's Hanging," *American Law and Economics Review*, 4, pp. 295–313 (interviews inmates and finds many are not deterred by sanctions); Greg Pogarsky, 2002, "Identifying 'Deterrable' Offenders," *Justice Quarterly*, 19, pp. 431–442 (distinguishing two classes of nondeterrables, "incorrigibles," and "acute conformists," based on a sample of 412 survey respondents); but see Bradley Wright et al., 2004, "Does the Perceived Risk of Punishment Deter Criminally Prone Individuals?," *Journal of Research in Crime and Delinquency*, 41, pp. 188, 206 (criticizing Pogarsky's circular method of identifying "acute conformists").

[39] Robert Cooter, 1984, "Prices and Sanctions," *Columbia Law Review*, 84, pp. 1532–1533.

function.[40] Dau-Schmidt relaxes a common assumption made by economists that preferences are exogenous, or taken as given, in order to account for the "moral dimension" of punishment. He argues that fundamental characteristics of the criminal law are best explained by regarding punishment not merely as a tax or price, but as a means of discouraging deviant preferences. Dau-Schmidt takes into account the moral point of view but from within a thoroughly economic framework: we rely on moral norms to shape preferences because the costs of policing externalities in an amoral society would be prohibitive.[41] Eric Posner also attempts to integrate social norms into an economic theory of the law. Rather than give independent weight to nonefficiency goals such as justice or fairness, which might otherwise seem to explain features of the law, he regards these values or norms as means by which individuals signal that they are desirable partners in cooperative endeavors and therefore as mechanisms to promote social utility.[42] He explains the decrease in shaming punishments such as branding and pillories by theorizing that shaming punishments may encourage deviant subcommunities, and are messy and unpredictable (leading, e.g., to mob lynchings), so there is no reason to believe that they provide "the proper level of deterrence" that efficiency theorists expect to observe.[43]

Although these internal criticisms of the standard economic model of law recognize that practices, norms, and moral values influence human behavior, economic explanations of the law remain problematic. Law-and-economics proponents, even those who modify the theory to account for social norms and apparently nonrational or altruistic behavior, often claim to explain why the law arose, when what they really seem to be doing is imputing reasons or offering justifications for features of the law. But they leave unclear why we should favor their explanations or reasons over others that are available. Glaeser and Sacerdote claim to explain why there are more severe punishments for arson or gang killings than for murders that occur following a romantic argument, and Posner explains why hanging was imposed for horse thievery in the American West (we should expect higher sentences when the apprehension rate is low, according to the expected-utility model).[44] Shavell claims to explain why the law does not allow a defense

---

[40] Kahan, "Social Meaning," p. 619; Dau-Schmidt, "Criminal Law as Preference-Shaping Policy"; Robert Frank, 2005, "Departures from Rational Choice: With and without Regret," in Parisi and Smith, *The Law and Economics of Irrational Behavior*, pp. 20–25; E. Posner, *Law and Social Norms*, pp. 5–6, 39, 49–53. See also Richard Murphy, 1996, "Property Rights in Personal Information: An Economic Defense of Privacy," *Georgetown Law Journal*, 84, pp. 2381–2417 (considering the "psychic" value of privacy as a "pure privacy preference," that one could enter into a utility calculation to determine privacy law).

[41] Dau-Schmidt, "Criminal Law as Preference-Shaping Policy," pp. 22, 28–30, 37.

[42] E. Posner, *Law and Social Norms*, ch. 6. But see Ernst Fehr and Simon Gächter, "How Effective Are Trust and Reciprocity-Based Incentives?," in Avner Ben-Ner and Louis Putterman, eds., 1998, *Economics, Values, and Organization*, Cambridge: Cambridge University Press, pp. 337–363 (providing conflicting evidence that norms are followed even when interactions are anonymous and so there is no possibility of signaling); and Ernst Fehr and Simon Gächter, 2002, "Altruistic Punishment in Humans," *Nature*, 415, pp. 137–140.

[43] E. Posner, *Law and Social Norms*, p. 93.

[44] Glaeser and Sacerdote, "Sentencing in Homicide Cases," p. 368; Posner, *Economic Analysis of Law*, p. 230.

for a criminal whose victim later condones the criminal (this would dilute deterrence and create an incentive to coerce victims into condoning).[45] Shavell, Posner, and Easterbrook claim to explain why we allow an insanity defense or reduce punishment for the "feeble-minded" (punishment is unlikely to deter and be efficient).[46]

But there are plausible competing accounts of most of these features of the law. We punish intentional crimes such as arson or gang killings more severely than crimes of passion because the former crimes are more blameworthy and their perpetrators more culpable and deserving of punishment. This explains, too, why we allow an insanity defense: not because punishment would not deter the insane, but because the insane are not blameworthy.[47] Lastly, the reason condoning is not a defense is that the point of legal punishment is to uphold community standards of justice and not to avenge the victim, and so the victim's feelings toward the criminal are beside the point from a moral point of view. In the face of competing explanations, something needs to be said about why one explanation is superior.

Laws and social practices arise for a number of reasons. Among the reasons legal punishment arose are to deter, incapacitate, express condemnation, stigmatize, rehabilitate, and vindicate the law. All of these may be reasons for acting within the practice and can explain some of its features. Deterrence and expected-utility theory may provide the most convincing account of some features of the practice, such as why horse thieves were hanged in the American West (for surely they did not deserve such harsh punishment).[48] The actual cause of the practice may be a question historians can best answer. But when we are dealing with complex practices that express ideals and involve purposeful action, practices that may have arisen for a multiplicity of reasons, we should not expect that a single goal such as economic efficiency or utility maximization will best explain all features of the practice. One reason to prefer economic explanations of the law would be if they pointed to a model that led to an optimal set of policies, but this shifts the debate away from merely descriptive and explanatory theory to normative theory; and there are reasons to be skeptical of a normative economic approach to law that excludes considerations other than those of an act utilitarian.

III. LIMITATIONS OF LAW AND ECONOMICS AS A NORMATIVE THEORY

I shall take as an exemplar of a normative theory in law and economics that takes a totalizing point of view the theory presented in Kaplow and Shavell's book *Fairness versus Welfare*. They argue that rules of law designed to comply with the principles of welfare economics leave (virtually) everyone better off than they would be under any other rule, whereas rules of law designed to comply with principles of fairness or justice would leave some or all of us worse off. It is important to recognize two

[45] Shavell, "Criminal Law," p. 1258.
[46] Ibid., pp. 1254–1255; Posner, "Economic Theory of Criminal Law"; Easterbrook, "Criminal Procedure," p. 325; compare Dau-Schmidt, "Criminal Law as Preference-Shaping Policy," pp. 26–27 (intent reveals a preference to deviate from norms).
[47] Mark Tunick, 1992, *Punishment: Theory and Practice*, Berkeley: University of California Press.
[48] Of course one might argue that executing horse thieves was really not a feature of, but an aberration from, the practice of legal punishment.

distinct sorts of criticisms that can be made of Kaplow and Shavell's approach. An internal criticism challenges their conclusions from within a law-and-economics framework by arguing that they fail properly to weigh the utility of justice or fairness in their economic calculations; in contrast, an external criticism challenges their fundamental assumption that welfare or social utility is the only valid criterion for deciding upon legal policy.

A. Internal Criticism

I first shall consider an internal criticism, focusing on their discussion of punishment. Their argument for rejecting nonutilitarian considerations such as retribution or fairness as independent grounds for deciding how to punish depends on their claim that a fair sanction is inferior to the sanction dictated by welfare economics. To reach this conclusion they offer a simple sanctioning model: They suppose that a crime causes harm of -100 utiles, that there is a 25 percent probability of apprehending the criminal, and that on conviction, the cost of the sanction is x to the criminal plus $2x$ to the public (to cover the cost of imposing punishment). They assume the fair sanction is equal to the harm caused (or -100 utiles), and that there are 1,000 people who obtain a benefit of more than 25 utiles if they commit the crime and who will therefore do so when the fair sanction of -100 is threatened, because their benefit from committing the crime will exceed the expected disutility of punishment (which is 25 percent of 100, or 25). On these assumptions, using the fair sanction will result in 1,000 crimes, and 250 people will be caught and punished. Each punishment has a disutility of 100 to the criminal and 200 to the society.

Whereas the fair sanction matches the punishment to the harm caused by the crime, the efficient sanction recommended by welfare economics, they argue, matches the expected disutility of punishment to the harm caused. In our example, the efficient sanction is -400 (as $400 \times 25\% = 100$), four times greater than the fair sanction. They then compare the total social utility of using the fair sanction with the total social utility of using the sanction recommended by welfare economics. With the fair sanction of 100, we find that 1,000 crimes will occur, creating $-100,000$ utiles. There will also be $-75,000$ utiles from punishing 250 people ($-25,000$ experienced by the criminals plus $-50,000$ in social costs), yielding a total of $-175,000$ utiles. Using the unfair but efficient sanction of -400, they argue, there will be no crime, and thus a total cost of 0. On this basis they conclude that an efficient sanction is superior to a fair sanction, and that punishing on the basis of retribution or fairness leads to individual suffering: noncriminals are worse off in that they are more likely to be crime victims, and criminals who are caught are worse off in that they would have been deterred if we had used the efficient sanction. On their view, only criminals who are not caught are better off when the sanction is fair, because they get the benefits of the crime, whereas if the sanction were -400, they would not, because they would have been deterred. They conclude that "[t]he actual consequence of fair punishment is to make all individuals worse off except for the criminals who are not caught."[49]

[49] Kaplow and Shavell, *Fairness versus Welfare*, pp. 317–322.

An internal criticism of this argument does not take issue with the use of a utilitarian calculus to determine how we should punish, but challenges some of the assumptions Kaplow and Shavell make. Consider the following example that modifies some of these assumptions while keeping the model simple. Suppose a crime still causes -100 utiles (which includes the harm to the victim and the secondary harm to society at large), and the probability of apprehension and conviction of those committing the crime remains 25 percent. The sanction is not costless to impose: assume it still costs $2x$ to impose a sanction of $-x$ utiles, a cost shared by society at large, so that the cost of the sanction to an individual member of the public averages $2x/N$, where N is the population. Suppose that half the members of society have a strong moral sense and oppose unfair punishment. If a person is sentenced excessively, half the population experiences a sense of demoralization, anxiety, and profound disappointment in and mistrust of their government, and for each unit of excessive punishment imposed on anyone in their society, they experience a disutility of -0.001 utiles. The total disutility from excessive punishment imposed in this society for each case of such punishment is expressed by $(0.5N)(ES - FS)(0.001)$, where FS is the fair sanction, equivalent to the disutility caused by the act, and ES is the efficient sanction that yields an expected disutility equal to the disutility caused by the act, or FS divided by the probability of apprehension and conviction.[50] With a crime resulting in -100 utiles, we have FS $= -100$, ES $= -400$. Assume also that if society imposes FS, then $N/500$ people will commit the crime, and that if society imposes ES, then $N/5000$ people will commit the crime. Kaplow and Shavell assume that no one will commit a crime if the expected utility of doing so is negative, but I have relaxed this assumption because it seems unrealistic.[51] There will be no disutility associated with excessive punishment when a fair sanction is imposed. On this model, using the preceding assumptions, society will be better off in terms of total utility using FS rather than ES if the population is larger than 9,000.[52]

The internal criticism of a law-and-economics approach takes into account preferences for fairness; and by assuming that crimes still occur when the expected utility of committing the crime is negative, it modifies the assumption that actors

---

[50] The marginal disutility of excessive punishment probably diminishes with increasing number of criminals excessively punished, but I assume a linear relationship to keep the model simple. Of course this assumption becomes increasingly unrealistic as N, and thus the number of offenders, increases.

[51] Kaplow and Shavell are inconsistent. They rely on the assumption that people will be deterred if expected utility is negative to establish that ES is superior to FS; but later they say "most individuals are unaware" of legal rules and even if they are, will not be influenced by them, due to their filtration through lawyers and other intermediaries (*Fairness versus Welfare*, p. 416).

[52] When FS is imposed, there will be $N/500$ crimes, yielding a disutility of $(N/500)(100)$, or $0.2N$. Of the $N/500$, 25 percent will be convicted and punished, yielding a disutility of $(N/500)(0.25)(100)$ for those punished, and of twice that for society. The total disutility of imposing FS is $0.2N + 0.15N = 0.35N$. When ES is imposed, there will be $N/5000$ crimes, yielding a disutility of $(N/5000)(100)$, or $0.02N$. Of the $N/5000$, 25 percent will be convicted and punished, yielding a disutility of $(N/5000)(0.25)(400)$ for those punished, and of twice that for society, or $0.06N$. There will be disutility associated with excessive punishment of $(0.5N)(300)(0.001)(N/5000) = 0.00003N^2$, so the total disutility when ES is imposed is $0.08N + 0.00003N^2$. Society will be worse off in terms of total utility using ES when $0.00003N^2 + 0.08N > 0.35N$, that is, for $N > 9000$.

are perfectly rational. The criticism is internal in that it works within the law-and-economics framework, according to which notions of fairness or corrective justice "receive no independent weight in the assessment of legal rules," and policy is made with the "exclusive use of welfare economics" – only individuals' well-being is factored into a policy decision.[53] External critics argue, in contrast, that the law-and-economics point of view does not adequately account for important considerations such as justice or fairness.[54] That concern is not necessarily met merely by including justice or fairness as preferences that receive weight in a utility calculation.[55] External critics challenge the assumption that social utility or individuals' well-being is the only valid criterion for deciding how one ought to act or what public policy ought to be.

B. External Criticism

The list of critics of Bentham's single-minded utilitarianism is legend, their criticism vituperative: Utilitarianism's most influential theorist is a "frightfully radical ass" (Goethe), a "worm... responsible for [civilization's] decay" (Keynes), his philosophy "stinking" (Emerson), "shallow" (Schumpeter), and "insipid" (Marx).[56] More recently, Martha Nussbaum criticizes the utilitarians' and economists' use of aggregate data, which fails to attend to the "diverse concreteness" of people – a criticism Dickens made with devastating effect in *Hard Times* in contrasting Gradgrind and Bounderby, utilitarians concerned only with facts, numbers, and self-interest, with the far more humane Sissy Jupe. For Nussbaum, the economic mind is blind "to the fact that human life is something mysterious and not altogether fathomable."[57]

Appeal to the mysterious and unfathomable is precisely the irrational move Kaplow, Shavell, and other law-and-economics proponents want to avoid and replace with clear-thinking and rational argument. But critics of utilitarianism

[53] Kaplow and Shavell, *Fairness versus Welfare*, pp. 4–5, 26.
[54] For example, Jules Coleman, 1985, "Crime, Kickers, and Transaction Structures," in J. Roland Pennock and John W. Chapman, eds., *NOMOS 27: Criminal Justice*, New York: NYU Press, pp. 323–4 (law and economics leaves out moral notions of guilt and fault and is "impoverished" because it analyzes behavior exclusively as exchange relations); Mark D. White, 2006, "A Kantian Critique of Neoclassical Law and Economics," *Review of Political Economy*, 18, p. 246 (law and economics ignores the "moral nature of punishment"); Stephen Schulhofer, 1985, "Is There an Economic Theory of Crime?," in Pennock and Chapman, *Criminal Justice*, p. 336 (in viewing punishment as simply a price, the law-and-economics approach leaves out the notion of fault); Debra Satz, 1995, "Markets in Women's Sexual Labor," *Ethics*, 106, pp. 69–70.
[55] Mark D. White is critical of Kaplow and Shavell for failing to take seriously the taste for fairness, and suggests that if that taste were made strong enough, their conclusions could be reversed (2004, "Preaching to the Choir: A Response to Kaplow and Shavell's *Fairness versus Welfare*," *Review of Political Economy*, 16, p. 512). But he also suggests an external criticism in asking us to challenge the assumption about the moral primacy of well-being (p. 514).
[56] Cited by Hanna Pitkin, 1990, "Slippery Bentham," *Political Theory*, 18, p. 104.
[57] Martha Nussbaum, 2001, "The Literary Imagination in Public Life," in Fred Kaplan and Sylvere Monod, eds., *Hard Times*, 3rd ed., New York: W.W. Norton, p. 433; compare Schulhofer, "Is There an Economic Theory of Crime?," p. 340 (Posner and Becker provide a limited perspective on the problem "what is man?").

have legitimate concerns when challenging the assumption that, in deciding what to do, we should appeal solely to welfare or preference satisfaction. One concern some of these critics raise is that we often regret our preferences; these critics ask, what is so valuable about seeing to it that individuals get the things they want?[58] Some values, the utilitarian critic might say, are "priceless," although it is better to say not that they are priceless, but that they are not readily measured and therefore are hard to take into account in a utilitarian calculation. Integrity (being able to live with oneself), having a sense of worth, living a meaningful life – none of which are reducible to preference satisfaction or individual well-being unless those concepts are so expanded as to make them vacuous – are not so mysterious as to be incoherent or unintelligible.[59] Because they cannot be measured as required by welfare economics, it is not surprising they are not taken seriously within a law-and-economics framework. But – and this is the key idea underlying the external criticism of normative law and economics I wish to present – we misconstrue the justification process if we think that the only way to recognize the force of a consideration is by giving it an economic measure of worth that is weighed in a calculation of net utility. The complex problems arising from the human condition of sharing a world with people holding conflicting values are not necessarily best resolved by forcing solutions merely because they can be arrived at using the tools available to the economist.

The following examples may suffice to show that there are reasons for rejecting policy prescriptions of law-and-economics proponents, or of act utilitarians – reasons that are not mysterious, unfathomable, or unintelligible, having been articulated following deliberation and defended against objections.

Disproportionate punishment. In a law-and-economics approach, disproportionately harsh punishment is prescribed because it is efficient in allowing reduced enforcement levels. By singling out the unlucky or especially inept criminal, society can purchase general deterrence cheaply. External critics of the law-and-economics approach object that this is unfair and, invoking Kant, that it treats the criminal merely as a means for furthering social goals, thereby failing to respect him also as an end in himself.[60] Kaplow and Shavell find this objection "incorrect" or at least "very misleading" because the convicts are not being used "merely" as a means, and by deterring others, innocent victims of crime have their humanity respected.[61] But to the external critic, in using aggregate data about overall deterrence, the utilitarian loses sight of the concrete individuals who are confined to prison for the rest of their lives in order to help promote a policy of general deterrence; and to

---

[58] Jules Coleman, 2003, "The Grounds of Welfare," *Yale Law Journal*, 112, pp. 1540–1541. Cf. Mark Sagoff, 1986, "Values and Preferences," *Ethics*, 96, p. 303: "Why is it good *in itself* that a person who wants a Mercedes succeeds in getting one?"

[59] On the danger of expanding or contracting the conception of "utility" so as to make utilitarian theory virtually useless, see Pitkin, "Slippery Bentham."

[60] Immanuel Kant, 1785/1964, *Groundwork of the Metaphysic of Morals*, trans. H. J. Paton, New York: Harper and Row, p. 95 (428 in Royal Prussian Academy edition) ("Now I say that man . . . exists as an end in himself, not merely as a means for arbitrary use by this or that will: he must in all his actions . . . always be viewed at the same time as an end"); cf. White, "Kantian Critique."

[61] Kaplow and Shavell, *Fairness versus Welfare*, pp. 333–335.

some external critics, the certain harm or disutility to the identifiable convict who is singled out for excessive punishment is a greater concern than the probabilistic harm or disutility to the unidentified victims of those who would not be deterred without a policy of excessive punishment. The tendency of law-and-economics proponents not to take seriously the rights of individuals because doing so would be nonoptimal from a utilitarian perspective is evident in a recent article that recommends severe penalties for juveniles, including death, as well as an enforcement policy that allows states to violate their rights and pay compensation later if a mistake is made, in the name of effective deterrence.[62] It is also evident in Easterbrook's defense of judicial discretion in sentencing; such discretion as a rule facilitates efficient pricing of crime. Although individual judges may be erratic and "out of line" with the going price, in general the market provides checks on "errant judges."[63] The argument asks us to compare paying the wrong price in a market with making individuals spend perhaps an extra year or more of their lives in prison, and these seem incomparable.

Privacy. A black man is photographed in a public place without his knowledge, and the picture appears on the cover of a national newsmagazine to illustrate a feature story about the black middle class, a story the man finds objectionable. He is embarrassed: perhaps he does not like his appearance, or does not want friends associating him with the article's message, or he simply likes to be anonymous. Should the law afford him a remedy?[64] One law-and-economics solution is that in such nonnewsworthy situations, individuals should control the right to publish their image as this will yield greater social utility – otherwise, anybody could threaten to publish a photograph of an individual, who might then have to negotiate with numerous parties to avoid publication.[65] The individual's disutility is great, whereas the publisher could easily and cheaply have gotten a different but equally suitable photo. If the image is newsworthy, however, the utility calculation ends up favoring the public.[66] *Ex ante*, the man's expected disutility may be unknowable: if he only cares about the photo once he sees it published, but could not be sure prior to its publication that a photographer would succeed in having it published in a prominent place, or if his disutility depended on factors beyond his control, such as the response of the public, friends, former acquaintances, or fellow workers, how could he determine *ex ante* the value of suppression he would be willing to pay prospective publishers? Still, we can surmise that the cost to the publisher of

[62] Moin Yahya, 2006, "Deterring Roper's Juveniles: Using a Law and Economics Approach to Show that the Logic of Roper Implies that Juveniles Require the Death Penalty More than Adults," *Penn State Law Review*, 111, pp. 53–106 (arguing that if juveniles have an inelastic demand for crime, being impulsive and less mature, the price of crime should be raised for them for the sake of efficiency).

[63] Easterbrook, "Criminal Procedure," p. 329.

[64] See *Arrington v. New York Times*, 449 N.Y.S. 2d 941 (1982) (ruling that the photographer and agent but not the publisher may have violated plaintiff's rights; the law was later amended to protect photographers and agents).

[65] Robert Cooter, 1999, *Strategic Constitution*, Princeton, NJ: Princeton University Press, p. 287; compare Joseph Siprut, 2006, "Privacy through Anonymity: An Economic Argument for Expanding the Right of Privacy in Public Places," *Pepperdine Law Review*, 33, pp. 324–325 (giving the public domain the right is "highly inefficient," putting the image in a lower-valued use).

[66] Siprut, "Privacy through Anonymity," p. 325.

granting the right of publication to the individual is not substantial, involving only the pursuit of someone willing to sign a consent form. But rather than think the issue is settled by a utility calculation, we might think that individuals, who may be unable to pay if the right to publish lay with the publisher, should not have to bargain for their privacy.[67] That this argument loses much of its force when the subject of the photograph is newsworthy does not mean that the value of privacy is reducible to utiles.

The exclusionary rule. The exclusionary rule prohibits the use of evidence against a defendant if the evidence was obtained in violation of the defendant's constitutional rights. Courts, consistent with a law-and-economics approach, have restricted the rule on the ground that it is thought to be justified solely as a deterrent to illegal searches, and in situations where the police would not be deterred, as when they act in good faith, the exclusionary rule should be waived.[68] But deterrence is not the only rationale for the exclusionary rule, which was originally defended by appealing to the value of judicial integrity.[69] Due process, and not just crime control, is an essential goal of the criminal law.[70]

Population policy. Richard Posner defends a policy in overpopulated societies that permits only one child per couple but that allows families who are more efficient in producing children to exceed the one-child limit by purchasing permits from less efficient families. It might cost family *A* less to produce a second child than it would cost family *B* to produce a first child "of the same quality," and so allowing *A* to buy *B*'s permit would be efficient.[71] The external critic objects to using a measurement for the quality of a child to support this policy prescription.[72]

Gun control policy. John Lott argues that regressions on crime data show that where people are allowed to have guns, there are fewer violent crimes.[73] From a utilitarian perspective this would seem to dictate that we ease gun restrictions. Let us leave aside the internal criticism that Lott can run his regressions only on the data he has available, and that had we better information, another regression might show his conclusion is wrong. To the external critic, Lott's argument is not decisive, because there are fathomable but nonquantifiable reasons to object to a community in which people carry concealed weapons.

The death penalty. Utilitarians prescribe the death penalty if its use would increase social utility. To retributivists, the appropriateness of the death penalty

---

[67] For nonutilitarian defenses of privacy see, for example, Charles Fried, 1968, "Privacy," *Yale Law Journal*, 77, pp. 475–493; Edward Bloustein, 1964, "Privacy as an Aspect of Human Dignity," *New York University Law Review*, 39, pp. 962–1007.

[68] *U.S. v. Leon*, 468 U.S. 897 (1984); Posner, *Economic Analysis of Law*, pp. 683–684 (although the exclusionary rule is needed to deter illegal searches, we should not apply it so as to overdeter, and a tort remedy is economically preferable).

[69] *Mapp v. Ohio*, 367 U.S. 643 (1961), 659.

[70] Herbert Packer, 1964, "Two Models of the Criminal Process," *University of Pennsylvania Law Review*, 113, pp. 1–68.

[71] Posner, *Economic Analysis of Law*, p. 156.

[72] See Margaret Jane Radin, 2001, *Contested Commodities*, Cambridge, MA: Harvard University Press.

[73] John Lott, 2000, *More Guns, Less Crime*, Chicago: University of Chicago Press.

depends on whether the criminal deserves it, and if society sometimes needs to invoke it to express blame, whether it did so would not depend on the empirical evidence about the marginal deterrent effect of the death penalty.[74]

In each of these examples, there are nonutilitarian reasons for a policy that do not seem mysterious, unfathomable, or unintelligible. The reasons may not convince the economist, but my purpose is to show not that they are decisive reasons, only that they are worth consideration.

Practices or institutions such as punishment, promising, marriage, private property, or voting arose in the pursuit of various ideals. These ideals became institutionalized, and this forces us to consider the costs of these institutions in deciding how much of society's limited resources should be devoted to their smooth functioning. But we should not lose sight of the ideals the practices either originally promoted, or have come to promote as practices evolve. Some practices, such as punishment, seek to promote multiple and even conflicting values.[75] Some values arise from no single practice in particular, such as the value of privacy, or of living in a community based on trust and not fear.

Human behavior is complex, and we should strictly scrutinize theories that try to make sense of it by appealing to a single principle. Bentham, Kaplow, Shavell, and Posner may be motivated to take a totalizing approach by a hope of "escaping the risks and disorders of human relationships, by reconceiving those relationships in the language now used for physical objects and mechanical movement."[76] But that approach is unlikely to be persuasive, because it takes as essential one consideration, the economics of our laws, practices, and institutions, and ignores other ideals that may account for why we have them in the first place, or that may be essential to our finding them acceptable.[77]

I am not arguing that we should be concerned only with justice and that we should not consider the consequences of our decisions. For example, if our court system would collapse if all defendants sought trials, and the only way to avoid this were to practice plea bargaining, then most of us will be persuaded that we need the practice even though plea bargaining raises questions from the point of view of justice (in cases where guilty defendants who cop pleas are punished for a lesser offense having no relation to their actual offense, and innocent defendants are punished for something they did not do). One need not reject consequentialist thinking merely because one is motivated by a concern for justice.[78]

---

[74] See, for example, Louis Pojman's discussion in Louis P. Pojman and Jeffrey Reiman, 1998, *The Death Penalty: For and Against*, Lanham, MD: Rowman and Littlefield; Walter Berns, 1979, *For Capital Punishment*, New York: Basic Books.

[75] Tunick, *Punishment*, pp. 177–179.

[76] Pitkin, "Slippery Bentham," p. 127.

[77] See Pitkin, *Wittgenstein and Justice*, pp. 186–188 (arguing that the contested character of justice derives from tensions resulting when ideas and purposes are institutionalized).

[78] Tunick, *Punishment*, pp. 143–145 (discussing plea bargaining); Mark Tunick, 1992, *Hegel's Political Philosophy*, Princeton, NJ: Princeton University Press, pp. 34–35, 135–138 (Hegel appeals to retribution as well as to consequences in his theory of punishment); Satz, "Markets" (opposes prostitution because it promotes unjust gender relations, but opposes criminalizing prostitution because doing so would not be beneficial).

IV. THE DEMAND FOR A FURTHER GROUND: CONNECTING
DESCRIPTIVE AND NORMATIVE THEORIES

Law-and-economics proponents who take a totalizing point of view that excludes moral points of view that are not act-utilitarian regard nonconsequentialist moral thinking as irrational or unintelligible. Any argument that appeals to justice or fairness, such as the argument that we should not punish the insane or impose disproportionate punishment such as $10,000 parking fines because doing so is unjust, to them begs the question "why be just or fair?"; and they deny that any further ground can be given for justice or fairness apart from the desire for those values. This demand for a further ground, which on their view is only provided by the principle of utility or a similar principle, is not a demand utilitarians themselves are able to satisfy when the demand is to explain why the principle of utility should be our criterion for acting. Kaplow and Shavell define welfare economics as the optimal approach to public policy, so that by definition any other approach is suboptimal. But they provide no reason for thinking welfare economics is the optimal approach, which is why critics characterize their argument as a tautology.[79] Even Bentham was unable to provide a further ground for the principle of utility.

Although Bentham did not think one can justify the principle of utility by pointing to any other ground, he did attempt to show that the principle of utility in fact guides us.[80] He offered an interpretation of existing practices that claims to show that their features, on the whole, can be explained as promoting social utility, and he criticized features of existing practice that failed to do this. In this way explanative and normative theory are connected. We are more likely to be persuaded by normative prescriptions that are based on principles that make sense of what we do, as they will cohere with judgments we already hold. A problem with the accounts of law given by Bentham and law-and-economics proponents is that their interpretations of existing practice are limited. In focusing only on some of the objectives of our practices and institutions, they leave aside others, and so their explanations and normative prescriptions do not fit with many of our settled understandings and convictions.[81]

Some may object to the view that descriptive or explanative theory of our practices can be the basis for a normative theory. In deciding what we ought to do, why should we be constrained by conventional understandings of existing practices?[82] I have pointed to two reasons. In some contexts, a justification is sought of an action within a practice, and only reference to the rules or purposes of the practice may satisfy the concern about the action. Of course, in other

---

[79] White, "Preaching to the Choir"; Coleman, "Grounds of Welfare," p. 1514; David Dolinko, 2002, "Review Essay: The Perils of Welfare Economics," *Northwestern University Law Review*, 97, p. 363.

[80] Bentham, *Principles*, ch. 14, § 28.

[81] See James Whitman, 2003, "A Plea against Retributivism," *Buffalo Criminal Law Review*, 7, pp. 104–105 ("we all know the distorted and eccentric picture of the legal world that results" from the simplified view of human behavior postulated by law-and-economics scholars).

[82] Kaplow and Shavell, *Fairness versus Welfare*, p. 296, n. 9 (ignoring "merely descriptive" theories claiming to articulate the meaning of legal practices such as punishment as not pertinent to those seeking a normative theory).

contexts, such as legislative debates about what the law should be, we need not be bound by existing law or the authority of tradition. But even in that context it is helpful to understand and acknowledge the nonutilitarian ideals our law and practices promote, not merely because individuals have sentimental attachment to these ideals – attachments that the economist might try to weigh in a utilitarian calculation – but because they are important in ways that cannot be measured in utiles. Among these ways, they may be part of a system of what most of us believe, a system in which some things are unshakable and some are more or less liable to shift, and what stands fast does so because "it is held fast by what lies around it."[83]

[83] Ludwig Wittgenstein, 1950–1951/1969, *On Certainty*, New York: Harper and Row, § 144; cf. §§ 96–99.

6 Numeraire Illusion: The Final Demise of the Kaldor–Hicks Principle

DAVID ELLERMAN

INTRODUCTION: PARETO VERSUS MARSHALL–PIGOU–KALDOR–HICKS

The Paretian revolution in normative economics established the possibility of defining efficiency (i.e., Pareto optimality, wherein no one can be made better off without making someone else worse off) without using interpersonal comparisons of utility or preferences. This treatment of efficiency is often seen as a weak form of a utilitarian or welfarist theory, that is, as a necessary condition for a maximum of "social welfare." But the notion of Pareto efficiency can also be seen as part of a rights-based approach[1] to normative economics that takes seriously the differences between persons and that accordingly eschews any given[2] social scalar ("social welfare") that morally ought to be maximized. Without any such scalar quantity to be maximized, the Paretian conditions are the necessary conditions for a vector maximization of the individual welfares.

The older Marshall–Pigou tradition in the economics of welfare was based on a fundamental distinction between the size and the distribution of the "social pie," for example, Pigou's "production" versus "distribution" of the "national dividend."[3] This social pie was *not* to be identified with overall welfare (e.g., Pigou's "economic welfare"), because the quantity of overall welfare could be affected by both the size and the distribution of the pie (e.g., Pigou's "national dividend"). The pie that economists would be professionally concerned with maximizing is an intermediate aggregate expressed in the measure of money and variously known as the national dividend (or product), net social benefits (e.g., in cost–benefit analysis), or social wealth (e.g., in the law-and-economics literature). An increase in *efficiency* was identified with an increase in the size of that social-wealth pie,

---

[1] See David Ellerman, 1992, *Property and Contract in Economics*, Cambridge, MA: Blackwell; David Ellerman, 2004, "The Market Mechanism of Appropriation," *Journal des Economistes et des Etudes Humaines*, 14, pp. 35–53.

[2] Persons can always come together, negotiate, and agree on certain common goals measured by a scalar quantity (e.g., profit in an economic enterprise), but those constructed goals are not ethically "given" independent of the common agreement.

[3] Arthur C. Pigou, 1960, *The Economics of Welfare*, 4th ed., London: Macmillan.

whereas the distribution of the pie was a question of *equity* outside the scientific bailiwick of economics.

Instead of taking the Paretian definition of efficiency in terms of vector maximization as an opportunity to explore nonwelfarist approaches to normative economics (e.g., rights-based theory), the economics profession has largely bridled at the "impracticality" of the definition. The rehabilitation of the Marshall–Pigou approach was inaugurated by the introduction of the Kaldor–Hicks (KH) principle[4] for a *potential* Pareto improvement (the winners in a proposed change could compensate the losers but do not necessarily do so) and by the modern treatment[5] of consumers' surplus. Kaldor was quite explicit about laying the groundwork to justify the older Marshall–Pigou way of thinking:

> This argument lends justification to the procedure, adopted by Professor Pigou in *The Economics of Welfare*, of dividing "welfare economics" into two parts: the first relating to production, and the second to distribution.[6]

The Marshall–Pigou tradition was thus modernized by Kaldor and Hicks, and the seemingly austere Paretian notion of efficiency[7] was broadened in the "Kaldor–Hicks (wealth maximization...) concept of efficiency."[8] Today any change that increases the "social wealth" according to the KH criterion is routinely interpreted as an "increase in efficiency," particularly in the law-and-economics literature, cost–benefit analysis, policy analysis,[9] and other parts of applied welfare economics.[10] In general, one could say that the closer economics is to being applied,

---

[4] See Nicholas Kaldor, 1939, "Welfare Propositions of Economics and Interpersonal Comparisons of Utility," *Economic Journal*, 49, pp. 549–552, and John R. Hicks, 1939, "The Foundations of Welfare Economics," *Economic Journal*, 49, pp. 696–712, for the original articles; and E. J. Mishan, 1964, *Welfare Economics: Five Introductory Essays*, New York: Random House, and John S. Chipman and John C. Moore, 1978, "The New Welfare Economics 1939–1974," *International Economic Review*, 19, pp. 547–584, for surveys of the KH criterion and later innovations. See Matthew D. Adler and Eric A. Posner, eds., 2001, *Cost–Benefit Analysis: Legal, Economic, and Philosophical Perspectives*, Chicago: University of Chicago Press, for a recent collection of viewpoints on cost–benefit analysis.

[5] The notion of consumers' surplus (Alfred Marshall, 1961, *Principles of Economics*, 9th ed., London: Macmillan) and the related notion of sellers' surplus are important tools in the Marshall–Pigou tradition, so Hicks's 1941 rehabilitation of consumer's surplus using utility-compensated demand curves ("The Rehabilitation of Consumers' Surplus," *Review of Economic Studies*, 8, pp. 108–116), and Robert D. Willig's 1976 justification of using Marshallian (uncompensated) demand curves as an approximation ("Consumer's Surplus without Apology," *American Economic Review*, 66, pp. 589–597), were important in reviving the thought patterns of that tradition.

[6] Kaldor, "Welfare Propositions," p. 551.

[7] Some authors assert that the KH principle will lead in the long run to a Pareto improvement. Aside from empirical problems, such a "defense" of the KH criterion is intellectually incoherent in that it attempts to reduce the KH condition to the Pareto or unanimity condition as if to admit that it was not an alternative after all. This chapter assumes that the KH condition is taken as a genuine alternative to the Pareto condition – as the foundation for economists to support some changes that will benefit some and hurt others on *efficiency* grounds.

[8] Richard Posner, 2001, "Cost–Benefit Analysis: Definition, Justification, and Comment on Conference Papers," in Adler and Posner, *Cost–Benefit Analysis*, p. 317.

[9] Edith Stokey and Richard J. Zeckhauser, 1978, *A Primer for Policy Analysis*, New York: W.W. Norton.

[10] See Richard E. Just, Darrel L. Hueth, and Andrew Schmitz, 1982, *Applied Welfare Economics and Public Policy*, Englewood Cliffs, NJ: Prentice-Hall.

the closer it comes to using the Marshall–Pigou approach with the modern KH refinements.

We will, however, show how the Marshall–Pigou–Kaldor–Hicks (MPKH) reasoning – based on the construction of a "pie" with the efficiency–equity parsing of changes in the pie's size and distribution – is fatally flawed.

I. NUMERAIRE ILLUSION AND SIMILAR SAME-YARDSTICK FALLACIES

Before considering the numeraire-illusion fallacy that vitiates the KH principle, it should be useful to consider a range of similar but simpler fallacies. The general fallacy involved here is the illusion that a statement is a substantive assertion when in fact it is only a tautological consequence of an arbitrary choice of numeraire, origin, or yardstick.

A "Proof" that Yardsticks Cannot Change

Suppose a yardstick is used to measure off a yard on a table. But is it really a yard? Perhaps the yardstick has expanded or contracted? Suppose that to check it, the distance is remeasured using the *same* yardstick, and sure enough (aside from negligible measurement error), the distance is indeed a yard. But this in fact gives no new information and simply reasserts the fact that the distance was originally measured by that same yardstick. Changes in a yardstick cannot be discovered by measurements using the same yardstick, and any conclusion of "no changes" based on such measurements would be illusory.

A "Proof" that Inflation Is Impossible

How much would a dollar buy in 1900? It would buy a dollar's worth of goods. How much would a dollar buy in 2000? It would again buy a dollar's worth of goods. Because a dollar buys the same "amount" of goods in 1900 and 2000, there has been no inflation between those two times. Because those two times were arbitrary, inflation is impossible.

What is wrong with this "proof"? Clearly the problem lies in using the same dollar measurement for what a dollar will buy at the two times. The seemingly substantive conclusion – "A dollar buys the same amount of goods at the two times" – is only a tautological restatement of the fact that the "amount of goods" is measured by what a dollar will buy.

A "Proof" that the Earth Does Not Move

Let $E(t)$ and $S(t)$ be respectively the coordinates of (the center of mass of) the earth and sun at time t when measured in geocentric coordinates. Then we check to see how the earth and sun move over the course of time. The investigation finds that indeed the sun's coordinates do change with the passage of time (in revolution around the earth) but that the earth's coordinates are constant. Therefore we can conclude that the earth does not move, because the sun does indeed move in rotation around the earth. The Church is vindicated and Galileo refuted.

What is wrong with this "proof"? Clearly the illusion lies in the attempt to draw seemingly substantive conclusions about the movement of the earth from the mere choice of geocentric coordinates. Instead of being an empirical statement, "the earth does not move" is only a tautological consequence of choice of geocentric coordinates.

A "Proof" that the Marginal Utility of Income Is Constant

The marginal utility of income is the marginal rate of change of utility with respect to a change in the consumer's income. Let $U(Q)$ be the utility level that results from a consumer maximizing utility at given prices and income. Because any monotonic transformation of a utility function is equally acceptable as a utility function, we consider the money-metric utility function $E(P,U(Q))$, which is the minimum expenditure necessary to reach the level of utility $U(Q)$ at the given prices and income. Then we consider the marginal change in the money-metric utility $E(P,U(Q))$ with respect to a change in income. We find that the minimum expenditure necessary to reach the level of utility $U(Q)$ reached with, say, a dollar increase in income is exactly a dollar, so we conclude that the marginal utility of income is in fact constant (with value unity).

What is wrong with this "proof" that the marginal utility of income is constant? Instead of being an empirical statement about the marginal utility of income, it is only a mathematical consequence of the use of the money-metric utility function to measure the marginal utility of income:

> [T]he money-metric marginal utility *of income* is constant at unity. For how could it be otherwise? If you are measuring utility by money, it must remain constant with respect to money: a yardstick cannot change in terms of itself.[11]

Indeed, "a yardstick cannot change in terms of itself" is a good statement of the general same-yardstick fallacy.

A "Proof" that an Apple Has the Same Value to Any Consumer

If John had an apple, what would be its value to John? In terms of apples as numeraire, it would be worth one apple to John. If Mary had an apple, it would also be worth one apple to Mary. Hence an apple has the same value to John or Mary or to any consumer, so a transfer of apples between two people can never increase or decrease value. The argument can be restated in terms of any commodity (changing the numeraire accordingly), so any commodity has the same value to any consumer. Hence all transfers of commodity cannot increase value and are thus of no value.

---

[11] Paul A. Samuelson, 1979, "Complementarity: An Essay on the 40th Anniversary of the Hicks–Allen Revolution in Demand Theory," *Journal of Economic Literature*, 12, p. 1264.

What is wrong with this "proof"? Clearly the problem lies in measuring the value of an apple to a person and also using apples as the numeraire. The statement that the apple has the same value to John and to Mary is only a tautologous consequence of the choice of apples as the numeraire. The "same value" statement was only a numeraire illusion.

A "Proof" that Commodity Transfers Do Not Change Social Wealth

Although the preceding apple argument may seem obvious, the main point of this chapter is that the basic KH reasoning that *money* compensation payments (to turn a potential Pareto improvement into an actual Pareto improvement) do not change total social wealth *as measured in money* is only the same sort of tautologous restatement of the consequences of the choice of numeraire. If the total value, or pie, is measured in terms of the numeraire X (apples or money or any other commodity), then any transfers in X will only seem to be a redistribution of the same total pie and never as an increase or decrease in the size of the pie. Hence the parsing of the total Pareto improvement into the efficiency part that changes the size of the pie and the equity part that only redistributes some of the X without changing the X-measured size of the pie is only a consequence of the choice of the X numeraire. Change the numeraire to Y, and the same transfers of X will then (in general) change the size of the Y-measured pie, so the parsing is not numeraire-invariant.

Restrict attention to a Pareto improvement that exchanges an apple for some money (or apples for nuts), and the parsing of the total exchange into the efficiency part and the equity part using one commodity as numeraire will reverse itself when the other commodity is used as numeraire. Hence the policy recommendation of the non-numeraire transfer on efficiency grounds (because the numeraire transfers in the potential exchange are only a question of equity) will reverse itself with reversed numeraires. Lacking any serious argument that the social pie as measured by dollars, gold, silver, BTUs, apples, or nuts is the "true" or "normatively significant" social pie, such policy recommendations based only on the use of one particular numeraire are groundless.[12]

II. NUMERAIRE ILLUSION AND OTHER CRITIQUES OF THE KALDOR–HICKS PRINCIPLE

The key step in going from Paretian reasoning to the MPKH reasoning was the parsing of the total Pareto improvement into efficiency and equity parts using the

---

[12] There sometimes seems to be a type of *money mysticism* in the MPKH tradition that attributes some unspoken normative significance to using that good as numeraire. Monetized net benefits, as opposed to net benefits revalued using a different numeraire, are treated as if they represented social welfare, a mistake that Pigou was careful to avoid. This money mysticism is absent in the Paretian exchange perspective, which views money as one of many goods, albeit a particularly useful one, that may or may not be involved in mutually beneficial transactions. See John R. Hicks, 1975, "The Scope and Status of Welfare Economics," *Oxford Economic Papers*, 27, pp. 307–26, for an interesting juxtaposition of the catallactics (exchange) approach in its Lausanne and Austrian versions with the "production and distribution of the national product" approach of the Marshall–Pigou tradition.

criterion that the equity compensations (paid in the numeraire) did not change the size of the social pie (measured using the same numeraire). But this in only what we have called the *numeraire illusion*: changes in the size of a yardstick cannot be revealed by using that same yardstick. The illusion is that attributes of a description based on one numeraire (usually money[13] or, abstractly, "purchasing power") are misinterpreted as if they were numeraire-invariant attributes of the underlying situation being described.

It may be useful to differentiate explicitly this numeraire-illusion critique of the MPKH tradition from some previous criticisms. For instance, Scitovsky[14] pointed out certain problems in the KH criterion (e.g., the project and compensation might have such strong income effects that the KH criterion then recommended a return to the original state). This criticism shows that in certain theoretical cases, income effects can lead to anomalies that complicate the use of the KH criterion. To the purist, these anomalies may be seen as "nails in the coffin" of the KH principle. But in applied economics, the anomalies in very special cases did as little to slow the use of the KH principle as the majority voting paradox did to slow the use of majority voting. In any case, the critique based on the numeraire illusion has nothing to do the Scitovsky-type anomalies, and the critique applies to *all* uses of the KH principle (i.e., to the underlying logic), not just to special cases.[15]

Within the MPKH tradition, there is also some controversy about the relative importance of efficiency-versus-equity questions – as if the efficiency–equity parsing were a numeraire-invariant matter. Some applied economists, such as A. C. Harberger,[16] have argued that equity questions should be firmly set to one side so that professional interest can be focused solely on what are considered efficiency questions; "a dollar's a dollar for all that." Other welfare economists, such as Boadway and Bruce[17] and Blackorby and Donaldson,[18] do not accept the sharp separation of efficiency and equity questions (e.g., due to general-equilibrium effects); such questions are more intertwined and should be considered more jointly by economists. The criticism developed here shows the lack of invariance in the whole construction of the "social pie" and the parsing – intertwined or not – into efficiency and equity questions. It is independent of the question of how general-equilibrium considerations might intertwine the so-called efficiency and equity parts of the total change.

It should also be noted that the critique based on the numeraire illusion has nothing to do with the old idea of a dollar having a different social welfare impact

---

[13] For our purposes the numeraire is only the commodity used as the units in which benefits and costs are stated. The results do not depend on the numeraire having any of the other usual characteristics of money (e.g., store of value or medium of exchange).

[14] Tibor Scitovsky, 1941, "A Note on Welfare Propositions in Economics," *Review of Economic Studies*, 9, pp. 77–88. Scitovsky's analysis generated a whole literature about such special cases, but it is not germane to our logical–methodological critique.

[15] Hence it is not just another nail in the coffin, but the last nail and final demise, of the KH principle.

[16] Arnold C. Harberger, 1971, "Three Basic Postulates for Applied Welfare Economics: An Interpretive Essay," *Journal of Economic Literature*, 9, pp. 785–97.

[17] Robin W. Boadway and Neil Bruce, 1984, *Welfare Economics*, Oxford: Basil Blackwell.

[18] Charles Blackorby and David Donaldson, 1990, "A Review Article: The Case against the Use of the Sum of Compensating Variations in Cost–Benefit Analysis," *Canadian Journal of Economics*, 23, pp. 471–94.

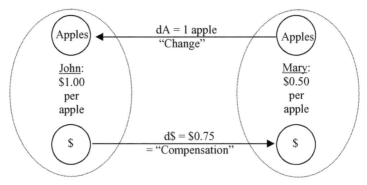

"Change" dA gives $0.50 = $1 − $0.50 = Δ$ increase in social $pie.
"Compensation" d$ gives $0 = $0.75 − $0.75 change in $pie.

Figure 6.1. The transfers described with $ as numeraire.

for the rich or poor, that is, the question of distributional weights in a supposed social welfare function. No notion of social welfare is used in this whole analysis and critique.

A. A Simple Generic Example

The MPKH reasoning is the basis for the maximization of "net social benefit" in cost–benefit analysis, as well as for the "social wealth" maximization at the foundation of the orthodox economic approach to law (the Chicago school of law and economics). For instance, consider the following pure example of numeraire illusion in cost–benefit analysis: "It should be emphasized that pure transfers of purchasing power from one household or firm to another per se should be typically attributed no value."[19]

In these contexts, it is not easy (though not impossible) to envisage a numeraire reversal, so the failure of numeraire invariance in hidden from normal view. But we are looking at the underlying economic logic of the MPKH tradition, and it can be applied to situations where numeraire inversions are trivial. Indeed, such examples are in law-and-economics textbooks themselves.

Consider the following simple but generic example from David Friedman's book *Law's Order*: Mary has an apple that she values at fifty cents, whereas John values an apple at one dollar. There might be a voluntary exchange where Mary sold the apple to John for, say, seventy-five cents. There are two changes in that Pareto improvement: the transfer of the apple from Mary to John, and the transfer of seventy-five cents from John to Mary (see Figure 6.1).

Let us apply social-wealth maximization reasoning to the transfer of the apple, using money as the numeraire. Because the apple was worth fifty cents to Mary and a dollar to John, social wealth would be increased by fifty cents by the apple

[19] Robin W. Boadway, 2000, *The Economic Evaluation of Projects*, Kingston, Canada: Queen's University, p. 30.

transfer from Mary to John. That is an increase in efficiency. The other change, the transfer of seventy-five cents from John to Mary, is a question of distribution or equity. Social wealth (measured in dollars and cents) would be unchanged by the mere transfer of seventy-five cents from one person to another:

> It would still be an improvement, and by the same amount, if John stole the apple – price zero – or it Mary lost it and John found it. Mary is fifty cents worse off, John is a dollar better off, net gain fifty cents. All of these represent the same efficient allocation of the apple: to John, who values it more than Mary. They differ in the associated distribution of income: how much money John and Mary each end up with.
>
> Since we are measuring value in dollars it is easy to confuse "gaining value" with "getting money." But consider our example. The total amount of money never changes; we are simply shifting it from one person to another. The total quantity of goods never changes either, since we are cutting off our analysis after John gets the apple but before he eats it. Yet total value increases by fifty cents. It increases because the same apple is worth more to John than to Mary. Shifting money around does not change total value. One dollar is worth the same number of dollars to everyone: one.[20]

Now describe exactly the same situation but from an inverted perspective with a numeraire reversal from dollars to apples. Changing the numeraire does *not* mean the trivial conversion of the net benefits in one numeraire to another one at some fixed public price ratio; it means summing again the benefits and costs, using each person's marginal rates of substitution.

Mary was at a point where her marginal rate of substitution of dollars for apples was one-half, so her marginal rate of substitution of apples for dollars would be the reciprocal, namely, two apples per dollar. John's marginal rate of substitution of dollars for apples was one, and its reciprocal is also one. Now apply the reasoning of social-wealth maximization (measured in apples) to the proposed change of transferring seventy-five cents from John to Mary. The seventy-five cents is only worth three-fourths of an apple to John, whereas the seventy-five cents is worth three-halves apples ($2 \times 0.75 = 1.5$) to Mary. Hence the social pie (which is now an apple pie) is increased by three-fourths of an apple by the transfer of seventy-five cents from John to Mary. Hence the *money* transfer is the efficient change (the increase in social wealth).[21] Whether or not an apple is actually transferred from Mary to John is now a question of equity or redistribution that leaves the social (apple) pie unchanged. Paraphrasing Friedman's statement of the numeraire illusion, one apple is worth the same number of apples to everyone: one. An apple's an apple for all that (see Figure 6.2).

There has been no change in Mary's or John's preferences; exactly the same underlying situation is described, first using dollars as numeraire and then using apples as numeraire. Yet the results of the social-wealth maximization reasoning

---

[20] David D. Friedman, 2000, *Law's Order: What Economics Has to Do with Law and Why It Matters*, Princeton: Princeton University Press, p. 20.

[21] Taking any commodity as numeraire, the MPKH logic similarly recommends on "efficiency" grounds the transfer of money from those who relatively like to those who relatively dislike the commodity.

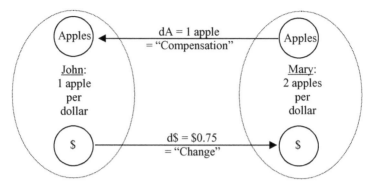

"Change" d\$ gives 0.75 = 1.5 − 0.75 = Δapples increase in social apple pie.
"Compensation" dA gives 0 = 1 − 1 = no change in apple pie.

Figure 6.2. Same transfers with apples as numeraire.

(and the underlying MPKH logic) have changed completely between the two descriptions. The efficiency part and the equity part of the total change reversed themselves under the numeraire reversal. In contrast, it might be noted that the weaker catallactic conclusion that the two changes together constitute a mutually beneficial exchange (a Pareto improvement) is invariant under numeraire change (see Table 6.1).

The argument that "a dollar is worth the same number of dollars to everyone: one" pinpoints the problem that we have called the numeraire illusion. Transfers in whatever is taken as the numeraire will always seem to not change the size of the pie and thus to be merely distributive. Changes in a yardstick will never be revealed by *that* yardstick; one needs to use a different yardstick.[22]

If the mutually beneficial exchange had been Mary's apple in exchange for John's three-fourths of a pound of nuts (instead of three-fourths of a dollar), then in terms of some third commodity such as dollars we could say symmetrically that John values the apple more than Mary and that Mary values the three-fourths of a pound of nuts more than John. But by computing in the metric of one of the goods involved in the potential exchange, we are misled to the asymmetric conclusion that one part of the exchange increases the social pie whereas the other is mere redistribution of the social pie – an illusion that is exposed by changing the numeraire.

B. A Pollution Example

Law and economics (specifically, wealth maximization) applies the same logic of David Friedman's apple example to legal rules: "We now expand the analysis by

---

[22] The idea of a different yardstick is present in the idea of a *relative* price, the price of x in terms of y. The only price that has no information content is the "self-price" of the numeraire, one. The numeraire's price is like the blind spot in an eye, the one place where no information is conveyed. Given a (differentiable) function $y = f(x)$, the derivative dy/dx tells one something about the function, but the derivative $dy/dy = 1$ tells one nothing about the function.

Table 6.1. *Reversal of efficiency and equity parts under numeraire reversal*

Change	Normal description (money as numeraire)	Inverse description (apples as numeraire)
Increase in size of "social pie"	Transfer of apple from Mary to John	Transfer of seventy-five cents from John to Mary
Redistribution of "social pie"	Transfer of seventy-five cents from John to Mary	Transfer of apple from Mary to John

applying Marshall's approach not to a transaction (John buys Mary's apple) but to a legal rule."[23] Because so much of this approach to the economic analysis of law grew out of Ronald Coase's analysis of pollution,[24] such an example may be used to represent the methodology of law and economics.

Take the first numeraire y to be money, and take x to be the number of pollution permits.[25] Our points are independent of the question of polluter's rights or pollutee's rights, one that has received much attention in the literature on Coase's theorem. Hence we initially take a pollutee's-rights perspective and then later take the opposite viewpoint. In our first example, person 1 is the polluter, initially endowed with much money and few pollution rights, whereas person 2 is the pollutee, with the opposite relative endowments.

At the endowment point it might well be that there could some mutually voluntary exchanges of dy money for dx pollution permits between the polluter and pollutee. So far so good; it is a Pareto improvement due to voluntary exchanges in the market for pollution permits, with no need for the KH criterion or wealth-maximization reasoning.

The problem comes when, say, a legal–economic analyst of the Chicago school (or "the planner"[26] of cost–benefit analysis) uses the MPKH reasoning to analyze the transfer in pollution rights dx as an increase in social wealth, whereas the payments dy are seen as a merely redistributive transfer with no effect on the size of social wealth (aside perhaps from minor income effects). Economists and economics-savvy lawyers can recommend the efficiency change, the increase in social wealth due to the dx transfer, because the dy redistribution (e.g., polluters paying for pollution permits) is left aside as a noneconomic question (all *as if* the efficiency–equity parsing were an invariant attribute of the underlying legal situation rather than just a consequence of the choice of numeraire). Moreover, the merely redistributive dy transfer might be plagued by deadweight transaction costs that would actually reduce social wealth. Hence the most efficient outcome would be to make the social-wealth-increasing transfer dx to the polluter – in effect, to switch that part of the endowment to the polluter – and avoid any of the social-wealth losses due to the costs of the dy transaction. This would "mimic

[23] Friedman, *Law's Order*, p. 20.

[24] Ronald H. Coase, 1960, "The Problem of Social Cost," *Journal of Law and Economics*, 3, pp. 1–44.

[25] See, for example, the SO_2 permits analyzed in Denny Ellerman et al., 2000, *Markets for Clean Air: The U.S. Acid Rain Program*, New York: Cambridge University Press.

[26] Boadway and Bruce, *Welfare Economics*, p. 9.

the market" in terms of increasing social wealth, while avoiding the deadweight transaction costs.

All of these arguments and conclusions – representative of the Chicago school[27] – are vulnerable to the mere redescription of the situation by exchanging the numeraires. Gains and losses are now to be expressed in terms of the measuring rod of pollution rights (x), and the transfers can be analyzed from the viewpoint of the new social x pie. The money payment dy from the polluter to the pollutee increases social wealth (now measured in x), whereas the dx transfer of pollution rights merely redistributes x with no effect on total social wealth as measured in x.[28] One pollution permit is worth the same number of pollution permits to everyone: one. Economists can recommend the social-wealth-increasing transfer of the money dy from polluter to pollutee, whereas the question of transferring the pollution rights dx is best left aside as a noneconomic question. There might even be some deadweight costs in social wealth associated with the transfer of the pollution rights dx, so the most efficient outcome would then be to just reassign the money dy from the polluter to the pollutee. That would also mimic the market in terms of increasing social wealth, while at the same time avoiding the deadweight transaction costs.

The flaws in the MPKH reasoning have nothing to do with the Coase theorem controversy. The numeraire inversion analysis applies as in the preceding example if we start with the polluter's-rights principle. Now take person 1 to be the pollutee, relatively well endowed with money but few pollution rights – the latter being assigned to person 2, the polluter. Again we might expect at the endowment point that there could be some mutually beneficial voluntary exchange where the pollutee buys pollution rights dx from the polluter for the money dy. In the literature, this is sometimes viewed as the pollutee "bribing" the polluter to reduce pollution, or it could be seen as the purchase of amenity rights to the good of less pollution.

The problem comes in the MPKH reasoning that would analyze the transfer of dx amenity rights from the polluter to the pollutee as an increase in the social y pie while the payment dy had zero effect on that pie. If there are deadweight transactions costs involved in the otherwise redistributive dy payments, then the most efficient outcome is the uncompensated transfer of the amenity rights dx from the polluter to the pollutee. But these "policy recommendations" are easily reversed simply by redescribing the same situation with reversed numeraires.

With the amenity rights x taken as the numeraire, the payment dy from the pollutee to the polluter increases the size of the social pie (now measured in amenity rights), whereas the transfer of rights dx from polluter to pollutee is a "wash" because one pollution permit has the same value in terms of pollution permits to each party. And if there are transaction costs associated with transfer in amenity rights dx, then the MPKH–Chicago reasoning would conclude that the

---

[27] Taking Chicago as the Mother Church in law and economics, we see here again a church mistaking a "does not move" statement (i.e., that social wealth "does not move" from transfers in the numeraire money or purchasing power) as a substantive assertion instead of a mere consequence of the choice of coordinate systems.

[28] See the appendix for a proof.

most efficient outcome is for the pollutee to make the bribe dy to the polluter but for the polluter to keep the pollution rights dx!

III. NUMERAIRE ILLUSION WITH CONSUMER AND SUPPLIER SURPLUSES

A. Summing Up So Far

There has been a long and rather exhausting debate in the law-and-economics literature about the KH principle, where the principle is often presented in the form of the wealth-maximization principle or, even, as the "efficiency norm."[29] In spite of the wide variety of arguments pro and con, the numeraire-illusion analysis seems to have escaped attention. Indeed, the numeraire-illusion analysis renders the debate rather moot. In an ultrasimple example such as the apple-and-money one, the wealth-maximization principle gives opposite results, depending on whether apples or money is taken as the numeraire. If money is the numeraire, then the apple transfer is wealth-increasing and the money transfer is not, but if apples are the numeraire, then the money transfer is wealth-increasing and the apple transfer is not. When the policy recommendation of the wealth-maximization principle reverses itself under a trivial redescription of exactly the same transfers, then the principle itself is rather incoherent – and the debate over it rather pointless.

The vulnerability of the MPKH reasoning to numeraire change is not as obvious in the usual context of law and economics or cost–benefit analysis, but the underlying logic is the same. In the law-and-economics literature, the "apple transfer" might be some proposed change in the law. In cost–benefit analysis, the "apple transfer" would be some complex project under consideration, and the numeraire illusion is the statement that "pure transfers of funds among households, firms and governments should themselves have no effect on project benefits and costs."[30] When the "apple transfer" is a proposed legal change or a proposed project, the flaw in the MPKH reasoning is more hidden from view.[31] Perhaps that is why such a simple methodological error has persisted for so long. The problem in the underlying MPKH reasoning is easily exposed in Friedman's simple apples-and-dollars example[32] – and how could the reasoning suddenly become valid when

---

[29] See, for example, the collections of opposing viewpoints in "Symposium on Efficiency as a Legal Concern" in vol. 8 of *Hofstra Law Review* (1980); Mark Kuperberg and Charles Beitz, eds., 1983, *Law, Economics, and Philosophy*, Totowa, NJ: Rowman and Allanheld; or Adler and Posner, *Cost–Benefit Analysis*.

[30] Boadway, *Economic Evaluation of Projects*, p. 35.

[31] At the end of the appendix, the general result is stated that for complex multicommodity and multiperson transfers that together form a Pareto improvement, the MPKH reasoning will recommend all the transfers except the transfers in the numeraire, because the effects of the latter seem to vanish because of the numeraire illusion. Change the numeraire to one of the other commodities, and then the MPKH reasoning will recommend all the transfers (including those in the old numeraire) except the transfers in the new numeraire.

[32] A more realistic example would be a land reform program with positive net monetized benefits of land transfers from, say, the rich to the poor. Revaluating the benefits and costs in terms of land as numeraire (which we might assume is of a uniform grade) yields the result that the compensation

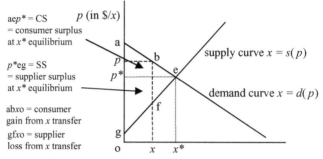

$aeg = CS + SS$ = consumer + supplier surpluses = increase in $pie from x^* transfer.
$0 = p^*ex^*o - p^*ex^*o$ = gain to x-supplier − loss to x-consumer from $\$p^*x^*$ transfer.

Figure 6.3. Standard supply-and-demand diagram.

apple transfers are replaced by more complex transactions in goods? Focusing on complex changes only fogs over the difficulties and does not resolve them. The "ostrich defense" – not looking at cases where the numeraire can be easily reversed – does not change the underlying logic (or the lack thereof).

B. The Standard Textbook Treatment

The numeraire illusion is hardly confined to the literature on cost–benefit analysis or the economic analysis of law. We will show how it arises in the standard textbook rendition of Marshall's consumer and supplier surpluses. There is a downward-sloping demand curve; the quantity of x demanded, x_d, is a function $x_d = d(p)$ of the price in dollars per unit x. And there is an upward-sloping supply curve; the quantity of x supplied is a function $x_s = s(p)$ of the price. Equilibrium occurs at a price p^* at which the quantities demanded and supplied are equal: $x^* = d(p^*) = s(p^*)$.

Leaving aside the fine-grained controversy about measuring the consumer and supplier surpluses as not germane to our analysis, the standard, or "naive," Marshallian definitions will be used. The total benefit to the consumer(s) in receiving x is measured in dollars by the area under the demand curve from 0 to x (see Figure 6.3). If px was paid out to receive x, then the net gain is the consumer's surplus. In a similar manner, the area under the supply curve from 0 to x represents the loss measured in dollars to the supplier(s) in giving up x. If px was received in return for x, then the net gain is the supplier's surplus.[33]

For the transfer of x from the supplier to the consumer, the total gain to the consumer is represented by the area abxo, whereas the total cost to the supplier is the area gfxo. The difference is the total social surplus, represented by the area abfg. If the consumer paid px (the area $p$bxo) to receive x, then the difference is

payments to the rich are also a project that increases social value but that the actual land transfers have no impact on social value (as measured in land).

[33] We might also give MPKH their best case by assuming just one consumer and one supplier. Thus the apostrophe is before the s in *consumer's* and *supplier's* surpluses.

the consumer's surplus from the transaction measured in dollars and represented by abp in the diagram. If the supplier was paid px to give up x, then the difference between that revenue and the cost (gfxo) is the supplier's surplus from the transaction, represented by the area pbfg. The sum of the consumer's surplus and the supplier's surplus is again the total social surplus: (abxo − pbxo) + (pbxo − gfxo) = abxo − gfxo.

The most efficient amount of x to transfer is the one that maximizes the increase in the social $ pie, which is the equilibrium value x^*. Many textbooks still use this MPKH reasoning to "explain" the "efficiency" of the competitive equilibrium (in this market, the exchange of x^* in return for p^*x^* dollars). The Paretian explanation of efficiency (using up all the opportunities for mutually beneficial exchange) is usually also given as if the two accounts were equivalent.

But the difference between the two accounts of efficiency becomes clear as soon as we take the MPKH reasoning seriously enough to ask about the efficiency role of the p^*x^* payment. From the Paretian viewpoint, it is necessary to make the exchange *mutually* beneficial, a Pareto improvement, so the x^* transfer without the p^*x^* transfer does not pass Paretian muster.[34] But from the KH efficiency point of view, the payment p^*x^* is redistributive; it does not change the size of the social $ pie. Thus numeraire illusion arises in this standard textbook account by picturing the x^* transfer as generating by itself the consumer and supplier surpluses, whereas the p^*x^* transfer is only redistributive.

In spite of this reasoning being developed to facilitate economics giving "professional" or "scientific" advice to public policy, the reasoning in fact reverses itself after a mere redescription of exactly the same market with reversed numeraires.

C. The Inverse Description

We now give an inverse description of the same market, reversing the roles of the commodity x and the revenue $R = px$. The supply curve provides the functional relationship giving the amount of x that is supplied if the revenue $R = s(p)p$ is paid for it. The seller of x goes to the market and demands money spent on x in exchange for x. Thus the x supplier is the R demander, and the reciprocal $p' = 1/p$ is the unit price of a dollar spent on x[35] in terms of x (where we may assume $0 < p < \infty$ and thus p' is in the same range). Thus the revenue demanded as a function of p' is $R_d(p') = R(1/p') = s(1/p')/p'$. This is the revenue (money spent on x) demand function in the redescribed market interpreting x supply as R demand:

$$\text{Revenue demand curve:} \quad R_d(p') = s(1/p')/p'.$$

---

[34] This highlights that the "mimic the market" rhetoric in Chicago-style law and economics selectively ignores the fact that market transactions involve payments.

[35] Intuitively, the commodity "dollars spent on x" could be thought of as money earmarked in a budget to be spent on x. The amount of this commodity supplied to or demanded from the market will depend on its price $p' = 1/p$ in terms of the numeraire x. Like an earmarked budget item, R units of this commodity can only be exchanged for $p'R$ units of x.

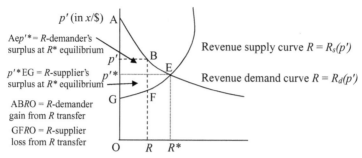

p' (in $x/\$$) A

$Aep'* = R$-demander's surplus at R^* equilibrium

$p'*EG = R$-supplier's surplus at R^* equilibrium

$ABRO = R$-demander gain from R transfer

$GFRO = R$-supplier loss from R transfer

p' B   E

$p'*$

G   F

O   R R^*

Revenue supply curve $R = R_s(p')$

Revenue demand curve $R = R_d(p')$

$AEG = AEp'* + p'*EG$ = total increase in social x-pie from $\$R^* = \$p^*x^*$ transfer.
$0 = p'*ER^*O - p'*ER^*O$ = gain to R-supplier – loss to R-demander of $p'*R^* = x^*$ transfer.

Figure 6.4. Inverse description of market as supply and demand for R using x as numeraire.

For the illustrative case of a linear supply curve $x_s = cp - d$ (with c and d nonnegative), the revenue demand curve is the downward-sloping curve (in the positive R, p' quadrant:

$$\text{Revenue demand curve for a linear supply:} \quad R_d(p') = \frac{c}{p'^2} - \frac{d}{p'}.$$

The x demand curve gives the functional relationship between the amount of x that is demanded and the money or revenue $R = d(p)p$ supplied for it. We might think of the x demander as a money-spent-on-x or revenue supplier. The revenue supplied as a function of its unit price p' is thus

$$\text{Revenue supply curve:} \quad R_s(p') = d(1/p')/p'.$$

Because the revenue $R(p) = d(p)p$ is the product of a decreasing and an increasing function of p, it is not necessarily monotonic, and the revenue supply curve might be backward bending (in the positive R, p' quadrant). In the illustrative case of a linear demand curve $x_d = -ap + b$ (with a and b nonnegative), the revenue supply curve is indeed backward bending:

$$\text{Revenue supplied for a linear demand curve:} \quad R_s(p') = \frac{b}{p'} - \frac{a}{p'^2}.$$

An illustrative redescription of the x-and-R market is given in the diagram in Figure 6.4.

The equilibrium price p'^* in the redescribed market is the p' where

$$R_s(p') = d(1/p')/p' = s(1/p')/p' = R_d(p').$$

Multiplying through by p', we find that equilibrium occurs at the p' where $d(1/p') = d(p) = x_d = x_s = s(p) = s(1/p')$, which are the original equilibrium conditions for p^*. The quantities x demanded and supplied are equal at the price p^*, the equilibrium price in the market for x, so $p'^* = 1/p^*$. At p'^*, the equilibrium amount of the revenue R^* is $R_s(p'^*) = d(1/p'^*)/p'^* = d(p^*)p^* = x^*p^*$. The amount of x paid for R^* is the price times the quantity: $p'^*R^* = x^*p^*/p^* = x^*$. Thus the redescribed market gives exactly the same equilibrium – just looked at in

Table 6.2. *Efficiency–equity reversal in standard competitive market analysis*

Kind of transfer	Normal description ($\$ =$ numeraire)	Inverse description ($x =$ numeraire)
Transfer that increased size of "social pie"	Commodity x^* from x supplier to x demander	Commodity $R^* = p^*x^*$ from R supplier (i.e., x demander) to R demander (x supplier)
Transfer that only redistributed "social pie"	Payment $R^* = p^*x^*$ from x demander to x supplier	Payment $p'^*R^* = x^*$ from R demander (i.e., x supplier) to R supplier (x demander)

the inverted way as the market for the supply and demand for money spent on x with the payments made in x.

It should not be surprising that the equilibrium properties of the model were unchanged by the mere redescription with reversed numeraire. However, the constructs of the MPKH reasoning change completely with the change in numeraire.

The area under the revenue demand curve (ABRO in the diagram) from 0 to R gives the total gain to the $\$$ demander (the x supplier), expressed in the numeraire x, from receiving R. The area under the revenue supply curve from 0 to R (GFRO) gives the total loss to the $\$$ supplier (the x demander) from giving up R. The difference gives the total social surplus, the increase in the social x pie, from the R transfer from the $\$$ supplier to the $\$$ demander. The transfer of the x payment for R, namely, $p'R = (1/p)px = x$, in the opposite direction is a mere redistribution of x that does not change the size of the social x pie.

The most efficient transfer of R is the amount that maximizes the increase in the social x pie – which is R^*. That transfer of $R^*(= p^*x^*)$ from the $\$$ supplier (x demander) to the $\$$ demander (x supplier) is the efficiency part of the transaction. The transfer of payment $p'^*R^* = (1/p^*)p^*x^* = x^*$ from the $\$$ demander to the $\$$ supplier does not affect the size of the social x pie, so it is the equity part of the total change – all according to the MPKH reasoning.

Thus in the textbook supply-and-demand competitive model, we have the ordinary description of the model with money as the numeraire (given in the textbooks), and we also have the inverse description with the commodity x as the numeraire (not given in textbooks). The underlying properties of the model (e.g., the equilibrium value of x^*, the equilibrium price ratio of $\$$ per x of p^*, and the equilibrium amount of money R^* transacted) are all the same under the redescription. But the MPKH parsing of the efficiency part and the equity part of the total change reverses under the redescription. The x^* transfer that is the efficient increase in the social $\$$ pie becomes a value-indifferent change in terms of the social x pie (i.e., the numeraire-illusion reasoning that "one unit of x has the same value in terms of x to everyone: one"). The $R^* = p^*x^*$ transfer of money, which was the value-neutral change in terms of the social $\$$ pie, becomes the efficient increase in the social x pie (see Table 6.2).

The numeraire-illusion analysis of the MPKH logic is not based on some esoteric special cases with little everyday relevance; the analysis applies to the simplest and most general textbook model of market equilibrium. Because the analysis in terms of efficiency (increased size of the social pie) reverses itself under the mere redescription of the same market with reversed numeraires, we see in the context of the standard textbook supply-and-demand model that recommendations based on MPKH efficiency reasoning are baseless. The MPKH shortcut to efficiency is a dead end.

What survives? The conclusion that is numeraire-invariant is that the mutual exchange of x^* for R^* is mutually voluntary, that is, that both transfers *together* are a Pareto-superior change. But this conclusion is based entirely on Paretian reasoning, and the MPKH efficiency–equity parsing and the wealth-maximization principle play no role.

FINAL REMARKS

One might ask: Where is economic reasoning misled by the numeraire illusion into making noninvariant conclusions? Where else have the "high priests" of economics habitually chosen to use "geocentric coordinates" and then "scientifically" drawn the conclusion that "the sun moves but the earth does not"? There is a whole research program to conduct an intellectual audit across economics to see where the numeraire illusion might lead to error as it did in the MPKH tradition of welfare economics.

Our focus here has been on Chicago-style (wealth maximization) law and economics, cost–benefit analysis, and other areas of applied welfare economics based on the MPKH reasoning. The common pattern is that a potential overall Pareto improvement is parsed into two parts: the proposed project or change, and the compensation of the losers that would make the total project cum compensation into a Pareto-superior change. Then the MPKH reasoning is used to represent the project by itself as an increase in the social pie measured by the money metric, and thus as something that can be recommended by economists on efficiency grounds. The compensation is represented as a redistribution of the social pie, a question of equity, not efficiency:

> The purpose of considering hypothetical redistributions is to try and separate the *efficiency* and *equity* aspects of the policy change under consideration. It is argued that whether or not the redistribution is actually carried out is an important but *separate* decision. The mere fact that is it possible to create potential Pareto improving redistribution possibilities is enough to rank one state above another on efficiency grounds.[36]

Richard Posner makes a similar point in the context of law and economics as well as cost–benefit analysis. He notes that KH efficiency leaves distributive considerations to one side:

> But to the extent that distributive justice can be shown to be the proper business of some other branch of government or policy instrument . . . , it is possible to set distributive considerations to one side and use the Kaldor–Hicks approach with a good conscience. This assumes . . . that efficiency in the Kaldor–Hicks sense –

[36] Boadway and Bruce, *Welfare Economics*, p. 97.

making the pie larger without worrying about how the relative size of the slices changes – is a social value.[37]

Posner seems unaware that "making the pie larger" gives completely opposite results depending on whether it is the dollar pie or the apple pie (the $ pie or the x pie). This pattern of reasoning – which assumes that the parsing of a proposed change into efficiency (size of pie) and equity (shares in pie) parts is a description-invariant property of the change – runs the length and breadth of the law-and-economics literature, and it is the warhorse of cost–benefit analysis and other parts of applied welfare economics.

As is clear from the numeraire reversals, there are simply no economic grounds to declare the project or change (e.g., x^* transfer) as an increase in efficiency and the compensation (e.g., $R^* = p^*x^*$ transfer) as a mere redistribution, rather than exactly the reverse. Both the project and the compensation are reallocations of resources that will each benefit some people and hurt others. The efficiency–equity analysis of the MPKH tradition does not provide valid economic grounds to claim that either partial change, which will benefit some and hurt others, can be recommended by itself on efficiency grounds.[38]

APPENDIX: THE ALGEBRA OF THE BASIC ARGUMENT

The controversies about measuring "consumers' surplus" or "aggregate willingness to pay" by integrating under Marshallian demand curves or Hicksian compensated demand curves are not germane to our point. Hence we will avoid those controversies by making the simple and basic point using differential changes (i.e., small changes at the margin) around a point prior to any integration over a path of finite changes.

There are two commodities X and Y involved in the changes. There are two *value systems* that give prices $P_1 > P_2 > 0$ of X in terms of Y that could be thought of as the marginal rates of substitution of Y for X of two different people, as the marginal rates of transformation of X into Y of two systems of production, or as resulting from any two different value systems in general. For example, the two prices might be the marginal rates of substitution of Y for X for persons 1 and 2:

$$P_i = MRS^i_{yx} = \frac{MU^i_X}{MU^i_Y} \quad \text{for } i = 1, 2$$

where $MRS^1_{yx} > MRS^2_{yx}$. Let P be any price between P_1 and P_2 that will function as a *public* rate of exchange between the two systems.

---

[37] Posner, "Cost–Benefit Analysis," pp. 318–319.

[38] Although beyond the scope of this chapter, it might be noted that this conclusion is congruent with the Wicksell–Buchanan perspective in political economy; see James M. Buchanan, 1999, *The Logical Foundations of Constitutional Liberty: The Collected Works of James M. Buchanan*, vol. 1, Indianapolis: Liberty Fund. Instead of using MPKH reasoning to supply an "efficiency" gloss to government planning decisions (e.g., cost–benefit analysis), it is the job of democratic politics to work out changes that are mutually voluntary on the part of all those whose rights are affected.

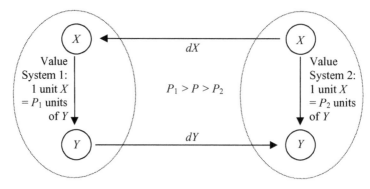

Figure 6.5. Two relative values for X in terms of Y.

We will further assume that these prices were determined by some prices of X and Y in terms of a third commodity Z. Let P_{1x} and P_{2x} be the prices of X in terms of Z that are *subjective*, or internal to the two systems, such that $P_{1x} > P_{2x}$, and let P_x be an intermediate public price of X in terms of Z. Similarly, let P_{1y} and P_{2y} be the prices of Y in terms of Z in the two systems such that $P_{1y} < P_{2y}$, and let P_y be an intermediate public price of Y in terms of Z. The previous prices of X in terms of Y are determined by the Z prices:

$$P_1 = P_{1x}/P_{1y} > P = P_x/P_y > P_2 = P_{2x}/P_{2y}.$$

The prices of Y in terms of X would be obtained by inverting the prices of X in terms of Y.

Thus we have three arrays of prices corresponding to the three different numeraires (X, Y, and Z). In the first description of transfers dX and dY between systems, or persons, 1 and 2, Y is the numeraire. Then we describe the same transfers with X as the numeraire. Both these descriptions will involve the numeraire illusion, because the numeraire is one of the commodities involved in the transfers being evaluated. The MPKH reasoning will apply to each of these cases but give opposite results. Then we evaluate the dX and dY transfers using a noninvolved commodity Z as the numeraire. Then no numeraire illusion arises, and the MPKH reasoning does not apply.

We start with the description using Y as the numeraire (see Figure 6.5).

If dX is transferred from where it has a lower value in 2 to where it has a higher value in 1, then the Y cost of taking dX out of 2 is $P_2 dX$, whereas the gain from adding dX to 1 is $P_1 dX$. Thus the increase in Y pie from the dX transfer is

$$\Delta Y = (P_1 - P_2)dX > 0.$$

Now suppose that $dY = PdX$ units of Y are transferred from 1 to 2. The cost to 1 is $dY = PdX$ units of Y, and the gain to 2 is dY units of Y, so the transfer of dY units of Y (or any other units of Y) yields no change in the size of the Y pie. The net change for 1 is $(P_1 - P)dX > 0$, and the net change for 2 is $(P - P_2)dX > 0$, so both 1 and 2 are better off, and the two positive slices add up to the Y pie:

$$(P_1 - P)dX + (P - P_2)dX = (P_1 - P_2)dX = \Delta Y.$$

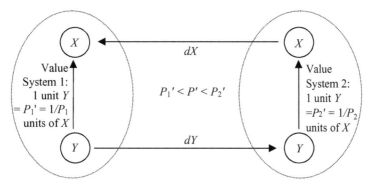

Figure 6.6. Two relative values for Y in terms of X.

The first term, $(P_1 - P)dX$, is the marginal version of X (consumer's surplus), and the second term, $(P - P_2)dX$, is the marginal version of X (supplier's surplus). The $dY = PdX$ transfers change the distribution of the Y pie between 1 and 2, but do not affect the size of the pie.

So far, this is just mathematics. Then the MPKH reasoning is misled by the numeraire illusion involved in measuring the effect of the dY transfer in terms of Y to conclude that the dY transfer added no value or wealth; it was only a redistribution. The value increase was all in the dX transfer, so it can be recommended on grounds of efficiency while the dY transfer can be treated separately as a question of equity.

But this asymmetric treatment of the dX and dY transfers is only a consequence of the asymmetric choice of one of the involved commodities as numeraire to evaluate the transfers. Reverse the choice of numeraires, and the conclusions will be reversed. Taking X as the numeraire, $P_1' = 1/P_1$ is the price of a unit of Y in units of X in system 1, and $P_2' = 1/P_2$ is the price of a unit of Y in terms of X in 2 (see Figure 6.6).

We now evaluate the results the same dY transfer from 1 to 2. The loss to 1 is $P_1'dY$, and the gain to 2 is $P_2'dY$, so, noting that $P_2' > P_1'$, we have the increase in the X pie from the dY transfer as

$$\Delta X = (P_2' - P_1')dY > 0.$$

Now taking $P' = 1/P$, we find that $P'dY = P'PdX = dX$ is the same dX units of X transferred from 2 to 1. The cost to 2 is dX units of X and the gain to 1 is dX units of X, so the transfer in dX units of X (or any other units of X) yields no change in the size of the X pie (i.e., the self-measuring yardstick records no change). But there is a change in the distribution of the pie. The net changes for 2 and 1 are respectively

$$(P_2' - P')dY > 0 \quad \text{and} \quad (P' - P_1')dY > 0,$$

so both 1 and 2 are better off, and the two positive slices sum to the X pie:

$$(P_2' - P')dY + (P' - P_1')dY = (P_2' - P_1')dY = \Delta X.$$

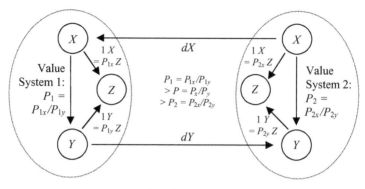

Figure 6.7. Two values for Y and for X in terms of Z.

The term $(P'_2 - P')dY$ is the marginal Y consumer's surplus, and the second term, $(P' - P'_1)dY$, is the marginal Y supplier's surplus.

These are the exact same underlying changes: the transfer of dX from 2 to 1 and the transfer of dY from 1 to 2. But the MPKH reasoning now yields the reverse conclusions. The dY transfer accounts for all the increase in the size of the X pie, so it can be recommended on efficiency grounds. The dX transfer merely redistributes the X pie, so that transfer can be treated as a separate question of equity.

One escapes the numeraire illusion only by evaluating the transfers in terms of some third commodity Z not involved in the transfers. We use the array of prices in terms of Z as assumed (see Figure 6.7).

The exchange of dX and $dY = PdX$ is equal-valued at the P_x and P_y prices, because $P_x dX = P_y dY$. But at the internal, or subjective, values in the two systems, the change in Z value from the dX transfer is $(P_{1x} - P_{2x})dX > 0$, and the change in Z from the dY transfer is $(P_{2y} - P_{1y})dY > 0$. The sum of the two increases is the total increase in the Z pie from the dX and dY transfers:

$$\Delta Z = (P_{1x} - P_{2x})dX + (P_{2y} - P_{1y})dY.$$

Because the exchange of dX and dY is made at the intermediate prices P_x and P_y, where

$$P_{1x} > P_x > P_{2x} \quad \text{and} \quad P_{1y} < P_y < P_{2y},$$

we can compute the surpluses in each system in terms of Z. In system 1, the gain from receiving dX is $P_{1x}dX$, while the cost of losing dY is $P_{1y}dY$, so the net benefit to 1 is

$$\Delta Z_1 = P_{1x}dX - P_{1y}dY$$
$$= (P_{1x} - P_x)dX + P_x dX - P_{1y}dY$$
$$= (P_{1x} - P_x)dX + P_y dY - P_{1y}dY$$
$$= (P_{1x} - P_x)dX + (P_y - P_{1y})dY > 0.$$

Similarly the gain in system 2 from receiving dY and giving up dX is

$$\Delta Z_2 = P_{2y}dY - P_{2x}dX = (P_{2y} - P_y)dY + (P_x - P_{2x})dX > 0,$$

and the two benefits sum to the total Z benefit:

$$\Delta Z = \Delta Z_1 + \Delta Z_2 = (P_{1x} - P_{2x})dX + (P_{2y} - P_{1y})dY,$$

where $(P_{1x} - P_{2x})dX > 0$ and $(P_{2y} - P_{1y})dY > 0$. Note that both transfers now contribute to the total benefit evaluated using a numeraire not involved in the transfers.

There is no simple multiplicative conversion of ΔZ into ΔX or ΔY, because the Z must be converted into X or Y at the different rates internal to system 1 or system 2.[39] For instance, $P_{1x}dX$ would be divided by P_{1y} to get the equivalent values in Y in system 1, while $P_{2x}dX$ would be divided by P_{2y} to get the equivalent Y value in system 2. Thus, to arrive at ΔY, we would have to divide the different terms in the expression for ΔZ by the appropriate Y prices for each system:

$$\left(\frac{P_{1x}}{P_{1y}} - \frac{P_{2x}}{P_{2y}} \right) dX + \left(\frac{P_{2y}}{P_{2y}} - \frac{P_{1y}}{P_{1y}} \right) dY = (P_1 - P_2)\, dX + (1 - 1)\, dY = \Delta Y.$$

Note how the numeraire illusion appears in the mathematics as the zeroing out of the dY coefficient, that is, $1 - 1$, in the calculation of ΔY (the increase in the Y pie from the transfers using Y as numeraire). In a similar manner we could convert ΔZ into ΔX, and the numeraire illusion would appear in the zeroing out of the dX coefficient in ΔX. When the numeraire illusion is avoided by evaluating the dX and dY changes in terms of some other *noninvolved* commodity Z, then we saw that both transfers added value.

With a noninvolved commodity as numeraire, the MPKH reasoning gets no illusionary foothold to recommend either dX or dY by itself on efficiency grounds.

At the cost of some complication, other commodities can be added to make the changes or project more complex. For instance, there might be other transfers dX^* from 2 to 1 and dY^* from 1 to 2 so all the transfers together were a Pareto improvement. Then with Y as the numeraire, the MPKH reasoning would recommend the dX, dX^*, and dY^* transfers on efficiency grounds. With X as the numeraire, the MPKH reasoning would recommend the dX^*, dY, and dY^* transfers on efficiency grounds.

The general result, which models a legal change or project as a set of multi-commodity and multiperson transfers (i.e., project cum compensation), is that when all the transfers together constitute a Pareto improvement, then the MPKH reasoning will recommend all the transfers except the numeraire transfers on efficiency grounds. Change the numeraire to one of the other commodities, and then the MPKH reasoning will recommend on efficiency grounds all the transfers *including* those in the old numeraire except the transfers in the new numeraire.

---

[39] This emphasizes the point that "changing numeraires" does not mean the trivial conversion of net benefits in one numeraire to another at some fixed public price ratio, but resummation of the benefits and costs when converted at each person's internal rate of substitution to the new numeraire.

When only two goods are involved in the transfers (as before), then the general numeraire-illusion flaw in the MPKH reasoning is illustrated in the simplest and most dramatic way as a *reversal* in the efficiency recommendations arising from a mere change in numeraire. The KH argument that efficiency does not require the numeraire transfers is only numeraire illusion. Changes in a yardstick cannot be revealed by the same yardstick – but can be revealed by changing the yardstick.

7   Justice, Mercy, and Efficiency

SARAH HOLTMAN

If one proposes to consider mercy and efficiency under the same heading, the aim surely must be to draw a contrast. For we associate mercy not only with leniency but with a fine sensitivity to circumstances and both the ability and the disposition to sympathize. No matter what the context in which we contemplate it, efficiency carries none of these associations. It requires no well-trained sensitivities or dispositions. These are time-consuming to develop and costly to employ. A mathematical formula, ready-to-hand and relatively simple to apply, much better suits efficiency's focus on savings.

This general division between mercy and efficiency carries over to their more specialized application in legal contexts. Here mercy urges attention to facts and circumstances that we might ignore if we focused solely on what strict justice requires or permits. It is, we might say, a virtuous disposition to leniency marked by a compassionate attention to the circumstances at hand.[1] Efficiency, in its relatively recent incarnation as the guiding principle of the law-and-economics approach to legal interpretation, is perhaps best understood as a means of wealth maximization. Depending on the context, we can use standards including Pareto superiority, the Kaldor–Hicks test, and the Coase theorem to determine what legal standards, or interpretations, will yield the most substantial gains. The chief concern of the economic approach is to achieve *Pareto-optimal* outcomes, those in which no distributional change could increase utility for one party without decreasing it for another. The measure of utility, of course, is individual preference, judged by parties' willingness to exchange positions or bundles of goods.[2]

---

[1] For a helpful overview of the features traditionally thought to characterize mercy, see Jeffrie Murphy's discussion in Jeffrie Murphy and Jean Hampton, 1988, *Forgiveness and Mercy*, New York: Cambridge University Press, p. 66.

[2] See, for example, Ronald Coase, 1960, "The Problem of Social Cost," *Journal of Law and Economics*, 3, pp. 1–44; Guido Calabresi, 1961, "Some Thoughts on Risk Distribution and the Law of Torts," *Yale Law Journal*, 70, pp. 499–553; and Richard Posner, 1973, *Economic Analysis of Law*, Boston: Little Brown. I should note that some distinctions, important in other contexts, are not significant

---

I owe thanks to Thomas E. Hill, Jr., Michelle Mason, and Martha Nussbaum for insightful comments on the discussion of mercy that follows. I am especially grateful to Gerald Postema, whose own thinking about mercy has been an invaluable resource. I have likewise benefited enormously from the volume editor's comments on the chapter as a whole.

Although I too aim to mark a contrast between mercy and efficiency, I will begin by noticing a similarity. Especially in the contexts of judicial decision making that will be my topic here, both mercy and efficiency enjoy what is at best a vexed relationship with justice. Mercy is said, famously, to season justice, to add something that tempers or strengthens justice in its application to particular cases. Yet the true nature of this relationship, just as famously, is drawn into question. To put the worry succinctly for now, how can mercy be consistent with justice, much less strengthen it, if it recommends a leniency that justice alone will not sanction?[3]

Likewise, it seems, for the proponent of the law-and-economics approach, efficiency (in the special sense there at issue) is not only what we and our legal system do seek, but what we have objective and decisive reasons for acknowledging as a chief aim. Legal decisions that maximize wealth, say advocates, are preferable to those made on grounds of justice, equity, or fairness alone.[4] Again, though, there seems to be a serious tension here, for the outcomes and, especially, the attitude or perspective that the economic approach recommends would seem potentially to conflict with justice. An unschooled outsider might suggest that proponents could eliminate these concerns by acknowledging that justice will trump efficiency in such cases. The suggestion would be unwelcome, though. Those advocating the economic approach do not merely claim that efficiency, though separate from justice, often can complement or add further value to otherwise just decisions. They claim that we best view considerations of justice as, at bottom, ones aimed at wealth maximization. Rules protecting property, enforcing contracts, prohibiting physical violence, and the like are not merely typically consistent with such maximization. They are rules we do, and should, endorse because of their relationship with this principal legal aim.[5] If this is the understanding of justice that the economic model endorses, though, we surely must worry that in cases of conflict the model will urge that we reassess the requirements of justice, revising those that do not serve the true underlying aim of this first virtue of institutions and laws.

Of course, "justice," "mercy," and "economic efficiency" are variously understood. The sections that follow attempt to develop enriched accounts that possess both wide appeal and the capacity to resolve apparent conflicts. The starting points for these discussions are the thinner and more basic accounts on which potential conflicts are readily apparent. So I begin here by understanding justice to

---

for the discussion that follows. One of these is the distinction between utility and a yet more narrow understanding of wealth. Views that differ as to the precise characterization of the value efficiency seeks to maximize nevertheless are strikingly similar in the simplicity of this characterization and in their focus on transactions.

[3] St. Anselm famously expresses this worry in a religious context; see *Proslogium* IX.

[4] See, for example, Guido Calabresi and Douglas Malamed, 1972, "Property Rules, Liability Rules, and Inalienability: One View of the Cathedral," *Harvard Law Review*, 85, pp. 1089–1128; and Richard Posner, 1985, "An Economic Analysis of the Criminal Law," *Columbia Law Review*, 85, pp. 1193–1231.

[5] See, for example, Richard Posner, 1983, *The Economics of Justice*, Cambridge, MA: Harvard University Press.

require a system of laws designed to protect and promote a freedom in each citizen that is compatible with a like freedom for all.[6] This freedom is multifaceted. It demands substantial protection and support for individual liberty and equal allocation among citizens of both liberties themselves and the burdens required to sustain them. On this view, self-government, or autonomy, also is central to justice. A just system of laws must meaningfully acknowledge each citizen's capacity for participating in just decision making within the community and for using liberty effectively (within the bounds of justice) to shape and secure an individual life.

On a traditional account, as mentioned, mercy is a virtuous disposition to leniency, prompted by compassion and guided by a deep sensitivity to the offender's circumstances. Notably, the merciful person acknowledges both that wrongdoing has occurred and that the offender is responsible for it and justly is subject to penalty. Mercy urges a significant reduction in this penalty on grounds of moral responsibility, or humanity, rather than right.[7] Although we also can characterize efficiency in many ways, there is far less room for initial variation once we limit ourselves to the law-and-economics model. Beyond the account already provided, it is worth noting that, with its focus on wealth maximization, the law-and-economics approach quite naturally characterizes the relationships and interactions to which laws apply as transactions. Exchanges thought to increase efficiency are voluntary ones based on full relevant information and unhindered by transactions costs. Thus the approach offers the aims of ensuring voluntariness and access to relevant information, and of reducing transactions costs, as explanations for various laws, practices, and interpretations. It also urges development of and appeal to such standards and interpretations as sources of, or means to, efficiency.

In what follows, then, I examine the relationship of mercy and efficiency to justice (all as previously characterized) in the context of judicial decision making. For it is in judicial contexts that conflicts with justice are most worrisome and potential benefits arguably most effectively implemented. In section I, after clarifying the potential incompatibility of thinner notions, I first develop enriched accounts of mercy and justice and examine the relationship between them. Appealing to a concrete example, section II suggests that, on these plausible, appealing, but not uncontroversial accounts, mercy indeed tempers, rather than undermines, justice. When we attempt a similar enrichment of efficiency in section III, though, we find that it cannot enjoy such a harmonious relationship with justice. Understanding why one conflict is seeming and the other quite real is instructive, because it helps us appreciate what we sacrifice when we adopt the economic model.

---

[6] Political theorists from a variety of eras and perspectives agree on this broad proposition. See, for example, Immanuel Kant, 1797/1996, *The Metaphysics of Morals*, Mary Gregor, ed. and trans., in *The Cambridge Edition of the Works of Immanuel Kant: Practical Philosophy*, New York: Cambridge University Press, pp. 355–603; John Rawls, 1999, *A Theory of Justice*, rev. ed., Cambridge, MA: Harvard University Press; Robert Nozick, 1974, *Anarchy, State, and Utopia*, New York: Basic Books; and Amartya Sen, 1999, *Development as Freedom*, New York: Anchor Books.

[7] See, for example, Murphy and Hampton, *Forgiveness and Mercy*, p. 166.

I. ENRICHING JUSTICE AND MERCY

A. The Chief Potential Conflict with Justice

Our account of central criteria for a just legal regime, outlined in the introduction, is compatible with a wide variety of views regarding the more specific demands of justice, both theoretical and more practical. It also squares with several popular understandings of our own legal system.[8] Although such views differ in their details, they broadly agree about the relationship between justice so conceived and the role of the judge within the legal system. Absent such a system – and the legislative, executive, and judicial authorities necessary to give it effect – we often may misinterpret or fail adequately to enforce the requirements of justice in the complex circumstances in which we find ourselves. Further, because more than one scheme may satisfactorily institute justice for our circumstances, we will risk acting on incompatible tenets of justice unless we have an authoritative set of laws and persons designated to interpret, apply, and execute them. Finally, once we have established a method that respects the autonomy of each citizen by unreasonably subjecting no one to the lawmaking authority of another, we cannot allow an individual, say in the person of a judge, to usurp that authority.[9]

Although there are several ways in which mercy and the demands of justice thus might collide, we usefully can think of them as reducing to one chief potential conflict, a conflict related to the autonomy considerations just mentioned. In contemporary judicial terms, we might capture this worry as one concerning the judge's institutional role. On a simplified account, sufficient for the moment, the judge's role within the modern state is to apply general laws to particular cases, always in the service of justice. The judge who mercifully imposes a lesser penalty than justice demands departs from his appointed function. If we further take a division of powers among branches of government itself to have its basis in considerations of justice, then a judge's departure from the required legal outcome on grounds of mercy is not merely an unauthorized deviation from this function, but is morally unjustifiable.[10]

Two further features of what we might term a merciful perspective seem to exacerbate this worry. For, as we have just seen, one who is merciful is, first, sensitive to the mitigating particulars of a situation, especially to emotions, intentions, and other matters internal to the individual. More, the merciful person's sensitivity to such particulars is due, in part, to a well-developed capacity for sympathy, pity,

---

[8] Ronald Dworkin's work provides an especially good example on the side of legal theory; see, for example, his 1986, *Law's Empire*, Cambridge, MA: Belknap Press. Martha Nussbaum likewise notes the significance of liberty, equality, and autonomy in both her political and her legal work; see her 2000, *Women and Human Development*, New York: Cambridge University Press; and 1995, *Poetic Justice*, Boston: Beacon Press. Of course, Rawls, Nozick, and Sen (ibid.) also provide fine examples of views that take liberty, equality, and autonomy as central to the just state.

[9] Immanuel Kant's political theory expresses these worries particularly well and takes them particularly seriously; see his *Metaphysics of Morals*, part II, section I. They are worries shared by Kant-based theories generally, but far from exclusively.

[10] Jeffrie Murphy also thinks of difficulties with judicial mercy in terms of the judge's institutional role; see *Forgiveness and Mercy*, pp. 173–180.

or compassion. If the particulars to which sympathy renders the merciful person sensitive are ones irrelevant to the questions of justice at hand, we seem to have particularly strong reason to worry that the merciful judge may render decisions at best unauthorized by his institutional role and, at worst, in conflict with those that role demands.

B. Justice Restated and the Judge's Role Clarified

As described thus far, then, justice requires a system of laws designed to protect and promote a freedom in each citizen that is compatible with a like freedom for all. This freedom is multifaceted. It encompasses extensive liberty of thought and action, equality of citizen burdens and benefits, and citizen autonomy. In order to respect autonomy in particular, justice demands a separation of legislative, executive, and judicial powers and limits the judiciary to interpreting and applying the law in service of the standards of justice embodied in the system. Might mercy season justice so conceived, most importantly in its judicial aspect, rather than urging departures from it? To see that it could, we first require richer accounts of both judicial justice and mercy.

A distinction undergirds the account of justice with which I began, for it is importantly different from two more familiar extremes. On the first character-ization, call it legalistic, justice simply demands that judges fulfill existing legal requirements. On the second, call it idealized, justice demands of the judge what-ever would be appropriate in a society whose laws, policies, and institutions were perfectly just. On this view, judges sometimes may ignore existing laws out of keeping with perfect justice.

Neither of these characterizes judicial justice as I am conceiving of it here. Rather, on this view, the just legal scheme is a sophisticated system in which interconnected standards work together to speak to various concerns of justice as they arise in our world. Thus, protection for basic interests in liberty of expression or equal treatment, procedural rules regarding limits on admissible evidence, general prin-ciples of punishment and exceptions to them, rules that favor compliance with formal contractual requirements – all of these properly address issues of justice as they arise in a complex and sometimes unjust world. Further, the special role of a judge in such a system is to do justice by interpreting and applying these standards in precisely that context. In short, justice as I am now conceiving it, and judicial justice as one aspect, is done only amidst, and with an eye to, the varied tangle of concerns that arise when real human beings interact with each other in our world.

So understood, justice is far more sensitive to context than some conceptions will allow. It must be, if it is to address central considerations of liberty, equality, and autonomy as they arise in the world in which we live. On this view, as we have said, justice is neither what human laws do require, nor what they would require in a more perfect world. It is what they must require given features of ourselves and our world. This is, first, because conflicts among human aims and interests in complex circumstances are the very subject of justice. Second, difficulties in determining and effectively applying justice's demands in such circumstances require that the structure and laws of the state be sensitive to worldly conditions that may thwart our efforts to make, interpret, and execute just laws. Thus in constructing and applying just laws, and in dealing with one another individually, we always must ask how to honor each as a citizen possessed of liberty and autonomy and due an equal voice in lawmaking and equal protection and regard from the laws themselves. This may require us to determine, for example, how to respect both a person's unrealized capacity for autonomy and her equality with others in circumstances where these may conflict. It further may require difficult decisions regarding conflicts between one person's liberty or autonomy and that of another. All of this demands sensitivity to case particulars.

Although the view does not make it a part of the conception of justice, it also allows the possibility that emotion, so central to mercy on a traditional account, might likewise have a role in judicial assessments of justice. Several recent discussions of the relationship between emotion and morality urge that emotion, properly constrained, can be crucial to awakening human agents to morally salient details.[11] Assuming for now that emotion indeed can inform moral decision making, a compassionate context sensitivity is an appropriate feature of the just person, and the just legal judge. What limits the connection between justice, especially in the guise of the judge, and both context sensitivity and emotion is any tendency these may have to tempt or mislead us in our efforts to do justice. Provided these features are shaped or limited in the service of justice foremost, they may be part of our account of the commitment to justice in judges and others. Indeed, we may expect that the judge who is possessed of these features, and is duly guided by principled commitment, will be more able to take justice-relevant particulars appropriately into account.

C. Mercy Refined

With this richer picture of judicial justice in hand, we can renew our inquiry regarding mercy as what we might call a judicial virtue. Our chief worry, again, is that a disposition to mercy might incline a judge to forsake his institutional role by urging a penalty or consequence less severe than that required even by a sophisticated and context-sensitive justice.

To undertake this inquiry, we require a characterization of mercy that goes somewhat beyond the general features of the traditional account. On this new understanding, mercy is reshaped to fit justice as described. The reshaping, however, is not *ad hoc*. The idea is to offer an account of mercy that, like that of justice, fits with an underlying moral commitment to freedom richly conceived. Certainly there may be other accounts of the underlying moral bases of mercy, exactly as there may be such accounts of the moral bases of justice. My aim here is simply to ask whether we can make sense of mercy as a moral helpmate to justice on a widely accepted view of the latter. This will only be possible if we understand mercy and

---

[11] See, for example, Martha Nussbaum, 1990, "Finely Aware and Richly Responsible: Literature and the Moral Imagination," in *Love's Knowledge*, New York: Oxford University Press, pp. 148–167; Marcia Baron, 1995, *Kantian Ethics almost without Apology*, Ithaca, NY: Cornell University Press, pp. 218–220.

justice to rest on the same moral foundations. That mercy conceived differently might conflict with justice as I characterize it here is unremarkable.

In this reshaping of mercy, we first add to the traditional features described earlier. For if there is to be any prospect of mercy as a judicial virtue, given our understanding of justice and institutional role, we must stipulate that not all penalty reductions accompanied by feelings of compassion (and otherwise meeting traditional criteria) can yield a genuinely merciful response. On our enriched view, the emotion or affective state that is an aspect of a merciful disposition must both guide and be shaped by moral principle.[12]

Most generally, on the new model, merciful responses must respect the wrongdoer as an autonomous agent. More specifically, we might now think of the traditional features of mercy as guided by a principled commitment to respect such agency by attending to the difficulties that can thwart or discourage right action in our human circumstances. This commitment is incompatible with a determination to deny a wrongdoer's responsibility for what he has done. On the present account, it is a hallmark of the autonomous agent that he can recognize and act in accord with moral requirements, even in the face of difficult circumstances, and thus properly is held accountable for his actions. Even on a traditional understanding, a commitment to mercy is a commitment at once to acknowledge the challenges human agents face in realizing their capacity for moral action and to hold agents responsible for moral wrongs. When we mercifully reduce a penalty in light of the challenges the wrongdoer faced, we do not deny his responsibility. We acknowledge that our capacity to do right goes hand in hand with physical, emotional, intellectual, and other limitations that sometimes can make it exceedingly hard for human agents to realize that capacity. Our attention to individual circumstances and willingness to reduce the penalty, while all the time maintaining a judgment of responsibility, can be seen as testimony to our genuine appreciation of what it is to be a human agent.[13] The enriched account captures this appreciation in a guiding principle in order to make explicit that a merciful disposition is always one grounded in a commitment to autonomous agency.

The question one is bound to ask, of course, is what the difference then is between our enriched account of justice and an account of mercy that shares its moral foundations. At first blush, they share much. The augmented account of justice I have described demands a commitment to honor each of our fellow citizens as equal, autonomous, and possessed of extensive personal liberty through the political and legal institutions of our society.[14] My augmented account also

---

[12] For helpful discussion see, for example, Baron, *Kantian Ethics almost without Apology*, ch. 6. We can find other acknowledgments of mercy's principled element in Murphy's discussion of Saint Anselm's second paradox in *Forgiveness and Mercy*, pp. 180–181, and, for example, in Claudia Card, 1972, "On Mercy," *The Philosophical Review*, 81, pp. 182–207.

[13] Seneca's *De Ira* expresses this potential relationship between mercy and an appreciation of the circumstances of human agents especially well. For an excellent discussion see Martha Nussbaum, 1995, "Equity and Mercy," in A. John Simmons et al., eds., *Punishment: A Philosophy and Public Affairs Reader*, Princeton, NJ: Princeton University Press, pp. 161–167.

[14] I assume throughout that judges and others operate in the context of an essentially just legal system. This, of course, is not always the case.

acknowledges that the agent most likely to act in ways that realize this commitment to justice may well possess a compassionate sensitivity to particulars. This
sensitivity, shaped by principle, will highlight salient details of particular lives and
circumstances to which the agent might otherwise be blind (or inadequately attentive). It thus will help him determine what actions are most likely to serve the
demands of justice in the context at hand. Mercy, we have said, requires a deep
commitment to respecting human agency by at once acknowledging the agent's
responsibility for his actions and the burdens that make it difficult for him to do
what is morally right. The merciful person gives voice to this commitment through
a disposition to leniency and informs himself of the particulars of individual lives
that are its subject through a compassionate context sensitivity. This sensitivity is
shaped, in turn, by a recognition that every human agent is a morally responsible
director of his own life.

Although justice and mercy so characterized indeed have much in common,
they are importantly distinguished both by the focus or perspective, and by the
character of the duty, that each involves. The focus of justice is on ensuring a
multifaceted freedom for each in social contexts. As we seek to do justice, we must
be attentive at once to the liberty, equality, and autonomy of an individual and
to the ways in which these affect the like interests of his fellows. The focus of
mercy, by contrast, is on the individual's struggle to act in accord with his moral
agency. The merciful person acknowledges how difficult it is for each of us to rise
above the challenges of daily life and to act morally despite the fatigue, depression,
desire, or emotion that urges the contrary. Justice, of course, also requires that
we acknowledge obstacles to right action in many cases and in various ways. In
doing so, though, it does not urge a general disposition to leniency focused on
the myriad challenges that confront individual moral agents. It rather demands
attention to the more limited circumstances in which we duly respect what is
central to citizenship in each person only by recognizing the special burdens and
barriers to just action that confront some.[15]

We can capture the difference in the character of each obligation through the
distinction, familiar from Kantian moral philosophy, between perfect and imperfect duties. A duty to act mercifully would be imperfect. To fulfill such a moral
obligation, one need not act on it – do what is merciful, benevolent, and the like –
whenever the opportunity to do so arises. Moreover, there is room for variation in
the manner in which one fulfills such an obligation. Not so the duty to act justly,
a perfect duty that must be fulfilled wherever implicated and that leaves far less
room for variation in method.[16]

---

[15] The view I suggest thus differs importantly from several recent discussions, all of which describe
mercy as a type or aspect of justice. In particular, Claudia Card develops such a connection in her
"On Mercy." So arguably do Nussbaum in "Equity and Mercy" and Alwynne Smart, 1968, "Mercy,"
Philosophy, 43, pp. 345–359. For criticism of accounts that fail to acknowledge the distinctness of
mercy and justice see Murphy and Hampton, *Forgiveness and Mercy*, pp. 169–177. My aim here,
of course, is not to prove that mercy is a virtue distinct from justice. Nevertheless, my inquiry has
implications for that other discussion.

[16] Elsewhere, I consider the possibility that Kantian duties of justice and virtue are distinguished, first
and foremost, by the urgency and primacy of the agency-centered concerns implicated in political

II. A MERCY THAT TEMPERS JUSTICE

With enriched accounts in place, we can explore the way in which mercy, as a settled disposition, might assist rather than thwart the judge in fulfilling his appointed function. If I am right, mercy may increase the judge's ability to take proper account of justice-relevant circumstances while avoiding errors that often undermine judicial justice. Because I want to ensure that this account of the relationship between mercy and justice rests on plausible understandings of both our moral psychology and our legal system, I develop it by appeal to a contemporary legal example. This allows me to explore the kind of interplay between moral psychology and complex legal issues that anyone developing an account of just adjudication must take seriously. It also paves the way for the discussion of efficiency that follows.

A. An Example

In 1997, a young woman named Louise Woodward was tried in Massachusetts for the murder of an infant boy. Specifically, the nineteen-year-old British *au pair* stood accused of shaking the baby in her care, causing serious injuries that led to his death. Woodward's case was the object of substantial public attention, most of it favorable to Woodward. When a jury found her guilty of second-degree murder, for which she faced a mandatory life sentence, the already substantial media attention and public outcry escalated. Reaction to the case was fueled by Woodward's youth and inexperience, by the severity and the inflexibility of the penalty, and by the fact that the jury's options had been limited (albeit on Woodward's own motion) to verdicts of murder or acquittal. Her attorneys had successfully argued that, were manslaughter an option, the jury might well convict her on that ground not on the basis of the evidence, but simply in an attempt to provide some solace to the grieving parents.

Hiller Zobel, the Massachusetts Superior Court judge who presided over the case, ultimately was asked to reduce the jury's verdict in accord with Rule 25(b)(2) of the Massachusetts Rules of Criminal Procedure.[17] This rule allows a judge, after a jury verdict and on the defendant's motion, to revisit a case in whole to determine whether justice requires a lesser verdict and thus a reduced penalty. Zobel's opinion, granting Woodward's motion under 25(b)(2), describes the circumstances surrounding her actions in careful detail. These were characterized, says Zobel, "by confusion, inexperience, frustration, immaturity and some anger.... Frustrated by her inability to quiet the crying child, she was 'a little rough with him,' under

---

contexts. This is why there is, on the Kantian view, so little play in our decisions about justice. Duties of virtue also involve matters important to agency. But unlike the concerns of justice, whose urgency requires that they be addressed through coercive legislation, many of these can be adequately taken into account through traits of character that make way for other considerations both moral and personal. See Sarah Holtman, 2001, "Justice, Welfare, and the Kantian State," *Proceedings of the Ninth International Kant Congress*, Volker Gerhardt, Rolf-Peter Horstmann, and Ralph Schumacher, eds., Berlin: Walter de Gruyter, pp. 152–160. Thus, at least from a Kantian perspective, the distinction between perfect and imperfect duties fits well with the account of mercy as a virtuous disposition and justice as achieved via the application of principles or laws.

[17] Massachusetts Rules of Criminal Procedure, Rule 25(b)(2), 43C M.G.L.A.

circumstances where another, perhaps wiser, person would have sought to restrain the physical impulse."[18] Although this kind of fine attention to circumstance is characteristic of one who is merciful, Zobel's decision makes clear that his grounds for reducing the *Woodward* verdict were – as 25(b)(2) required – ones of justice. Missing from the prosecution's case against Woodward, said Zobel, was the showing of malice that is a legally necessary element of second-degree murder. The fact that her own attorneys successfully had argued to restrict the jury's choices to a verdict of murder or acquittal did not change the fact that she had not been proven guilty of murder. Massachusetts law allowed Zobel to alter the verdict in such circumstances, and that is what he did.[19]

B. The Context

As criticisms make apparent, though, it would oversimplify Zobel's decision to stop here. In particular, some critics contend that, once Woodward's own attorneys had succeeded in limiting the charges the jury could consider, she and the judge were legally bound to abide by that limitation. Woodward gambled and lost.[20] Zobel's departure from the demands of just laws, say the critics, was due to the improper role of mercy. His actions suggest that he went beyond what was owed Woodward by way of justice and improperly allowed the details of her case, colored by pity, to ground a decision to reduce the verdict and thus the penalty. Zobel's own words, spoken as he prepared to announce his decision, confirm the charge: "I do, however, recognize that mercy is not less than appropriate. It is time to bring the judicial part of this extraordinary matter to a compassionate conclusion."[21]

A possible explanation for Zobel's appeal to mercy, of course, is that he is no philosopher. We may carefully distinguish mercy from justice and then hew strictly to that distinction in our choice of words. The average judge does not. This explanation seems all the more likely given the similarities between justice and mercy that our earlier discussion acknowledges. Though Zobel's language lacks philosophical precision, it may nonetheless suggest a noteworthy sensitivity to the relationship between mercy and justice. To see what I have in mind, first remember that it is not always clear what justice, embodied in laws, requires in a given case. A variety of factors can contribute to this uncertainty: evidence may be open to conflicting interpretations; legal standards may seem to pull in different directions; some relevant law may be essentially unjust; or personal bias or societal pressure may threaten judgment.

---

[18] *Commonwealth v. Woodward*, Massachusetts Superior Court, Criminal No. 97-0433 (10 November 1997), p. 8. Memorandum opinion of Judge Zobel retrieved from ABCNEWS.com, and pagination follows that version.

[19] *Woodward*, Criminal No. 97-0433, pp. 6–10.

[20] Some also criticized Zobel for reducing Woodward's sentence to time served. I do not mention that complaint here, because on appeal even the state was unwilling to argue that this was legal error. As Massachusetts's Supreme Judicial Court (SJC) reiterated on appeal, the sentence was evidently in keeping with state guidelines. See *Commonwealth v. Woodward*, 694 N.E. 2d (1998), pp. 1277–1301, 1296–1297.

[21] "Au pair freed after judge reduces verdict," *The Chicago Tribune* (evening), 10 November 1997.

In *Woodward*, Zobel faced each of these concerns. The facts surrounding the infant's death were far from clear.[22] Woodward's successful effort to limit jury options perhaps conflicted with her later appeal to 25(b)(2).[23] The worries that make some condemn mandatory sentencing as unjust certainly were present. More, as press coverage makes abundantly clear, *Woodward* brought strong biases to the fore in many quarters. True, some saw the case as one of regrettable but comprehensible error on Woodward's part and, at most, of a nonculpable misjudgment on the part of the baby's parents. It was, they determined, a tragedy born of human failings. Others saw the case differently and cast the grieving parents, especially the mother, in the role of wrongdoer. For some of these, the wealthy parents were guilty of exploitation; hoping to avoid high child-care costs by employing an inexperienced foreign teenager, they reaped the consequences of their greed. For others, the prime fault lay with the baby's mother, who selfishly pursued her career as a physician rather than fulfill her maternal duties by raising her own child.[24] Thus Zobel made his decision in a public atmosphere hardly conducive to justice.

C. Justice and Mercy

When there are so many concerns that press for attention, the potential is high that one will overlook some relevant fact, make some error in reasoning, fail to give due consideration to a strong, perhaps innovative, argument, or fall prey to personal or pubic bias. Judges like Zobel, who work with a sophisticated legal system and have good training and long experience, are better equipped to avoid such difficulties than the average person. A good legal system serves justice, in part, by assisting decision-makers to separate one question from another and to focus only on evidence or arguments relevant to the issue at hand. Moreover, as we have seen, the best judge is aided in his just application of laws to facts by a compassionate attention to circumstance.

Even with such assistance, though, one issue or concern may cloud thinking about another nonetheless. A judge may view the facts of the case in a way less favorable to the defendant from an underlying sense that she created her own difficulties through legal maneuvering. He may see them more favorably than he otherwise would from a sense that mandatory sentencing laws are deeply unjust (even if the remedy for this injustice does not lie with the judge at the trial level), or from personal bias, or from a desire to court public opinion. In every case, the judge's duty to do justice by applying existing laws, sensitively interpreted, will demand that he try to separate issues and rid himself of inappropriate tendencies toward favor or prejudice. The problem is that the very effort to do this may

---

[22] See Zobel's summary of the evidence in *Woodward*, Criminal No. 97-0433, p. 2.

[23] The SJC ultimately determined that Zobel's decision not to penalize Woodward for her attorney's trial strategy was in keeping with Massachusetts law. Although it held Zobel in error for having refused to instruct the jury on manslaughter in the first place, it found that the prosecution's case sustained no damage, because the jury returned a verdict of second-degree murder. See *Woodward*, 694 N.E. 2d, pp. 1282–1284, 1298.

[24] For a description of the press coverage see Susan Chira, 1998, *A Mother's Place: Rewriting the Rules of Motherhood*, New York: HarperCollins, ch. 1.

make it more difficult for him to see the facts clearly. Bent on rightly interpreting and applying relevant standards, or on thrusting undue favor or prejudice from his mind, the judge may be less sensitive to the facts (or the evidence supporting them) than he otherwise would be. The difficulty of his legal task and his own effort to honor institutional role may, in challenging circumstances, silence or confuse the compassionate context sensitivity that typically joins and informs his commitment to justice.

Yet suppose, as we have reason to suspect, that Zobel is not only a just judge but also a merciful person. He is not only committed to working for justice within the legal system as his prime institutional duty, but is disposed, in his individual capacity, to mercy. He regularly responds to others with a compassion shaped by a principled commitment to appreciating each as a fellow human being faced by challenges to autonomous agency. This disposition highlights some circumstances as grounds for leniency even when justice would permit, if not require, a harsher verdict.

What I want to suggest is that the hallmark of mercy as we have most fully described it – the compassionate attention to circumstances that challenge agency – might assist a judge attempting to see the facts clearly in a complex situation like Zobel's. Where concerns of justice themselves make the judge uncertain of what the circumstances might be, his disposition to mercy might, allowed for awhile to govern his thinking, put those facts or the varying evidence supporting or disconfirming them in sharper focus. Having attained that sharper focus, though, the judge need not act on any conclusion he reaches about the moral value of leniency. Indeed, such inaction is in keeping with the characterization of some duties, mercy among them, as imperfect. Rather, accepting his obligation to do justice and the inappropriateness of a merciful response given his institutional role, the judge might carry this clearer picture of the details, internal and external, back to the interconnected standards of justice that are our law. Here he may ask, now seeing clearly, whether or not malice has been adequately proven. Mercy, I suggest in short, sometimes may season justice not by coming in to alter the just sentence, but by helping us to see justice-relevant considerations more truly or more clearly.[25]

III. A PARALLEL COURSE FOR EFFICIENCY

A. Mercy and Efficiency

Section II appeals to enriched accounts of justice and mercy and explores the possibility that, so enriched, mercy can temper judicial justice without threatening

---

[25] The lesson to take away from our example thus far is one about the complexity of our capacity to render moral judgment. Not only are we capable of recognizing relevant details (including both surrounding circumstances and mental states) and of grasping their actual or potential moral relevance; the principles and attitudes that are our moral character or disposition may work side by side. They allow us, at times, to see the morally appropriate outcome without being fully certain of what reasons support it and to express relevant attitudes and traits of character, as it were, in our hypothetical rather than final judgment.

the demands of institutional role. Our question now is whether we might be able to describe a similar relationship between justice and efficiency. Toward an answer to this question, we will first return to the kind of comparison between mercy and efficiency with which we started.

A natural way to begin this inquiry is by identifying the features of mercy most central to a tempering relationship with justice. These, it seems, are two. First, mercy is not only grounded in moral principle but is essentially tied to moral considerations that are central to appreciation of, and respect for, human agency. Even on a traditional account, the compassionate reduction in penalty that it rec- ommends must be consistent with acknowledging the offender's responsibility for wrongdoing. On our enriched account, any genuinely merciful decision is expressly grounded in a commitment to respect autonomous agency. This commitment both limits cases in which mercy can be appropriate and guides its recommendations. Second, the duty to act mercifully is imperfect. This means that it does not require action in every case to which it applies. I can possess a disposition to mercy, be properly characterized as a merciful person, yet not display mercy in every instance where this would be possible. Moreover, as we have seen, mercy is best understood as a character trait or disposition. Our commitment to mercy evidences itself in a developed capacity for compassion, a sensitivity to morally relevant circum- stances, and a tendency to endorse leniency where together these inform us that moral considerations warrant such an outcome.

It is largely due to these features that a commitment to mercy (a merciful character) can inform and improve justice rather than undermine it, at least where justice is founded on the multifaceted conception of freedom described earlier. Deeply sensitive to the very conditions of humanity that are central to justice, the merciful person has special access to relevant information, a refined capacity for moral evaluation, and the developed ability to set recommendations of leniency aside where these would breach moral demands that underlying commitments show to be more basic.

Whether we can expect to discover a similar compatibility between justice and efficiency will depend partly on whether commitments to efficiency and mercy are similar in these respects. Understood in a colloquial sense, the commitment to efficiency might seem to display some of these features. Thrift, or perhaps better a commitment to conservation, might find its foundations in underlying moral demands that could be shared with justice as generally understood here. We can also conceive thrift as a moral disposition with the accompanying features described.

In the hands of law-and-economics proponents, though, the judge's commit- ment to economic efficiency is not one to thrift, or conservation. Understood as a commitment to wealth maximization via decisions that achieve, or approximate, Pareto optimality, it need not involve any moral foundation at all. One can, of course, propose such a foundation. Some form of consequentialism would be an obvious candidate, a possibility I will take up in the next section. It is important to note, though, that the idea that the recommendations of economic efficiency should be limited or guided by an underlying moral commitment in the legal context is not traditionally part of the theory. Proponents sometimes argue that efficiency as they conceive it serves consequentialist aims, but they seldom look to these for guidance in reshaping the conception of efficiency.[26] More important, as we will see in the next section, a commitment to efficiency is at best loosely tied to the kinds of agency considerations central to justice as we are now conceiving it.

Second, the person (in particular the judge) who is committed to efficiency on the law-and-economics model is not well conceived as possessed of an imperfect duty that gives way, or could be temporarily set aside, when fundamental moral considerations pull in another direction. More, unlike mercy, economic efficiency is not conceived by proponents as first and foremost a disposition of individuals to be assessed through examination of actions over time. It is a feature of institutions, laws, and the outcomes of particular cases, which we honor, or fail to honor, in each instance of potential application. Further, even the judge who is committed to economic efficiency is not a person possessed of a special trait of character. He is committed to a principle to be consciously applied (or not) to the case at hand.

B. Moral Foundations – Possibilities and Problems

Toward a parallel with mercy, one might posit moral foundations for economic efficiency. Again, some form of consequentialism is the most obvious possibility here. Many philosophers have noted, though, that the conception of persons and behavior central to the economic model is too simple to capture the nature of ourselves and our moral relationships, even as most consequentialists conceive these.[27] Whatever the particular brand of that theory, the utilitarian, for example, neither reduces value to what one would pay, nor attempts to cast all questions of allocation in terms of economic transactions. There is ample space within that theory to acknowledge that assessing and comparing levels of happiness or satisfaction may require means far more complex than any account of wealth-maximizing transactions. The economic model, applied to law in general, and to judicial decisions in particular, could at most provide a highly imperfect method for achieving underlying consequentialist aims. We might be justified in appealing

---

[26] On the general issue of providing normative justification for the economic approach see Jules Coleman, 1988, "Efficiency, Utility, and Wealth-Maximization," in *Markets, Morals, and the Law*, New York: Cambridge University Press, pp. 93–132.

[27] Martha Nussbaum addresses the oversimplifications of the contemporary law-and-economics approach generally and points out the greater sophistication both of post-Benthamite utilitarianism and of much contemporary economic analysis; see her 1997, "Flawed Foundations: The Philosophical Critique of (a Particular Type of) Economics," *University of Chicago Law Review*, 64, pp. 1197–1214. She argues that complicating its conceptions of persons, utility, preference, and the like would render economic analysis of law more realistic and more useful. For an excellent discussion of the purpose, usefulness, and limitations of idealized economic models that simplify our conception of persons in various ways, see Amartya Sen, 1977, "Rational Fools," *Philosophy and Public Affairs*, 6, pp. 317–344. I do not intend to question, here, the value of idealization of the sort common in economics; I mean to emphasize the limitations of the highly simplistic model that characterizes the law-and-economics approach. To the extent that that model is made less simplistic, it might, as Nussbaum suggests, become more useful and more compatible with justice. How far the model could be taken in this direction, when it could be useful, and whether some changes might best be thought of as proposing a new descriptive and normative legal theory are questions I do not address here.

to it at some times and for some purposes. But the appeal would always be subject to scrutiny and to revision or abandonment in favor of another course of action.

If we further enrich our understanding of human moral psychology and moral requirement, the limitations of the economic model only become more evident. The notion that there are matters whose value cannot be captured in terms of any form of comparison, much less in the narrow context of economic exchange, extends over a wide variety of moral theories.[28] Accounts of justice that have their foundations in such theories typically capture the values in question via conceptions of right and obligation to which any notion of transaction or exchange is antithetical. On these accounts, a legal theory that assesses fundamental rights by asking about willing exchange fails to appreciate what is at issue. To take classic examples, whether and to what extent I have a right of free thought or expression cannot be determined by considering whether I would exchange the right so defined for some alternative.[29] To treat a person justly is to respect such rights. They are not the proper subjects of transaction or exchange.

Of course, if we understand justice (and our legal system) to protect and promote the multifaceted conceptions of freedom and agency described in section II, the failing of the economic model will be most significant of all. Some level of wealth is necessary to realize agency so conceived. At most, though, wealth is a means to the ends of liberty, equality, and autonomy. Significantly (and notoriously), it is a means that can undermine those ends if not carefully managed and divided among citizens. From this perspective the law-and-economics model is inadequate not only because it conceives of value too narrowly, or even because it misconceives of basic moral and legal elements like individual rights. Beyond these failings, it misunderstands what is central to personhood, and so to citizenship and to the justice of laws and institutions. Law and economics supposes this to be wealth, or perhaps better the satisfaction of preferences as expressed by my willingness to buy and sell, rather than my liberty to choose and pursue those preferences, my autonomous participation in the choices that form and affect my life, and the state's equal regard for me and my fellow citizens.[30]

The point here is not to suggest that efficiency, as conceived on the law-and-economics model, can be intimately joined with justice only on some accounts. It is to offer reasons to think it unsuited to such a position. Efficiency so conceived lacks the rich conceptions of persons, capacities, and interests that are central to a moral disposition like mercy. Because a merciful disposition shares these conceptions with justice and increases our sensitivity to them, it enhances our ability to recognize justice-relevant considerations and to appreciate their implications. Efficiency, as conceived by law-and-economics proponents, grossly oversimplifies these conceptions. So far from improving justice by increasing our sensitivity to,

---

[28] Among these, of course, are moral and political theories put forward by Aquinas, Kant, and Locke, and more contemporary work that takes any of these as its foundation.

[29] On the inability of the economic approach to account for fundamental aspects of the criminal law see Jules Coleman, 1988, "Crimes, Kickers, and Transaction Structures," in *Markets, Morals, and the Law*, pp. 153–165, especially pp. 161–165.

[30] For one example see Richard Posner, 1979, "Utilitarianism, Economics, and Legal Theory," *Journal of Legal Studies*, 8, pp. 103–140. For commentary see Coleman, "Efficiency, Utility, and Maximization."

and appreciation of, relevant concerns, such a commitment to efficiency is likely
to lead us to endorse what justice cannot countenance. The conceptions of persons
and values with which the economic model is equipped are too limited to accommodate even those moral theories with which it arguably has most in common,
and too limited to allow it a tempering relationship with justice.

C. Woodward Again

To ground these observations in something more concrete, I return briefly to
Woodward. The role of mercy in that decision, I suggested, was to keep Judge Zobel
alert to those facts relevant to a just decision. In particular, in order to fulfill his
institutional role, Zobel was required to assess whether the prosecution had proven
that Woodward acted with malice in the baby's death. Absent such a showing, she
lacked the *mens rea* legally required for second-degree murder.

In characterizing Zobel's decision process, and the role mercy might have played
within it, we focused on the multifaceted nature of our commitments of justice
and on the consequent complexity of just decision making. *Woodward* brought to
the fore a panoply of justice-related concerns: the centrality of state of mind to
criminal responsibility; the need for proportionality between the seriousness of a
crime and the severity of the corresponding penalty; the irrelevance of personal or
social bias to a criminal verdict; and the inappropriateness of manipulating legal
procedures to suit one's purposes.

Even if we posit no rich or consistent explanation of the way in which each of these
implicates justice, we can recognize that considerations of efficiency are unlikely
to explain them all. Criminal decisions that ignore *mens rea* or are infected with
bias may be unlikely to identify those who can be discouraged from further crime
through punishment. Thus they may provide little or no reduction in the costs that
criminal activity imposes on citizens and society. The extent to which this is true,
though, is uncertain. More importantly, lack of savings hardly explains the strength
or character of these demands. Zobel (and Massachusetts's Supreme Judicial Court)
deemed the demand that *mens rea* be established clearly to override other concerns
(including that involving rule manipulation, which certainly implicates efficiency).
The fiercest criticism of Zobel concerned the possibility that he was biased against
the parents and in favor of Woodward, a criticism expressed with an outrage that
efficiency does not explain and could not be expected to answer. In short, to suggest
that efficiency concerns underlie these features of justice is revisionist at best.

Our consideration of Zobel's decision, and of the role mercy played within it,
also reveals much about the variety and complexity of human capacities, our moral
psychology foremost. It suggests not only that we can take account of much more
in the realm of persons and values than law and economics recommends, but that
we have strong reason to do so. What we value and what we can achieve go far
beyond anything the transaction-based model recognizes, protects, or encourages.
We need not embrace the freedom-based model I suggested, in either its original or
its enriched version. We have every reason, though, to support a basis for laws and
legal decisions that approaches a realistic picture of human capacities and values
more nearly than the gross simplicity of the economic model possibly could.

CONCLUSION

I began with the observation that mercy and efficiency share a questionable relationship with justice. More specifically, neither can claim an uncontroversial place among the judicial virtues. What I hope now to have shown is not so much that mercy deserves such a place whereas efficiency does not. It is, rather, the deeper point that the economic model falls far short in its understanding of laws and persons and of the aspirations we realistically can have for them. Although there surely is a place for efficiency concerns in a good legal system, and in the decisions its judges render, these cannot properly lead us in our understanding and development of our laws or ourselves. They must instead be led by conceptions that are richer and more true.

8 Bounded Rationality and Legal Scholarship

MATTHEW D. ADLER

Any normative framework that has the structure of recommending that decision-makers advance certain goals, and that they do so in accordance with decision theory (DT), runs into the problem of bounded rationality. The problem is how to refine DT so as to be usable by a bounded decision-maker – someone with limited cognitive resources, for whom the full evaluation of her choices is impossible or at least very expensive.

This chapter has two aims. The first, pursued in sections I and II, is to discuss the problem of bounded rationality in general terms. The second, pursued in section III, is to show why the problem creates a gap at the foundations of legal scholarship. In *Fairness versus Welfare*, Louis Kaplow and Steven Shavell propose a welfarist methodology for legal scholarship.[1] They may be wrong to think that morality is wholly welfarist, but a normative program that says that social welfare is one of a plurality of criteria by which legal scholars should evaluate laws and policies is plausible. But we have no good normative handle on how legal scholars who are bounded in their cognitive abilities should implement a welfarist or pluralistic program.

I. THE PROBLEM OF BOUNDED RATIONALITY

The term "bounded rationality" is sometimes used by psychologists to describe or explain certain decision-making processes without endorsing or criticizing them. By contrast, the problem of bounded rationality that I discuss in this chapter is *normative*. I am interested in the problem that human cognitive limits create for our attempts to flesh out normative frameworks.

A. Instrumentalist Normative Frameworks and Decision Theory

A normative framework furnishes recommendations for some class of decision-makers. Some normative frameworks furnish *moral* recommendations, others

[1] Louis Kaplow and Steven Shavell, 2002, *Fairness versus Welfare*, Cambridge, MA: Harvard University Press; henceforth *FW*.

Thanks to Christoph Engel, Jeff Rachlinski, Adrian Vermeule, and Mark White for comments.

nonmoral recommendations (for example, recommendations concerning what the decision-maker should do in light of her interests). In either event, let us call a normative framework *instrumentalist* if it is oriented toward goals.[2] One such framework is *Humeanism*, which recommends to each individual that she pursue whatever preferences she happens to have. Another is *welfarism*, a moral framework, which recommends that decision-makers promote the goal of social welfare.

An instrumentalist normative framework will not be very helpful unless it furnishes procedural norms for the decision-makers within its scope, explaining how they should go about implementing the stipulated goals. Call these procedural norms the *procedural component* of the normative theory. The argument I will be developing in the next two sections of the chapter is this: *human cognitive limitations pose serious difficulties for using DT as the procedural component for an instrumentalist normative framework.*

Understood as a set of procedural norms, DT enjoins the decision-maker to think of any choice situation at some time t as an outcome set $O = \{o_1, o_2, \ldots\}$, an action set $A = \{a_1, a_2, \ldots\}$, and a state set $S = \{s_1, s_2, \ldots\}$.[3] An outcome is a normatively relevant description of some way the world might be – a description in terms of the goals of the normative theory that DT is fleshing out. Equivalently, an outcome is a proposition or a set of possible worlds. Actions are what the decision-maker can do at t.

States, like outcomes, are propositions. But, in a well-framed description of a choice situation, states are causally independent of actions – it should not be possible for an action to cause a state[4] – and so each state is most naturally thought of as a possible past history of the world, together with causal laws. Further, in a well-framed choice situation, the states are mutually exclusive and collectively exhaustive. The decision-maker does not know which state is the true one – but one must be, only one can be, and the decision-maker knows that. Finally, there are necessary connections among the states, the actions, and the outcomes, which again the decision-maker knows. The conjunction of a state and an action entails one and only one outcome in the outcome set (see Figure 8.1).[5]

DT also enjoins the decision-maker to follow certain norms in ranking outcomes and actions. To begin, the decision-maker is enjoined to have a *complete* and

[2] What exactly this means is a complicated question. Within moral theory, that question has been extensively discussed with reference to the distinction between consequentialist and nonconsequentialist moral frameworks. For purposes of this chapter, I do not need to take a firm stand on the question. The crucial point is that some frameworks, such as Humeanism, or welfarism, or consequentialist moral frameworks more generally, *are* thus oriented and therefore naturally employ DT as their procedural component – in turn leading to the problem of bounded rationality.

[3] In my discussion of DT, I have relied heavily upon James M. Joyce, 1999, *The Foundations of Causal Decision Theory*, Cambridge: Cambridge University Press.

[4] See Joyce, *The Foundations of Causal Decision Theory*; James M. Joyce and Allan Gibbard, 1998, "Causal Decision Theory," in Salvador Barbera et al., eds., *Handbook of Utility Theory*, vol. 1, Dordrecht: Kluwer, pp. 627–666.

[5] This formulation assumes that the decision-maker gives zero probability to the possibility of indeterministic causal laws. Refining DT for the possibility of indeterminism raises complicated issues that I cannot consider here. See David Lewis, 1981, "Causal Decision Theory," *Australasian Journal of Philosophy*, 69, pp. 5–30. But it is hard to see why DT, thus refined, would not confront problems of bounded rationality similar to those discussed in this chapter.

States

		s_1	s_2	s_3	...
	a_1	$o(a_1, s_1)$	$o(a_1, s_2)$	$o(a_1, s_3)$	
Actions	a_2	$o(a_2, s_1)$	$o(a_2, s_2)$	$o(a_2, s_3)$	
	a_3	$o(a_3, s_1)$	$o(a_3, s_2)$	$o(a_3, s_3)$	
	...				

Figure 8.1. How DT conceptualizes a choice situation. *Note:* $o(a_i, s_j)$ is the outcome in the outcome set **O** that would result if action a_i were performed in state s_j.

transitive ranking of the outcomes. Another such norm is *consequentialism*: if, in each state, two actions produce the very same outcome, then the decision-maker should be indifferent between the two actions. Another is *dominance*: if one action produces no worse outcomes than a second action in all states, and better outcomes in some, then the first action must be ranked better.[6] Yet another is *independence*. Imagine that two actions produce the same outcome o^* in state s', the same outcome o^{**} in state s'', and so forth, for a collection of states $\{s', s'', \ldots\}$ which is a subset of the state set **S**. Then the independence norm requires that a second pair of actions that is identical to the first pair except that both actions in the second pair produce $o+$ rather than o^* in s', $o++$ rather than o^{**} in s'', and so forth, should be ranked the same way as the first pair.

DT is sometimes offered, not as a set of procedural norms, but as a set of substantive criteria for normatively appropriate choice.[7] In this guise, the theory takes an "as if" form; it is agnostic about the procedure the decision-maker actually uses, and instead says that – whatever that procedure might be – he should pick the choices that he would have selected, had he used DT as his procedure.

I do not know whether DT, in its substantive version, runs afoul of human cognitive limits. But, as already stated, any normative framework is incomplete if it lacks a procedural component. How helpful will it be to state some goal for some agent, but not tell her what to do to implement the goal? And DT, in its procedural form, clearly does run afoul of bounded rationality, as I will show in a moment.

But why even think, then, of using DT as the procedural component of a normative framework? The answer is that DT is far and away the best-developed account of rational choice. DT meshes particularly well with instrumentalist normative frameworks. A goal is just a norm for identifying a set of outcomes that matter and ordering its elements. DT then tells the agent how to orient his choices toward these outcomes, given uncertainty, in a plausible way: by thinking systematically about how his possible actions and possible prior states might interact to cause different outcomes.

---

[6] More precisely, some of the states in which the first action produces better outcomes must be *nonnull*, that is, have positive probability.

[7] See Frederic Laville, 2000, "Foundations of Procedural Rationality: Cognitive Limits and Decision Processes," *Economics and Philosophy*, 16, pp. 117–138.

In addition, Leonard Savage showed that the choices of a decision-maker who satisfies DT's norms (and several other more technical axioms) can be represented as maximizing the expectation of a utility function.[8] There is some probability function assigning numerical probabilities to states, and some utility function assigning numerical utilities to outcomes, such that the decision-maker's ranking of actions corresponds to their expected utility (where the expected utility of an action is the sum of the utilities of its possible outcomes, each utility discounted by the probability of the state that, together with the action, produces that outcome). Reciprocally, if the decision-maker consciously maximizes the expectation of a utility function, then she automatically satisfies the axioms of DT. So it is not too much of an exaggeration to say that DT and expected-utility theory are one and the same account of rational choice.

B. DT and the Specification of Outcomes, Actions, and States

What, then, is the problem of bounded rationality for DT? Humans are cognitively limited, in various ways. They have limited memories and computational abilities (even when aided by computers), make logical and mathematical errors, and so forth. But how does this implicate the framework for decision making set forth by DT?

The key difficulty, as I see it, has to do with the *specification* of outcomes, actions, and states. The sets of outcomes, actions, and states can be *fully specified* or *incompletely specified*. Start with outcomes: Remember that an outcome is a proposition or set of possible worlds. An outcome is fully specified, for purposes of some instrumentalist normative framework, if any two worlds within the outcome are equally good in terms of the goals of that framework. In other words, a fully specified outcome provides a description of what might occur that is sufficiently complete that nothing of relevance to the framework is left out.

Consider, for example, a Humean framework that tells decision-makers to maximize their preferences. Imagine that the decision-maker, Jim, cares only about his annual income and the number of friends he has each year. Then, if a given outcome *o* describes Jim's annual income in each year that he is alive, it is incompletely specified. If it describes his annual income and the number of his friends each year, it is fully specified.

A fully specified outcome set is a set of mutually exclusive and collectively exhaustive outcomes, each of which is fully specified. A fully specified action set consists of every possible action the decision-maker could undertake at the time of choice. A fully specified state set consists of states that are (again) mutually exclusive and collectively exhaustive, and are sufficiently well described to do what state sets are supposed to do in DT: Each action, together with a state, entails one and only one outcome in the outcome set.

An unbounded decision-maker can produce a fully specified outcome, action, and state set instantly and at zero cost (she can do so *internally* without mental

---

[8] For an accessible discussion, see David M. Kreps, 1988, *Notes on the Theory of Choice*, Boulder and London: Westview Press.

strain and without paying for expensive computers and software). DT is therefore most plausibly understood as providing the following specification norm for an unbounded decision-maker: Use a fully specified outcome, action, and state set. Why is this so? Consider, first, the unbounded decision-maker who uses an incompletely specified action set. In other words, she considers some of the actions that she might perform at this moment, but not all of them. Is this not arbitrary? The benefits of adding an action to the set of actions she already considers is that the new action might be preferable to those she already considers; the costs (given her unbounded abilities) are nil. So why not consider it?

Consider, next, the unbounded decision-maker who uses a fully specified action set, but an incompletely specified outcome set. Where outcomes are incompletely specified, the basic norms of DT lose their intuitive plausibility. I will show why this is so, using the norm of consequentialism; a similar analysis applies to the other basic norms.

Let us continue with the example of Jim. O' is an incompletely specified outcome set, where outcomes are described just in terms of Jim's income, not his friends. Imagine that Jim reasons in terms of this outcome set; identifies a matching state set (sufficiently detailed to determine which member of O' would result for every action he might perform at present); and ascertains that there are two actions, a and $a+$, that result in the same member of O' in each state. In s_1, a results in o^*, and $a+$ also results in o^*; in s_2, a results in o^{**}, and $a+$ also results in o^{**}; and so forth for every state. The norm of consequentialism tells Jim to be indifferent between a and $a+$. But why should he be? After all, it is possible that, in some states, a leads to a different number of friends for Jim than $a+$. And Jim cares about the size of his group of friends, not just his annual income. So why should Jim consider a and $a+$ as equally good, given that it is costless for him to replace O' with a fully specified set O whose members specify what happens along both the income and the friendship dimensions, and to think about his choice in terms of that outcome set?

Consider, finally, an unbounded decision-maker who uses a fully specified action and outcome set, but an incompletely specified state set. This could mean two things. First, it might mean that the state set is insufficiently rich for a conjunction of an action and a state to always entail one and only one outcome in the outcome set. A choice situation, thus framed, is one in which the decision-maker lacks relevant information about his choice – and, in the case of the unbounded decision-maker, this is a pointless gap, one that he could costlessly rectify through a more detailed consideration of possible prior histories of the world together with causal laws.[9] Second, an incompletely specified state set might not be exhaustive. Although each member of the action set, together with each member of the state set, leads to some determinate member of the outcome set, there is some possible state that the decision-maker ignores. Were he to consider that state, he might find that he accords it nonzero probability, and that adding it to the analysis changes his evaluation of the possible actions. So why not consider it?

---

[9] Again, this assumes that the decision-maker gives zero credence to the possibility of indeterminism; see the discussion in note 5.

C. Specification and Bounded Decision-Makers

It is therefore quite straightforward to determine the content of DT's specification norm in the case of unbounded decision-makers: use fully specified outcome, action, and state sets. The difficulty arises once we allow that it may be costly or plain impossible for the decision-maker to produce a fully specified outcome, action, and state set. What specification norm should DT contain for this sort of decision-maker – a bounded one? The specification norm cannot be to use fully specified outcome, action, and state sets. More precisely, given any instrumentalist normative framework with a sufficiently rich goal to generate a very large set of fully specified outcomes, DT coupled with a full-specification norm will be a highly implausible candidate to be the procedural component of this framework.

Consider the example of welfarism. For purposes of the general discussion of bounded rationality, this is simply one example of a normative framework that cannot be plausibly fleshed out as advising decision-makers to use fully specified outcome, action, and state sets. For purposes of the methodology of legal scholarship, as we shall see in section III, this is a key example.

Welfarism is really a family of moral theories, which tell the decision-maker to aim at some mix of overall well-being and the equitable distribution of well-being.[10] The most plausible variants of welfarism understand individual well-being as the attainment of various objective goods or (what is essentially the same thing) as the attainment of those things everyone with full information would converge in self-interestedly preferring. The most plausible variants of welfarism adopt an impartiality constraint: everyone's well-being matters equally, or at least the well-being of everyone within a large population of interest does (all members of the society, for example). In characterizing outcomes, we should not limit ourselves to the well-being of a single dictator or members of a small oligarchy, and if two outcomes differ only with respect to the identity (proper names) of individuals attaining particular welfare levels, they should be seen as equally good.

Consider DT as the procedural component of welfarism with an impartiality constraint and a reasonably extensive list of objective goods. Imagine, for example, a U.S. governmental official, June, who attends to the well-being of all current and future U.S. citizens and considers the following goods: longevity, consumption, health, happiness, and social relations. June presides over a pollution control agency and, at the present moment, has the power to regulate some toxin.

A fully specified outcome set O, for June, would be such that each o_i in this set consists of a list of individuals who are U.S. citizens now or in the future; a consumption history for each individual, specifying what goods she consumes for every moment she is alive; a health history for each individual, specifying her health state for every moment she is alive; a happiness history, specifying her affective states for every moment she is alive; and a social history, specifying how

[10] See, for example, Matthew D. Adler and Chris William Sanchirico, 2006, "Inequality and Uncertainty: Theory and Legal Applications," *University of Pennsylvania Law Review*, 155, pp. 279–377; Matthew D. Adler and Eric A. Posner, 2006, *New Foundations of Cost–Benefit Analysis*, Cambridge, MA: Harvard University Press, pp. 25–61.

many friends she has at each moment, what her social status is, and so forth. A fully specified action set **A**, for June, would consist of every possible regulation she might issue to limit the toxin. The outcome (in **O**) produced by a given regulation would depend on the causal laws of toxicology (which determine the direct impacts of the toxin on health and longevity); the laws of economics (which determine how firms, consumers, and workers will react to a given regulation, thereby affecting consumption and other items); and the laws of psychology and sociology (which determine how an individual's health, longevity, and consumption will influence her affective states, and how the distribution of consumption and other items affects social relations). Thus, each state will consist of a combination of a particular toxicological model, economic model, psychological model, and sociological model, plus a specification of prior facts relevant to all the models, sufficiently detailed to lead determinately to one member of **O** for each member of the action set.

This level of specification massively exceeds the detail about possible regulations, outcomes, and causal models currently employed by regulators in even the largest and most deliberate rulemakings.[11] I suggest that it would be normatively unwarranted for June to attempt to follow a full-specification norm in implementing her welfarist goals. The effort might never end and, if it did, would surely consume large amounts of time and resources. So what *is* the normatively appropriate procedure for June to follow? That, as I see it, is the question of bounded rationality, to which DT currently offers no good answer.

To be clear, I do not mean to suggest that the problem of providing a procedural norm that bounded decision-makers should follow in implementing an instrumentalist normative framework is unanswerable. *Cognitivists* believe that there are normative truths and facts; *noncognitivists* deny this, and think that normativity is at bottom just a matter of what norms we wish to endorse. Although my sympathies are cognitivist, this chapter can remain neutral on the issue, because the problem of bounded rationality arises for both cognitivists and noncognitivists. The cognitivist must decide which normative framework she believes to be correct and, within that framework, which procedural component she believes to be correct, given humans' cognitive limitations. The noncognitivist must decide which normative framework she wishes to endorse and, within that framework, which procedural component she wishes to endorse.

How do the cognitivist and noncognitivist settle these issues? Both can, I think, avail themselves of John Rawls's method of *reflective equilibrium*. We should decide what normative framework we believe is correct (the cognitivist spin), or what normative framework we wish to endorse (the noncognitivist spin), by striving for an internally coherent framework that respects (as much as possible) both our pre-equilibrium beliefs regarding general normative principles or our pre-equilibrium endorsements of such principles, and our pre-equilibrium intuitions about particular cases. "Solving" the problem of bounded rationality, for a given

---

[11] For a discussion of the ways in which cost–benefit analysis and other regulatory decision procedures need to be – and, in practice, are – structured to be sensitive to decision costs and delay costs, see Adler and Posner, *New Foundations of Cost–Benefit Analysis*, pp. 62–100.

instrumentalist framework, means modifying DT as a procedural norm, or perhaps replacing it with an entirely different kind of norm, so that the framework now has a procedural component that is acceptable in reflective equilibrium.

Such a solution may well exist; I do not claim otherwise. Rather, my claim is that the scholarly literature on decision making has not yet arrived at a solution, or even come close. Let us now survey current candidate solutions and see where they fall short.

II. SOLUTIONS TO THE PROBLEM OF BOUNDED RATIONALITY?

A. Uncertainty versus Bounded Rationality

Uncertainty and bounded rationality are distinct problems. Although DT has solved the problem of providing attractive norms for choice where the only obstacle to good choice is uncertainty, these features of the view give us zero traction in addressing bounded rationality.

To see the distinction between uncertainty and bounded rationality, observe that the decision-maker with limitless ability to conceptualize actions, states, and outcomes might be uncertain which state obtains. Indeed, the central contribution of DT is to help us see what the procedural component of an instrumentalist normative framework appropriate for *partly* ideal agents – ideal in the sense of having limitless mental abilities, nonideal in the sense of being nonomniscient – would consist of. In the static case, this decision-maker has a fully specified outcome set, a complete and transitive ranking of outcomes, and a fully specified action set. But she does not know which outcome would, in fact, result from a given action. So she does just what DT suggests. She asks herself: How might the history of the world, including causal laws, have proceeded up to this point? Which outcome would each action map onto, given each such state? And how strongly do I believe in the various states?

In the dynamic case, this unbounded but nonomniscient decision-maker is considering securing more information about the states – at some cost. For this case, one well-established aspect of DT – *value-of-information* (VOI) *analysis* – comes into play.[12] The basic idea is that the decision-maker can use his outcome set and an appropriately enriched state set[13] to evaluate information-seeking actions as much as other sorts of actions. To see the basic idea in a simple case (shown in Figure 8.2), imagine that the outcome set has four outcomes, one with utility L (low), one with utility H (high), one with utility $L-K$, one with utility $H-K$. There are two ordinary actions, a_1 and a_2, that the decision-maker, Phil, can take: In the first state, s_1, a_1 leads to the outcome with utility H and a_2 leads to the outcome with utility L. In the second state, s_2, it is a_2 that produces the H-utility

---

[12] On VOI, see, for example, Robert L. Winkler, 2003, *An Introduction to Bayesian Inference and Decision*, 2nd ed., Gainesville: Probabilistic Publishing, pp. 267–350; Jack Hirshleifer and John G. Riley, 1992, *The Analytics of Uncertainty and Information*, Cambridge: Cambridge University Press, pp. 167–208.

[13] That is, a state set sufficiently specified so that each state combined with each experiment entails one and only one outcome in the outcome set.

States

	s_1 and signal X if experiment	s_1 and signal Y if experiment	s_2 and signal X if experiment	s_2 and signal Y if experiment	**Expected Utility**
	$P = .54$	$P = .06$	$P = .04$	$P = .36$	
Actions					
a_1	utility H	utility H	utility L	utility L	$.6H + .4L$
a_2	utility L	utility L	utility H	utility H	$.6L + .4H$
a_3	utility $H{-}K$	utility $L{-}K$	utility $L{-}K$	utility $H{-}K$	$[.9H + .1L] - K$

Phil attaches utility to a_3 as follows. He reasons that, if he were to undertake the experiment and the true state of the world is s_1 with a propensity to send signal X, he would receive signal X. He would at that point update his probabilities in Bayesian fashion and ascribe probability $0.54/0.58$ to s_1 with a propensity to send X, 0 to s_1 with a propensity to send Y, $0.04/0.58$ to s_2 with a propensity to send X, and 0 to s_2 with a propensity to send Y. With these new probabilities, he would choose action a_1, which leads to utility $H{-}K$ in state s_1 with a propensity to send X. Similar reasoning allows him to attach utilities to a_3 in the other three states.

Figure 8.2. Value-of-information (VOI) analysis.

outcome and a_1 that produces the L-utility outcome. Phil gives the first state a probability of 0.6 and the second a probability of 0.4. There is an experiment Phil can undertake to get better information about which state obtains, but at some fixed cost K in utility. The experiment is action a_3. Phil believes that if s_1 obtains, the experiment sends signal X with probability 0.9 and Y with probability 0.1. If s_2 obtains, the experiment sends signal Y with probability 0.9 and X with probability 0.1. In effect, there are four states: s_1 with a propensity to send signal X, s_1 with a propensity to send signal Y, s_2 with a propensity to send signal X, and s_2 with a propensity to send signal Y. The probabilities of these states are, respectively, 0.54, 0.06, 0.04, and 0.36. This enriched state set (together with the assumption that Phil would respond to the experiment by updating his beliefs about the states in a Bayesian fashion, and then choose a_1 or a_2 using these updated beliefs) suffices to produce a determinate outcome in the outcome set for each of the three actions, that is, for the two ordinary actions and the experiment. If K is sufficiently small and the difference between H and L sufficiently large, the experiment is worth undertaking – otherwise not.

VOI is a very potent tool, but it simply does not address the problem of specification. It takes as given an outcome set; takes as given an action set, one that includes some experiments and other information-gathering measures; and gives guidance in thinking through how a particular information-gathering measure might be understood (like an ordinary action) as a distribution across different elements of the outcome set, producing different outcomes in different states.

Nor does it seem fruitful to try to adapt VOI for the task of determining optimal specification. Consider the problem of optimally specifying an outcome set. Imagine starting with some underspecified set of outcomes **O**. Among the actions that the decision-maker could take at t are not only ordinary actions a_1, a_2, and so forth, but also the deliberative action d of thinking about these ordinary actions using a more fully specified outcome set O'. So we might imagine a value-of-specification analysis that marries O with this expanded action set – in other words, it predicts the effects of ordinary actions $\{a_1, a_2, \ldots\}$ *and* the deliberative action d in the initial outcome set O.

We would need to enrich the state set so that each state, combined with d, produces one and only one outcome in O. One way to do that is to combine the initial state set $\{s_1, s_2, \ldots\}$, sufficient for determining the outcomes in O of the ordinary actions, with statements about what would occur if the decision-maker were to think about the ordinary actions with a more refined outcome set O'. So the state set becomes something like $\{s_1$, and if I were to use outcome set O' in choosing among the ordinary actions, I would pick a_1; s_1, and if I were to use outcome set O' in choosing among the ordinary actions, I would pick $a_2; \ldots; s_2$, and if I were to use outcome set O' in choosing among the ordinary actions, I would pick a_1; s_2, and if I were to use outcome set O' in choosing among the ordinary actions, I would pick $a_2 \ldots\}$. And the decision matrix now looks like Figure 8.3.

Note that this device allows the decision-maker to consider undertaking action d and using a more refined outcome set, without actually incurring the costs of doing d. (If she decides just to undertake one of the ordinary actions $\{a_1, a_2, \ldots\}$ rather than doing d, she never actually chooses among the ordinary actions using the more refined outcome set.) So this seems like a promising start to the problem of analyzing the value of refining an outcome set.

But there is a problem: from an initial outcome set O, there may be many different refinements. Consider our decision-maker June, who cares about individuals' well-being, which is understood to depend on their longevity and moment-to-moment consumption sequences, health sequences, happiness sequences, and social relations. She starts with an outcome set where each outcome specifies individuals' longevity and annual consumption. She could undertake action d_1, which means using a refined outcome set that specifies individuals' moment-to-moment (rather than annual) consumption; or do d_2 and use a different refined set that specifies individuals' annual consumption and average annual health; or do d_3 and use yet a different refined set that specifies individuals' moment-to-moment consumption and moment-to-moment happiness; and so forth. There are a very large number of such d_i. Considering all of them will be costly for the bounded decision-maker; but there is nothing in the VOI framework, either directly or by analogy, that suggests how to limit the set of deliberative actions $\{d_1, d_2, \ldots\}$ that the decision-maker considers.

A similar point is that the decision-maker can start with different outcome sets. June might start with ordinary actions $\{a_1, a_2, \ldots\}$ and a initial outcome set O that specifies individuals' consumption, and from that starting point think about the outcomes in O of deliberative actions that pick among the ordinary actions using some refinement of O. Or June might start with ordinary actions $\{a_1, a_2, \ldots\}$ and an initial outcome set O^* that specifies individuals' happiness, and from *that* starting point think about the outcomes in O^* of deliberative actions that pick among the ordinary actions using some refinement of O^*. Again, there is nothing in VOI, directly or by analogy, that helps guide June in determining which outcome set she should start with.

Original choice situation, with ordinary actions

States

	s_1	s_2
Actions		
a_1	o	$o*$
a_2	$o**$	$o***$
...		

New choice situation, with ordinary actions plus deliberative action d of refining outcome set from $\boldsymbol{O}$ to $\boldsymbol{O'}$

States

	s_1 and if I were to use $\boldsymbol{O'}$ to choose among $\{a_1, a_2, ...\}$, I would pick a_1	s_1 and if I were to use $\boldsymbol{O'}$ to choose among $\{a_1, a_2, ...\}$, I would pick a_2	...	s_2 and if I were to use $\boldsymbol{O'}$ to choose among $\{a_1, a_2, ...\}$, I would pick a_1	s_2 and if I were to use $\boldsymbol{O'}$ to choose among $\{a_1, a_2, ...\}$, I would pick a_2	...
Actions						
a_1	o	o		$o*$	$o*$	
a_2	$o**$	$o**$		$o***$	$o***$	
...						
d	$o+$	$o++$		$o+++$	$o++++$	

Every outcome in this matrix is an outcome in the original outcome set $\boldsymbol{O}$. Note that $o+$ and o need not be the same outcome. That is, the outcome in $\boldsymbol{O}$ of simply picking a_1 (outcome o) need not be the same as the outcome in $\boldsymbol{O}$ of picking a_1 after deliberating among the ordinary actions using a refined outcome set $\boldsymbol{O'}$ (outcome $o+$). Outcome $o+$ may well reflect the increased deliberational expenses that flow from choosing d rather than one of the ordinary actions. Similarly, $o++$ need not be the same outcome in $\boldsymbol{O}$ as $o**$, $o+++$ need not be the same outcome as $o*$, and so on.

Figure 8.3. "Value of Specification" analysis?

B. Optimal Search

Economists since George Stigler have entertained the notion of optimal search. Consider the individual who wants to buy a good, has found some willing sellers with various asking prices, and is trying to decide whether to look for a seller with a lower asking price, given that the costs of searching are positive. Stigler's suggestion is that, in this sort of case, the rational individual searches only if doing so increases expected utility – given expected search costs, the probability of finding a seller with a lower asking price, and the expected benefit of doing so.[14]

The optimal-search notion seems sensible enough in the case of a decision-maker with zero analytic costs but positive costs of searching in the sense of

[14] See George J. Stigler, 1961, "The Economics of Information," *Journal of Political Economy*, 69, pp. 213–225.

States

	s_1 and if I were to add x_1 to my choice set, I would choose a_1	s_1 and if I were to add x_1 to my choice set, I would choose a_2	...	s_1 and if I were to add x_1 to my choice set, I would choose x_1	...	s_2 and if I were to add x_1 to my choice set, I would choose a_1	...
Actions							
a_1	o	o		o		o'	
a_2	$o*$	$o*$		$o*$		$o**$	
...							
e	$o+$	$o++$		$o+++$		$o++++$	

Figure 8.4. Analyzing the value of expanding a choice set.

making physical efforts to locate goods. Such a decision-maker can consider every possible sequence of bodily movements he might make, every possible choice situation that might eventuate along each sequence, the choices he would make in each such situation, and the possible results of each such choice – and then decide whether to initiate some sequence of bodily movements, as opposed to engaging in an immediate act of consumption, by determining which action maximizes expected utility. It is harder to see how the optimal-search notion is helpful for the decision-maker with positive analytic costs.

Consider adapting the notion to the specification of choice sets (where it seems, at first blush, applicable). How exactly does this work? Building on the discussion in the previous part, perhaps we might say this (see Figure 8.4). The decision-maker's outcome set O is fixed. He has some initial choice set $\{a_1, a_2, \ldots\}$, and there are additional options $\{x_1, x_2, \ldots\}$ not in the initial choice set. Rather than just considering those, he considers a *choice-set-expansion* choice e. Performing such a choice means expanding the initial choice set $\{a_1, a_2, \ldots\}$ in some way. For example, e might mean expanding $\{a_1, a_2, \ldots\}$ to $\{a_1, a_2, \ldots, x_1\}$. The decision-maker evaluates the outcomes of a choice such as e in the outcome set O with an appropriately enriched state set – one with conditionals of the form "Were I to consider this expanded choice set, I would choose this action."

But this procedure is perverse for a decision-maker with positive analytic costs (at least absent an intrinsic preference for the very process of decision analysis). The analytic costs of considering an expansion option e – the option of supplementing the initial choice set $\{a_1, a_2, \ldots\}$ with some choice x_1 – are greater than the analytic costs of just adding x_1 to the choice set without thinking about it and then choosing among $\{a_1, a_2, \ldots, x_1\}$. In order to evaluate $\{a_1, a_2, \ldots, e\}$ in terms of our fixed outcome set O, the decision-maker must have a set of mutually exclusive and collectively exhaustive states sufficiently richly described so that: each state maps each of the initial actions $\{a_1, a_2, \ldots\}$ onto one and only one element of O; each state maps the choice e onto one action in the choice set $\{a_1, a_2, \ldots, x_1\}$, that is, each state determines which action in the expanded set the decision-maker would choose, were she to expand the set; and, in each state where expanding the choice set would lead the decision-maker to choose x_1, x_1 is mapped onto one and only element of O. In order to evaluate the choice set $\{a_1, a_2, \ldots, x_1\}$ in terms of our fixed outcome set O, the decision-maker needs a less elaborate state set: she needs a set of mutually exclusive and collectively exhaustive states such that each state maps each of the initial actions $\{a_1, a_2, \ldots\}$ onto one and only one element of O, and each state maps x_1 onto one and only one element of O. Simply adding x_1 to the choice set without thinking and then choosing from the expanded set is less analytically laborious than thinking about adding x_1 to the choice set – so why not just take the first course?

A second and equally serious difficulty for the proposal now under discussion is this: If we start with some subset $\{a_1, a_2, \ldots\}$ of the totality of actions open to the decision-maker right now, there are a large number of choice-set-expansion options $\{e_1, e_2, e_3, \ldots\}$, where each e_i expands the initial subset in a different way. And there is nothing in the optimal-search literature that I am aware of that explains how the bounded decision-maker should narrow the choice-set-expansion options being considered – in effect, how he should narrow down the set of possible searches and think about only some of them.

C. Tversky and Kahneman and the Heuristics-and-Biases Program

Amos Tversky, Daniel Kahneman, and their collaborators have shown that real-world individuals are characterized by a variety of *heuristics and biases*,[15] and this now famous research has, in recent years, generated much legal scholarship under the banner of *behavioral law and economics*. One heuristic identified by Tversky and Kahneman, *prospect theory*, involves a framework for decision making that directly violates DT. In brief: decision-makers do not think in terms of the value of outcomes, but rather in terms of the value of losses and gains relative to some reference point. The value function for losses is convex, the value function for gains is concave, and the loss function is steeper than the gain function. Where the possible losses and gains resulting from a choice are uncertain, individuals do not weight the value of possible losses and gains by their probabilities, but rather by a weighting function that is an S-shaped transformation of the probabilities.

A different set of heuristics involve *judgments* rather than choice. These are processes by which individuals form beliefs – in particular, processes by which individuals make probability judgments. The three judgment heuristics originally identified by Tversky and Kahneman were *representativeness*, *availability*, and *anchoring and adjustment*. In brief: The representativeness heuristic involves judging whether some possible state of the world is true, given some data, by focusing on whether

---

[15] For reviews of this scholarship, see, for example, Jonathan Baron, 2000, *Thinking and Deciding*, 3rd ed., Cambridge: Cambridge University Press; Reid Hastie and Robyn M. Dawes, 2001, *Rational Choice in an Uncertain World*, Thousand Oaks: Sage Publications; Gideon Keren and Karl H. Teigen, 2004, "Yet Another Look at the Heuristics and Biases Approach," in Derek J. Koehler and Nigel Harvey, eds., *Blackwell Handbook of Judgment and Decision Making*, Malden, MA: Blackwell Publishing, pp. 89–109; Daniel Kahneman, 2003, "Maps of Bounded Rationality: Psychology for Bounded Economics," *American Economic Review*, 93, pp. 1449–1475.

the data is representative of the state; the prior probability of the state is ignored. Availability means ascribing higher probabilities to states whose instances are easier to recall from memory. Anchoring and adjustment means making probability judgments (or other magnitude estimates) by starting from some arbitrary initial value.

Sometimes, the heuristics identified by Tversky, Kahneman, and their successors are termed instances of "bounded rationality." But do these heuristics in fact help solve the *normative* problem of bounded rationality as I have described it here? To begin, it should be noted that Tversky, Kahneman, and others working in this tradition generally seem to see the heuristics and biases they identify as *departures* from rationality – as deviations from the true norms of choice, embodied in DT, and the true norms of judgment, embodied in probability theory.[16]

To be sure, prospect-theoretic choice, and probability judgments driven by representativeness, availability, or anchoring and adjustment, *could* really be part of the correct procedural component of the correct normative framework, whatever Tversky and Kahneman think. Although that is true, these heuristics are not particularly relevant to the issue at hand: namely, how to revise DT, and the norm of full specification, so as to make them usable by bounded decision-makers. Prospect theory is just orthogonal to that question. It tells the decision-maker to transform outcomes into losses and gains from a reference point, and to transform the probabilities of states by an S-shaped function. How to characterize outcomes in the first place (the problem of specifying an outcome set), and which actions to consider (the problem of specifying an action set), are not a part of the theory.

The judgment heuristics, too, give no guidance about how to specify an outcome, state, or action set. However, these heuristics could be seen as an important adjunct to DT revised for the bounded decision-maker. They might be an appropriate way for that decision-maker to economize on the analytic costs of assigning probabilities to states, at least in the case of "small" decisions. But, intuitively, all or at least many instrumentalist normative frameworks will identify a class of "large" decisions where it would be unwarranted for the decision-maker not to think more systematically about her decisions. (I am pointing to intuitions because, on a reflective-equilibrium account of normative reasoning, intuitions matter.) The whole apparatus of probability theory and statistics is a methodology for thinking more systematically about our probability ascriptions. Consider welfarism: within the framework of welfarism, are there not at least some decisions – in particular, governmental decisions to issue statutes or regulations that govern many individuals – where the deployment of this apparatus is the right thing to do?

I will not try to identify this class of "large" decisions more precisely, using criteria that a bounded decision-maker could employ. I do not see how I could do so except as part of a more general normative account of decision making by bounded actors – the very problem that no one has yet managed to solve. But it is implausible, I suggest, to think that the class is null or small, and thus implausible to

[16] See Gerd Gigerenzer et al., 1999, *Simple Heuristics that Make Us Smart*, New York: Oxford University Press, pp. 25–29; Kahneman, *Maps of Bounded Rationality*, p. 1456.

take representativeness, availability, anchoring and adjustment, and similar "quick and dirty" judgment heuristics as anything like full solutions to the question of how bounded individuals should make probability ascriptions.

D. Simon and Satisficing

Herbert Simon is the pioneer in normative work on choice by bounded agents.[17] He rightly and famously argued that computational costs undermine expected-utility theory as a general account of rational choice. But – notwithstanding all the credit Simon is owed for initiating this field of inquiry – he did not, I suggest, succeed in solving the problem of bounded rationality.

Simon proposed that bounded agents rationally "satisfice."[18] Satisficing, generally, means setting a threshold or aspiration level for a choice. Rather than constructing a full action set, consisting of every option open to her, the decision-maker begins to enumerate these options (systematically or not) and chooses the first one that is good enough – that meets the aspiration level. Satisficing is, therefore, directly responsive to the problem that constructing a full action set may be infeasible or hugely expensive for the bounded agent.

But is satisficing a normatively attractive solution to this problem? That depends on how the aspiration level is set. Some scholars (not Simon) suggest that an aspiration level might be set in terms of expected utility.[19] For this proposal to be workable, we would need to solve the problem of simplifying the outcome set. Calculating the expected utility of an action by identifying its possible outcomes in a fully specified outcome set, developing a matching state set, and then assigning utilities to the outcomes and probabilities to the states would be infeasible or at least unwarranted if the fully specified outcome set is very large. We would also, of course, need to provide a normatively attractive proposal for setting the aspiration level while economizing on computation costs (relative to doing DT with a fully specified outcome set). I am not aware of plausible suggestions on these two fronts.

A different possibility is to set an aspiration level for choices in terms of some nonutility features of choices – for example, deciding which house to purchase by looking for houses until one meets a price cutoff and a size cutoff. But how do we do this where the impact of choices on the outcomes we care about is uncertain?

Simon, in his original work on satisficing, offered a simple suggestion: take every *outcome* and make a binary judgment that the outcome is either satisfactory (a value of 1) or unsatisfactory (a value of 0). A choice, then, meets the aspiration level if it has a satisfactory outcome in every state.

---

[17] See generally Herbert Simon, 1982, 1997, *Models of Bounded Rationality,* vols. 1–3, Cambridge, MA: MIT Press; Herbert Simon, 1979, 1989, *Models of Thought,* vols. 1–2, New Haven: Yale University Press.

[18] See Herbert Simon, 1955, "A Behavioral Model of Rational Choice," in both *Models of Bounded Rationality* and *Models of Thought.* For discussions of satisficing by other scholars, see Michael Byron, 1998, "Satisficing and Optimality," *Ethics,* 109, pp. 67–93; Michael Byron, ed., 2004, *Satisficing and Maximizing,* Cambridge: Cambridge University Press.

[19] See Byron, "Satisficing and Optimality."

This solution (upon examination) leaves untouched the problem of specifying an outcome set. Are we supposed to consider whether the possible outcomes of an action in the fully specified outcome set are always 1 or 0? In many cases, this will be infeasible or hugely expensive. Reciprocally, once we fix an incompletely specified outcome set appropriate for the problem at hand, it will sometimes – for some "large" decisions – be appropriate to order these outcomes on some finer scale than a binary one.

A different solution is to pick certain aspects or dimensions of outcomes that are relevant to the goals adopted by our normative framework, produce a simplified set of outcomes that differ with respect to *these* dimensions, and set an aspiration level for choice in terms of the expected value of choices with respect to the selected dimensions. (For example, Fred may care about his income, his living space, his aesthetic experience, his happiness, and many other things. He focuses just on income and living space, and decides to bid on the first house whose expected cost is no more than $300,000 and whose expected living space is at least 2,000 square feet.) If the simplified outcome set is sufficiently simplified, this may reduce to a case of choice under certainty. (Fred will, in fact, know what the contract price and the living space of a given house are.)

One difficulty here is identifying the dimensions of outcomes to focus upon. Intuitively, we want to pick the most important dimensions – but identifying those dimensions, while economizing on analytic costs, may prove tricky, as I shall discuss in a moment. Quite apart from this issue, the variant of satisficing now under consideration still faces the problem of specifying a nonarbitrary aspiration level.

E. Gigerenzer, Take the Best, and Noncompensatory Choice Procedures

A body of recent work on bounded rationality has focused on *noncompensatory* heuristics. Much of this scholarship has been undertaken by Gerd Gigerenzer,[20] who is notable for his endorsement of heuristics as *rational*. He sees their use, not as a deviation from rationality, but as a rational response to computational demands.

Gigerenzer and his collaborators have focused on judgment rather than choice – in particular, on prediction tasks – and have analyzed a heuristic they call *Take the Best* (TTB).[21] Imagine that there is a population of objects. The individual is given pairs of objects, and tries to predict which object has a higher value on some criterion. Each object in the population has a series of *k* binary cues. The predictor (in the simplest case) knows whether each object he is presented has a negative or positive value for each of the *k* cues, and knows the ecological validity of each cue – that is, the frequency, across all pairs of objects where one object has a positive

[20] See Gigerenzer et al., *Simple Heuristics that Make Us Smart*; Gerd Gigerenzer, 2000, *Adaptive Thinking: Rationality in the Real World*, New York: Oxford University Press; Gerd Gigerenzer and Reinhard Selten, eds., 1999, *Bounded Rationality: The Adaptive Toolbox*, Cambridge, MA: MIT Press; Gerd Gigerenzer, 2006, "Heuristics," in Gerd Gigerenezer and Christoph Engel, eds., *Heuristics and the Law*, Cambridge, MA: MIT Press, pp. 17–44.
[21] See, for example, Gigerenzer et al., *Simple Heuristics that Make Us Smart*, pp. 75–95.

cue value and the other not, with which the positive-value object has the higher criterion value.

TTB tells the individual to follow this procedure in predicting which object in a pair has a higher criterion value: order the cues in the order of their validity, and if the most valid cue assigns a positive value to one object and a negative value to the other, choose the first object; otherwise, move on to the next most valid cue and, if that does not differentiate, the next, ultimately picking randomly among the objects if no cue differentiates. TTB is a noncompensatory rule in the sense that the information about a pair of objects provided by a higher-validity cue can never be outweighed by the information provided by lower-validity cues. Gigerenzer's research finds TTB to be surprisingly accurate in a variety of prediction tasks.

TTB is closely related to noncompensatory choice procedures that other scholars have studied.[22] Much of this work has focused on choice under certainty. Now, there are multiple choices, not necessarily a pair; the choices have values on k dimensions; the decision-maker's true preference is some weighted sum of the values on the k dimensions. One sort of noncompensatory procedure in this context is the *lexicographic* rule – the analogy of TTB in the prediction context. Order the dimensions by their weights, top to bottom. Given a choice situation, pick the choice with the highest value on the top dimension. If there are multiple choices tied for the highest value on the top dimension, pick among these using the next-to-top dimension; and so forth. A different, even simpler noncompensatory procedure is to choose using only the top dimension – and then pick randomly among choices tied for the highest value on this dimension.

These ideas, in turn, can be generalized to the case of choice under uncertainty, and to the case of any instrumentalist normative framework (not just the Humean framework), along something like the following lines. The goals of the framework define a fully specified outcome set. The goals also order the outcomes and allow the assignment of a utility to each outcome, representing its place in the ordering. Assume, further, that these utilities are the weighted sum of an outcome's *subutilities* along k dimensions or aspects of the outcomes. The top-value rule says this: Define a simplified outcome set, where outcomes differ only with respect to the top dimension (the dimension with the largest weight). Use a DT framework, framed in terms of that simplified outcome set, to choose between the alternatives – and if doing so produces multiple actions tied for best, choose randomly among them. The lexicographic rule says: Define a simplified outcome set, where outcomes differ only with respect to the top dimension. Use a DT framework to choose among the alternatives, using that simplified outcome set. If two or more are tied for best, choose among those by moving on to the next-best dimension and framing a DT problem in terms of an outcome set specified with respect to that dimension.

---

[22] See John W. Payne et al., 1993, *The Adaptive Decision-Maker*, Cambridge: Cambridge University Press; Robin M. Hogarth and Natalia Karelaia, 2007, "Heuristic and Linear Models of Judgment: Matching Rules and Environments," *Psychological Review*, 114, pp. 733–758; Barbara Fasolo et al., 2007, "Escaping the Tyranny of Choice: When Fewer Attributes Make Choice Easier," *Marketing Theory*, 7, pp. 13–26.

If two or more remain tied for best, move on to the third-best dimension to choose between these, and so on.

An initial difficulty with such lexicographic or single-value procedures is that they do not help with the problem of specifying an action set. But do they not at least give us some traction in simplifying the outcome set? One difficulty is that the utilities that the normative framework assigns to outcomes may not be representable as the weighted sum of subutilities along k dimensions. The literature on multiattribute utility theory shows that a linear decomposition of preferences (and, more generally, goals) presupposes special conditions that are not, plausibly, general requirements of rationality.[23] Absent a linear decomposition, it may not be meaningful to say that one dimension or aspect of outcomes is weightier than another in terms of the framework. A different and obvious problem is that, even if the utility numbers that the framework assigns to fully specified outcomes are linearly decomposable into a weighted sum of subutilities along k dimensions, the bounded individual may not know what those weights are.

A third and distinct problem is this: noncompensatory procedures are not perfectly accurate and, in some environments, may be sufficiently less accurate than compensatory procedures as to be inadvisable. Robin Hogarth and Natalia Karelaia have undertaken substantial research on the accuracy of noncompensatory prediction and choice procedures.[24] Although the answer is complicated, one important determinant of whether noncompensatory procedures are much less accurate than compensatory procedures is (not surprisingly) the true weights of the cues or dimensions. If the true value or utility of an item is the weighted sum of k cue values or subutilities, and if one cue or dimension has a much larger weight, then a noncompensatory procedure using that cue or dimension will tend to be quite accurate. If the weights are closer to equal, then a noncompensatory procedure will tend to be less accurate.

Consider, then, a decision-maker facing a large choice: one in which, it seems, it is rational to expend substantial decisional costs to get the decision right. And imagine that our decision-maker believes that there is no one dimension of fully specified outcomes that dominates the others, in terms of the goals she is trying to attain. Imagine, for example, our official June, who cares about individuals' well-being, and believes that well-being is a matter of longevity, consumption, health, happiness, and social relations, with none taking lexical priority over the others. June is overseeing the issuance of a major rule, which (she thinks) will change the well-being of many individuals over many years. June finds that one version of the rule maximizes population attainments with respect to the dimension of well-being she takes to be most important – say, health. But the difference between the best rule and the next best in terms of population health is small, and June is wondering whether to consider how the rules compare on the other dimensions. Would she not be rational to consider that – at least if the other dimensions are measurable without huge expense and there is no emergency requiring immediate issuance of the rule?

[23] See Detlof von Winterfeldt and Ward Edwards, 1986, *Decision Analysis and Behavioral Research*, Cambridge: Cambridge University Press, pp. 331–334.
[24] See Hogarth and Karelaia, "Heuristic and Linear Models," and their prior scholarship cited therein.

In short, although noncompensatory strategies may well be normatively advisable in an important range of cases – for small decisions, or cases in which the decision-maker believes there is a dominant dimension in the framework's ordering – they are more problematic in others (large decisions without dominant dimensions).

F. Departing from DT: Dropping the Norms or Dropping the Structure

DT consists of a certain structure for thinking about decisions, plus a set of norms. The attractiveness of these norms has been challenged. It has been suggested that the rational decision-maker might only have a partial rather than complete ordering of outcomes.[25] It has also been argued (particularly in the context of social choice) that it might be appropriate to violate the independence norm.[26] Finally, some have even suggested that violations of transitivity are rational.[27]

But these discussions are largely orthogonal to the problem of bounded rationality. As long as the decision-maker is supposed to think about her choice in terms of outcomes – whether or not her ranking of those is supposed to be complete or even transitive, and whether or not she is supposed to comply with independence – the problem remains that we have no good theory for how to simplify the outcome set to make it tractable for bounded decision-makers.

A more radical revision of DT would be to change its structure. Might we develop a procedural component for our normative frameworks that enjoins or permits the decision-maker to ignore outcomes entirely (and therefore, also, to ignore states), and to focus just on her actions? There is a literature on noninstrumentalist approaches to decision making, which I will not attempt to survey here.[28] Such approaches might avoid or mitigate the problem of bounded human cognitive abilities. But they would sit uneasily with instrumentalist normative frameworks, such as welfarism, other consequentialist moral frameworks, or any other normative framework that is oriented toward some goal. Indeed, they would sit uneasily with pluralist normative frameworks, which incorporate both goals and other requirements (e.g., a hybrid moral view that tells the actor to maximize social welfare within deontological side constraints). Anyone attracted to any instrumentalist or pluralist normative framework should hesitate to adopt a procedural norm that tells the actor to ignore outcomes.

III. LEGAL SCHOLARSHIP

At this point, the reader is surely growing impatient. What on earth does the problem of bounded rationality have to do with the methodology of legal scholarship? The connection is this: *the problem of bounded rationality will stymie any attempt to provide an instrumentalist methodology for prescriptive legal scholarship.*

---

[25] See, for example, Adler and Posner, *New Foundations of Cost–Benefit Analysis*, pp. 161–162.

[26] See Adler and Sanchirico, "Inequality and Uncertainty," pp. 334–350.

[27] See Larry S. Temkin, 1996, "A Continuum Argument for Intransitivity," *Philosophy and Public Affairs*, 25, pp. 175–210.

[28] See Elijah Millgram, ed., 2001, *Varieties of Practical Reasoning*, Cambridge, MA: MIT Press.

Legal scholarship may be *prescriptive*, providing recommendations to legislators, judges, and other legal officials; or it may be *nonprescriptive*, seeking to describe or explain the behaviors of various actors. A methodology for legal scholarship furnishes norms for legal scholars themselves. In the case of prescriptive legal scholarship, it tells legal scholars how to go about making recommendations to legislators, judges, and other legal officials. A methodology for prescriptive legal scholarship is *instrumentalist* if it tells legal scholars to make those recommendations by determining which laws and policies maximize some goal.

If legal scholars were cognitively unbounded, an instrumentalist methodology for prescriptive legal scholarship would naturally incorporate DT as its guidance for legal scholars – with the further guidance, on the crucial issue of specification, that legal scholars employ fully specified outcome, action, and state sets. It would instruct the scholar making recommendations to some class of legal officials to consider all possible actions that the officials might undertake; to evaluate each action with reference to an outcome set that is fully specified in light of the goal of the methodology; to do so using a fully specified state set (containing mutually exclusively and collectively exhaustive states, each of which maps a given action onto a single outcome); and to do so consistently with the norms of DT: completeness, transitivity, consequentialism, dominance, and independence.

However, because legal scholars are not cognitively unbounded, it is difficult to say what norms an instrumentalist methodology for prescriptive legal scholarship should contain on this crucial issue of specification. This is one implication (among many) of the general analysis presented in sections I and II. The general problem is that reflection about appropriate decision making – by economists, philosophers, decision theorists, and others who study decision-making norms – has not yet reached a point of reflective equilibrium with respect to how bounded decision-makers should use the apparatus of DT. The implication of this problem for legal scholarship is that anyone reflecting on the appropriate methodology for legal scholarship will have difficulty reaching reflective equilibrium with respect to how legal scholars giving advice to decision-makers should use DT to formulate that advice.

It would be absurd to suggest that the implications of bounded rationality for legal scholarship are its most important or interesting implications. I certainly do not claim that. Cognitive limitations are a pervasive feature of humans, and thus bounded rationality is a pervasive problem for attempts to specify normative frameworks for aspects of human life – including but hardly limited to legal scholarship. Still, legal scholars should understand that bounded rationality *is* a pervasive problem, which will stymie their own efforts to rationalize their own activities. I do not believe this point has been sufficiently understood, and it is one worth articulating in a book on the methodology of law and economics.

I will elaborate the implications of bounded rationality for legal scholarship by focusing on Kaplow and Shavell's *Fairness versus Welfare* (*FW*), the most sustained attempt, in recent years, to provide a methodology for prescriptive legal scholarship. Although *FW* is, to some extent, addressed to governmental officials, it consists, first and foremost, of guidance for legal scholars and other policy analysts:

Our object has been to convince legal policy analysts to pursue a research agenda focused on identifying which legal rules best promote individuals' well-being. . . . It should be clear . . . that our claim concerns legal academics and other policy analysts, not ordinary individuals who must make decisions in everyday life. . . . We [also] acknowledge that the problem of government officials is complicated by the fact that their constituents may not always be able to understand proper analyses of legal rules (or of many other government policies). Nevertheless, we believe that responsible government decision-makers will be able to make better policy decisions if those who analyze legal policy devote themselves to identifying the effects of legal rules on individuals' well-being – that is, if they employ welfare economics rather than base their analysis on notions of fairness.[29]

The normative framework that *FW* adopts is welfarism. *FW* argues that legal scholars should identify and recommend the legal rules that advance the goal of social welfare – meaning the overall well-being of some population of interest, but potentially also the distribution of well-being in the population.[30] To put this formally, legal scholars should identify the legal rules that maximize a *social welfare function*: a utility function that assigns a utility number to each outcome as a function of individuals' well-being numbers in that outcome, and that does so without reference to the identity of the individuals (no dictatorship or proper names), and with the understanding that these well-being numbers are interpersonally comparable.[31] By well-being, *FW* means the satisfaction of fully informed preferences.[32] *FW* criticizes the traditional approach to law-and-economics scholarship, which is to evaluate laws and policies with reference to wealth maximization or Kaldor–Hicks efficiency.[33] *FW* also famously recommends that legal scholars should ignore extra-welfarist or "fairness" considerations.

FW, although lengthy, is incomplete. A fully developed welfarist methodology for prescriptive legal scholarship would have a full procedural component, explaining in greater detail how scholars should pursue the task of identifying welfare-maximizing legal rules.[34] But any attempt to do that, I suggest, would run headlong into the problem of bounded rationality.

The conundrum of a legal scholar trying to identify the legal rules that maximize social welfare is quite analogous to that of our hypothetical welfarist governmental official June. Just as June needs to somehow narrow down the set of possible legal rules that she might *promulgate*, so the scholar must somehow narrow down the set of possible legal rules that he might *investigate*. The scholar, like June, wants to evaluate a given legal rule by considering the different outcomes that the rule might have, depending on the state of the world – ignoring non-well-being facts about outcomes and focusing just on facts about well-being. But, again, an outcome set

---

[29] *FW*, p. 472; see generally pp. 382–402.
[30] *FW* does not take a position on the membership of this population; see p. 26, n. 19.
[31] Ibid., pp. 24–28.
[32] Ibid., pp. 18–24, 410–413.
[33] Ibid., pp. 35–38, 458–461.
[34] *FW* itself, it should be noted, does not discuss the problem – which I take to be crucial – of how legal scholars should construct outcome, action, and state sets. There is a brief discussion of how welfarist scholars should reach conclusions under uncertainty, which does not address the problem. See pp. 457–458.

consisting "just" of outcomes fully specified with respect to well-being facts would
be huge – given that each individual's well-being is multidimensional, and given
that social welfare is a function of everyone's well-being (not just the well-being of
a single dictator). As Kaplow and Shavell explain:

> The notion of well-being used in welfare economics is comprehensive in nature.
> It incorporates in a positive way everything that an individual might value –
> goods and services that the individual can consume, social and environmental
> amenities, personally held notions of fulfillment, sympathetic feelings for others,
> and so forth. Similarly, an individual's well-being reflects in a negative way harms
> to his or her person and property, costs and inconveniences, and anything else
> that the individual might find distasteful. Well-being is not restricted to hedo-
> nistic and materialistic enjoyment or to any other named class of pleasures and
> pains.[35]

Finally, like June, the scholar must somehow whittle down his state set. Policies
produce outcomes (inter alia) by affecting human behavior. So a computationally
unbounded scholar predicting the effect of a given policy on a given set of outcomes
would consider every possible model of human behavior to which he ascribes
some nonzero probability – not just the traditional model of expected-utility
maximization, and prospect theory, but every alternative. More precisely, if there
are N individuals in the population, and a (presumably very large) finite number
M of behavioral models to which he ascribes a nonzero probability, he should
consider every composite model that says that individual i behaves in accordance
with model j – leading to M^N composite models. This is an overwhelming task for
bounded scholars.

As an illustration of the difficulty I am describing, consider optimal-tax scholarship – the main area in which scholars have explicitly used social welfare functions
to evaluate policies and, on Kaplow and Shavell's view, the model for normative legal scholarship.[36] James Mirrlees, in his original, Nobel Prize–winning work,
sought to determine the optimal income tax schedule, given the following assumptions (as described by Matti Tuomala):

> Imagine an economy where individuals have the innate ability to transform
> working-time into a single consumption good, which is called income. Each indi-
> vidual's utility is a numerical function that depends only on his net income and
> the quantity of labour he supplies. Thus his preferences are personal. Individuals
> are regarded as identical except that they vary in their ability to supply labor.
> Thus they can be grouped by productivity types. For the same number of hours
> worked, a more able person naturally can produce more income. Each individual
> decides how much labour to supply, calculating what will maximize his utility. All
> these labour supply decisions taken together determine the output of the econ-
> omy.... [Government] cannot monitor the number of working hours a person
> chooses to work, but can only observe a person's income. For this reason the only

[35] Ibid., p. 18.
[36] Ibid., p. 31, n. 31.

policy the government can execute is to impose a tax schedule. The government chooses the income tax schedule which maximizes its social welfare function, knowing the manner in which individuals of any productivity type will respond.[37]

We see, here, a radical simplification in the characterization of outcomes. Well-being is a function of income and leisure, nothing else. We also see a radical simplification in the state set. In particular, prospect theory and every other non-expected-utility model of individual behavior are ignored. And a very simplified model of the economy is adopted (each worker is unable to change his productivity, and his wage rate is solely a function of his productivity). Finally, Mirrlees in his original work ignored the possibility of optimizing a social welfare function by combining an income tax schedule with other policies.

These were understandable simplifications. Even Mirrlees is human and faces computational limits. The problem is that we lack a persuasive normative account to tell us whether the simplifications Mirrlees adopted were the right ones – whether he simplified too much, or too little, or along the right dimensions.[38]

Some readers of early drafts of this chapter have been puzzled by my focus, here, on the bounded rationality of *scholars*. Is that not a secondary problem or meta-problem? *FW* instructs legal scholars to identify the laws and policies that maximize social welfare. In order to do so, scholars must predict how different laws and policies will affect the well-being of individuals in the population. Those effects will depend, inter alia, on the behavior of legal officials and private citizens. Officials and citizens may have cognitive limitations, and may deviate from the model of expected-utility maximization posited by traditional economics. Is it not this deviation – rather than the cognitive limitations of legal scholars themselves – that constitutes the primary threat to *FW*'s welfarist methodology for legal scholars?

I think not. If legal scholars were unboundedly rational, the fact that non-scholars – private citizens or legal officials – might deviate from expected-utility maximization would not frustrate *FW*'s program for legal scholarship. In general, DT articulates norms of rationality for a decision-maker; but it is agnostic about the nature of the causal models driving the human actors or nonhuman processes in the decision-maker's environment.[39] Likewise, DT as a framework for prescriptive legal scholarship imposes norms of rationality on the scholar herself; but it is agnostic about the nature of the causal models that determine the effects of legal rules, including causal models of the behavior of individuals and government officials. Unboundedly rational legal scholars using DT's state–outcome–action

[37] Matti Tuomala, 1990, *Optimal Income Tax and Redistribution*, Oxford: Oxford University Press, pp. 4–5; see also pp. 86–105. For the original paper, see James Mirrlees, 2006, *Welfare, Incentives, and Taxation*, Oxford: Oxford University Press, pp. 131–173.

[38] To be sure, some of the simplifications have been dropped in subsequent optimal-tax work, but subsequent work still contains many simplifications that would not characterize scholarship by unbounded scholars. For a survey of subsequent work, see Tuomala, *Optimal Income Tax*.

[39] There is a different and larger question here, about whether DT can be used for *strategic* rather than parametric choice – that is, in situations in which the effects of the decision-maker's choices depend on other actors who are themselves choosing with reference to the decision-maker's choices. I believe the answer is yes, but cannot pursue the point here.

framework could, without difficulty, be sensitive both to the possibility that some or all citizens and officials might conform to expected-utility maximization, and to the possibility that some or all citizens or officials might fail to conform. In one (improbable) state within the state set, all conform; in another state, none do; in other states, some do and some do not.

Of course, prescriptive legal scholars are addressing their recommendations to government officials. But I do not see why the bounded rationality of the addressees would stymie FW's program if the legal scholars themselves were unboundedly rational. In short, it is the bounded rationality of *legal scholars* – not citizens and officials – that poses a grave difficulty for FW's welfarist program for legal scholarship.[40]

What are the possible responses to this difficulty? One response, of course, is to reject FW's welfarist program for legal scholarship. But this is trickier than it sounds. Much of the criticism of FW involves its rejection of fairness criteria. If this indeed is a deficiency in FW, and we correct it by adopting a pluralist program – recommending that legal scholars evaluate policies with respect to both social welfare and some set of fairness criteria – the problem of bounded rationality remains (at least) with respect to the welfarist part of this program. A different response is to adopt a wholly nonwelfarist framework, which enjoins legal scholars to focus solely on fairness criteria or other nonwelfarist considerations, and ignore overall well-being or the distribution of well-being. Such a framework might be easier to square with legal scholars' cognitive limits, but it would be normatively unattractive: social welfare is surely one significant part of the moral landscape. Finally, we might return to the traditional criteria adopted by law and economics: wealth maximization or Kaldor–Hicks efficiency. But these criteria are much less attractive (on their own, or as part of a pluralistic framework) than social welfare as FW understands it. And, in any event, cost–benefit analysis – the traditional technique for implementing wealth maximization and Kaldor–Hicks efficiency – faces exactly the same problems of explaining how to simplify action, state, and outcome sets that the application of a social welfare function does.[41]

Nor will the problem be solved by shifting away from FW's preferentialist theory of well-being. What compounds the problem of bounded rationality is not preferentialism but multidimensionality. Any theory that recognizes multiple sources of well-being (be they multiple objective goods, multiple kinds of good mental states, or the multiple things people prefer), and cares about the well-being of many people, will tend to generate a particularly large fully specified outcome set.

A different response is to endorse welfarist goals for legal scholars (either solo, or as part of a larger pluralist program), but to adopt one of the possible solutions to the problem of bounded rationality discussed in section II. I have criticized those solutions already, and will not repeat the criticism here.

---

[40] It might be objected that FW is arbitrary to address its recommendations just to legal scholars. Welfarism is either the right moral framework for everyone or for no one. Still, the point remains that the viability of FW, qua methodology for legal scholarship, is chiefly threatened by the cognitive limitations of legal scholars.

[41] See Adler and Posner, *New Foundations of Cost–Benefit Analysis*, pp. 68–73.

Yet another response is to point to the collective nature of legal scholarship. One might say, "Each legal scholar should try to identify laws and policies that maximize social welfare. But, in doing so, each scholar should coordinate with other scholars, rather than acting as if she were the sole researcher pursuing the welfare-maximization goal." This leads us into the murky waters of rule-consequentialist revisions to DT. Rather than asking which policy she should investigate, so as to maximize one or another social welfare function, the scholar might ask something like the following: what rule for the community of scholars, if followed by everyone in the community, would maximize that social welfare function? But, whatever the attractions of rule consequentialism, it does not seem a fruitful solution to the problem of bounded rationality. There is a large set of possible rules to structure the community's research that might be followed, each to be evaluated in light of a large set of outcomes and states.

Finally, it might be pointed out that some legal scholars are engaged in nonprescriptive scholarship. They aim, not to recommend laws and policies to government officials, but simply to describe and explain how individuals behave (specifically, to understand how individuals respond to legal rules).

There is a clear sense in which descriptive/explanatory legal scholarship does *not* need an account of bounded rationality. Imagine that, as a descriptive or explanatory scholar, I believe that human behavior in some domain is produced by some computationally cheap heuristic such as those identified by Tversky and Kahneman or by Gigerenzer: availability, representativeness, anchoring and adjustment, Take the Best, and so forth. I need not take a position about whether this behavior is rational.[42] My aim is not to endorse or criticize the behavior, but to explain it; the heuristic, I claim, does so. Why do I need to take a position on whether compliance with the heuristic is normatively appropriate?

A harder question is whether legal scholars engaged in descriptive or explanatory scholarship confront the problem of bounded rationality in structuring their own research activities. Will any methodology for nonprescriptive legal scholarship be stymied by the cognitive limitations of legal scholars? Any such methodology will give guidance to legal scholars in deciding which questions about human behavior to investigate. Odd as it may sound, one such methodology – at least in principle – is welfarist. That methodology tells scholars to pursue those research projects into human behavior that have the greatest expected positive impact on social welfare – in virtue of the information the projects might produce, the probability of producing that information, and the relevance of the information to well-being.[43] Such a methodology would, pretty clearly, be hampered by scholars' bounded rationality. However, there may be plausible nonwelfarist accounts of how scholars should undertake descriptive or explanatory work that are feasibly implemented by bounded scholars.

---

[42] See Allan Gibbard, 2002, "Normative Explanations: Invoking Rationality to Explain Happenings," in Jose Luis Bermudez and Alan Millar, eds., *Reason and Nature: Essays in the Theory of Rationality*, Oxford: Oxford University Press, pp. 265–282.

[43] See Philip Kitcher, 2001, *Science, Truth, and Democracy*, New York: Oxford University Press, pp. 117–135.

I will not try to address these questions about the foundations of descriptive or explanatory legal scholarship. Bounded rationality may not be a gap in the foundations of such scholarship, but it *is* a large and unresolved gap in our understanding of how prescriptive legal scholars should conduct their activities. *FW* may be right that prescriptive legal scholarship should focus solely on identifying legal rules that maximize social welfare. At a minimum, it is surely true that social welfare is one of the criteria that prescriptive legal scholarship should use to evaluate legal rules. But we currently lack any normative handle on how cognitively limited scholars should undertake that analysis: on how incomplete action, state, and outcome sets should be structured so that the analysis is both sufficiently intensive, and yet neither computationally infeasible nor overly expensive, given the welfare stakes of the rules being evaluated.

9 Emotional Reactions to Law and Economics, Market Metaphors, and Rationality Rhetoric

PETER H. HUANG

This chapter makes three fundamental points about law and economics. First, some people have strong, negative emotional reactions to utilizing microeconomics to analyze nonbusiness areas of law,[1] whereas others have no such reactions.[2] This chapter advances the hypothesis that people who do not view the world through an economics lens are likely to experience negative feelings toward applying microeconomics to nonbusiness law areas, whereas people who view the world through an economics lens are unlikely to do so.[3] Second, while law and economics remains an uncontroversial subfield of applied microeconomics, it has become a dominant yet controversial field of scholarship in legal academia.[4] This chapter proposes that differences in how most academic and professional economists perceive law and economics versus how most academic and professional lawyers perceive law and economics are due primarily to differences in how familiar they are with microeconomics presented in a mathematically rigorous fashion. Third, much research considerably and significantly qualifies many well-known and often quoted alleged benefits of competitive markets and unbounded rationality.[5] People who comprehend this research appreciate that the extent to which markets and rationality are socially desirable is more complicated than people who do not understand this research often suggest. This research involves traditional

---

[1] Austan Goolsbee, 2006, "The 486th Convocation Address: 'Why People Hate Economists (and Why We Don't Care),'" *The University of Chicago Record*, 41, pp. 18–19, available online at http://www.uchicago.edu/about/documents/chicagorecord/pdfs/41-1.pdf.

[2] Kevin M. Murphy, 2006, "The 485th Convocation Address: 'Seeing the World through the Economics Lens,'" *The University of Chicago Record*, 41, pp. 12–13, available online at http://www.uchicago.edu/about/documents/chicagorecord/pdfs/41-1.pdf.

[3] Drew Westen, 2007, *The Political Brain: The Role of Emotion in Deciding the Fate of the Nation*, New York: Public Affairs.

[4] Nicholas Mercuro and Steven G. Medema, 2006, *Economics and the Law: From Posner to Postmodernism and Beyond*, 2nd ed., Princeton: Princeton University Press.

[5] Hugh Schwartz, 2000, *Rationality Gone Awry?: Decision Making Inconsistent with Economic and Financial Theory*, New York: Praeger.

Thanks to David Hoffman, Amy Sinden, Rick Swedloff, Mark White, and audiences of the Psychology and Economics Theme Seminar, School of Social Science, Institute for Advanced Study and of the Methodology of Law and Economics panel at the Eastern Economics Association 2006 Annual Meeting for their helpful comments.

microeconomics,[6] behavioral economics,[7] cognitive psychology,[8] social psychology,[9] and neuroeconomics.[10]

I. EMOTIONAL AND UNEMOTIONAL REACTIONS
TO LAW AND ECONOMICS

It is uncontroversial to apply economics to analyze business-related law fields. Most applications of economics to law utilize microeconomics, but a few applications of macroeconomics to law exist.[11] Law and economics began its rise to prominence in legal academia by applying microeconomics to every subject in the first-year law school curriculum, namely civil procedure, constitutional law, contracts, criminal law, property, and torts. Some applications remain controversial, such as the assertion that the socially optimal amount of litigation is positive;[12] the concept of a socially optimal extent of liberty;[13] that the socially optimal number of contract breaches is positive;[14] that the death penalty deters violent crimes by raising their price;[15] that the socially optimal quantity of accidents is positive;[16] and that the socially optimal magnitude of pollution is positive.[17]

It has always been and remains today controversial among most noneconomists and those who do not see the world through an economic lens to apply microeconomics to nonbusiness fields of law. For example, a seminal article that applied microeconomics to analyze child adoption generated much controversy.[18] More generally, applying microeconomics to analyze family law remains controversial

---

[6] David D. Cremer et al., eds., 2006, *Social Psychology and Economics*, Mahwah, NJ: Lawrence Erlbaum Associates.

[7] Peter Diamond and Hannu Vartiainen, eds., 2007, *Behavioral Economics and Its Applications*, Princeton: Princeton University Press.

[8] Don Ross, 2005, *Economic Theory and Cognitive Science: Microexplanation*, Cambridge, MA: MIT Press.

[9] Paul A. M. Van Lange, ed., 2006, *Bridging Social Psychology: Benefits of Transdisciplinary Approaches*, Mahwah, NJ: Lawrence Erlbaum Associates.

[10] Colin F. Camerer, 2007, "Neuroeconomics: Using Neuroscience to Make Economic Predictions," *Economic Journal*, 117, pp. C26–C42.

[11] Mark Kelman, 1993, "Could Lawyers Stop Recessions? Speculations on Law and Macroeconomics," *Stanford Law Review*, 45, pp. 1215–1310; Steven A. Ramirez, 2003, "The Law and Macroeconomics of the New Deal at 70," *Maryland Law Review*, 62, pp. 515–572; Steven A. Ramirez, 2002, "Fear and Social Capitalism: The Law and Macroeconomics of Investor Confidence," *Washburn Law Review*, 42, pp. 31–77.

[12] Robert G. Bone, 2002, *Civil Procedure: Economics of Civil Procedure*, New York: Foundation Press.

[13] Robert D. Cooter, 2002, *The Strategic Constitution*, Princeton: Princeton University Press.

[14] Victor Goldberg, 2007, *Framing Contract Law: An Economic Perspective*, Cambridge, MA: Harvard University Press.

[15] Susan Bandes, 2008, "The Heart Has Its Reasons: Examining the Strange Persistence of the American Death Penalty," *Studies in Law, Politics and Society*, 42, pp. 21–52.

[16] Thomas J. Miceli, 1997, *Economics of the Law: Torts, Contracts, Property and Litigation*, Oxford: Oxford University Press.

[17] Ibid.

[18] Elisabeth M. Landes and Richard A. Posner, 1978, "The Economics of the Baby Shortage," *Journal of Legal Studies*, 7, pp. 323–348; see also Chapter 2 by Dorff and Ferzan in this volume.

among legal scholars to this day,[19] but is uncontroversial among economists[20] and lawyers.[21]

Most economists have no emotional reactions toward applying microeconomics to nonbusiness areas of law, but many noneconomists have quite strong emotional reactions to doing so. Emotional reactions vary across the negative-to-positive spectrum, ranging from such negative reactions as discomfort, disgust, and shock, to such positive reactions as admiration, comfort, and pleasure. Other emotional reactions include amusement, anger, bewilderment, irritation, and exasperation. For example, vocal critics of cost–benefit analysis (CBA) view it as a strongly inappropriate methodology for promulgating environmental, health, and safety regulations,[22] whereas practitioners of CBA view it as merely a weak form of social rationality for ensuring that benefits of regulations exceed their costs.[23]

The home page of the Cultural Cognition Project describes it as "a group of scholars from Yale and other universities interested in studying how cultural values shape the public's risk perceptions and related policy beliefs. Cultural cognition refers to the tendency of individuals to conform their beliefs about disputed matters of fact (e.g., whether global warming is a serious threat; whether the death penalty deters murder; whether gun control makes society more safe or less) to values that define their cultural identities. Project members are using the methods of various disciplines – including social psychology, anthropology, communications, and political science – to chart the influence of this phenomenon and to identify the mechanisms through which it operates. The Project also has an explicit normative objective: to identify processes of democratic decision making by which society can resolve culturally grounded differences in belief in a manner that is both congenial to persons of diverse cultural outlooks and consistent with sound public policymaking."[24] Its current research projects find in a variety of settings that laypeople's perceptions of risk involve cultural cognitions and worldviews as opposed to merely probability assessments.[25]

Kahan observes that some individuals experience negative feelings about evaluating risks based upon CBA and its associated welfarist policymaking.[26] Huang observes that such people are likely to feel equally negative toward applying CBA

[19] Margaret F. Brinig, 2005, "Some Concerns about Applying Economics to Family Law," in Martha Albertson Fineman and Terence Dougherty, eds., *Feminism Confronts Homo Economicus: Gender, Law, and Society*, Ithaca, NY: Cornell University Press, pp. 450–466.

[20] Donald A. Wittman, 2005, "The Internal Organization of the Family: Economic Analysis and Psychological Advice," *Kyklos*, 58, pp. 121–144.

[21] Rhona Mahoney, 1995, *Kidding Ourselves: Breadwinning, Babies, and Bargaining Power*, New York: Basic Books.

[22] Frank Ackerman and Lisa Heinzerling, 2005, *Priceless: On Knowing the Price of Everything and the Value of Nothing*, New York: The New Press.

[23] Richard O. Zerbe, Jr., and Allen S. Bellas, 2006, *A Primer for Benefit–Cost Analysis*, Northampton, MA: Edward Elgar.

[24] http://culturalcognition.net.

[25] Dan M. Kahan, 2008, "Two Conceptions of Emotion in Risk Regulation," *University of Pennsylvania Law Review*, 156, pp. 741–766.

[26] Ibid.

to a riskless environment,[27] because these negative feelings are responses to not just risks, but also calculations,[28] commensurability,[29] and contested commodities.[30] As Kenneth Arrow points out, "[o]ne of the oldest critiques of economic thinking has been its perceived disregard of the deeper and more sacred aspects of life."[31]

CBA strives to be, often appears to be, and usually is a cold and unemotional, technocratic method of (assisting) human decision making. CBA, like other forms of commensuration, such as rankings of academic institutions, employers, places to live, Web sites, and wines, certainly appears to fill an understandable human desire for objectivity and precision. Many lawyers obsess over numerical rankings, ranging from student rank in law school, to the annual *U.S. News & World Report* ranking of law schools, to rankings of law firms according to such criteria as associates' first-year salaries, annual bonuses, and quality of life. But some critics of CBA believe this appearance is a mere illusion.[32] Most people understandably experience stress from deliberating over and having to make tragic choices,[33] such as those depicted in the movie *Indecent Proposal* and the book *Sophie's Choice*.[34] CBA makes trade-offs explicit and transparent.[35] Some people often experience negative feelings and find it hard to face when they have to explicitly make certain types of trade-offs.[36]

A psychologically sophisticated theory provides an explanatory framework for taboo trade-offs.[37] This theory integrates two other theories, one that posits four fundamental models of social relations,[38] and one about value pluralism and trade-offs.[39] This theory suggests that taboo trade-offs are not just cognitively

---

[27] Peter H. Huang, 2008, "Diverse Conceptions of Emotions in Risk Regulation" (in response to ibid.), *University of Pennsylvania Law Review PENNumbra*, 156, pp. 435–447.

[28] Claire A. Hill, 2004, "Law and Economics in the Personal Sphere," *Law and Social Inquiry*, 29, p. 224, n. 11.

[29] Eric A. Posner, 1998, "The Strategic Basis of Principled Behavior: A Critique of the Incommensurability Thesis," *University of Pennsylvania Law Review*, 146, pp. 1185–1214.

[30] Margaret J. Radin, 2001, *Contested Commodities*, Cambridge, MA: Harvard University Press. See Peter H. Huang, 1998, "Dangers of Monetary Commensurability: A Psychological Game Model of Contagion," *University of Pennsylvania Law Review*, 146, pp. 1701–1722, for a psychological–game-theoretic model of contested commodities.

[31] Kenneth J. Arrow, 1997, "Invaluable Goods," *Journal of Economic Literature*, 35, p. 757.

[32] Emma Coleman Jordan and Angela P. Harris, 2005, *Economic Justice: Race, Gender, Identity, and Economics*, New York: Foundation Press, pp. 379–384.

[33] Guido Calabresi and Philip Bobbitt, 1978, *Tragic Choices: The Conflicts Society Confronts in the Allocation of Tragically Scarce Resources*, New York: W. W. Norton.

[34] *Indecent Proposal*, 1993, Paramount Pictures; William Styron, 1979, *Sophie's Choice*, New York: Vintage, pp. 483–484.

[35] Harold Winter, 2005, *Trade-offs: An Introduction to Economic Reasoning and Social Issues*, Chicago: University of Chicago Press.

[36] Mary F. Luce et al., 2001, *Emotional Decisions: Trade-off Difficulty and Coping in Consumer Choice*, Chicago: University of Chicago Press.

[37] Alan Page Fiske and Philip E. Tetlock, 1997, "Taboo Trade-offs: Reactions to Transactions That Transgress the Spheres of Justice," *Political Psychology*, 18, pp. 255–297.

[38] Alan Page Fiske, 1992, "The Four Elementary Forms of Sociality: Framework for a Unified Theory of Social Relations," *Psychological Review*, 99, pp. 689–723.

[39] Philip E. Tetlock et al., 1996, "Revising the Value Pluralism Model: Incorporating Social Content and Context Postulates," in Clive Seligman et al., eds., *The Psychology of Values: The Ontario Symposium*, vol. 8, Hillsdale, NJ: Erlbaum, pp. 25–51.

confusing, but also trigger negative behavioral and emotional reactions. It hypothesizes that people facing, and being forced to make, taboo trade-offs feel agony, ambivalence, anger, anxiety, denial, discomfort, distress, indignation, moral outrage, offense, and uneasiness. But for individuals who see the world through an economic lens, no trade-off is taboo, because all values can be and so are reduced to a single metric, namely that of utility. For people who do not see the world through an economic lens only, some trade-offs are taboo because they violate deeply held intuitions and social-relational constraints on what should be considered fungible.[40] Such people would like to protect certain values from being part of trade-offs.[41] People's reluctance to make such trade-offs explicitly instead of implicitly helps explain people's resistance to CBA.[42] Expressive views of law interpret choices among incommensurable options and processes by which societies make those choices as signals of those societies' identities or aspirations.[43] Such views of social decision making are related to psychological models of individual self-signaling.[44]

Some people feel that for particular issues, other criteria should or do trump CBA. For example, in the movie *Class Action*,[45] a car manufacturer decides to not recall a defectively designed automobile, after comparing the cost of redesigning that model with the benefit of saving human lives. This plot mirrors how the Ford Motor Company used CBA in deciding to not move the location of gas tanks in the Pinto model.[46] An empirical study found that mock jurors penalize business defendants who engaged in CBA of potential safety improvements.[47] Another example of CBA some people are likely to find troubling is utilizing it to decide whether to torture a suspected terrorist for information that could save innocent lives. A final example is that some people may feel that insider trading and securities fraud should be illegal even if they generate benefits like greater informational efficiency that exceed costs like reduced market liquidity.

People sometimes choose to not utilize CBA for particular choices by adopting rules or principles.[48] CBA of environmental, health, and safety regulations is based

---

[40] A. Peter McGraw and Philip E. Tetlock, 2005, "Taboo Trade-offs, Relational Framing, and the Acceptability of Exchanges," *Journal of Consumer Psychology*, 15, pp. 2–15.

[41] Jonathan Baron and Mark Spranca, 1997, "Protected Values," *Organizational Behavior and Human Decision Processes*, 70, pp. 1–16.

[42] Robert J. MacCoun, 2000, "The Costs and Benefits of Letting Juries Punish Corporations: Comment on Viscusi," *Stanford Law Review*, 52, pp. 1821–1828.

[43] Elizabeth Anderson, 1995, *Value in Ethics and Economics*, Cambridge, MA: Harvard University Press; Philip Harvey, 2004, "Aspirational Law," *Buffalo Law Review*, 52, pp. 701–726.

[44] Ronit Bodner and Drazen Prelec, 2003, "Self-Signaling and Diagnostic Utility in Everyday Decision Making," in Isabelle Brocas and Juan D. Carrillo, *The Psychology of Economic Decisions, Volume I: Rationality and Well-Being*, Oxford: Oxford University Press, pp. 105–123; Drazen Prelec and Ronit Bodner, 2003, "Self-Signaling and Self-Control," in George Loewenstein et al., eds., *Time and Decision: Economic and Psychological Perspectives on Intertemporal Choice*, New York: Russell Sage Foundation, pp. 277–298.

[45] *Class Action*, Twentieth Century-Fox Film Corporation, 1991.

[46] Douglas Birsch and John H. Fielder, 1994, *The Ford Pinto Case: A Study in Applied Ethics, Business, and Technology*, Albany, NY: State University of New York Press.

[47] W. Kip Viscusi, 2000, "Corporate Risk Analysis: A Reckless Act," *Stanford Law Review*, 52, pp. 547–597.

[48] Drazen Prelec and R. J. Herrnstein, 1991, "Preferences or Principles: Alternative Guidelines for Choice," in Richard Zeckhauser, ed., *Strategy and Choice*, Cambridge, MA: MIT Press, pp. 319–340.

upon taking account of measurable costs and benefits, determined via revealed preference techniques, such as hedonic pricing methodology, or stated preference techniques, such as contingent valuation methodology. One criticism of CBA is that it is often incomplete about benefits but complete about costs, because many costs are monetary and easy to measure, whereas those benefits that are left out are perceived to be difficult for government regulators to quantify and verify. But, even for regulations that are desirable regardless of their quantifiable benefits, regulators can adopt the most cost-effective regulations. For example, regulators can apply cost-effectiveness analysis to ration health care.[49]

Lord Kelvin famously stated that: "[w]hen you can measure what you are speaking about, and express it in numbers, you know something about it; but when you cannot measure it, when you cannot express it in numbers, your knowledge is of a meager and unsatisfactory kind."[50] The mathematician Philolaus "put it even more bluntly in the fifth century BC: 'Everything that can be known has a number.'"[51] But numbers can also provide us with the illusion of knowledge and offer corporate or political leaders a false sense of authority.[52] A popular nickname for economics is the queen of the social sciences,[53] partly because economics is like a certain style of physics due to the mathematical nature of economic theories and its econometric testing. A mathematical economist and game theorist found experimental survey evidence that teaching microeconomics by emphasizing the mathematics of constrained optimization problems encourages individuals toward profit maximization.[54] I remember, as a Ph.D. student of Kenneth Arrow's, listening to Arrow and Frank Hahn have a conversation about how those who choose to study economics differ from those who do not. Hahn said that he chose to go into economics because he realized he was not as gifted in mathematics as physicists and mathematicians. Arrow replied that that sort of thinking in terms of comparative advantage is already of an economic nature.

Does exposure to economics change one's behavior and expectations of how others behave? Several empirical and experimental studies examine whether being exposed to economics changes people's behavior. There is evidence that economists behave more selfishly than noneconomists in prisoner's dilemma games, and that learning introductory microeconomics from professors emphasizing prisoner's dilemmas and self-interested behavior is correlated with students choosing less cooperative responses in questionnaires about their behavior in hypothetical

[49] Peter A. Ubel, 2000, *Pricing Life: Why It's Time for Health Care Rationing*, Cambridge, MA: MIT Press.
[50] Sir William Thomson (Lord Kelvin), 1889, "Electrical Units of Measurement," lecture delivered to the Institution of Civil Engineers on May 3, 1883, in *Popular Lectures and Addresses*, vol. 1, London: McMillan, p. 73.
[51] John M. Henshaw, 2006, *Does Measurement Measure Up?: How Numbers Reveal and Conceal the Truth*, Baltimore, MD: Johns Hopkins Press, p. x.
[52] David Boyle, 2004, *The Sum of Our Discontent: Why Numbers Make Us Irrational*, New York: Texere.
[53] Uskali Mäki, "The Dismal Queen of the Social Sciences," 2003, in Uskali Mäki, ed., *Fact and Fiction in Economics: Models, Realism, and Social Construction*, Cambridge: Cambridge University Press, p. 3.
[54] Ariel Rubinstein, 2006, "A Sceptic's Comment on the Study of Economics," *Economic Journal*, 116, pp. C1–C9.

ethical dilemmas.[55] These findings have been replicated and extended to Canadian undergraduates, focusing on differences between economics majors and others, such as psychology majors.[56] But there is also evidence that real-world behavior of undergraduates in economics courses is actually substantially more cooperative than that of undergraduates in other courses.[57] There is also evidence that professional economists are significantly more cooperative about paying their professional association dues than professional political scientists and sociologists.[58] Further empirical evidence contradicts an indoctrination hypothesis that learning and practicing microeconomics leads to more calculating behavior in everyday life, and instead supports a selection hypothesis that individuals who are sympathetic to applying the price system are drawn to economics.[59] Nonetheless, recent experiments found that participants who were only primed to think about money preferred to play alone, work alone, and put more physical distance between themselves and new acquaintances.[60]

It would be of interest to resolve the open empirical question whether law students in actual and hypothetical ethical dilemmas, prisoner's dilemmas, and other experimental situations behave differently according to whether they took courses from professors who are supportive or critical of law and economics. Therefore, this chapter proposes empirically testing if those who see the world through an economics lens experience neutral or positive emotional reactions to applying microeconomics to nonbusiness areas of law, and those who do not see the world through an economics lens experience negative emotional reactions from doing so. This unsettled question can be resolved empirically by conducting surveys of academic and professional economists, academic and professional lawyers, economics graduate students, law students, and laypeople who view the world through an economic lens and those who do not. A hypothesis is that people who view the world through an economics lens will feel neutral or positive emotional reactions to applying microeconomics to nonbusiness areas of law, whereas people who do not will feel negative emotional reactions to doing so.

II. HOW MOST ECONOMISTS – AS OPPOSED TO MOST LAWYERS – VIEW LAW AND ECONOMICS

Most academic and professional economists without a J.D. know less about substantive law and legal procedure than most academic and professional lawyers.

[55] Robert H. Frank et al., 1993, "Does Studying Economics Inhibit Cooperation?" *Journal of Economic Perspectives*, 7, pp. 159–171; Robert H. Frank et al., 1996, "Do Economists Make Bad Citizens?" *Journal of Economic Perspectives*, 10, pp. 187–192.

[56] Tammy James et al., 2001, "Are Economists Rational, or Just Different?" *Social Behavior and Personality*, 29, pp. 359–364.

[57] Anthony M. Yezer et al., 1996, "Does Studying Economics Discourage Cooperation? Watch What We Do, Not What We Say or How We Play," *Journal of Economic Perspectives*, 10, pp. 177–186.

[58] David N. Laband and Richard O. Beil, 1999, "Are Economists More Selfish than Other 'Social' Scientists?" *Public Choice*, 100, pp. 85–101.

[59] Bruno S. Frey et al., 1993, "Economics Indoctrination or Selection: Some Empirical Results," *Journal of Economics Education*, 24, pp. 271–281; Bruno S. Frey and Stephan Meier, 2003, "Are Political Economists Selfish and Indoctrinated? Evidence from a Natural Experiment," *Economic Inquiry*, 41, pp. 448–462.

[60] Kathleen D. Vohs et al., 2006, "The Psychological Consequences of Money," *Science*, 314, pp. 1154–1156.

But much of substantive law and legal procedure is to a large degree arbitrary and the result of human conventions, as evidenced by the fact that at different times within any one country, and in different countries at any one time, there is usually much variation in substantive law and legal procedure. By virtue of their education in graduate school, most academic and professional economists share common training in microeconomics, involving routine application of a set of mathematical methods. In contrast, most academic and professional lawyers do not share that instruction unless they also have successfully completed a Ph.D. in economics or an economics-related field. Instead, most academic and professional lawyers have a J.D. and thus have their first year of required law school courses in common. Knowledge in microeconomics among most academic and professional lawyers is vastly more heterogeneous than among most academic and professional economists.

Most academic and professional lawyers do not know any microeconomics whatsoever. A few academic and professional lawyers know only whatever they have read in popular trade books about law and economics,[61] or microeconomics.[62] Fewer academic and professional lawyers know microeconomics at the level of a freshman undergraduate principles course, using high school algebra and geometry. Even fewer academic and professional lawyers know microeconomics at the level of an intermediate course for economics undergraduate majors, utilizing calculus. A few academic and professional lawyers know microeconomics at the level of a course specifically designed for lawyers.[63] Even fewer still academic and professional lawyers know microeconomics at the level of a first-year graduate school core sequence course, utilizing multivariable calculus and linear algebra. Finally, of course, the fewest academic and professional lawyers know microeconomics at the level of a second-year graduate school advanced microeconomic theory or mathematical economics field course, utilizing differential topology, functional analysis, and measure theory.

Because of differences in their professional training, most academic and professional lawyers without a Ph.D. in economics or an economics-related field know less formal mathematical microeconomic theory than most academic and professional economists. Ironically, most law-and-economics researchers at what is considered the birthplace of law and economics, the University of Chicago law school, apply microeconomics only at the level of at most the first-year microeconomics graduate course. I remember while being a first-year law student at the University of Chicago law school thinking of writing a review of game-theory books for legal scholars,[64] focusing on a just-published book that then dean of the University of Chicago law school Douglas Baird coauthored, explaining how legal

[61] David D. Friedman, 2001, *Law's Order: What Economics Has to Do with Law and Why It Matters*, Princeton: Princeton University Press.

[62] Steven D. Levitt and Stephen J. Dubner, 2006, *Freakonomics: A Rogue Economist Explores the Hidden Side of Everything*, rev. ed., New York: William Morrow.

[63] Richard A. Ippolito, 2005, *Economics for Lawyers*, Princeton: Princeton University Press.

[64] Peter H. Huang, 1995, "Strategic Behavior and the Law: A Guide for Legal Scholars to *Game Theory and the Law* and Other Game Theory Texts," *Jurimetrics: Journal of Law, Science, and Technology*, 36, pp. 99–114.

scholars can apply game theory to analyze legal rules and institutions.[65] He graciously invited me to lunch at the University of Chicago faculty club. En route to our
table, several other University of Chicago law school professors congratulated him
on the recent publication of his book, but also questioned why legal scholars had to
learn any modern game theory, because all of law and economics is just marginal
"this and that," for which all one required was calculus. It is unclear whether this
comment was made jokingly or not, but such a viewpoint certainly exists among a
number of law-and-economics practitioners: that all of microeconomics is merely
the study of single-person constrained optimization problems.

A related but different viewpoint is that microeconomics is the mere formal-
ization of three commonsense and intuitive notions, namely, that individuals are
rational, markets are socially desirable, and government regulations are harmful.
This viewpoint was also certainly prevalent among some, if not most, law-and-
economics researchers at the University of Chicago. Other related viewpoints that
are most associated with the University of Chicago include these: if one looks hard
enough, there is a rational explanation for any seemingly irrational behavior,[66] people are primarily motivated by monetary incentives,[67] microeconomics explains
many apparent paradoxes of life,[68] and one can find examples of microeconomics
in action everywhere by just observing people in their ordinary lives.[69]

Crossing the Midway while returning from the University of Chicago faculty
club to the University of Chicago law school after another lunch with Dean Baird,
he asked me whether I thought it was more important for one to be correct or first
in publishing research. I replied that if it was too much to ask for both, the history
of ideas has valued being first more than being correct. He said that neither was as
important as what is most important, namely being controversial. Not only is much
of the application of microeconomics to nonbusiness areas of law by University
of Chicago law school professors controversial outside the University of Chicago
law school, but apparently part of the University of Chicago culture is to not care
that people outside the University of Chicago find the relentless application of
(simple) price theory in a nonbusiness realm to be often inappropriate and in bad
taste. As University of Chicago Graduate School of Business economist Austan
Goolsbee stated: "We know that everyone hates us. The reason we do not care
is that we are too busy arguing with each other to pay attention."[70] Apparently
some University of Chicago law school professors actively seek out controversy.
Being controversial is related to another part of the University of Chicago ethos:
being misunderstood by those who are not part of the University of Chicago. En

---

[65] Douglas G. Baird et al., 1994, *Game Theory and the Law*, Cambridge, MA: Harvard University Press.
[66] Tim Harford, 2008, *The Logic of Life: The Rational Economics of an Irrational World*, New York: Random House.
[67] Tyler Cowen, 2007, *Discover Your Inner Economist: Use Incentives to Fall in Love, Survive Your Next Meeting, and Motivate Your Dentist*, New York: Dutton.
[68] Tim Harford, 2007, *The Undercover Economist: Exposing Why the Rich Are Rich, Why the Poor Are Poor – and Why You Can Never Buy a Decent Used Car!* New York: Random House.
[69] Robert H. Frank, 2007, *The Economic Naturalist: In Search of Explanations for Everyday Enigmas*, New York: Basic Books.
[70] Goolsbee, "Why People Hate Economists," p. 18.

route to a third lunch with Dean Baird, he described how difficult it is to secure letters from external reviewers who would understand the research conducted by a University of Chicago law school assistant professor. Indeed, as van Overtveldt writes, "Chicago's scholars have always been engaged in developments that were described elsewhere as 'crazy,' 'on the lunatic fringe,' 'a dead-end street,' and/or 'useless.'"[71]

A barrier to entry into graduate school in economics or an economics-related field is knowledge of multivariable calculus and linear algebra, and successful completion of graduate school in such fields requires successfully mastering some rudimentary elements of convex analysis, decision theory, dynamic programming, game theory, and topology. Undergraduate economics majors have to complete such mathematically rigorous courses as econometrics and intermediate microeconomics, quite often in addition to game theory and mathematics for economists. There is no equivalent mathematically rigorous course requirement for being a pre-law undergraduate major. In contrast, pre-med undergraduates are required to complete a year-long course in calculus and other rigorous courses such as organic and physical chemistry.

Mathematics is a language that most in law school are uncomfortable speaking or even hearing. Whether one admires or bemoans it,[72] there is no denying that mathematics is the language of contemporary microeconomic theory as well as that of empirical and experimental (micro)economics. This is because the language of mathematics offers levels of abstraction, precision, and rigor that do not exist in the language of anecdotes, metaphors, rhetoric, and stories, the way economists argued before the advent of mathematical economics. With the presentation of formal economic models in the language of mathematics that the Arrow–Debreu canonical model of general equilibrium started, economics came to be perceived as a mathematical science as opposed to a branch of moral philosophy.[73]

Economist Marcus Berliant provides five reasons for why modern economists continue to expand the depth and breadth of their use of the language of mathematics: "First, and perhaps foremost, mathematics makes communication between researchers succinct and precise. Second, it helps make assumptions and models clear; this bypasses arguments in the field that are a result of different implicit assumptions. Third, proofs are rigorous, so mathematics helps avoid mistakes in the literature. Fourth, its use often provides more insights into the models. And finally, the models can be applied to different contexts without replicating the analysis, simply by renaming symbols."[74]

Most Nobel laureates in economics who have made pioneering and seminal contributions in microeconomics or finance did so by formulating models of human behavior utilizing the language of mathematics. A clear hierarchy exists

---

[71] Johan van Overtveldt, 2007, *The Chicago School: How the University of Chicago Assembled the Thinkers who Revolutionized Economics and Business*, Chicago: University of Chicago Press.

[72] Donald A. R. George, "Consolations for the Economist: The Future of Economics Orthodoxy," *Journal of Economic Surveys*, 21, pp. 417–425.

[73] E. Roy Weintraub, 2002, *How Economics Became a Mathematical Science*, Durham, NC: Duke University Press.

[74] Foreword to Norman Schofield, 2004, *Mathematical Methods in Economics and Social Choice*, Berlin: Springer-Verlag.

among economists, with mathematical economists having the highest status.[75] But, precisely because mathematical economists deeply understand the mathematics of economic models, they also appreciate the limitations of economic models much more than people who do not understand the mathematics. Economist Stephen Marglin wrote: "Kenneth Arrow, among the great economists of the twentieth century, was recognized with one of the very first Nobel Prizes given in economics for his work on, among other things, general equilibrium theory. Arrow once said to me that the chief virtue of deep study of the theory of general equilibrium was that it revealed how stringent are the requirements for market outcomes to be socially desirable."[76]

The apparently sensible notion that financial market innovation is always socially desirable provides an example of how a lack of knowledge about mathematical models can lead people to believe in a falsehood. Because a complete set of asset markets will result in a Pareto-efficient allocation of risk,[77] it follows that completing asset markets by adding sufficiently many assets so as to have as many nonredundant assets as there are states of nature is Pareto-improving. But a central insight of theoretical research in the general-equilibrium theory of incomplete markets is that if asset markets remain incomplete after the addition of assets, then competitive market allocations typically not only are Pareto-inefficient, but also can be improved upon by a benevolent central planner who is constrained to utilize the set of existing incomplete asset markets.[78] This research formally proves that an intuition that many people have about the unambiguous social desirability of financial innovation – namely, that the introduction of asset markets will always and monotonically improve the welfare of consumers and investors – is demonstrably wrong and is actually only correct if a society is just one market short of complete asset markets.

III. QUALIFICATIONS REGARDING MARKETS

Economist Donald Wittman stated that "[m]ost controversies in the social sciences are ultimately arguments over the nature of the market. Marxist sociologists believe that both economic and political markets are characterized by poorly informed, possibly irrational consumers and voters who are exploited by monopolist suppliers of goods and policy."[79] For some people, markets can evoke negative images of unsympathetic robber barons and selfish capitalists exploiting hard-working

---

[75] Axel Leijonhufvud, 2004, "Life Among the Econ," *Western Economic Journal*, 11, pp. 327–337.

[76] Stephen A. Marglin, 2008, *The Dismal Science: How Thinking Like an Economist Undermines Community*, Cambridge, MA: Harvard University Press, p. 292. Some current economics research investigates whether there is a normative justification for competitive market allocations even when consumer preferences are not coherent; see, for example, Robert Sugden, 2004, "The Opportunity Criterion: Consumer Sovereignty without the Assumption of Coherent Preferences," *American Economic Review*, 94, pp. 1014–1033.

[77] Kenneth J. Arrow, 1963–1964, "The Role of Securities in the Optimal Allocation of Risk-Bearing," *Review of Economic Studies*, 31, pp. 91–96.

[78] Peter H. Huang, 2000, "A Normative Analysis of New Financially Engineered Derivatives," *Southern California Law Review*, 73, pp. 471–521.

[79] Donald A. Wittman, 1995, *The Myth of Democratic Failure: Why Political Institutions Are Efficient*, Chicago: University of Chicago Press.

laborers,[80] and recall the infamous scene in the film *Wall Street*,[81] in which Gordon Gekko made the notorious speech about how greed is good.[82] Such depictions make for colorful stories of and reflect suspicions toward markets. Academic and professional lawyers routinely tell stories, make analogies, and use metaphors,[83] as do academic and professional economists.[84] Human cognition at its heart involves narratives, analogies, and metaphors.[85] Of course, there are limits to the appropriateness or aptness of market metaphors.[86] There are related negative and positive metaphors about marketing.[87] To be sure, there are positive metaphors about markets, the most famous being Adam Smith's notion of an invisible hand.

But Milton Friedman famously defended markets, not in terms of Pareto efficiency of competitive allocations, but instead in terms of promoting freedom.[88] Friedman contrasted market allocation with allocation by governments under majority rule, where a majority can impose its will on individuals. Friedman viewed markets as ways to avoid the tyranny of the majority. As he eloquently stated, a "characteristic feature of action through political channels is that it tends to require or enforce substantial conformity. The great advantage of the market, on the other hand, is that it permits wide diversity. It is, in political terms, a system of proportional representation. Each man can vote, as it were, for the color of tie he wants and get it; he does not have to see what color the majority wants and then, if he is in the minority, submit."[89] But it is well known in the subfield of economics known as industrial organization that for heterogeneous instead of homogeneous products, markets with sizable fixed costs of production result in a socially inefficient amount of product differentiation.[90] For consumers

[80] William D. Casebeer, 2008, "The Stories Markets Tell: Affordances for Ethical Behavior in Free Exchange," in Paul J. Zak, ed., *Moral Markets: The Critical Role of Values in the Economy*, Princeton: Princeton University Press, pp. 3–15.

[81] *Wall Street*, Twentieth Century-Fox Film Corporation, 1987.

[82] David Ray Papke et al., 2007, *Law and Popular Culture: Text, Notes, and Questions*, Newark, NJ: LexisNexis, pp. 433–439.

[83] Ruth Anne Robbins, 2006, "Harry Potter, Ruby Slippers, and Merlin: Telling the Client's Story Using the Characters and Paradigm of the Archetypal Hero's Journey," *Seattle University Law Review*, 29, pp. 767–802; Lloyd L. Weinreb, 2005, *Legal Reason: The Use of Analogy in Legal Argument*, New York: Cambridge University Press; Pamela Samuelson, 1996, "The Quest for Enabling Metaphors for Law and Lawyering in the Information Age," *Michigan Law Review*, 94, pp. 2029–2057.

[84] Sara Ann Reiter, 1997, "Storytelling and Ethics in Financial Economics," *Critical Perspectives on Accounting*, 8, pp. 605–632; H. Thoben, 1982, "Mechanistic and Organistic Analogies in Economics Reconsidered," *Kyklos*, 35, pp. 292–306; Hanna Skorczynska, 2006, "Readership and Purpose in the Choice of Economics Metaphors," *Metaphor and Symbol*, 21, pp. 87–104.

[85] Mark Turner, 1998, *The Literary Mind: The Origins of Thought and Language*, New York: Oxford University Press; Dedre Gentner et al., 2001, *The Analogical Mind: Perspectives from Cognitive Science*, Cambridge, MA: MIT Press; George Lakoff and Mark Johnson, 1980, *Metaphors We Live By*, Chicago: University of Chicago Press.

[86] Jeffrey R. Henig, 1994, *Rethinking School Choice: Limits of the Market Metaphor*, Princeton: Princeton University Press.

[87] John A. Quelch and Katherine E. Jocz, 2008, *Greater Good: How Good Marketing Makes for Better Democracy*, Cambridge, MA: Harvard Business School Press.

[88] Milton Friedman, 1962, *Capitalism and Freedom*, Chicago: University of Chicago Press.

[89] Ibid., p. 15.

[90] Michael Spence, 1976, "Product Differentiation and Welfare," *American Economic Review*, 66, pp. 407–414; Michael Spence, 1976, "Product Selection, Fixed Costs, and Monopolistic Competition," *Review of Economic Studies*, 43, pp. 217–235.

with atypical preferences, such as African Americans, Asian Americans, Hispanics, other ethnic and racial minorities, people suffering from rare allergies or diseases, and individuals living in remote places, there can be a tyranny of markets.[91] Empirical examples of markets having suboptimal product diversity include those for local daily newspapers,[92] local radio stations,[93] and local television stations.[94]

A related appeal to markets for promoting freedom occurs when the phrase "a marketplace of ideas" is invoked in order to advocate freedom of expression or speech. This fundamental human right is guaranteed under the First Amendment of the U.S. Constitution, Article 19 of the Universal Declaration of Human Rights, and Article 10 of the European Convention on Human Rights. The underlying appealing and intuitive notion is that from unrestricted competition among different ideas in free and transparent public discourse, the best policy or truth will prevail. A 1967 Supreme Court opinion first contained the phrase "a marketplace of ideas" in stating "[t]he classroom is peculiarly the 'marketplace of ideas.'"[95] A broad concept and metaphor of "a marketplace of ideas" is usually attributed to a dissenting opinion by Justice Oliver Wendell Holmes, Jr., where he never used that actual phrase, but implied that notion: "Persecution for the expression of opinions seems to me perfectly logical. If you have no doubt of your premises or your power and want a certain result with all your heart you naturally express your wishes in law and sweep away all opposition. . . . But when men have realized that time has upset many fighting faiths, they may come to believe even more than they believe the very foundations of their own conduct that the ultimate good desired is better reached by free trade in ideas, . . . that the best test of truth is the power of the thought to get itself accepted in the competition of the market, and that truth is the only ground upon which their wishes safely can be carried out. That at any rate is the theory of our Constitution."[96]

The preceding theoretical research and empirical evidence demonstrating that markets with large fixed costs have too few or too many products, of course, naturally should qualify any faith one may have about whether the outcome from a marketplace of ideas will be optimal. The production of ideas, like information generally, has aspects of public goods, including substantial fixed costs and low if not zero marginal costs. In addition to the question of whether a marketplace of ideas will produce an outcome with too few or too many ideas, "ideas do not develop in a vacuum. Ideas need networks through which they can be shared and nurtured, organizations to connect them to problems and to diffuse them to

[91] Joel Waldfogel, 2007, *The Tyranny of the Market: Why You Can't Always Get What You Want*, Cambridge, MA: Harvard University Press.

[92] Lisa George, 2006, "The *New York Times* and the Market for Local Newspapers," *American Economic Review*, 96, pp. 435–447; Lisa George and Joel Waldfogel, 2003, "Who Affects Whom in Daily Newspaper Markets," *Journal of Political Economy*, 111, pp. 765–784.

[93] Steven T. Berry and Joel Waldfogel, 1999, "Free Entry and Social Inefficiency in Radio Broadcasting," *RAND Journal of Economics*, 30, pp. 397–420; Joel Waldfogel, 2003, "Preference Externalities: An Empirical Study of Who Benefits Whom in Differentiated-Product Markets," *RAND Journal of Economics*, 34, pp. 557–568.

[94] Joel Waldfogel, 2004, "Who Benefits Whom in Local Television Markets?" *Brookings-Wharton Papers on Urban Affairs*, 5, pp. 257–284.

[95] *Keyishian v. Board of Regents*, 385 U.S. 589, 605–606 (1967).

[96] *Abrams v. United States*, 250 U.S. 616, 630 (1919).

political actors, and patrons to provide resources for these supporting conditions. Of greater significance, the market for ideas is one in which incumbents have substantial resources with which to frustrate the challenges of competitors, regardless of how compelling their ideas are. In short, though there is a 'market' for ideas, it is one that is institutionally sticky and requires entrepreneurial activity to give it life. For this reason, intellectual history is necessary but not sufficient."[97] There are related other concerns based upon the concept of a meme, which is an information pattern, and the field of memetics, which theoretically and empirically studies how memes replicate, spread, and evolve.[98] Examples of memes include fashions, ideas, practices, songs, technologies, theories, and traditions.

Austan Goolsbee stated that "[i]n our world, it does not matter where you got a degree or how old you are or where you are from. It just matters what your ideas are. And that's how it should be."[99] He is making a positive statement about how the University of Chicago is a marketplace of ideas and also a normative statement about how that is desirable. Economist Colin Camerer once joked that if you present a talk at most places, the audience is gracious and polite, treating you like a dinner host, but if you present a talk at the University of Chicago, the audience is rowdy and unruly, treating you like an emergency room patient on whom the audience has to perform triage. Law-and-economics scholar Steven Shavell presented a talk in the University of Chicago law school's law-and-economics workshop in the fall of 2001 when I was a visiting assistant professor there. The first slide that he put up was one that was numbered in the twenties because he wanted to make sure that he would be able to cover it. After five minutes of audience members bickering among themselves and interrupting him, he simply turned off the overhead projector, stating that he should have known better than to think any differently. As Goolsbee stated: "It's who we are. We live to argue. How does the world work? Where should we eat lunch? Anything."[100] He added, "Come to a seminar any week of the year in economics, and you will find scholars in the thick of a debate that would long since have been considered 'checked out' anywhere else. It's actually quite thrilling."[101]

Although some people may be in love with the idea of a marketplace of ideas in academia, the reality in economics is that both type I and type II errors occur as to which articles are published in peer-refereed journals.[102] With respect to law reviews, second- and third-year law students make the decisions about which articles get published. There usually is not blind submission, because law students typically use the law school affiliation and alma mater of an author as informative signals for the "quality" of authors and perform searches on authors in the two

[97] Steven M. Teles, 2008, *The Rise of the Conservative Legal Movement: The Battle for Control of the Law*, Princeton: Princeton University Press, pp. 3–4.
[98] Richard Dawkins, 1976, *The Selfish Gene*, Oxford: Oxford University Press; Susan Blackmore, 2000, *The Meme Machine*, new ed., Oxford: Oxford University Press.
[99] Goolsbee, "Why People Hate Economists," p. 18.
[100] Ibid.
[101] Ibid., p. 19.
[102] Joshua S. Gans and George B. Shepherd, 1994, "How Are the Mighty Fallen: Rejected Classic Articles by Leading Economists," *Journal of Economic Perspectives*, 8, pp. 165–179.

primary databases of legal publications, Lexis and Westlaw, to see the "quality" of their law review publications. Most law students rank law reviews according to how the associated law schools are ranked annually by *U.S. News & World Report.* It is also common for law professors to include with their submissions cover letters, resumes, reprints, suggested optional external reviewers, and even photographs. Simultaneously submitting to many law reviews is also standard, whereas such a practice is unacceptable in economics, medicine, and other fields. Finally, one can try to trade up an acceptance from a lower-ranked law review by asking higher-ranked law reviews for expedited reviews. This has led some law reviews to offer exploding offers with a deadline of twenty-four hours, the close of the business day, or even two hours.

Law review editors are likely to be twenty-five years old; do not necessarily know anything about microeconomics, statistics, and other fields besides law, nor even the area of law that a submission is about; and have neither the interest nor the time required to read thoroughly each of several thousand unsolicited submissions that they annually receive to fill up the four to six issues of a typical law review volume, with each issue having space for only several articles. When I taught at the University of Pennsylvania law school, articles editors there confided that they read few submissions, and they only read the abstract, first couple of pages, and conclusion to see how it felt. One particular law review articles editor said that he and other articles editors decided to publish a law review article because, even though they could not determine whether it was correct in terms of its (very simple) microeconomics, that article was by a well-known University of Chicago law professor with a famous history of being quite controversial in applying economics to nonbusiness areas of law, and they could tell from just reading its abstract and conclusions that it was a highly controversial article certain to draw attention to it directly, and their law review indirectly.

Facing such a marketplace for law review articles, most law professors freely admit in private that placement in law reviews is a highly random crap shoot. Several law professors repeatedly submit articles to all the top twenty law reviews twice a year for several years until one of them publishes those articles, which they can do because most law reviews have no institutional memory. Each February or March, law reviews choose new editorial boards and begin accepting submissions. They continue to do so until the end of the law school year or until they fill the first part of their available slots, whichever happens first. They then break for the summer and fill the remaining slots when they return in August from their summer associate jobs. When Mark Ramseyer was a professor at the University of Chicago law school, he said that an article of his was rejected three times by the law review at UCLA, twice after it had already been published in a higher-ranked law review, because two successive generations of UCLA articles editors found it in the law review office without realizing it already was published.

Another problem with the legal academic marketplace for ideas is that quantity is often confused with or valued over quality. After I presented a job talk at George Mason University law school, Lloyd Cohen told me that when he was a John M. Olin Research Fellow at the University of Chicago law school from September 1988 to July 1990, people were discussing who was likely to be a future Nobel laureate

in economics. Lloyd suggested Ronald Coase, at which point prolific legal scholar
Cass Sunstein said that Coase only had one good idea. Upon hearing this, Lloyd
said that Coase had at least two good ideas. (I said to Lloyd that Coase had two
more good ideas than most academics.)

The likely inefficiency of the marketplace for ideas has consequences not just
for legal scholars, but also for government regulation and public policy. As the
famous macroeconomist John Maynard Keynes famously wrote in the conclusion
of his celebrated book *The General Theory of Employment, Interest, and Money*:
"The ideas of economists and political philosophers, both when they are right and
when they are wrong, are more powerful than is commonly understood. Indeed,
the world is ruled by little else. Practical men, who believe themselves to be quite
exempt from any intellectual influences, are usually the slaves of some defunct
economist. Madmen in authority, who hear voices in the air, are distilling their
frenzy from some academic scribbler of a few years back. I am sure the power of
vested interest is vastly exaggerated compared with the gradual encroachment of
ideas."[103]

The discipline of law also respects the force of precedent and is quite tradition-
bound, meaning that good and bad ideas can live for quite a long time before they
get competed away. As Keynes also wrote in the preface to his *General Theory*:
"The difficulty lies, not in the new ideas, but in escaping from the old ones, which
ramify, for those brought up as most of us have been, into every corner of our
minds."[104] In other words, new ideas can only take hold when old ideas die, but
old ideas die hard and slowly. Thus the progress of economics, like the progress of
science, is not by a gradual and linear accumulation of new ideas, but instead via
episodic paradigm shifts.[105] A behavioral economist observes that "academia is a
nasty environment, strewn with hidden traps and populated by hostile, territorial
tribes protecting their ideas with a ferocity akin to what one would expect a parent
to direct at someone trying to steal his baby."[106]

IV. CONCERNS ABOUT RATIONALITY

As Kenneth J. Arrow eloquently stated, "An economist by training thinks of himself as the guardian of rationality, the ascriber of rationality to others, and the
prescriber of rationality to the social world."[107] Neoclassical economics assumes
that because people are rational, economists can infer an individual's private, subjective, and unobservable preferences from that individual's public, objective, and
observable behavior in terms of market choices. This revealed-preference approach
requires that preference orderings are well-behaved, not only in the sense of satisfying certain mathematical axioms, such as the weak axiom of revealed preference,

[103] John Maynard Keynes, 1936, *The General Theory of Employment, Interest, and Money*, London: Macmillan, p. 383.
[104] Ibid., p. vii.
[105] Thomas S. Kuhn, 1962, *The Structure of Scientific Revolutions*, Chicago: University of Chicago Press.
[106] George Loewenstein, 2007, *Exotic Preferences: Behavioral Economics and Human Motivation*, New York: Oxford University Press, p. xiii.
[107] Kenneth J. Arrow, 1974, *The Limits of Organization*, New York: Norton, p. 16.

but also more crucially in the sense of being stable across contexts and over time. Naturally, a number of microeconomic theorists have conducted research in search of weaker conditions for being able to perform revealed-preference analysis.[108] But much of recent behavioral and experimental economics research by consumer researchers, marketing professors, and psychologists empirically demonstrates that preferences are to a large degree inchoate, being constructed from, and quite sensitive to, anchors or reference points, external cues, situational contexts, and social norms.[109] It is clear that individual preferences are culturally and socially constructed in addition to being malleable in response to advertising, experience, imitation, and persuasion. One legal scholar suggested that elections and voting should not be seen as the mere aggregation and tabulation of exogenous and given individual citizens' preferences, but instead as processes for the deliberation and persuasion of endogenous and tentative individual citizens' preferences.[110]

Economists have a methodological preference for, or bias toward, building models that have as their data or inputs variables that can be objectively measured and verified, such as initial endowments of physical capital, labor, land, energy, and financial resources. These variables are quantifiable, and when markets function smoothly, they can also be priced. But there are two categories of variables that economists also treat as exogenous parameters, and that are trickier for economists to measure: producers' technologies and consumers' tastes. Economic models about how firms and societies engage in and can foster research and development, growth, and innovation obviously do not assume that production possibilities and technological constraints are fixed and immutable.

An understandable concern, at least among noneconomists, about CBA is that it privileges economics in policy evaluation by framing costs and benefits as positive or negative, which economists can then simply add or subtract. But economists already enjoy privileged roles in public policy and have done so for quite a while now, as evidenced for example by the Council of Economic Advisers (CEA), which consists of three independent economists who prepare an annual overview of U.S. economic progress known as the Economic Report of the President, with the aid of approximately twenty academic economists and four permanent economic statisticians. On the other hand, there is not now, nor is there likely to be anytime soon, a corresponding Council of Psychological Advisers.[111]

Many economists and policymakers prefer objective measures over subjective measures, and measures that are behaviorally generated and thus observable to and verifiable by others over measures that are self-reported, unobservable, and

[108] Botond Kőszegi and Matthew Rabin, 2007, "Mistakes in Choice-Based Welfare Analysis," *American Economic Review*, 97, pp. 477–481.

[109] Sarah Lichtenstein and Paul Slovic, 2006, *The Construction of Preference*, Cambridge: Cambridge University Press.

[110] James Gardner, 2007, "Deliberation or Tabulation? The Self-Undermining Constitutional Architecture of Election Campaigns," *Buffalo Law Review*, 54, pp. 1413–1482.

[111] Max H. Bazerman and Deepak Malhotra, 2006, "Economics Wins, Psychology Loses, and Society Pays," in Cremer et al., *Social Psychology and Economics*, pp. 263–280.

unverifiable. A recent proposal is to evaluate environmental policy upon the basis of experienced utility measures.[112] Financial and securities regulations can also be promulgated in the hope of influencing based upon their impacts upon investors' and others' experienced affect, happiness, and trust.[113] A possible concern about experienced utilities is that they are temporary psychological effects that dissipate with experience or practice. There is psychological evidence that people adapt over time, both faster and more than they and others expected, to happiness and some types of unhappiness.[114] The affective-forecasting literature in social psychology finds that people overestimate both the duration and the intensity of their future hedonic responses to changes in their external circumstances.[115] Such affective overestimation can be due to a number of sources, including a focusing illusion, a distinction bias, immune neglect, and an intensity bias.[116] Regardless of its cause, people inaccurately anticipate their adaptation upon a hedonic treadmill, and also incorrectly predict other people's hedonic adaptation, with numerous attendant legal implications.[117]

Indeed, because of inaccurate forecasting and memories about experienced utility,[118] two scholars advocated basing and evaluating policy upon measures of actual experienced utility.[119] Two other scholars presented convincing arguments that hedonic adaptation presents difficulties for using experienced utility as a welfare criterion for evaluating policy.[120] But what is crucial to note is that people make decisions based upon their systematically inaccurate affective forecasts, some of

[112] Daniel Kahneman and Robert Sugden, 2005, "Experienced Utility as a Standard of Policy Evaluation," *Environmental and Resource Economics*, 32, pp. 161–181.

[113] Peter H. Huang, 2008, "How Do Securities Laws Influence Affect, Happiness, and Trust?" *Journal of Business and Technology Law*, 3, pp. 257–308.

[114] Philip Brickman et al., 1978, "Lottery Winners and Accident Victims: Is Happiness Relative?" *Journal of Personality and Social Psychology*, 36, pp. 917–927.

[115] Daniel T. Gilbert, 2006, *Stumbling on Happiness*, New York: Knopf; Daniel T. Gilbert and Timothy D. Wilson, 2000, "Miswanting: Some Problems in Affective Forecasting," in Joseph P. Forgas, ed., *Feeling and Thinking: The Role of Affect in Social Cognition*, Cambridge: Cambridge University Press, pp. 178–197.

[116] Daniel Kahneman and Richard H. Thaler, 2006, "Utility Maximization and Experienced Utility," *Journal of Economic Perspectives*, 20, pp. 221–234; Daniel Kahneman et al., 2004, "A Survey Method for Characterizing Daily Life Experience: The Day Reconstruction Method," *Science*, 306, pp. 1776–1780; Christopher K. Hsee and Jiao Zhang, 2004, "Distinction Bias: Misprediction and Mischoice due to Joint Evaluation," *Journal of Personality and Social Psychology*, 86, pp. 680–695; Daniel T. Gilbert et al., 1998, "Immune Neglect: A Source of Durability Bias in Affective Forecasting," *Journal of Personality and Social Psychology*, 75, pp. 617–638; Roger Buehler and Cathy McFarland, 2001, "Intensity Bias in Affective Forecasting: The Role of Temporal Focus," *Personality and Social Psychology Bulletin*, 27, pp. 1480–1493.

[117] Richard Layard, 2005, *Happiness: Lessons from a New Science*, London: Allen Lane; Jason Riis et al., 2005, "Ignorance of Hedonic Adaptation to Hemo-Dialysis: A Study using Ecological Momentary Assessment," *Journal of Experimental Psychology: General*, 134, pp. 3–9; Jeremy A. Blumenthal, 2005, "Law and the Emotions: The Problem of Affective Forecasting," *Indiana Law Journal*, 80, pp. 155–238; Samuel R. Bagenstos and Margo Schlanger, 2007, "Hedonic Damages, Hedonic Adaptation, and Disability," *Vanderbilt Law Review*, 60, pp. 745–797.

[118] Daniel Kahneman and Alan B. Krueger, 2006, "Developments in the Measurement of Subjective Well-Being," *Journal of Economic Perspectives*, 20, pp. 3–24.

[119] Kahneman and Sugden, "Experienced Utility."

[120] George Loewenstein and Peter A. Ubel, 2008, "Hedonic Adaptation and the Role of Decision and Experience Utility in Public Policy," *Journal of Public Economics*, 92, pp. 1795–1810.

which are irreversible or costly to reverse. Even if experienced utility is transitory or people can adapt to affective reactions, affect can have irreversible and permanent consequences upon individual behavior and such traditional economic variables as levels of aggregate consumption, investment, stock prices, and stock volume. More generally, both correct and incorrect affective forecasts will influence any forward-looking behavior, such as commercial real estate purchases, commercial and personal borrowing, consumer durable expenditures, mortgage financing and refinancing, new home construction, and residential real estate purchases. Expectations concerning the future affect many economic decisions in the present.[121] Of course, there is more to life and policy than just affect or mood.[122] Issues of identity and meaning can and should also be taken into account in evaluating policies and regulations.

Unlike most other social scientists, most economists have traditionally been quite skeptical of the accuracy, precision, and reliability of questionnaires and other self-descriptions.[123] But recently, a number of economists have begun to utilize survey data involving self-reported measures of happiness and subjective well-being (SWB), and economists have developed statistical techniques to examine how external factors affect SWB.[124] For example, economists found that an individual's own reported utility losses from terrorism far exceed terrorism's purely economic consequences; another pair of researchers estimated the monetary value of the disutility from airport noise.[125]

Another study, involving a sample of nine hundred employed women, found that commuting to and from their work produced among the lowest levels of retrospective well-being out of a list of nineteen activities.[126] The stress from daily commuting is a bona fide disutility that can be quite large. Commuters may also feel anger toward their fellow commuters for clogging up roads, but such anger or road rage is at least conceptually distinct from driving stress, though stress might be related to such feelings as anger, boredom, despair, frustration, or loss of control. Other economists found that changes in macroeconomic variables, such as a nation's gross domestic product and inflation rate, are correlated with reported SWB; these economists also found that mere fear about unemployment is correlated with large reductions in SWB.[127]

---

[121] Kenneth J. Arrow, 1978, "The Future and the Present in Economic Life," *Economic Inquiry*, 16, pp. 157–169.

[122] Loewenstein and Ubel, "Hedonic Adaptation."

[123] Truman F. Bewley, 1999, *Why Wages Don't Fall during a Recession*, Cambridge, MA: Harvard University Press.

[124] Bruno S. Frey, 2008, *Happiness: A Revolution in Economics*, Cambridge, MA: MIT Press; Andrew E. Clark and Andrew J. Oswald, 2002, "A Simple Statistical Method for Measuring How Life Events Affect Happiness," *International Journal of Epidemiology*, 31, pp. 1139–1144.

[125] Bruno S. Frey et al., 2007, "Calculating Tragedy: Assessing the Costs of Terrorism," *Journal of Economic Surveys*, 21, pp. 1–24; Bernard M. S. van Praag and Barbara E. Baarsma, 2005, "Using Happiness Surveys to Value Intangibles: The Case of Airport Noise," *Economic Journal*, 115, 224–246.

[126] Kahneman et al., "Characterizing Daily Life Experience."

[127] Rafael Di Tella et al., 2003, "The Macroeconomics of Happiness," *Review of Economics and Statistics*, 85, pp. 809–827; Rafael Di Tella et al., 2001, "Preferences over Inflation and Unemployment: Evidence from Surveys of Happiness," *American Economic Review*, 91, pp. 335–341.

The findings of the preceding studies, in conjunction with the literature on affective misforecasting, demonstrate that people often make choices that do not maximize their experienced utilities. Such behavior naturally raises the question of why people continue to act irrationally. As Kenneth Arrow explained:

> Any argument seeking to establish the presence of irrational economic behavior always meets a standard counterargument: if most agents are irrational, then a rational individual can make a lot of money; eventually, therefore, the rational individuals will take over all the wealth. Hence, rational behavior will be the effective norm. There are two rebuttals to the counterargument: (1) Not all arbitrage possibilities exist. For example, corporate profits, even though down, are distinctly positive in real terms, after all necessary adjustments, including taxes. Yet there seems no way by which the average investor in corporate securities can get a positive real rate of return. (2) More important, if everyone else is "irrational," it by no means follows that one can make money by being rational, at least in the short run. With discounting, even eventual success may not be worthwhile. Consider for example a firm that engages in research and development, which depresses the current profit and loss statement. Irrational investors look only at this information, and therefore the price of the stock is below the expected value of future dividends based on the profitable outcomes of the research and development. In a perfectly working market with rational individuals, stock prices would gradually rise as the realization date approaches, but prices in the actual market would be constant. A rational investor would understand the future value of the stocks, but he or she could not realize any part of the gain during the gestation period. While the rational investor may get rewarded eventually if the stock is held long enough, he or she is losing liquidity during an intervening period which may be long. Hence, the demand for the stock even by the rational buyers will be depressed. As Keynes argued long ago, the value of a security depends in good measure on other people's opinions.[128]

Persistence of irrationality raises at least a potential role for other actors, such as profit-seeking firms or benevolent government regulators, to help individuals make better decisions with respect to achieving higher levels of experienced utilities.[129] But there is also the possibility that it would be more profitable for firms or more advantageous for governments to exploit, rather than mitigate, persistent instances of irrationality.[130] There is currently a lively debate among some academic

[128] Kenneth J. Arrow, 1982, "Risk Perception in Psychology and Economics," *Economic Inquiry*, 20, pp. 7–8.
[129] Peter H. Huang, 2008, "Authentic Happiness, Self-Knowledge, and Legal Policy," *Minnesota Journal of Law, Science, and Technology*, 9, pp. 755–783; Peter H. Huang and Jeremy A. Blumenthal, forthcoming, "Positive Law and Policy," in *Encyclopedia of Positive Psychology*, Shane J. Lopez, ed., New York: Blackwell Publishing; Peter H. Huang and Jeremy A. Blumenthal, forthcoming, "Positive Institutions, Law, and Policy," in *Handbook of Positive Psychology*, 2nd ed., Shane J. Lopez, ed., Oxford: Oxford University Press; Peter H. Huang and Rick Swedloff, 2008, "Authentic Happiness and Meaning at Law Firms," *Syracuse Law Review*, 58, pp. 341–356; Richard H. Thaler and Cass R. Sunstein, 2008, *Nudge: Improving Decisions about Health, Wealth, and Happiness*, New Haven: Yale University Press; Richard H. Thaler and Cass R. Sunstein, 2003, "Libertarian Paternalism," *American Economic Review*, 93, pp. 175–179.
[130] Edward L. Glaeser, 2006, "Paternalism and Psychology," *Regulation*, 29, pp. 32–38.

economists and legal academics over what sort of paternalism can be justified by irrational behavior.[131]

CONCLUSION

In conclusion, this chapter has made three major points about law and economics. First, people have strong negative emotional reactions or no emotional reactions toward applying microeconomics to nonbusiness areas of law; such emotions are responses to taboo trade-offs and protected values. Second, within the field of economics, law and economics is an uncontroversial subfield of applied microeconomics, but within legal academia, it has become a forceful and contested school of thought; these different outcomes reflect differences in familiarity with microeconomics presented mathematically. Third, much research substantially qualifies many familiar and often cited purported benefits of markets and rationality, and those familiar with this research realize that there are intricacies and subtleties to markets and rationality that people unfamiliar with it often do not.

---

[131] Jeremy A. Blumenthal, 2007, "Emotional Paternalism," *Florida State University Law Review*, 35, pp. 1–72; Colin Camerer et al., 2003, "Regulation for Conservatives: Behavioral Economics and the Case for 'Asymmetric Paternalism,'" *University of Pennsylvania Law Review*, 151, pp. 1211–1254; Richard A. Epstein, 2006, "Behavioral Economics: Human Errors and Market Corrections," *University of Chicago Law Review*, 73, pp. 111–132; Claire A. Hill, 2007, "Anti-anti-anti-paternalism," *NYU Journal of Law and Liberty*, 2, pp. 444–454; Jonathan Klick and Gregory Mitchell, 2006, "Government Regulation of Irrationality: Moral and Cognitive Hazards," *Minnesota Law Review*, 90, pp. 1620–1663; Gregory Mitchell, 2005, "Libertarian Paternalism Is an Oxymoron," *Northwestern University Law Review*, 99, pp. 1245–1277.

10   Pluralism, Intransitivity, Incoherence

WILLIAM A. EDMUNDSON

> For the real problem of morality, and of the point or meaning of existence, is not in discerning the basic aspects of human well-being, but in integrating those various aspects... [into] one or another of the many admirable forms of human life.[1]

I. ETHICS OUT OF LAW AND ECONOMICS?

The methodologies of economics have cast revealing, if garish, light upon legal institutions and processes. In response to the criticism that those methodologies rely upon unrealistic assumptions about human rationality, the field of law and economics has lately taken an empirical turn. The *bounded* nature of our reasoning powers, with the implications of that boundedness, has moved from the fringes toward the center of discussion. But the methods of economics have also been taken in a different and more abstract direction recently: they have been applied to questions about the metaphysical nature of value that lie in the department of ethics that philosophers sometimes refer to as *axiology*. If economics is purged of its seemingly crude assumptions about what is valued, it may have a lot to tell us about the structure of value. Or such is the hope. The focus of this chapter is on the question of whether value in its plural nature can be held to behave in ways amenable to economic methods.

II. PLURAL VALUES

Experience reveals to us a host of things that we respond to as good or as bad. That tiramisu I had for dessert at dinner last week was good. That cruel remark I made to a friend one evening years ago, that was bad. The carnage of the third battle of Ypres was very bad. That removal of a property qualification for voting in my state

[1] John Finnis, 1986, *Natural Law and Natural Rights*, Oxford: Clarendon Press, p. 31.

I am indebted to a number of people for advice and encouragement at the formative stage of this chapter: chief among these is the late Susan Hurley. I also owe gratitude to Liz Ashford, Bruce Chapman, Jeremy Farris, Iwao Hirose, David McCarthy, Kevin Roberts, and Mark White. None of them has given an imprimatur to anything I write here, and none is to blame for my misunderstandings.

was good. That kind word from my spouse the other day, when I needed one, was good, but in a different way. Many different things and events are experienced as good or bad, and the ways in which they present themselves as good or bad are various. The way in which that soufflé Aunt Louise served at the family reunion is good is different from the way in which the smile of the Mona Lisa is good, or the emancipation of the serfs in Russia was good.

So, many things are good, but not all in the same way; and so also with things that are bad. This leads us to appreciate another pervasive fact of experience: some things are better than others, and some worse. More specifically, some good things are better than other good things, just as undeniably as good things are better than bad things. Similarly, some good things are better than other good things in some ways, and not as good in other ways. For example, that chardonnay I had last month was a better wine than the pinot grigio I had last week, but it was not as good a value. So also with bads.

So, it is easy to know that some things are good and others bad, and that some goods are better than others. It is easy to know that some things are better than others in some ways, but not in others. But, as John Finnis points out in the epigraph, it is not as easy to specify how we put these facts together into a coherent plan of living.

Another kind of common experience is that of judging that the good of a thing or option outweighs what is bad about it. This, put together with the experience of finding some goods greater than other goods, suggests the idea that what appear to be various goods are in fact different manifestations of a single good. Bads, then, can be seen either as lackings or deprivations of this single good. The problem of responding to the good could then be enormously simplified. What one ought to do is simply to act in a way that will achieve the greatest amount of good available, given one's options. This idea of maximizing a single value must be supplemented by an account of what this single good is, and how its various manifestations contribute to it. One account, hedonism, was familiar to the Greeks. Pleasure is the good, and the problem of life is simply to maximize the amount of pleasure one enjoys, or brings about, net of costs in pains. One may dispute the hedonists' account of good while accepting the basic idea that various goods are good in virtue of something they share, call it goodness, or value.

The view outlined in the last paragraph can be termed *monism*. Value, or the good, is one thing, variously manifested in various degrees. Pluralism asserts that there is value but denies that value is one thing. The problem of living is not solvable by maximizing some one value, but by integrating plural values. The pluralist account makes better sense of familiar experiences, such as balancing family and career. It is not that family and career both possess a single kind of value, and that balancing is simply a matter of measuring which has the greater amount of that value. It is more complicated than that, and it is incredible that there should be a uniquely optimal way of balancing the two. Moreover, there is no reason to think that family and career are the only aspects of human well-being; there are others, such as recreation, reflection, education, and so forth. Although it is tempting to think that these several values are simply vessels that contain some master value, like pleasure, that idea does not jibe with experience.

Another aspect of experience that monism does not jibe with is the experience of regret. I may, for example, choose to stay home with my ailing spouse rather than attend a concert. I see more good in doing that than in the alternative, but I regret not having gone to the concert. If monism were correct, my sense of regret would be irrational,[2] for I will have chosen to bring about the greater good. Regretting not having chosen the lesser is, on a monistic view, as irrational as it would be to regret not having had only a half glass of wine, after having chosen to drink a full glass (with no ill effect).

Pluralism about value is not committed to denying that there is better and worse. That is, pluralism need not deny that instances of different values are comparable.[3] Pluralism can readily admit that a wink is as good as a nod, or that a modest raise is better than a poke in the eye with a sharp stick. There may indeed be incomparabilities, but a pluralist need not insist that they are pervasive. Nor should a pluralist want to defend such a position, for it is contrary to the familiar experience of confidently choosing a greater good of one kind over a lesser of another. All the pluralist has to say is that comparability between instances of different values is not premised on their expressing different amounts of some single, underlying value.

III. THE PARADOX OF PLURALISM

Pluralism about values has (as one might expect) many attractions. The hard part for pluralism lies in explaining how we might coherently integrate the plurality of values that claim our attention. Finnis speaks of integrating the plural aspects of well-being (itself one among many values, and comprising many) into one or another of a plurality of "admirable forms of human life." But this is already to stake a claim for integration as desideratum; and another, surely, is rationality.

Values can be understood as sources of reasons for action. Rationality can be understood as a capacity to respond appropriately to those reasons. But a moment's reflection will convince us that rationality is a constrained response to reasons. As Joseph Raz has pointed out, responsiveness to all reasons is neither possible nor desirable. Rationality is a capacity to respond to reasons in the right way, and the right way is at least partially to be characterized in terms that limit the ways in which rational persons respond to reasons.

A general sketch of the constraints that constitute rationality is beyond the scope of this chapter. What I will focus on here are certain aspects that in particular bear on the question: how ought one rationally to respond to (a plurality of) reasons? One reasonable expectation is that a rational creature will perceive reasons and, having perceived a number of them, will put them in some sort of order. A rational creature will also be cognizant of salient options before her, and their correspondence to

[2] Robert Sugden, 1985, "Why Be Consistent? A Critical Analysis of Consistency Requirements in Choice Theory," *Economica*, 52, pp. 167–183.

[3] Donald Regan, 1997, "Value, Comparability, and Choice," in Ruth Chang, ed., *Incommensurability, Incomparability, and Practical Reason*, Cambridge, MA: Harvard University Press.

C_1	C_2	C_3
x	y	z
y	z	x
z	x	y

Figure 10.1.

the reasons she has. Perceiving a multiplicity of options, a rational creature will attempt to sort them into better and worse, according to the reasons each would fulfill or frustrate. Finally, a rational creature will form an intention to act on the best option available to her, and will act appropriately. Although conscious deliberation is not always involved, this process of converting values into action is one that is subject to criticism insofar as it deviates from certain canons of practical rationality. One such canon, plausibly, is that if the actor perceives that A is better than B, and that B is better than C, she should infer that A is better than C. "Whatever decisions we make, we shall always be guided by logic to preserve the transitivity of the comparative.... Logic requires betterness to be transitive...."[4] This is the familiar – but, as discussed in the following, controversial – requirement of *transitivity*. Its being a constraint on rationality is not the same as its being a constraint on the reasons there are, however. Just as we cannot respond to all the reasons there are (as Raz points out), it may be that we cannot expect moral reality to be as well behaved as we insist our reasoning about it to be – if, that is, we are truly pluralist about value. Let me explain.

At least since Condorcet, the rationality of collective decision making in democratic assemblies has been known to be problematic. Whenever voters vote by ranking three or more options by preference, intransitivities can arise. Majorities may prefer A to B, B to C, and C to A even though no individual voter's preference ordering is so perverse. If the pattern of preferences falls out in this intransitive way, no choice can be made that seems entirely rational; for a majority will prefer something other than the chosen option, whatever it might be. This possibility is well known as Condorcet's *voting paradox*. It arises, generally, where the matrix of criterial orderings contains a Latin square configuration, of the form shown in Figure 10.1.[5]

Interpret the C_i's as voters and x, y, and z as candidates: it is clear that transitivity fails if voters are asked to rank the candidates in order of preference, and the winner is determined by compiling the rankings. Two-thirds of the voters prefer x to y, two-thirds prefer y to z, but two-thirds prefer z to x.

---

[4] John Broome, 1995, *Weighing Goods*, Oxford: Blackwell, pp. 12, 136.
[5] From Bruce Chapman, 2001, "Pluralism in Tort and Accident Law: Towards a Reasonable Accommodation," in Gerald Postema, ed., *Philosophy and the Law of Torts*, New York: Cambridge University Press, p. 285.

Kenneth Arrow's *Impossibility Theorem* generalizes the structural difficulty Condorcet first recognized. Arrow showed that, given certain plausible assumptions, a *social welfare function* is impossible. A social welfare function is a mapping of individual preferences onto social choices (preference serving as a proxy for welfare). A social welfare function would represent an ordering of outcomes, which is to say that the arguments would be comparable and the function connected and transitive over the range of arguments. Here is Luce and Raiffa's explanation:

> Arrow has shown that five seemingly innocuous requirements of "fairness" for social welfare functions are inconsistent (i.e., no social welfare function exists which satisfies all of them). The five conditions are: (1) universal domain (the function has to resolve all conceivable profiles of preference patterns); (2) positive association of individual values; (3) independence of irrelevant alternatives; (4) citizen's sovereignty (or non-imposition); and (5) non-dictatorship.[6]

Another way of stating Arrow's result is to say that if all five requirements are satisfied, then either the preference relation fails to be transitive or a contradiction results. The less controversial of these requirements are (2), (4), and (5), and the more controversial are (1) and (3). Yet another way of stating Arrow's result is to say that any social welfare function that satisfies the first three conditions must be "either imposed or dictatorial."[7]

At the risk of oversimplifying, the following characterizations motivate these requirements. Requirement (2), "positive association of individual values," is essentially a reasonableness condition that assures that if alternative x is preferred to alternative y under a given social welfare function, for a given profile of individual preferences, it will remain so for any profile that differs only in that x receives higher rankings for some profiles. Requirement (4), "citizen's sovereignty (or non-imposition)," states that for any pair of alternatives x and y, there is a profile of individual orderings such that the social welfare function ranks x above y (assuring that the social welfare function is responsive to individual preferences, however they happen to fall out, and thus is not "imposed"). Requirement (5), "non-dictatorship," assures that no one individual's preferences are decisive regardless of the preferences of others. (The two more controversial requirements call for more detailed discussion, but I will reserve that until after I have set out an intrapersonal version of Arrow's impossibility result, which will throw into relief what I call the "paradox of pluralism.")

The practical impact of Arrow's result and the Condorcet paradox is limited. The paradox arises only when individual preferences happen to present themselves in unfortunate configurations. The more general Arrow result is demonstrable only with the assistance of strong assumptions, particularly the universal-domain requirement. *Universal domain* requires the social welfare function to take as arguments all possible preference profiles in a population, and this will mean taking seriously perverse preferences that no reasonably representative group is likely to

---

[6] R. Duncan Luce and Howard Raiffa, 1985, *Games and Decisions: Introduction and Critical Survey*, New York: Dover, p. 368.
[7] Ibid., p. 339.

hold. Moreover, democratic voting can be structured in various ways to avoid a Condorcet paradox where the underlying pattern of preferences would produce it. Voters might be asked to pick a favorite rather than to rank all candidates, for example; or the candidates might be winnowed down to two by a series of head-to-head contests (for example, z might be seeded and x and y required to face each other to determine who advances to challenge z).

One focus of this chapter is the circumstance that the rationality of individual decisions that reflect a plurality of values is affected in a similar, and surprisingly little-discussed, way.[8] The structure that generates the Condorcet paradox can easily be adapted to the case of an individual who is motivated by reasons arising from plural values. In the context of a particular choice, values may stand in for voters, and may rank options in a way that exactly mirrors Condorcet's conditions. Interpreting the C_i's to stand not for voters but for values, or criteria of choice, and x, y, and z as options, it is evident that the compilation of rankings will be intransitive: x outranking y according to two criteria, y similarly outranking z, and z outranking x. Kenneth May gave this illustrative example: let C_1 = entitlement, C_2 = equality, and C_3 = excellence. A doctor has to choose which of three patients (x, y, and z) to treat, and can only treat one. Entitlement ranks them x, y, then z, because x is a patient of long standing, y a referral from a colleague, and z a walk-in. Equality ranks them y, z, then x, because y is neediest, z less needy, and x needs nothing other than treatment. Finally, excellence ranks them z, x, then y, because z will contribute wonderfully to humankind once cured, x less so, and y hardly at all. The doctor can of course break out of the resulting intransitive cycle – the point is that nothing *a priori* prevents her finding herself caught in one.[9]

Rational agents perform that act, among the options open to them, that they have most reason to perform – but plural values, under reasonable assumptions, can create circumstances in which, in a simple-minded sense, each of several incompatible option has greater rational weight than its rivals. As May points out, transitivity is in effect a sixth condition assumed by Arrow. Combining an assumption of transitivity with an assumption of value pluralism leads to contradiction – for present purposes, taking the conjunction of nondictatorship and nonimposition as capturing an essential condition of genuine pluralism. Either transitivity or pluralism must be given up if paradox is to be avoided. I call this situation the *paradox of pluralism*, which comes in two forms: a strong (Arrovian) form, and a weaker form, which I will discuss later.

IV. AVOIDING THE ARROVIAN (STRONG) PARADOX

An intrapersonal (or "intraprofile") analogue of the Arrow result rests on the assumption that, *ceteris paribus*, A is preferred to B if there are more reasons favoring A than B. In the social case, the parallel assumption is that it is more

---

[8] Susan L. Hurley, 1985, "On Intrapersonal Analogues of Arrow's Theorem," *Mind*, pp. 501–525; Susan L. Hurley, 1989, *Natural Reasons*, Oxford: Oxford University Press.

[9] Kenneth O. May, 1954, "Intransitivity, Utility, and the Aggregation of Preference Patterns," *Econometrica*, 22, pp. 1–23.

rational to satisfy more people than fewer, assuming each counts for one and none for more than one.[10] Similarly, it is hard to see how it could not be the case that if A satisfies two desiderata and B only one, then normally there is more reason to choose A than B – unless, of course, there is some basis for preferring some desiderata to others, or if the desideratum that both satisfy is satisfied to a greater degree by A. But if these conditions are present, nonimposition and nondictatorship, which are necessary to any genuine pluralism, assure that indeed this is the case. Given these pluralistic conditions, more *reasons* favoring A to B amounts to greater *reason* to elect A than B, and it is an obvious canon of rationality that one ought to choose the option there is greater reason to choose.[11] Susan Hurley has explained what is at stake:

> We may regard the majority-of-criteria method of deliberation as crude and unappealing, so we may not be alarmed when it turns out to be inadequate. But the generalized claim, that there is no function from orderings of alternative by specific criteria to an all-things-considered ordering that meets certain conditions [viz., transitivity], may indeed be alarming. . . . According to coherence accounts, what ought to be done is some function of the various specific reasons that apply to the alternatives in question; deliberation involves a process of constructing hypotheses about the content of the function. If May's reinterpretation of Arrow's framework accurately represents the constraints on a deliberator who seeks coherence in the face of conflicting reasons, then there is no question but that the sought-after coherence function does not exist.[12]

The existence of such a (nondictatorial) coherence function is essential to value pluralism, Hurley continues, for if none exist,

> We must conclude that, despite their attractions, non-lexicographic pluralistic theories, which recognize conflicting values and give priority to different values in different circumstances rather than simply arranging them in a rigid hierarchy, cannot be coherent.[13]

Hurley's view is that although the problem May identified is a serious one, it can be defused by relaxing one or more of the stronger Arrovian assumptions needed to set up an intraprofile analogue of the Arrow Impossibility Theorem. In particular, the unrestricted-domain assumption is in her view unwarranted in the intraprofile case. This assumption (variously called the "richness" condition or the "rectangular field" assumption) assures that the domain of the preference function is rich in the sense that it contains every possible array of preferences. As David McCarthy explains it:

> Roughly speaking, the rectangular field assumption guarantees that the domain of the relation in question is like a box, or more precisely, a Cartesian product.

---

[10] T. M. Scanlon, 1975, "Preference and Urgency," *Journal of Philosophy*, 72, pp. 655–669.

[11] William A. Edmundson, 2007, "Adding Reasons Up," in Barbara Montero and Mark D. White, eds., *Economics and the Mind*, London: Routledge, pp. 180–200.

[12] Hurley, *Natural Reasons*, p. 230.

[13] Ibid., pp. 230–231.

Suppose for example that we are interested in a relation which holds between n-tuples of different lives. Then a version of the rectangular field assumption says that if $l_1, l_2, \ldots, l_n$ are each possible lives considered separately, then there is some n-tuple of lives $[l_1, l_2, \ldots, l_n]$. I.e. if the lives are separately possible, then they are jointly possible.[14]

In the intraprofile case, the universal-domain assumption guarantees that the domain includes not only all possible counterfactual pairings, but all "countercriterial" ones as well. Not only is the valuer represented as ranking unavailable as well as available options, she is represented as ranking all options in all possible orders – preferring, as it were, the destruction of the Earth to the pricking of her thumb somewhere in the domain, as well as the reverse elsewhere. The effect of this is that somewhere in the domain there are bound to be Latin square configurations. To paraphrase Bruce Chapman, the Arrow assumptions taken together seemingly convert

> a "not generally possible" result for some particular counterfactual ordering (available only as a logical matter, perhaps, because of universal domain) into a "generally not possible" result for all possible criterial orderings, including the much more limited profile of criterial orderings that exists as a matter of fact.[15]

Hurley convincingly argues that the assumptions of universal domain and independence of irrelevant alternatives – necessary to deriving a general intraprofile impossibility result – are improper for the intraprofile case. Universal domain, in particular, violates supervenience, for it posits a range so rich as to contain differing preferences with respect to identical states of the world. Supervenience allows assigning differing values only where there is some nonevaluative difference between states. In the course of her discussion, Hurley explains that

> we must distinguish the domination of a particular theory about values over others on theoretical grounds from the dictatorial status of a single value . . . [moreover] a coherence function's success and the justification it provides for certain resolutions of conflicts shouldn't be confused with the dictatorship of one of the values the theory is about [as though] any successful coherence function could immediately be reinterpreted as a dictatorial argument of a simpler function. . . . The analogous confusion for social welfare functions doesn't arise because functions of individuals' preferences have no tendency to materialize into individuals whose dictatorial status would be a matter of concern.[16]

So, for example, if the ingredients of utility are genuinely plural, we ought not to twit utilitarians as monists who stand for the dictatorship of a favored value.

But the question remains, in what way are the genuinely plural ingredients of utility (or happiness, or virtue, etc.) to be integrated (even if we draw back from thinking of the integration as formulable as a "coherence function")? The hostility of supervenience to a universal-domain assumption in the intraprofile case does not guarantee that intransitivities will never otherwise appear in a profile.

---

[14] In correspondence with the author.
[15] Chapman, "Pluralism in Tort and Accident Law," p. 284.
[16] Hurley, *Natural Reasons*, p. 233.

Supervenience guarantees that there are no (real) evaluative differences unless there is some subvening nonevaluative difference: it does not guarantee that there are no real intransitivities. And there do seem to be actual nonevaluative intransitivities: an example being the "is preferred to" relation understood in the psychological sense. Supervenience does not even guarantee that evaluative intransitivities (if any) supervene upon some nonevaluative intransitivity. One might reasonably hold, for example, that preference, as a psychological phenomenon, supervenes upon neurophysical phenomena. But that is no ground for assuming that the psychological relation of preference maps onto some relation (transitive or otherwise) inhering in the neurophysical substrate. It seems unlikely that it would, although it might (which is an empirical question).

V. WEAK PARADOX: THE PERSISTENT POSSIBILITY OF INTRANSITIVITY

A persistent possibility of a Latin square creeping in seems to affect both the domain of rationality and preference and the domain of moral reality. As argued in the preceding section, an appeal to supervenience cannot, alone, exclude this possibility from the domain of real values. Can anything? It is natural to look for treatments that have been devised for the domain of rational preference. With a modest assist from the assumption that the logical behavior of real values mirrors that of rational preference, what works in the latter case could be applicable to the former. But how well-behaved is rational preference? Kenneth May was skeptical:

> [T]he question is no longer "Are preferences transitive?" but rather "Under what conditions does transitivity fail?" Of course, the whole issue may be avoided by simply asserting transitivity as part of the definition of "rational behavior." The question then is whether rational behavior as so defined has very much importance, either descriptive or normative. Still another way of avoiding inconvenient circularities is to define troublesome alternatives as "not comparable." But it is just these "non-comparable" cases that are of interest. Comparison only of alternatives in which one is superior to another in every respect makes for a simple but rather trivial theory. Incidentally, the relation of non-comparability is itself intransitive! There seems no way to avoid considering intransitivity as a natural phenomenon.[17]

In this passage May anticipates the respective approaches of John Broome (stipulating transitivity) and John Finnis (invoking incomparability), which I discuss in the following.

A. Preference Intransitivity

It is worthwhile having a closer look at an apparent intransitivity-of-preference case. Amos Tversky shows how intransitivity of preferences attaches to certain

---

[17] May, "Intransitivity," p. 8.

Dimensions

		I	II
	x	2ε	6ε
Alternatives	y	3ε	4ε
	z	4ε	2ε

Figure 10.2.

modes of decision making, whereas others are immune. Tversky distinguishes what he terms *additive* from *additive difference* models.[18] Roughly, an additive model evaluates alternatives singly, summing the several value-giving qualities of each, then assigning an overall value. Only then are alternatives compared. Assuming that the model otherwise behaves as it should, transitivity can be demonstrated to hold. In contrast, an additive-difference model is one in which evaluative dimensions are taken first, and alternatives compared as to each, in turn. Depending upon how the decision-maker processes the dimensional evaluations, intransitivities may indeed arise.

Consider Figure 10.2: In this example, Tversky describes a hypothetical selection among three job candidates.[19] Intelligence is the chief criterion (dimension I), but where two candidates do not differ significantly in measurable intellect, the more experienced is preferred (dimension II). Stipulating that differences no greater than 1ε are negligible, an intransitivity can arise if values fall out in certain ways. If the values shown are assigned, the decision rule yields a cycle of preferences: x is preferred to y because the difference in intelligence is insignificant whereas that in experience is not. Similarly, y is preferred to z. Transitivity would dictate that x be preferred to z, but if x and z are compared directly, z is preferred because the difference in intelligence is not negligible.

The decision heuristic in Tversky's example satisfies the additive-difference model rather than the additive model. Is the lesson, then, that decision heuristics that satisfy only the additive-difference model are irrational? Tversky argues to the contrary, on the ground that additive-difference methods often have practical advantages.

---

[18] Amos Tversky, 1969, "Intransitivity of Preferences," *Psychological Review*, 76, pp. 31–48.
[19] Ibid., p. 32.

B. Real Intransitivity

The further question is about the structure of value, and only indirectly about the psychology of valuers. As a matter of axiology, the relative ease by which some additive-difference heuristics can be applied in practice is neither here nor there. Larry Temkin and Stuart Rachels offer a kind of counterexample to transitivity that does not involve heuristics, although (as I will show) it has a similar structure.[20] The example goes like this. Let us agree (or stipulate) that a person's death is worse than that person's becoming a quadriplegic. We can also agree that, *ceteris paribus*, it is worse if two die than if one only dies. It seems reasonable, though, to say that there is some number n of quadriplegias such that n quadriplegias is worse than one death. That might be a large number, but it need not be so large that quadriplegia amounts to death because there are no nonquadriplegics left to care for the quadriplegics. Say, a million quadriplegias is worse than one death. Better surely that one die, than that a million be rendered quadriplegic (imagine a large trolley hurtling out of control, etc.).

But, by the same token, a quadriplegia is not as bad as some number n' of paraplegias. And, in turn, there is some number n'' of broken hips that is worse than a single paraplegia; and there is some number n''' of bruised hips that is worse than a single broken hip, and so on. If transitivity is assumed, then we are required to conclude that it is better that one die than that n''' suffer a bruised hip. But that seems false. No? Continue the construction until we reach some extremely large number of mild headaches. Though Broome would trust transitivity and the numbers,[21] surely the intuitive response is that it is better that there be a gazillion mild headaches than one death – transitivity fails over such distances.

Temkin's example seems not to fit Tversky's model. Or does it? Return to Figure 10.2.

Let dimension I be "grade one harm avoided" and dimension II be "grade two harm avoided." Temkin essentially argues that there is an ε such that the difference between one death and n quadriplegias is less than ε. But the difference between n quadriplegias and $n + 1$ quadriplegias is greater than ε, and this is what registers in dimension II. So $x > y$ despite the fact that x involves a death and y does not. Similarly, $y > z$ for some n. Then we get the mild headaches numbering some huge n, but the difference between the badness of one death and n mild headaches exceeds ε, so $z > x$, violating transitivity.

So, I think it is correct to say that Temkin's example is a form of Tversky's. It differs in that dimension I is not assumed to be a noisy proxy for value, but value itself. There just is some number n of quadriplegias that is worse than a single death. The denial is counterintuitive, but to make the admission is to step onto the slope of transitivity. But transitivity leads to the counterintuitive conclusion that one life is less valuable than the avoidance of some multitude of mild headaches. In

[20] Larry S. Temkin, 1996, "A Continuum Argument for Intransitivity," *Philosophy and Public Affairs*, 25, pp. 175–210; Stuart Rachels, 1998, "Counterexamples to the Transitivity of *Better Than*," *Australasian Journal of Philosophy*, 76, pp. 71–83.
[21] John Broome, 2004, *Weighing Lives*, Oxford: Oxford University Press, pp. 55–62.

the same way, insisting on transitivity in Tversky's example would require choosing the aged dimwit over the whiz kid. The difference between the two examples is that in Tversky's, dimension II comes into play due only to the imperfectness of the dimension I proxy for intelligence. In Temkin's example, grade one harm avoidance is not serving as a proxy for something else: it is the very thing.

VI. AVOIDING WEAK PARADOX IN THE REAL DOMAIN

The persistent possibility of unruly preferences was shown, in the last section, to be mirrored in the world of real values. Any value pluralism that is realist about values has therefore to worry that a world of plural values is an incoherent world. I will now look at three solutions, due to John Broome, John Finnis, and Bruce Chapman, respectively. Each fails.

A. Broome's Way: Transitivity as Conceptual Truth

Following his general approach to extracting from economics what is of durable value to ethics, Broome eschews preference and utility in favor of goodness; or, more precisely, he eschews the relations "is preferred to" and "has greater utility than" in favor of "is better than." What, then, of the apparent intransitivities pointed out by Pettit,[22] Schumm,[23] Sugden,[24] Temkin,[25] and Tversky[26]? If betterness cannot shake free of them, value pluralism courts incoherence.

In the face of such apparent intransitivities of the betterness relation, Broome insists that it is a conceptual truth that betterness is transitive. But what reason is there to believe that betterness (as opposed to preference) is transitive? If it is conceded that "is preferred to" may be intransitive, whereas "is greater than" may not, what ground can there be for assimilating betterness to "greater than" rather than to "preferred to"? If we are realists about values, should we not be open to the possibility of intransitivities? If we are, instead, going to stipulate that the semantics of English demands that betterness can never be cyclical, it is not easy to see how that posture can be squared with naturalism or with pluralism. Broome concedes that "ought" may indeed be intransitive, but insists that the transitivity of betterness may be detached and maintained, even in a teleological ethics that treats the "ought" as, one way or another, a product of betterness.[27] Decoupling the right and the good in this way seems a desperate expedient; but it is true that the possibility of cycles of betterness is an additional problem insofar

[22] Philip Pettit, 1991, "Decision Theory and Folk Psychology," in Michael Bacharach and Susan Hurley, eds., *Foundations of Decision Theory: Issues and Advances*, Oxford: Blackwell, pp. 147–175.

[23] George F. Schumm, 1986, "Transitivity, Preference, and Indifference," *Philosophical Studies*, 52, pp. 435–437.

[24] Sugden, "Why Be Consistent?"

[25] Larry S. Temkin, 1987, "Intransitivity and the Mere Addition Paradox," *Philosophy and Public Affairs*, 16, pp. 138–187; Temkin, "Continuum Argument."

[26] Tversky, "Intransitivity of Preferences."

[27] Broome, *Weighing Lives*, pp. 59–60.

as there may be realms of choice into which the mandatory "ought" does not reach – where we have genuine options.[28] It is in this optional realm that we feel we make most of our decisions, whether momentous or trivial. Here we also aspire not only to openness to genuine values but also to integrity or coherence in some sense.

B. Finnis's Way: Rejecting Comparability

Finnis recoils from the horrors to which comparability – by itself and especially if propelled by transitivity – would lead. Accordingly, he insists that basic values are incomparable. He grudgingly admits that there may be comparability across bearers of a single basic value, and he admits that trade-offs between basic values are sometimes inescapable. He, like May, regards choice between a dominant and a dominated alternative as trivial, and goes farther to say that such a choice is hardly worth counting as a case of rational deliberation.

The aspects of existence that constitute the basic values are easily discerned, Finnis says; but the trick (if the problem of life and its meaning can be so called) is in "integrating those various aspects . . . [into] one or another of the many admirable forms of human life." Finnis finesses the difficult challenge of saying when and how conflicts are to be resolved. Instead, he posits a constraint against choosing "directly" against a basic value. This constraint is underived, and in that sense is like the basic values themselves, but is not itself a basic value. The distinction between direct and nondirect choosings creates space for deontological moves like the doctrine of double effect, which (depending on how it is formulated) might allow one to choose to bring about a net greater good where the costs that must be netted are merely foreseen and not intended, or are mere side effects rather than means.

How is one to choose among various competing basic goods, which may be chosen in various proportions, without violating the deontological constraint against direct choosings-against? Finnis does not even hint at how choices between the remaining eligibles are to go. He indicates that there are "many admirable forms of human life," which is to say that there are genuinely plural ways of integrating genuinely plural values without acting directly against any of them. There is then of course no coherence function of any kind, for there is no mapping the constellation of values and options available to one onto a unique outcome (action, disposition, or rule of thumb). But Finnis surely does not mean to say that "anything goes" so long as one chooses among basic values and never directly against any of them. Not just any hodgepodge can count as an "admirable form of life" representing an integration rather than a mere assortment of tokens of the basic values. Or can it?

Some characters possess certain virtues (manifest certain values) in high degree, but others in such modest degree that the whole person is less than admirable. (The description of Rooney Lee in *The Education of Henry Adams* comes to mind: his initially impressive "habit of command" ceased to impress as his lack of intelligence

---

[28] See Shelley Kagan, 1989, *The Limits of Morality*, Oxford: Clarendon Press.

became evident.) Is the lesson that an admirable life cannot be one that – though it does not act against any basic value – manifests one of them in too modest a degree? That promising suggestion ignores the difference between an admirable integration and a not-as-admirable dilettantism. More bluntly, the dilettante is not admirable. Nor can the dilettante attain admirability by being serious about everything. Worse than having a natural aptitude for every worthy pursuit is uniform seriousness in the exercise of those aptitudes. Finnis knows this, for he speaks of "many admirable forms" rather than a maximally admirable ideal combining all the virtues in the highest compossible degree.

But this brings us no closer to an understanding of how to distinguish admirable integrations from less-than-admirable accumulations. (To treat integratedness rather as a separate, basic value is not a starter. For one thing, it would have to be integrated with other basic values, which suggests both double counting and incoherence.) Perhaps knowing how to tell the difference between integration and accumulation is an ineffable aspect of *phronesis*, the practical wisdom that the practically wise exhibit as second nature, but that eludes any formulation.[29] (Is one practically unwise, perhaps, precisely to the extent that one needs a formulation?) It might be true that incomparable, plural basic values cohere or fail to cohere in ways not susceptible to further analysis. But it would be disheartening to believe that no matter how scrupulously one honors the basic values, whether one's life as whole hangs together or falls apart is intrinsically a piece of luck, and that a happy result is one that no amount of reasoning might determine.

C. Chapman's Way: Appeal to Natural Structures

Insisting on the incomparability of basic values is one way of avoiding both the incoherence that comes with intransitivity and the antipluralism that comes with dictatorship. But it seems to invite the charge of arbitrariness, even of obscurantism. "Are there no natural orderings among plural values?" one has to ask. Some choices just seem naturally prior to others. Suppose it is evening and there is time (or budget) for dinner or for a movie but not both. The choice whether to go out to dinner or to go out to a movie instead seems to be a question prior to the questions which restaurant to go to (if it is dinner) and which movie to see (if it is the movies). It might seem perverse to debate about the relative merits of the various movies in town until it has been settled whether it is to be dinner or a movie. Similarly, one might think it is naturally more sensible to decide whether to reform a policy or stick with the status quo before deciding between two distinct reform proposals. But it is a familiar experience to condition the choice between dinner and a movie on what the movie is (or the dinner options are), and to condition the choice whether to reform or to continue a policy on which of two reforms is to be instituted if there is a change.

Bruce Chapman points out that, often, certain criteria are *jurisdictionally decisive* with respect to certain alternatives. In other words, if, within a certain decisive subdomain, the pair x and y rank in the same order as w and z, those rankings may

---

[29] Thomas Nagel, 1979, *Mortal Questions*, Cambridge: Cambridge University Press, pp. 134–137.

be conclusive even though the all-things-considered rankings deviate. As Chapman puts the point:

> If different criteria can be separated into different domains where they reign supreme, perhaps because the criteria are in some sense a good match for the alternatives considered there, then it might seem that some of the conflict between criteria, so characteristic of pluralism, can be avoided.[30]

So a "conceptual ordering" of pluralistic choice might be a way of working out a "jurisdictional separation strategy" that mitigates or avoids incoherence. The strategy accepts the path dependence of rankings not as a troublesome anomaly but as reflecting the nature of the values and domains in play. "After all, path dependence is simply partition dependence with a temporal dimension."[31] The task becomes one of exhibiting the ordered sequence as not arbitrary but rather manifesting an underlying conceptual structure.

The procedure Chapman pursues appears, however, to be less a matter of unearthing any conceptually dictated ordering than of imposing one. Chapman says as much:

> We might *impose* a form of value restriction on pluralistic criteria by way of appropriate institutional design ... even if the criterial orderings do not satisfy the requirement spontaneously or as a matter of brute fact.[32]

He goes on to describe the "sequenced structure" that is to be imposed:

> First, for any possible triple of alternatives, the idea is to have the criteria compare, and choose between one of the three alternatives considered on its own and the other two alternatives considered as a packaged pair. Then, if the packaged pair is chosen, the criteria can go on to consider and choose, which of the previously packaged alternatives in particular is to be the final choice.[33]

The trick is in the packaging. The unpackaged alternative is privileged in the sense that it need not face the packaged alternatives singly. The packaged alternatives are privileged in the sense that they, too, need not face the unpackaged alternative singly. In that sense, the sequencing does not seem prejudicial. But the packaging is equivalent to privileging the dimensions of choice that are decisive in the first round; and the prejudicial effect of that is not symmetrically canceled out. The tactic is commonly referred to as a "sequential elimination agenda" and is one viewed with suspicion in the social-choice literature as often giving the agenda setter (actual or hypothetical) what amounts to near-dictatorial power over outcomes.[34]

---

[30] Chapman, "Pluralism in Tort and Accident Law," p. 286.
[31] Ibid., p. 290.
[32] Ibid., p. 296 (emphasis in original).
[33] Ibid.
[34] Peter C. Ordeshook and Thomas Schwartz, 1987, "Agenda and the Control of Political Outcomes," *American Political Science Review*, 81, pp. 179–200.

To return to Tversky's example, if intelligence is assigned a priority over experience, choosing the additive over the additive-difference method of comparison
determines whether or not intransitivities can arise. But the more serious difficulty
lies in justifying the decision to assign the intelligence dimension a priority over
experience. It is not obvious why the priority should not be the reverse. So it is also
with other cases in which one dimension of choice is deemed to be lexically (or,
more properly, lexicographically) prior to another. As Chapman worries, "Have
we not simply substituted a new form of criterial conflict, one now focused on the
particulars of a choice sequence, for the original one that focused on the choice of
final alternatives?"[35] He resists this dire conclusion by insisting that "some choice
sequences (or paths), or choice packages (or partitions of the alternatives), simply
make more sense than others, at least in a given context where real alternatives are
standing in for the merely lettered abstractions x, y, and z."[36]

The particular context that concerns him is accident law. As to this, he stakes
the claim that the "natural" approach to the question of reform of accident law
follows this sequence: (1) change or no change? (2) if change, then what form
of change? and (3) of that chosen form, what extent of change? To the obvious
objection that the questions of the form and extent of change are inextricably
wound into the decision whether to maintain the status quo or depart from it,
Chapman responds: "I prefer our proposed choice sequence [proceeding from the
general to the particular] to the alternative choice sequence [from particulars to
the general question whether to change or not] because it preserves a coherence
that should exist between the *conceptual* (partition dependent) ordering of issues
and the *value* restrictions which are imposed on criteria."[37] But all this seems but
a fancy way of saying that the sequence one chooses should be one that responds
to the desire that motivated sequencing in the first place, namely to maintain
coherence and avoid intransitivity.

Tversky, to the contrary, maintained that the value of a heuristic is not to be
judged solely by its avoidance of intransitivities. Any heuristic has to be judged
by how it performs in two dimensions: accuracy and usability. The usability of
a heuristic is not necessarily destroyed by its generating intransitivities. True, in
the abstract, one might be made into a "money pump" by another who can be
imagined to be positioned to exploit one's use of a heuristic – just as one can
be made to look infinitely credulous for embracing näive (Cantorian) set theory.
Tversky, like Wittgenstein, regards such vulnerabilities as largely valetudinarian.
We deal with latent intransitivities in our reasoning the way we deal with latent
contradictions in our beliefs: when a real need arises.

On the dimension of accuracy, there is reason to believe that there are no
contradictory pairs within the set of all truths about nature: the contrary cannot
be imagined. But what reason is there, for a value pluralist who is also a realist
about values, to insist that there are no intransitive triples in the set of all true

---

[35] Chapman, "Pluralism in Tort and Accident Law," p. 298.
[36] Ibid.
[37] Ibid., pp. 300–301 (emphasis in original).

comparative judgments? It is not because a self-contradiction can be derived, nor is it because the contrary cannot be imagined. Nor is such an occurrence in conflict with supervenience. If it is simply semantic bedrock that betterness is transitive, then so much the worse for value pluralism. The avenues of escape seem all to lead to monistic dictatorship in one guise or another.

CONCLUSION

Bernard Williams made these remarks about Isaiah Berlin's pluralistic political philosophy:

> [I]f there are many and competing genuine values, then the greater the extent to which a society tends to be single-valued, the more genuine values it neglects or suppresses. More, to this extent, must be better . . . even if we grant the important qualification that not all values *can* be pluralistically combined, and that some become very pale in too much pluralistic company. There are [however] logical, psychological and sociological limits on what range of values an individual can seriously respect in one life, or one society respect in the lives of various of its citizens.[38]

The limits Williams adverts to, "logical, psychological and sociological," may or may not confine an individual's response to genuine values in ways that assure a coherent, much less an admirable, combination. Nor is there any assurance that the admirable combinations are one and all coherent. Dictatorial combinations, though, are ruled out, for those "neglect or suppress" genuine values. But "principles of rational choice"[39] do not, unless by stipulation, guarantee coherence, whether the question is one's "plan of life" or one's plan for the evening.

Thus Nozick: "For each person, so far as objective criteria of goodness can tell (insofar as these exist) there is a range of very different kinds of life that tie as best; no other is objectively better for him than any one in this range, and no one in the range is objectively better than any other."[40] Reference to "kinds of life" (Nozick) or "admirable forms of human life" (Finnis) might suggest that at an ultimate stage the individual faces a choice between alternative plans that are themselves internally coherent. The motive for clearing the incoherent plans from the field of choice would presumably operate at the ultimate stage as well – the rational agent will pick one plan from among the internally coherent alternatives: no mixing. But this suggestion would assume that at a penultimate stage coherence had somehow been assured, while at the same time the genuine plurality of values had been respected. This, I have argued, is an illegitimate assumption.

Once transitivity of preference is called into question on descriptive grounds, it is tempting to impose it as a conceptual or a normative requirement. But no compelling case has been made for regarding such an imposition as a demand of rationality. Must a world of (objective) plural reasons, then, nonetheless exhibit

---

[38] Bernard Williams, 1978, "Introduction," in Isaiah Berlin, *Concepts and Categories*, Princeton: Princeton University Press, p. xix (emphasis in original).

[39] John Rawls, 1971, *A Theory of Justice*, Cambridge, MA: Harvard University Press, p. 408.

[40] Robert Nozick, 1973, *Anarchy, State, and Utopia*, New York: Basic Books, p. 310.

a characteristic that rationality in responding to such a world does not? I have suggested that there is no ground for insisting it should. A world of genuinely plural values may well happen to be an unruly world of real intransitivities; and the more genuine values there are in a world, the likelier that world is to be unruly. To paraphrase Williams: more, to this extent, must be more unruly. Value pluralists who are realists must be prepared to follow where these commitments lead. If economic methods lack needed traction in such slippery territory, expectations of what they can contribute to the study of value must be revised downward.

11 Law and Economics and Explanation in Contract Law

BRIAN H. BIX

INTRODUCTION

Law-and-economics scholars have offered theories that purport to compete with other theories of law, and with other theories of particular doctrinal areas of law. This chapter will explore what it means to have a theory of a particular area of law, using contract law as an example, and will then consider the way in which law-and-economics theories succeed or fail in explaining contract law.

Section I offers a brief overview of the problems and possibilities inherent in theories about a doctrinal area of law (like contract law). Section II addresses the question of whether theories are or should be general and universal rather than particular. Section III introduces the law-and-economics approach, and section IV discusses the role of historical or causal explanation, both in general theorizing about doctrinal areas and in the law-and-economics approach. Section V looks at some less ambitious variations of doctrinal theories from law-and-economics writers, and section VI outlines some critiques and responses to the law-and-economics approach.

I. THEORIES, EXPLANATION, AND JUSTIFICATION

What does it mean to have "a theory of law" or "a theory of contract law"? Such jurisprudential theories sit uneasily between theories of the humanities and theories of the social sciences. And theories of doctrinal areas do not obviously fit into the more familiar sorts of theories one finds from the physical sciences, declaring the certain causes and effects of objects in their interaction. Nor are they the sorts of theories one finds commonly in the social sciences: evaluating or predicting human behavior based on observations and statistical analysis. Although there is a need and a use for studies (say) describing the frequency with which different sorts of contract claims prevail, theories of contract law are usually an entirely different sort of project. If anything, theories of contract law may be closer to certain kinds

I am grateful to Mark D. White for his comments and suggestions on an earlier draft.

of theories within the humanities – conceptual theories in political science and philosophical theories.[1]

If one says that a theory "explains contract law," what is being explained, and what is meant by "explanation"? The meaning of "explanation" seems like one of those inquiries so basic that it is difficult to make headway: one can speak of reducing the complex to the simpler, displaying deep structure, and showing the connection between concepts, but it is not clear that any of these phrases make the objective clearer. One suspects that explanation is a foundational notion, such that any effort to discuss it in other terms will confuse more than clarify. At the same time, one can note that however we think of explanation, it seems to fill different sorts of roles in different areas of study, as will become clearer in the following.

As already noted, one should not expect a theory of contract law to be like a theory in physics – or even like one in history – which might link two factors as a matter of physical causation, or at least, strong statistical correlation, though one should not exclude the possibility of such a theory altogether. One could certainly imagine a kind of crude Marxist theory of law that claimed that all rules and court decisions – including those in contract law – could be shown to serve directly the interests of the wealthy and powerful classes. However, theories of contract law are not usually simple causal theories of that sort, but rather partake in a combination of descriptive and evaluative tasks. This reflects the fact that such theories are usually presented as both descriptive of, and participating in, the project of practical reasoning that we call "law."

Michael Moore has nicely summarized the motivations of theorizing at the level of areas of law: that it is in part entailed by the moral requirement that we treat like cases alike; that it helps to determine the proper outcome in novel cases; and that it is entailed by our assumption – or hope – that the law coherently pursues worthy objectives.[2] These are important moral (and psychological) forces pushing us toward having a general theory for an area of law, but it may be that some areas are too various and inconsistent to ground a general theory, despite those reasons for theory.[3]

One can also ask questions about the subject of theories of areas of law, along a different axis: do these theories purport to explain the results of cases, the reasoning of cases, or something else? Theories often refer to particular legal doctrines,[4]

---

[1] The core jurisprudential question, "what is law?," quite clearly parallels other humanities inquiries, like "what is art?" or "what is literature?," and is usually thought to be a similarly conceptual inquiry. See Brian H. Bix, 2006, "Joseph Raz and Conceptual Analysis," *American Philosophical Association Newsletter on Philosophy and Law*, 6, pp. 1–7, http://www.apaonline.org/publications/newsletters/Vol06n2/Law.pdf.

[2] Michael S. Moore, 1990, "A Theory of Criminal Law Theories," *Tel Aviv University Studies in Law*, 10, pp. 115–185; Michael S. Moore, 2000, "Theories of Areas of Law," *San Diego Law Review*, 37, pp. 731–741.

[3] I have elsewhere argued that contract law may be one area for which multiple, more parochial theories may be preferable to a general and universal theory. See Brian H. Bix, 2007, "Some Reflections on Contract Law Theory," *Problema*, 1, pp. 143–201, available at http://www.juridicas.unam.mx/publica/librev/rev/filotder/cont/1/pr/pr6.pdf.

[4] Peter Alces is emphatic: "Contract theory, whether deontological, consequentialist, or pluralist, begins and must end with the doctrine, and must have something to say about doctrine that serves a

but doctrines are just shorthand used by commentators (as well as judges, law professors, and law students) to summarize past and future court decisions in individual cases. (Some doctrines are based on, or modified by, statutes, or get codified in statutes, but one can still argue that the full meaning of these general rules is not understood until one sees how they are applied in individual cases.)

One problem (perhaps more familiar, or at least more immediate, to law students writing exams than to high-level theorists about the common law) is that explaining the doctrine cannot be easily translated into explaining the case outcomes. One need not accept the old critical-legal-studies claim about radical legal indeterminacy[5] to see that doctrine often underdetermines case outcomes. For those who believe that contract theory should be about doctrine, what should be said about these instances? One possibility is simply to shrug, saying that doctrine does not operate in such cases,[6] or one could say that how doctrine operates requires the fuller elaboration and specification in the case decisions. In such situations, at least, the focus needs to be on case outcomes, at least as a supplement.

Law-and-economics theories of contract law are frequently criticized on the basis that they do not track the way that participants in the legal system (judges, lawyers, and perhaps also legal commentators) talk about contract law.[7] Where legal practitioners speak in terms of particular doctrines, or more generally about morality and obligation, or consent and freedom of contract, law-and-economics theories frequently refer only, or primarily, to efficiency.

One potential response is that the terms in which contract-law cases are debated in court, or decisions are discussed in judicial opinions, should not be the primary objects for explanation. What is, or should be, the primary focus for explanation are the outcomes of cases, the actual decisions of who wins and who loses in contract-law disputes. This view has been forcefully argued by Jody Kraus.[8] He presses the point that a theory that explains the judicial reasoning but is contrary to the actual outcomes (or would work equally well on given cases both with the actual outcome and the opposite outcome) fails as a matter of justification, and that justification is a central aspect of what these sorts of theories do – and should be doing.[9]

---

heuristic purpose . . . " (2007, "The Moral Impossibility of Contract," *William & Mary Law Review*, 48, p. 1647).

[5] See Lawrence B. Solum, 1987, "On the Indeterminacy Crisis: Critiquing Critical Dogma," *University of Chicago Law Review*, 54, pp. 462–503.

[6] Cf. Alces, "Moral Impossibility," p. 1663, n. 47.

[7] See Stephen A. Smith, 2004, *Contract Theory*, Oxford: Oxford University Press, pp. 108–136; Nathan B. Oman, 2007, "The Failure of Economic Interpretations of the Law of Contract Damages," *Washington & Lee Law Review*, 64, pp. 829–875.

[8] Jody S. Kraus, 2007, "Legal Determinacy and Moral Justification," *William & Mary Law Review*, 48, pp. 1773–1787; Jody S. Kraus, 2007, "Transparency and Determinacy in Common Law Adjudication: A Philosophical Defense of Explanatory Economic Analysis," *Virginia Law Review*, 93, pp. 287–359.

[9] It is on this basis that Kraus ("Transparency") constructs an argument that an economic approach to contract law may be defensible despite its less good fit (than that of deontological theories) with the bilateralism of contract law specifically, and, more generally, with the way participants perceive and characterize contracts and contract doctrine. It is important to note that Kraus's argument depends, in part, on an assumption "that economic analysis in fact yields more determinate explanations of case outcomes than deontic theories" (p. 302). That economic theories may have somewhat

Kraus has argued that deontological and consequentialist (economic) theories differ in that deontological theories give priority to justification whereas consequentialist theories give priority to explanation.[10] This leads to a separate question: is explanation something different from justification? Of course, in the abstract, the two are separate, but one might argue that the two cannot be separated in the specific context of common-law legal reasoning. This ties into the fact, already discussed, that theories of doctrinal areas of law play a role in legal reasoning, both directly and indirectly.

II. UNIVERSAL THEORIES AND PARTICULAR THEORIES

To have a theory of contract law is, implicitly, to assert that contract law is a category about which something of interest can be said (just as a similar claim about law is implicit in those who offer general or universal theories of law[11]). Do the theorists believe that there is some category "contract law" that is in some way independent of human belief and practices, in the way that, for example, the chemical structure of gold creates a natural kind, independent of human belief and practices? Or if contract law is not a Platonic idea or a natural kind, perhaps theorists assume it to be an accidental category, about which we just happen to have interesting things to say. Neither alternative seems attractive, but theorists rarely offer any alternative justification for theorizing about contract law as a general category.

In any event, for most law-and-economics theorists, it is probably not entirely accurate to say that they have "a theory of contract law." More often, such theorists offer a economics analysis theory of (all) legal rules, or perhaps a theory of private law or common law, of which contract law is but a subset or an example or application.[12] Not that there is necessarily anything wrong with that. That view certainly does not require a naive belief in the homogeneity of law. To say that one seeks efficiency in tort law, constitutional law, and contract law is not to assert that one expects the rules in all three areas to be identical: what efficiency requires in the area of regulating safety will be predictably different from what it will require in general government structure and in commercial transactions.

---

greater *relative* determinacy may not be controversial ("is it efficient?" perhaps yielding more consensus answers on most questions than "is it fair?"), but, as noted in the text following, many scholars, including many sympathetic to the law-and-economics movement, find efficiency analysis in contract law to be significantly indeterminate. To the extent this is true, this may undermine some of the power of Kraus's argument here.

[10] Jody S. Kraus, 2002, "Philosophy of Contract Law," in Jules Coleman and Scott Shapiro, eds., *The Oxford Handbook of Jurisprudence and Philosophy of Law*, Oxford: Oxford University Press, pp. 694–696. In the same piece, he argues that economic theories tend to focus on case outcomes, whereas deontological theories focus on doctrine (p. 696).

[11] Bix, "Conceptual Analysis."

[12] See generally Richard A. Posner, 2007, *Economic Analysis of Law*, 7th ed., New York: Aspen Publishers; Steven Shavell, 2007, *Foundations of Economic Analysis of Law*, Cambridge, MA: Harvard University Press; Cento Veljanovski, 2007, *Economic Principles of Law*, Cambridge: Cambridge University Press. For example, we read in Posner, *Economic Analysis of Law*: "we have seen that the law of property..., of contracts, and commercial law, of restitution and unjust enrichment, of criminal and family law, and of admiralty law all can be restated in economic terms that not only explain the principal doctrines, both substantive and remedial, in these fields of (largely) judge-made law but also demonstrate their economic unity" (p. 249, footnote omitted).

On the other hand, some law-and-economics scholars do seem to imply that there is something distinctive about a category called "contract law." They speak of what is, or what should be, distinctive of this area. At the same time, were such theorists to be pressed regarding the issue of universal versus particular theories, they could respond that this is not an issue on which they need to take a stand, and that their theories would serve the same purpose were they to be redescribed as, say, "theories of American contract law" or "theories of American, English, and Canadian contract law" or "theories of Minnesota contract law."

Such theorists might (again, this is speculation) respond that there is reason to believe that their theories aspire to more general application – that what functions to improve efficiency in commercial and interpersonal transactions in one location will likely do so in other locations as well. They may argue that economic analysis is grounded in human nature and the nature of social institutions, and that these are unlikely to vary greatly from one location (and one time) to another. (Some nonconsequentialist theorists, by contrast, seem quite wedded to there being a particular category, contract law, which – they imply, more than assert – would be constant across jurisdictions and over time. The justification here might be that if contract law is connected in some essential way to, say, promise[13] or corrective justice, then that connection would not vary by location.)

I have discussed elsewhere, at some length,[14] the issues surrounding whether there is or should be a general and universal theory of contract law. The question is whether a single theory should cover contract law in all times and places (the alternative I argue for is making theory narrowed to a particular jurisdiction and time; another alternative is the claim that theory is untenable even at this localized level). It is likely that if one sees one's subject for theorizing to be all contracts, or all contract law, crossing boundaries of time and place, the tendency will necessarily be toward references to "essential characteristics" and "necessity." Theorizing narrowed to a particular time, and perhaps a particular type of transaction, may be able to veer more toward the descriptive, and less towards the conceptual.

III. LAW-AND-ECONOMICS THEORIES

At its most basic, law and economics is the application of the tools of economics to legal rules, institutions, and actors. Sometimes the application is relatively basic, for example, involving talk of incentives and disincentives, and the rational-actor model. One major difference between economic analysis in this context and in more conventional contexts involves the assumption (developed most fully by Gary Becker[15]) that economic analysis can be fruitfully applied to noncommercial activity. The more intricate approaches and tools of game theory[16] and public

---

[13] See Charles Fried, 1981, *Contract as Promise: A Theory of Contractual Obligation*, Cambridge, MA: Harvard University Press; Charles Fried, 2007, "The Convergence of Contract and Promise," *Harvard Law Review Forum*, 120, pp. 1–9, http://www.harvardlawreview.org/forum/HLRforum.shtml.

[14] See Bix, "Some Reflections."

[15] Gary S. Becker, 1976, *The Economic Approach to Human Behavior*, Chicago: University of Chicago Press.

[16] See, for example, Douglas G. Baird, Robert H. Gertner, and Randal C. Picker, 1994, *Game Theory and the Law*, Cambridge, MA: Harvard University Press.

choice theory[17] may also be brought to bear. Finally, there are forms of analysis distinctive to the economic analysis *of law*, including, famously, the Coase theorem.[18]

A separate problem which one sometimes comes across in law-and-economics theories (though, arguably, it was more likely to affect the early theorists than the most recent works) is that some of the theories are not as clear as they might be about the nature of the claims being made: are they meant to be descriptive/explanatory, a rational reconstruction, or pure prescription? The terminology alone can create confusion, with analysis that purports to be neutral, but that often uses terms with strong normative overtones (e.g., "rational" and "efficient"). Of course, one might note that this is a problem generally for doctrinal legal analysis, and especially with common-law subjects, where no clear line separates the law that is from the law that (we think, or the judges think) ought to be.

There is one particular idea within, or about, contract law that is associated with, and arguably distinctive of, the economic analysis of contract law: the idea of *efficient breach*.[19] The concept is that the law effectively gives the promisor the option whether to perform or pay damages – as payment of expectation damages is the near-universal remedial standard, with orders of specific performance allowed only in extraordinary cases, and supracompensatory damages unavailable (and penalty provisions unenforceable). The reference to efficient breach means that the law can be seen as implicitly encouraging parties to breach their contracts when an alternative transaction would be so much more profitable that the original contracting party could be paid full expectation damages and the breaching party would still be better off.

One standard response to the doctrine of efficient breach by critics of economic analysis is that it improperly conflates what the law gives permission to do and violations of duties that require compensation.[20] To use an analogy from a different legal context, paying a fine and paying a tax may have the same financial consequences, but they are normatively distinct, and a theory that conflates them is for that reason a worse theory.

IV. HISTORICAL EXPLANATION: TRADITIONAL AND ECONOMIC

It is a common experience of contract-law scholars, as well as teachers and students of the area, that some doctrines seem difficult to explain: they neither cohere well with other contract-law doctrines and principles, nor do they seem to be independently justifiable. In such circumstances, commentators and teachers do not (usually) stop talking. They instead alter the nature of the explanation they offer. Instead

---

[17] See, for example, Daniel A. Farber and Philip P. Frickey, 1991, *Law and Public Choice: A Critical Introduction*, Chicago: University of Chicago Press.

[18] Ronald H. Coase, 1960, "The Problem of Social Cost," *Journal of Law and Economics*, 3, pp. 1–44.

[19] For example, Charles J. Goetz and Robert E. Scott, 1977, "Liquidated Damages, Penalties, and the Just Compensation Principle," *Columbia Law Review*, 77, pp. 554–594.

[20] For example, Jules L. Coleman, 2007, "Some Reflections on Richard Brooks's 'Efficient Performance Hypothesis,'" *Yale Law Journal Pocket Part*, 116, pp. 416–422, http://www.thepocketpart.org/2007/07/23/coleman.html.

of a theory that offers a rational reconstruction to give coherence and justification to the rules and principles, the theories offered are more in terms of causal explanations: explaining how we came to have the rules and principles we do have. Most often, these are straightforwardly historical explanations, indicating the accidents or arbitrary choices of the past that led to one path being chosen rather than another. For example, A. W. B. Simpson[21] and J. H. Baker[22] have intricate stories to tell about how we came to have the doctrine of consideration in English law.[23]

Another kind of causal story – historical, in a sense – comes from some law-and-economics theorists, who argue that certain processes occurring over time have led to our having the private-law doctrines we do. The processes that concern these economic theorists are ones that (they argue) lead to increasingly greater efficiency for private-law rules (e.g., the rules for contract law, tort law, and property law). Richard Posner famously once argued that the common-law doctrines developed by judges in the nineteenth and twentieth centuries followed, as though by an invisible hand, a path to ever greater efficiency.[24] (Posner still proffers a slightly diluted version of that claim,[25] though it is not an analysis that is as commonly supported or as seriously considered as it was when first proffered 30 years ago.[26])

In George Priest's 1977 version of the argument,[27] inefficient rules are more likely to be challenged through litigation than efficient rules, and thus inefficient rules were more likely to get changed to efficient rules than the other way around (even if judges were not trying to make the rules more efficient). Over time, the argument goes, the increase in efficient rules would be solidified by judicial precedential reasoning, whereby judges would also incorporate (perhaps unconsciously) the efficiency norm that underlay a growing percentage of the private-law doctrines.

This evolutionary or invisible-hand theory argues that contract-law doctrines (and doctrines in other private-law areas) came to be the way they are today because of forces that pushed the doctrine in particular directions (toward greater efficiency). This theory, narrowly understood, is an explanation, not a justification,

---

[21] A. W. B. Simpson, 1975, *A History of the Common Law of Contract*, Oxford: Clarendon Press, pp. 316–326.

[22] J. H. Baker, 1981, "Origins of the 'Doctrine' of Consideration, 1535–1585," in Morris S. Arnold et al., eds., *On the Laws and Customs of England: Essays in Honor of Samuel E. Thorne*, Chapel Hill: University of North Carolina Press, pp. 336–358.

[23] For a good example of historical explanation (in competition with philosophical explanation), from tort law, see Guido Calabresi, 1998, "Supereditor or Translator: Comments on Coleman," in Brian Bix (ed.), *Analyzing Law*, Oxford: Oxford University Press, pp. 107–115, especially pp. 113–114.

[24] Richard A. Posner, 1983, *The Economics of Justice*, Cambridge, MA: Harvard University Press, pp. 103–107.

[25] See Posner, *Economic Analysis*, pp. 249–253; see also Richard A. Posner, 1990, *The Problems of Jurisprudence*, Cambridge, MA: Harvard University Press, pp. 353–374.

[26] See, for example, Richard Craswell, 2003, "In that Case, What Is the Question? Economics and the Demands of Contract Theory," *Yale Law Journal*, 112, pp. 903–924: "this descriptive hypothesis has fallen out of favor, in the sense that it is rarely discussed and even more rarely defended in the legal literature" (p. 904).

[27] See George L. Priest, 1977, "The Common Law Process and the Selection of Efficient Rules," *Journal of Legal Studies*, 6, pp. 65–82; see also Kraus, "Transparency," pp. 349–352; compare Paul H. Rubin, 1977, "Why Is the Common Law Efficient?" *Journal of Legal Studies*, 6, pp. 51–63. Priest seems largely to have abandoned the theory not long after publishing it; see George L. Priest, 1980, "Selective Characteristics of Litigation," *Journal of Legal Studies*, 9, pp. 399–421, especially pp. 409–415.

though it is proffered by theorists who are generally committed to the notion that greater efficiency is a valuable objective – and perhaps the primary objective in commercial transactions.

There remain many obstacles to this type of claim: for example, to show that the contract rules (and other private-law rules) *are* efficient, or at least much more efficient than they once were. This has proven difficult. Additionally, some within the law-and-economics movement argue that approaches of this kind fail to apply the insights of law and economics to the actors at the center of the legal–historical narrative: that relevant decision-makers are themselves subject to incentives working on preferences, in ways that make it unlikely that legal regimes will be simple conduits for ever greater efficiency.[28]

Jody Kraus has recently revived a version of this argument – or, more precisely, has tried to show why such an approach would be viable.[29] Beyond whatever success there might be in economics as a *causal–historical* explanation – how we came to have the doctrines we have – Kraus has important arguments to offer regarding why economic analysis might be necessary at least as a supplementary *descriptive* explanation of (certain) contract-law doctrines. Kraus asserts that moral–philosophical concepts are too vague to either describe or prescribe contract-law doctrines in specific enough ways to determine case outcomes. The notions of autonomy, fairness, and corrective justice cannot specify the exact contours of the rules of (say) substantial performance, adequate assurances, mutual mistake, remedial rights, and so on.[30] Through conscious or subconscious choices, judges, over time, have – or at least may have – filled out the content of general moral standards with an eye toward greater efficiency.

V. OTHER VERSIONS OF ECONOMIC ANALYSIS AND CONTRACT LAW

Sometimes what is being offered in a law-and-economics discussion of contract law is something arguably less ambitious than a theory of the whole doctrinal area (or a theory of all of law, with applications to particular doctrinal areas). Consider the following from Victor Goldberg's recent work:

> The economic analysis here focuses on the transaction. I ask: Why might reasonable, profit-seeking actors structure their relationship in a particular way? How should the answer to that question affect the interpretation of a contract or suggest the appropriate contract law rule?[31]

---

[28] For example, Francesco Parisi, 2004, "Positive, Normative, and Functional Schools in Law and Economics," *European Journal of Law and Economics*, 18, pp. 259–272; and Chapter 3 by Klick and Parisi in this volume.

[29] Kraus, "Transparency"; see also the discussion of his argument in note 9.

[30] Here Kraus's argument tracks that of Richard Craswell, 1989, "Contract Law, Default Rules, and the Philosophy of Promising," *Michigan Law Review*, 88, pp. 489–529.

[31] Victor Goldberg, 2006, *Framing Contract Law: An Economic Perspective*, Cambridge, MA: Harvard University Press, p. 2. He adds: "Like virtually all contracts scholars, I start with the presumption that the purpose of contract law is to facilitate private ordering. The parties are the best judges of their interests, and the law should, as much as possible, stay out of the way. There are exceptions – there might be good reasons to discourage or prohibit certain classes of promises . . . or to be suspicious of the manner in which agreements have been reached. . . . Still, the facilitation of voluntary exchange remains the primary goal of contract law."

Goldberg is offering economic analysis (or, perhaps more precisely, the standard of efficiency) as a guide for interpreting contracts,[32] and also, it seems, as a guide for setting default rules to fill in gaps in commercial contracts.

A related claim is that economic analysis should not be seen as offering a theory (or a description) of contract law, but rather a partial analysis, potentially useful to judges and other lawmakers: to the extent that one is interested in (certain aspects of) efficiency, one should prefer this rule; or, to the extent that one wants to discourage breach or encourage precautions, this is the right set of remedies to use, and so on.[33]

VI. CRITIQUE AND RESPONSE

A growing line of argument against law-and-economics theories of contract law (and tort law) is that this approach fails, at least for these areas of law, because it is incompatible with the bilateral nature of these causes of action.[34] This argument is connected to the one raised earlier, that there is a disconnect between the law-and-economics scholars' focus on efficiency and the terms in which participants describe contract-law practices and rules. The argument goes: if our primary purpose in fact were to maintain efficient levels of performance (and of reliance), one would not, for example, tie the breaching party's level of liability so closely to the nonbreaching party's circumstances. A nonbreaching party's fortuitous ability to mitigate should (usually[35]) not reduce the disincentive the other party has to perform.

Jody Kraus has argued that this critique is overstated.[36] For example, there may be reasons of administrative convenience (efficiency) to structure regulation of industry through civil litigation, and alternative approaches might create greater problems of over- or underdeterrence. However, one might still believe that a certain presumption lies with theories that incorporate the structural elements of private law generally, and contract law in particular, in contrast to theories that might be able to explain them away.

As noted, some law-and-economics theorists shrug off any critique focused on descriptive or explanatory objectives, arguing that, whatever the claims of earlier law-and-economics theorists, the approach of contemporary theories is primarily evaluative and prescriptive.[37] However, even if the focus is on the prescriptive or evaluative question of which rule would best serve efficiency, there are theorists

---

[32] By its own terms, the argument would seem to work best with commercial agreements, or other agreements with a clearly pecuniary focus. It is not clear how useful such a perspective would be with agreements with quite different objectives, like premarital agreements.

[33] See Craswell, "Economics and the Demands of Contract Theory," pp. 910–915.

[34] See Smith, *Contract Theory*, pp. 108–136; Oman, "Failure of Economic Interpretations." A similar critique is commonly made regarding the law-and-economics view of tort law: see, for example, Jules Coleman, 2001, *The Practice of Principle*, Oxford: Oxford University Press, pp. 13–24.

[35] One can imagine that there are categories of cases where a certain level of mitigation is consistently available, and it may be that, for such categories, the incentives of the other party to perform should take that consistent mitigation into account.

[36] See Kraus, "Transparency."

[37] See Ian Ayres, 2003, "Valuing Modern Contract Scholarship," *Yale Law Journal*, 112, pp. 881–882; Craswell, "Economics and the Demands of Contract Theory," pp. 903–907.

even within the law-and-economics movement who question whether judges and legislators will usually have access to the kind of information (e.g., transaction costs, administrative costs, levels of risk neutrality or risk aversion) necessary to make the evaluation.[38]

A different line of critique (again directed against law and economics generally, rather than its particular application to contract law) questions the model of human behavior (rational-actor model) on which economic analysis is grounded, claiming that experimental evidence shows the model to deviate in significant ways from actual behavior; reference is made to "cognitive biases" and "bounded rationality."[39] This in turn has led some to argue that economic analysis needs to modify its prescriptions for legal rules, including rules in contract law.[40] The response from economists (and libertarian fellow travelers) is usually to concede the validity of the findings of cognitive psychology, but argue that there are still good reasons for following policy prescriptions consistent with a rational-actor assumption.[41]

CONCLUSION

This chapter has explored the intersection between theories of doctrinal areas of law, law and economics, and contract law. There are inherent complications and uncertainties in the idea of "theories of contract law" and "explaining contract law" – in part grounded in the mixture of description, interpretation, and pre-scription in such theories, and in part grounded in the question of whether to focus broadly and universally or more narrowly.

Although some law-and-economics theorists, especially in the early years of the movement, seemed to be offering theories of contract law meant to com-pete, at historical–causal levels, descriptive levels, and interpretive levels, with

---

[38] Eric A. Posner, 2003, "Economic Analysis of Contract Law after Three Decades: Success or Failure?" *Yale Law Journal*, 112, pp. 829–880; Craswell, "Economics and the Demands of Contract Theory," pp. 907–909; Ian Ayres and Kristin Madison, 1999, "Threatening Inefficient Performance of Injunc-tions and Contracts," *University of Pennsylvania Law Review*, 148, pp. 56, 87, 91. For a comparable critique focused on tort law, and emphasizing activity levels, transaction costs, and risk neutral-ity, see Jon D. Hanson and Melissa R. Hart, 1996, "Law and Economics," in Dennis Patterson, ed., *A Companion to Philosophy of Law and Legal Theory*, Oxford: Blackwell Publishers, pp. 311–331.

[39] See Daniel Kahneman, Paul Slovic, and Amos Tversky, 1982, *Judgment under Uncertainty: Heuristics and Biases*, Cambridge: Cambridge University Press. Although "bounded rationality" is often used loosely to refer to all the deviations from the rational-actor model behavior that experimenters have found, it is also sometimes used more narrowly to refer to Herbert A. Simon's work – work dealing with the limits on people's ability to analyze data and remember facts and the methods people use to respond to those limitations. See, for example, Herbert A. Simon, 1955, "A Behavioral Model of Rational Choice," *Quarterly Journal of Economics*, 69, pp. 99–118; and Chapter 8 by Adler in this volume.

[40] For example, Cass R. Sunstein, ed., 2000, *Behavioral Law and Economics*, Cambridge: Cambridge University Press; Oren Bar-Gill, 2008, "The Behavioral Economics of Consumer Contracts," *Min-nesota Law Review*, 92, pp. 749–802, discussing consumer contracts in particular.

[41] See, for example, Richard A. Epstein, 2008, "The Neoclassical Economics of Consumer Contracts," *Minnesota Law Review*, 92, pp. 803–835, responding to Bar-Gill, "Behavioral Economics."

nonconsequentialist theories, these theories often conflated descriptive and pre-scriptive claims, and made little effort to justify the lack of fit between economic analyses and the understanding of contract law by participants in the practice. Although recent efforts may show that a descriptive theory of contract-law doc-trine grounded in economic analysis may yet be salvageable, most contemporary law-and-economics theorists disclaim any such ambition, speaking instead of lim-ited normative goals. To the extent that the primary focus of law and economics is partial and prescriptive ("if one wants a rule that will encourage more efficient transactions, this is the rule to choose"), it is wrong to compare those theories with descriptive or explanatory theories, or to judge the two types of theories under the same criteria.

12   Welfare, Autonomy, and Contractual Freedom

GUIDO PINCIONE

Advocates of contractual freedom typically use either welfarist or autonomy-based arguments. Also typical is their shared belief that welfarism and autonomy-based theories are both fundamentally distinct and divergent in their policy implications. The welfarist argument rests on proofs that a perfectly competitive market is Pareto-efficient (henceforth, *efficient*), that is, no one can be made better off without worsening someone. Because, by definition, a market is a network of voluntary exchanges, the welfarist case for perfectly competitive markets is simultaneously a case for contractual freedom. The autonomy-based argument holds that by freely controlling their legitimate holdings, individuals exercise their autonomy, that is, their ability to pursue life plans of their own. This line of thought sees contracts as legal devices to express unanimous consent to new allocations of resources.[1] Unlike hedonistic utilitarianism, which demands the sacrifice of persons for the sake of aggregate happiness, the autonomy-based argument insists on the moral separateness of persons, both as sources and as pursuers of life plans.

I argue in this chapter that both welfarist and autonomy-based considerations support a strong presumption of contractual freedom. I will call this the *convergence thesis*. The presumption asserted by the convergence thesis is strong enough to exclude invalidation of contracts for reasons other than the classical defenses of fraud, mistake, duress, and necessity. I further contend that the convergence thesis is in turn grounded in a more fundamental commitment to contractual freedom itself (the *contractarian thesis*). The contractarian thesis explains why the convergence thesis yields such a strong presumption of contractual freedom.

My argument purports to be more than a critique of the claim that maximal welfare by definition excludes respect for, or promotion of, personal autonomy. Thus, it differs from Jules Coleman's critique of Louis Kaplow and Steven Shavell's attempt to portray fairness-based policies, including policies sensitive to personal autonomy, as detrimental to everyone's welfare.[2] Coleman notes that Kaplow and

---

[1] See Randy E. Barnett, 1986, "A Consent Theory of Contract," *Columbia Law Review*, 6, pp. 269–321.
[2] So their 2002 book, *Fairness versus Welfare* (Cambridge, MA: Harvard University Press), is a sustained attempt to rebut the convergence thesis.

I am grateful to Martín Hevia, Lawrence H. White, and Mark White for their helpful comments on earlier drafts. Work on this chapter was supported by the Social Philosophy and Policy Center, Bowling Green State University.

Shavell's case for welfare-based policies amounts to an uninteresting tautology: Kaplow and Shavell ensure by definition that maximal welfare and fairness cannot coexist.[3] They assert that any impression that welfarist arguments and autonomy-based arguments have the same policy implications results from redefinitions of autonomy that make it collapse with welfare.[4] For Kaplow and Shavell, *typical* fairness-based policies fail to conform to *ideal contracts*, that is, contracts made by fully informed, competent, and noncoerced persons, and for this reason such policies diminish everyone's welfare. I will argue, instead, that the very notion of an ideal contract *nontrivially* embodies features that figure in any attractive conception of personal autonomy. Some policies that Kaplow and Shavell take to be typically advocated by fairness theorists deprive persons of contract opportunities, and to that extent they diminish both everyone's welfare and everyone's autonomy. More generally, I want to outline a theoretical framework that, unlike Kaplow and Shavell's logical equivalences and incompatibilities, is rich enough to perform justificatory functions.[5]

In section I, I offer my core argument for the convergence thesis. To that end, I introduce a notion of manipulation that helps us see that both welfarist and autonomy-based arguments for a strong presumption of contractual freedom ultimately rest on the normative force of a hypothetical constitutional contract. This amounts to saying, in my terminology, that the convergence thesis is grounded in the contractarian thesis. Section II expounds and rejects what I take to be the most challenging objection to the convergence thesis, namely, the idea that the state may refuse to enforce otherwise valid contracts without prejudice to personal autonomy, on the grounds that they are *unconscionable* contracts. If this argument for the unconscionability doctrine were sound, there would be cases in which the principle of efficiency would require the state to enforce an unconscionable contract despite the fact that failing to enforce it would not be detrimental to personal autonomy. In other words, contractual freedom, understood (as I argue we should) as a freedom to enter agreements enforceable by the state, would be required by efficiency but not by autonomy. Section III expands the theoretical framework introduced in section I with an eye to showing that neither the contractarian thesis nor the convergence thesis is, or trivially relies on, uninteresting tautologies; on the contrary, both theses are grounded in moral theories that are not immediately obvious. Indeed, the economic theory embraced by the parties to the ideal constitutional contract is opaque to most people – a fact that should help my contractarian justification of the convergence thesis avoid charges of triviality.

I. A CONTRACTARIAN APPROACH TO MANIPULATION

To see how exactly the welfarist and the autonomy-based arguments converge on a strong presumption of contractual freedom, we need to say more about personal

---

[3] Jules Coleman, 2003, "The Grounds of Welfare," *Yale Law Journal*, 112, pp. 1528, 1540–1541.

[4] See, for example, Kaplow and Shavell, *Fairness versus Welfare*, p. 164, n. 24.

[5] Coleman says that Kaplow and Shavell's siding with welfarism against fairness-based criteria rests on conceptual platitudes ("The Grounds of Welfare," pp. 1540–1541).

autonomy and its relation to welfare.[6] Personal autonomy excludes manipulation by others. Let us say that action A, performed by x, *manipulates* y's choice if and only if (i) y takes A as a decisive reason to do something, (ii) A worsens y's situation in terms of y's preference ranking, and (iii) x performs A in order to worsen y's situation. The classical contract-law defenses are means to correct, or discourage, manipulation in the formation of the contract. Thus, condition (ii) is satisfied if x misleads y into thinking that the brakes of the car y is contemplating to buy from x are more durable than in fact they are. We can also state this point by resorting to the notion of an ideal contract. In an ideal contract, y knows all the features of the car that determine y's decision whether to buy it or not at a given price. Fraud induces an agent to make a choice that is worse than the choice she would make in an ideal contract, where, by construction, the agent knows all her alternatives and their outcomes. In the present example, x's deceit makes y choose an alternative that is in fact worse for y than it appears to be, because y prefers not to buy the car as it really is at that price. Or consider, as another example, duress. If x coerces y into signing a contract with x, then y's situation worsens vis-à-vis a situation in which x does not interact with y at all.[7]

Not all actions that worsen our alternatives manipulate our choice.[8] My willingness and ability to pay for a certain thing depend on my budget constraints, and these in turn depend on previous market prices, including the wages I earned. It follows that my choice sets are to a large extent determined by the actions of others. But these actions may not have been performed with an eye to worsen my situation – hence the point of condition (iii) in the preceding characterization of manipulation. The equilibrium price of a product I cherish may rise, thereby worsening my situation, without anyone seeking to harm me thereby. As Adam Ferguson observed in the eighteenth century, many aggregate outcomes (e.g., prices) result from actions pursuing local objectives, without such outcomes being intended by anyone.[9] This distinction between local intentions and overall effects is crucial to a normative theory of manipulation. No one can be held responsible for competitive equilibrium prices, because no one can – either single-handedly or in concert – set competitive equilibrium prices. Competitive firms have no market power: they cannot change the prices of their products and subsist. Because market prices are the unplanned milieu in which our contractual relationships take place, competitive sellers do not manipulate consumers' options any more than nature does.

---

[6] Horacio Spector has recently offered a cogent contractarian defense of a strong presumption of contractual freedom in 2006, "A Contractarian Approach to Unconscionability," *Chicago-Kent Law Review*, 81, pp. 95–118. I will endeavor to uncover three aspects of the contractarian argument that lie beyond Spector's purposes while being, as far as I can see, compatible with his claims: (a) the combined force of tragedy-of-the-commons and tragedy-of-the-anticommons considerations in support of contractual freedom as part and parcel of a regime of strong property rights, (b) the forms of manipulation condoned by the unconscionability doctrine, and (c) the nontriviality of the convergence thesis.

[7] I discuss coercion in more detail in section III.

[8] This is convenient, yet slightly obscure, talk. What I have in mind is that not all actions that induce another agent to make a choice whose outcome is worse for A than the outcomes of A's previous alternatives manipulate A's choice.

[9] See Adam Ferguson, 1767, *An Essay on the History of Civil Society*, part 3, section 2.

Absence of manipulation fits well into an attractive conception of autonomy, one that praises self-rule and so disapproves of domination by others. It might seem, however, that a regime of contractual freedom sanctions a great deal of manipulation. Firms *strive to* drive competitors out of the market. New technologies, publicity, and other means are employed *in order to* acquire competitive advantages, that is, *in order to* worsen competitors' situations. To be sure, we might distinguish between goals and foreseen effects of the means used to achieve such goals. Elimination of competitors can perhaps be described as a foreseen effect of the means (e.g., a new technology) used to maximize profits. Still, it would be far-fetched to portray all of the disadvantages visited on others by agents making permissible moves in a free market as merely foreseen. Monopolists can by definition decide whether a product will be available or not, and as a result they can manipulate consumers' choices to an extent that competitive producers cannot. Indeed, a monopolist can literally *direct the life* of a consumer who urgently needs her products, by requiring a variety of specific sorts of behavior as a component of the implicit price of those products.

Does the fact that a monopolist can manipulate a consumer's choice undermine the convergence thesis? Does, in other words, a regime of contractual freedom sanction manipulation by monopolists, polluters, and other agents involved in what economists call market failure? I have already said that perfectly competitive markets are demonstrably efficient: perfect competition leads to an equilibrium where no one can be made better off without thereby worsening others. Parties to an *ideal constitutional* contract would accordingly try to mimic the workings of a perfectly competitive market, by designing institutions capable of yielding outcomes attainable in perfectly competitive markets. Thus, to cope with environmental market failures, they will figure out how polluters and victims of pollution would have bargained for certain amounts of pollution and compensation in the absence of transaction costs (a corollary of the Coase theorem). More generally, parties to an ideal constitutional contract would arguably provide for a broadly free market, along with political structures with built-in incentives to overcome market failures. They would choose an arrangement that will minimize both market failure and government failure (such as that originated in rent seeking or pork barrel spending).

We can imagine a hierarchy of ideal contracts. Thus, we might speculate that in a world like ours but for the absence of transaction costs and the existence of full information, both producers who are currently banned from certain polluting activities and the potential victims of such pollution would consent to a repeal of the ban coupled with changes in procedural law to the effect that lawyers be given the right to bring environmental class actions to the courts. Highest in the legal hierarchy, and most distant from the real-world barriers to informed and free consent, everyone would consent to mutually advantageous constitutional rules, the details of the decision rule (e.g., maximization of expected utility, maximin) and the relevant metric (e.g., utility, wealth) depending on the details of the contractarian setting. With regard to pollution, an inclusive, ideal constitutional contract signed by parties knowledgeable of the theories of market failure and government failure may well *reject* bans on, or taxation of, polluting activities, compulsory environment-friendly technologies, and the other sorts of direct regulation favored by many environmental activists. Ideal constitutional contractors may not favor such restrictions on everyday contractual freedom, even if they anticipate market failure, because they may also anticipate that the government failure involved in devising and implementing such restrictions will be even worse, given the information and incentive problems under which governments operate.[10] This is why they may settle for something like the mentioned class-action example. A similar logic demands market-friendly corrections of monopolistic markets – a presumption in favor of, say, repealing barriers to entry rather than special taxes or mandatory breach into separate units.

In any event, no method that *effectively* overcomes market/government failure invades personal autonomy. A market/government failure is a failure to exploit possibilities for mutual advantage. Because our concept of manipulation entails that persons have a second-order preference not to have their first-order preferences manipulated (e.g., by a monopolist in the ways already described), a market failure is a failure to fulfill persons' higher-order preferences, the preferences we tend to ascribe to their autonomous selves.[11] The ideal constitutional contract is, then, a common platform for welfarist and autonomy-based considerations that converge on justifying a strong presumption of contractual freedom.

It is crucial to distinguish between the contractarian argument that I have just outlined and some ostensibly contractarian arguments, such as John Rawls's, which in effect embody independent principles of political morality.[12] Ronald Dworkin plausibly sees Rawls's theory of justice as ultimately resting on a principle of "equal concern and respect" that implicitly guides Rawls's description of the "original position," a hypothetical setting where people deliberate behind a "veil of ignorance" that induces them to select impartially the principles that will govern society's "basic institutions."[13] To be sure, the ideal contracts that I have in mind are hypothetical too, because they depict the preferences that real-world persons *would* have *if* well informed and free. But these are still the preferences that recognizably real-world persons, with their specific desires, needs, and commitments, would have if well informed and free. Ideal *constitutional* contractors are no exception. No external authority overrules their judgments on what is wise, fair, or noble to accept in that setting. Ideal constitutional contracts, then, fit the individualistic, nonpaternalistic, and nonperfectionist tenets of liberal, autonomy-based political morality; they also meet the conditions under which people's fully informed and free preferences can be satisfied.

---

[10] For an account of governmental information and incentive problems in relation to environmental policies, see William C. Mitchell and Randy T. Simmons, 1994, *Beyond Politics: Markets, Welfare, and the Failure of Bureaucracy*, Boulder: Westview Press, pp. 146–162.

[11] To use a classical example, we regard the individual who unsuccessfully seeks to get rid of her addiction to hallucinogens as lacking in personal autonomy – she is a "slave" of her addiction. For an overview of the literature on hierarchical analyses of autonomy, see James Stacey Taylor, 2005, "Introduction," in Taylor, ed., *Personal Autonomy: New Essays on Personal Autonomy and Its Role in Contemporary Moral Philosophy*, New York: Cambridge University Press, pp. 4–10.

[12] John Rawls, 1971, *A Theory of Justice*, Cambridge, MA: Harvard University Press.

[13] Ronald Dworkin, *Taking Rights Seriously*, Cambridge, MA: Harvard University Press, ch. 6.

II. THE UNCONSCIONABILITY OBJECTION AND CRITIQUES

The courts have been using the unconscionability doctrine to invalidate contracts deemed to be grossly unfair, or *unconscionable*. Imagine, for example, that a borrower cannot repay a loan, and as a result the creditor wants to foreclose on her home. Crucial to the borrower's plight was the fact that most competent adults could not have fully understood the contract's provisions for adjustments in the interest rate. Seana Shiffrin favors judicial decisions that take such contracts to be unconscionable and, as such, unenforceable by the state.[14] She argues that the unconscionability doctrine grounds restrictions on contractual freedom without trampling on personal autonomy. By refusing to enforce unconscionable contracts, she says, the state avoids complicity in evildoing. In Shiffrin's view, the state does not substitute its judgment for the promisor's as to whether it is wise to enter such contracts. The state does not *prohibit* citizens from drawing up, or even complying with, unconscionable contracts. Avoiding complicity in evildoing (understood as the exploitative behavior of the promisee), rather than paternalism or perfectionism, is, Shiffrin argues, the motivation behind the unconscionability doctrine. She concludes that liberals, and generally those who value personal autonomy, can consistently embrace this doctrine.[15] If she is right, some restrictions on contractual freedom that are innocuous to personal autonomy lack welfarist support, because they seek to avoid complicity in evildoing rather than overcoming a market failure.

The unconscionability doctrine differs from legal prohibitions in ways that matter to personal autonomy. When the state bans drug dealing, it thereby announces it will send the police to apprehend drug dealers, who are thereby coerced into abstaining from selling drugs. In contrast, when judges rule that a contract is unconscionable, they thereby say that they are *not* prepared to put in motion the coercive apparatus of the state to compel compliance. Saying that the unconscionability doctrine is a restriction on contractual freedom may therefore sound Pickwickian.[16]

[14] Seana Shiffrin, 2000, "Paternalism, Unconscionability Doctrine, and Accommodation," *Philosophy and Public Affairs*, 29, pp. 205–250. Arthur Allen Leff distinguishes between procedural and substantive unconscionability. Procedural unconscionability obtains when the formation of the contract was not fully consensual. The classical contract-law defenses are intended to cure procedural unconscionability. Substantive unconscionability obtains when contract terms are unfair or exploitative. (See Arthur Allen Leff, 1967, "Unconscionability and the Code – The Emperor's New Clause," *University of Pennsylvania Law Review*, 115, pp. 485–547.) I will henceforth refer to unconscionable contracts in the substantive sense only, because this is the sense relevant to Shiffrin's discussion.

[15] The U.C.C., § 2-302, (1) extends the scope of the unconscionability doctrine to justify judicial revision of contract terms: "If the court as a matter of law finds the contract or any term of the contract to have been unconscionable at the time it was made the court may refuse to enforce the contract, or it may enforce the remainder of the contract without the unconscionable term, or it may so limit the application of any unconscionable term as to avoid any unconscionable result." Such revisions can be construed as (partial) refusals to enforce a contract.

[16] Shiffrin offers a related thought: "Unlike many of the commonly cited examples of paternalism (such as drug prohibitions or seat-belt laws), the putatively protected, benefited agent does not resist or oppose the result or the procedure enacted by the paternalism. Here, the relevant agent actively endorses the supposedly paternalist conduct. This may seem puzzling" ("Paternalism," p. 210).

There is, however, a natural use of "freedom" under which the doctrine does reduce contractual freedom. Philosophers distinguish between *negative* and *positive* freedom. Roughly put, we are negatively free just in case others do not interfere with our desires or plans; I am now negatively free to write on my computer, because nobody is preventing me from doing so. Notice that this usage forces us to say that a person whose legs are accidentally crippled is free to walk if nobody is preventing him from doing so. Examples of this latter sort led some philosophers to advocate a positive conception of freedom, according to which an agent is free to do something just in case she *can* do it. This usage also allows us to say that I am free to write on my computer, but, in harmony with our intuition that freedom is valuable, it prevents us from saying that the crippled person is free to walk.[17]

I have been using the term "contractual freedom" in the positive sense all along. This conforms to usage, since contractual freedom is normally conceived of as the ability to make enforceable agreements. More importantly, it conforms to our sense of what is valuable about contract *law*. There is no contractual freedom in the Hobbesian state of nature, where people live without police, courts, and presumably all other kinds of reliable enforcement mechanisms. As a result, people cannot enter into enforceable agreements, and so cannot pursue the multifarious aims that such agreements alone make possible – nobody could count on others' promises as securely as if such promises were backed with the threat of overwhelming force. The unconscionability doctrine restricts, then, (positive) contractual freedom. (I will continue to use the term *contractual freedom* in this positive sense.) An appropriate assessment of Shiffrin's liberal defense of the unconscionability doctrine depends, then, on whether restrictions on contractual freedom involve judgment substitution or manipulation – on whether or not, in short, they trample on people's autonomy. Shiffrin's negative answer poses a challenge to the convergence thesis: if she were right, welfare considerations would warrant a more extensive contractual freedom than would a concern for autonomy.

A. The Morality of Enforcement

I have four replies to the objection from unconscionability. First, the unconscionability doctrine does nullify the promisee's *weighing of the reasons* for and against enforcing the contract. The promisee has weighed all the considerations, moral and prudential, that she deemed relevant, and arrived at an overall judgment. The state's refusal to enforce the contract ignores that judgment. It is not merely that the state *disagrees* with that judgment. It *thwarts* the promisee's plans, for which the expectation of state assistance in enforcing the contract if necessary was a crucial ingredient, and it does so on the grounds that those plans disregard the reasons that *ought* to govern her behavior – the ("genuine") demands of morality.

---

[17] See Isaiah Berlin, 1969, *Four Essays on Liberty*, Oxford: Oxford University Press; Lawrence Crocker, 1980, *Positive Liberty: An Essay in Normative Political Philosophy*, London: Martinus Nijhoff; and Horacio Spector, 1992, *Autonomy and Rights: The Moral Foundations of Liberalism*, Oxford: Clarendon Press, pp. 12–48.

It is useful to compare the kind of judgment substitution involved here with paternalistic interventions licensed by autonomy-based theories, even if such interventions target consenting adults. To the extent that paternalistic treatment of consenting adults preserves, or even promotes, personal autonomy, such treatment overrides those adults' *prudential*, as opposed to moral, judgments. We do not infringe on a person's autonomy if we forcibly stop him from stepping onto a bridge about to collapse, if this is the only means to save him from serious injury.[18] Given the agent's desire to get home and his belief that crossing the bridge is a cost-effective means to satisfy that desire, he correctly concluded that he should step on the bridge. He is a competent, though misinformed, adult. His decision is not prompted by any conscious weighing of moral considerations: neither his desire to go home nor his belief that crossing the bridge is the best means to satisfy that desire possesses inherent moral significance. Here paternalism involves overriding of prudential beliefs, and to that extent it advances the agent's goals, as he set them for himself. A paternalistic intervention challenges the agent's epistemic authority – it takes him to be a bad judge of the means available to him to achieve his ends. By contrast, the unconscionability doctrine challenges the promisee's *moral* judgment. She has weighed both the prudential and the moral reasons pertaining to her situation, at least by ignoring whatever moral considerations militate against enforcing the contract. A state that overrules this morally charged judgment embraces perfectionism, and consequently poses a more serious threat to personal autonomy than a paternalistic state does: unlike substitution of prudential judgment, substitution of moral judgment cannot even allege a concern for the overall autonomy of the agent – a concern, that is, for the fulfillment of her freely chosen goals.

There may well be no clear-cut divide between morally relevant and morally irrelevant considerations, but some cases do clearly fall well within one of those categories. On an ordinary understanding of morality, the considerations pertaining to the agent's decision to cross the fragile bridge are prudential, not moral, whereas the considerations regarding the use of coercion, especially to enforce promises, are moral in nature. I conclude, then, that rulings based on the unconscionability doctrine substitute the court's own moral convictions (in Shiffrin's account, a moral revulsion at its complicity in exploitation) for those of the promisee.

To be sure, a liberal state *must* sometimes substitute its moral judgment for that of its citizens. A liberal state abides by the harm principle, which allows the use of coercion or violence only to defend oneself or others from harm. To the extent that the harm principle expresses, or implements, a recognition that personal autonomy has paramount value, it is the only moral principle that a liberal state is authorized to substitute for citizens' (illiberal) moral views. Liberals reject paternalism toward competent and well-informed adults because it affronts their autonomous *weighing* of reasons for and against their freely chosen courses of action and life plans. The liberal commitment to personal autonomy is not merely a disposition to respect a person's autonomous decisions – it is fundamentally a commitment to respect the autonomous deliberative process that yielded those

---

[18] John Stuart Mill famously uses a similar example in *On Liberty* (1859), chapter V.

decisions.[19] Liberals want to respect a person's autonomous decision even if she is mistaken – even if, that is, her beliefs about the cost-effective means to achieve her goals are false. Thus, we feel we ought not to thwart a competent adult's informed decision to study law rather than medicine, even if we know that such a decision will ruin his life. It is the autonomous weighing of reasons, as opposed to the wisdom of the judgment that results from it, that liberals want to protect.

The practical authority that liberal thought confers on me as an autonomous agent excludes, at a minimum, that others are authorized to decide on my behalf, or to override my decisions. It follows that, within the limits of the harm principle, I have ultimate practical authority. Now unconscionable contracts cannot as such harm the promisor – if they did, the harm principle would suffice to invalidate them. "Consented harm" is an oxymoron. It follows that contractors have practical authority over the exercise of their contractual rights, including their right to have their contracts enforced. Denying them such authority involves perfectionism – that is, substituting, for the purpose of using public coercion, the state's moral views on exploitation, usury, or any other moral defect that allegedly taints the promisee's decision to enforce the contract, for the promisee's all-things-considered reason to enforce it. Unlike paternalistic interventions, which sometimes can (as in the fragile bridge case) be accommodated within a liberal outlook, perfectionist interventions substitute the interferer's conception of what is worth pursuing in life for that of the agent. They do not challenge the agent's epistemic authority, but rather her practical authority, her autonomous choice of courses of action or life plans.

B. Manipulation and Reliance

My second reply to the unconscionability objection points to the manipulation of the promisee's *choice set*. Courts that void unconscionable contracts flout their general promise to enforce contracts as agencies of a legal system that (we are assuming) upholds contractual freedom. Unlike legal regulations that restrict contractual freedom (say, by licensing judicial reduction of "abusive" interest rates), the unconscionability doctrine leaves untouched citizens' expectations that contracts will generally be enforced – promisees are assumed to retain their legal rights to resort to the state's enforcement apparatus in the event of breach. There is an inherent tendency for the unconscionability doctrine to mislead promisees into believing they have entered enforceable contracts. Given the open texture and essential contestability of the notion of an unconscionable contract, from the point of view of reasonable contractors unconscionability may well emerge *ex post*, often unexpectedly, as a reason to void their contracts. If so, the unconscionability doctrine, as opposed to well-defined defenses in contract law, induces promisees to rely too much on promisors. To that extent, the state manipulates the promisees' choice sets.

Ironically, the unconscionability theorist might try to resist this conclusion by appealing to an ideal constitutional contract. We saw in section I that parties to an

---

[19] See Gerald F. Gaus, 2003, *Contemporary Theories of Liberalism*, London: SAGE, pp. 162–164.

ideal constitutional contract would uphold various kinds of restrictions on every-day contractual freedom. They may predict, for example, that enforcing certain contracts will have negative externalities on compassionate people. If they also pre-dict that transaction costs will be too high to induce contractors to internalize such externalities, they will set limits on the enforceability of such ("unconscionable") contracts. Now this picture is highly speculative, and in any event it faces a fun-damental difficulty: The notion of an unconscionable contract cannot guide the behavior of the courts, and derivatively the behavior of potential contractors. The doctrine has by necessity retroactive effects, because it is intended to apply to contractual provisions that, by hypothesis, were enforceable at the time the par-ties accepted them. It introduces open-textured exemptions to *binding* contracts. If we make the plausible assumptions that (a) the courts will rule few contracts unconscionable, (b) the concept of unconscionability is highly contestable, and (c) part of the state's motivation for adopting the unconscionability doctrine, as opposed to explicit legislative restrictions on contractual freedom, is to preserve the public's belief that contractual freedom is still the rule, it seems safe to conclude that most decisions based on the unconscionability doctrine will manipulate the promisees' considered expectations that they can count on the state's assistance in the enforcement of their contracts.

This point is not weakened by the fact that prospective contractors may cor-rectly assign a *probability* to the courts' embracing the unconscionability doctrine. Based on such probability estimates, prospective contractors will bargain for bet-ter terms. It would seem that such bargains would shield prospective promisees against manipulation, because they will take measures (e.g., price adjustments) to make up *ex ante* for the expected frustration of their expectations *ex post*. The problem with this argument is that *any* contract has some probability of being voided for whatever reason, including judicial mistake. Price will be sensitive to such perceived probabilities, yet we do not conclude that utterly arbitrary (though correctly perceived as probable) rulings (or, for that matter, perfectionist rulings) do not substitute the courts' judgments for those of the parties. Even though the *content* of the contractual obligations assumed by the parties may be partly deter-mined by the perceived probability of judicial refusal to enforce those obligations, the fact remains that the parties autonomously decided to assume them. In refusing to enforce such contracts, the courts override *those* autonomous decisions.

It might be replied that a state determined to avoid complicity in exploitation may refuse to make *its* enforcement apparatus available to the promisee while tolerating *private* enforcement. Promisees need not be misled, then, by the state's general promise to enforce contracts, for they will resort to private enforcement agencies (perhaps at the promisor's expense). On this view, private enforcement restores the promisee's choice set: for all practical purposes, the promisee's options (e.g., how much to invest in information about the promisor's reliability) are the same as under a legal system that provides for unexceptional enforcement by the state. The suggested conclusion is that no manipulation of the promisee's decision obtains.

One preliminary difficulty with this objection is that it jettisons the initial impe-tus of the liberal argument for the unconscionability doctrine. We saw that Shiffrin urges the state not to enforce an unconscionable contract in order to avoid complicity in exploitation or other forms of evildoing. Presumably, then, there must be something wrong with *enforcing* such contracts. On a natural understanding of the unconscionability doctrine, it does not assert that there is something distinctively wrong with *the state's* enforcing unconscionable contracts, as opposed to private agents enforcing them. If so, the avoiding-complicity-with-evil rationale for the doctrine does not easily cohere with the state's acquiescing in private enforcement.

But even if this worry could somehow be dispelled, a fundamental inconsistency would remain. We are told that, in order to avoid complicity in evildoing, the state ought not to enforce an unconscionable contract, yet in order to avoid the charge of manipulation, the state ought to allow private enforcement. Third parties must then be legally forbidden to prevent the promisee, or the enforcement agencies he had contracted with, from enforcing the contract. We must assume, that is, that the promisee has a *legal claim* to enforce the contract, either single-handedly or with the aid of private enforcers, a claim that places others under a duty to let him or the private enforcers enforce the contract.[20] (He *must* have that claim-right if the objection under consideration is to avoid the charge of manipulation.) But this is tantamount to saying that the state is prepared to enforce such a claim: it is, after all, a *legal* claim. The state remains, then, in the background, threatening to use force in support of the legal claims entailed by a right to private enforcement. Or, to put it in more precise terms, the legal availability of private enforcement entails that the promisee has a state-backed legal claim against third parties' interfering with his attempt to enforce the contract, along with various layers of legal claims and powers to enforce whatever contracts he made with private enforcement agencies. It is hard to see how the liberal supporter of the unconscionability doctrine can consistently exonerate the state from complicity in evildoing here.

C. Prudential Authority

I turn now to my third reply against the challenge from unconscionability: the unconscionability doctrine disregards the promisor's authority to determine where her interests lie and how to fulfill them. We saw in the last section that contractual freedom (understood as the freedom to make enforceable agreements) involves recognition of persons' practical authority. It follows that the unconscionability doctrine cannot, consistently with liberal principles, uphold judicial revisions of contractual terms – terms that by hypothesis include a mutual understanding that an enforceable agreement was being made. Such revisions would substitute the court's assessment of the reasons for and against enforcing the contract for the promisor's reasons to enter it.

It might be objected that I am unduly privileging the promisor's perceived interests at the time she entered the contract, instead of her perceived interests

---

[20] I am relying here on Wesley Newcomb Hohfeld's classification of legal rights; see Hohfeld, 1913/1964, *Fundamental Legal Conceptions as Applied in Judicial Reasoning*, ed. W. W. Cook, New Haven: Yale University Press. Arguably, the promisee has other rights as well – for example, what Hohfeld would call a legal "power" to make (enforceable) contracts with private enforcers.

at the time the promisee requests compliance. Why not regard the defendant's current decision to breach an unconscionable obligation as more authoritative than her previous decision to assume that obligation?

When is a decision authoritative for present purposes – when can we forcibly interfere with a course of action, or break our promises, without infringing on other people's autonomy? My argument in section I suggests that a moral system centered on personal autonomy may prohibit only those actions that manipulate the choices made by others. It must therefore confer authority on the practical reasons leading to *non*manipulative actions, especially if those are the reasons of well-informed, free, and competent adults. On this view, denying authority to a promise that does not affect others is inimical to personal autonomy. Such a denial would ignore the promisor's authority to assume contractual obligations as a means to pursue life plans of his own. Indeed, the liberal unconscionability theorist herself must presuppose the promisor's prudential authority, if only because the doctrine does not call for a ban on (the enforcement of) unconscionable contracts. Nor does it treat the promisee as an offender. It bears repeating that the unconscionability doctrine is about nonenforcement, not prohibition.

It might seem that this account is incompatible with the claim, based on welfare economics, that specific performance (and so fulfillment of a contractual promise) is usually an inefficient remedy for contractual breach – an incompatibility that would threaten the convergence thesis. There is a welfarist case for the adoption of expectation damages as a remedy for contractual breach. Briefly, efficiency requires everyone to take account of the total costs of their actions. This requirement is met by making the party who breaches a contract pay an amount of damages that leaves the other party as well off as if the contract had been fulfilled. The issue is complicated by the fact that an efficient amount of contract breach need not coincide with an efficient amount of contract *signing*: the latter is achieved by means of a remedy known as *reliance damages*, according to which the party who breaches must make the other party as well off as if they had never signed the contract. Breach of a particular contract may be efficient under expectation damages consistently with the fact that it was inefficient to sign that contract in the first place. It is a tricky matter how to combine the two remedies so that contractors are given the right incentives both to breach and to rely.[21] For present purposes, the point to bear in mind is this: whereas efficiency condones some breaches of contract, the understanding of contractual freedom that I have been adopting seems to ask for unexceptional enforceability of contractual obligations. This divergence poses a challenge to the convergence thesis.

We have also seen in section I, however, that only ideal constitutional contractors are fully autonomous. In that capacity, they will agree on the conditions under which the courts will award expectation damages or specific performance. Any other constitutional provision for the event of contractual breach, including the unconscionability doctrine, will deprive citizens of contract opportunities that, by hypothesis, are better from their own (ideal constitutional) perspectives, and for

---

[21] For a brief and useful discussion, see David D. Friedman, 2000, *Law's Order: What Economics Has to Do with Law and Why It Matters*, Princeton: Princeton University Press, pp. 164–168.

this reason it will be manipulative. A *rule* that worsens everyone would have no place in either welfarist or autonomy-based political moralities, because it would not be chosen by ideal contractors.[22] It seems to me that the burden of proof that judicial endorsement of the unconscionability doctrine will not deprive people of contract opportunities falls on the unconscionability theorist, especially if we believe that parties to an ideal constitutional contract will provide for a vigorous market for insurance against the kinds of misfortunes that the unconscionability theory aims to mitigate.

At this juncture, the unconscionability theorist may try again to play the card of private enforcement, this time to underscore the promisor's authority to make binding contracts. Only if the promisor's authority over her decisions to exercise her rights is recognized – only if the agent has the final say on the choices protected by such rights, which includes transferring those rights through enforceable agreements – can enforcement be permissible under a morality responsive to the value of personal autonomy. The state may nevertheless want to avoid complicity in exploitation, and the unconscionability doctrine is the legal means it finds available to preserve its moral purity. On this view, then, the unconscionability doctrine not only allows the state to avoid complicity in exploitation, but also expresses its commitment to the promisor's authority to alienate her rights through agreements enforceable by the promisee or other private enforcers. Facing a dilemma between flouting its general promise to enforce contracts and assisting in evildoing, the state chooses to preserve as much as possible its moral purity by transferring to others the *direct* responsibility for enforcing an unconscionable contract.[23]

A careful assessment of this objection would require us to take sides on complex empirical issues that I cannot pursue here except for the following rough remarks. If the costs of enforcement fall on the promisee, he will find promises less valuable; some contracts that would be mutually beneficial given state enforcement would accordingly not be made. This suggests that the unconscionability doctrine ignores the promisor's authority to assume higher risks of enforcement (maybe in exchange for better contract terms), as expressed in an ideal constitutional contract where the promisor would have *insisted* on having such contract opportunities available. Consequently, this line of defense of the unconscionability doctrine would be vulnerable too to the welfarist and autonomy-based objections derivable from my contractarian argument. Saying that there is something wrong with public enforcement while leaving open the possibility that private enforcement would be sanctioned by ideal constitutional contractors not only amounts to a Pyrrhic victory for a position that invokes the authority of the breaching promisor – it also deprives (at least some) prospective promisors of the contract opportunities they value most.

---

[22] Thus, I reject Kaplow and Shavell's distinction between the autonomy-based, promise-keeping approach, which they take to justify performance instead of expectation damages as a remedy for breach, and the welfarist approach (Kaplow and Shavell, *Fairness versus Welfare*, pp. 191–192). I hasten to add that the nature of my disagreement here is not merely terminological or otherwise trivial. I will postpone, however, until section III a defense of the claim that the convergence thesis relies on interesting policy implications, as opposed to trivial tautologies.

[23] The state would still be responsible for enforcing the private enforcement agreements discussed in the previous subsection.

D. Where Evildoing Lies

It is time now for my fourth and final reply to the unconscionability objection. Kaplow and Shavell write: "Notions of fairness that would penalize or compensate for reasons unrelated to the promotion of individuals' well-being will fail in their purpose (because of contract price adjustments) or prove perverse (because the combination of the behavioral effects and contract price adjustments will detrimentally affect promisors and promisees)."[24] Notice how undemanding the normative assumptions of this passage are. They are even weaker than the Pareto principle, for they just demand that public policies not harm *everybody*. An implication of Kaplow and Shavell's position is that the unconscionability doctrine, which is in effect a rule followed by the courts, will inflict uncompensated harm. The plaintiff who sues for breach of an "unconscionable" contract is not responsible for such harm, even conceding, for the sake of argument, that she is somehow involved in evildoing. The state is the only agent to be blamed for instituting such a rule, for it is the only agent capable of instituting it. In doing so, it perpetrates an obvious sort of evildoing. It follows that the liberal argument for the unconscionability doctrine, premised on the moral need to avoid complicity in evildoing, founders.

The unconscionability theorist might object that a *one-time* application of the unconscionability doctrine will not give rise to such perverse incentives, especially if the case is so exceptional, and the court's opinion so detailed and *ad hoc*, that for all practical purposes it sets no precedent. Such a decision would not harm future contractors. The unconscionability theorist might even hold that the doctrine is so plastic and contestable that no fixed list of well-defined *types* of contractual obligations qualifies for the category of unconscionable obligations.[25] If we also assume that, whatever its definiteness, the class of unconscionable contracts is negligibly small in comparison with the total class of contracts people are inclined to make, we seem compelled to conclude that the unconscionability doctrine would not make much of a difference to people's decision to make the contracts they would otherwise be inclined to make. The suggested conclusion is that citizens will for all practical purposes perceive all rulings based on the unconscionability doctrine as marginal departures from a still-strong presumption of contractual freedom; as such, they would not give rise to the perverse incentives that Kaplow and Shavell find so worrying.

Let us grant, for the sake of argument, that a one-time nullification of an unconscionable contract would not give rise to perverse incentives. Still, judicial decisions grounded on an objective notion of evildoing (i.e., one that is independent of the

---

[24] *Fairness versus Welfare*, p. 202.

[25] Moral particularists argue that moral judgment does not presuppose principles, although it typically relies on reasons of varying force and valence, according to context. See Jonathan Dancy, 2004, *Ethics without Principles*, Oxford: Clarendon Press. If moral particularism is true, it may be plausible to say that judicial decision making relies on reasons but not on principles. Thus, feature F may be a reason to regard obligation O as unconscionable under circumstances C, even if F does not always weigh in favor of the claim that O is unconscionable; indeed, sometimes F may undermine such a claim. Anthony Kronman's defense of the virtue of "practical wisdom" in judicial reasoning can be seen as a legal reflection of moral particularism. See Anthony Kronman, 1995, *The Lost Lawyer: Failing Ideals of the Legal Profession*, Cambridge, MA: Belknap Press, pp. 53–108.

parties' desires and life plans, as expressed in an ideal contract) will raise liberal concerns. Such decisions may be based on reasons of distributive justice (e.g., those stemming from a theory of exploitation) that resist interpretations in terms of the contractarian argument I am advocating here (as opposed to the morally laden contractarian arguments alluded to in section I). It might be countered that our ideal counterparts would prefer to live in an exploitation-free society at the cost of worsening everyone's overall situations. Now this strikes me as unpersuasive as a speculation about our well-informed and free preferences. I have argued elsewhere that many policies seen as responsive to certain values or principles are counter-productive in ways that no reasonable political morality can endorse. In particular, no reasonable deontological or distributive concern can plausibly be adduced to fight exploitation at the price of even more severe and widespread poverty (due to higher unemployment and reduced production).[26] Ideal constitutional contrac-tors will arguably take account of these facts. Although the empirical issues here are, again, complex, I find it unrealistic to hypothesize that such contractors will be more absorbed in fighting exploitation, at least on conventional understandings of it, than in averting abject poverty. And even if they will, doubts will remain as to whether they, knowledgeable as we assume them to be about the dangers of discretionary power (including judicial power), will adopt the unconscionability doctrine rather than, say, a negative income tax, or a repeal of barriers to entry in markets for insurance against "unconscionable" enforcement of debts for which the classical contract-law defenses will be ineffective.

A detailed contractarian argument along the lines I have been suggesting in this chapter should show how rational and well-informed contractors would forestall deviant interpretations of legal rules, including constitutional rules. Indeed, it is far from obvious that they will favor a blanket literal guarantee of contractual freedom, if only because the concept of freedom is notoriously contestable and so vulnerable to rent-seeking interpretations.[27] My critique of the unconscionability doctrine was not meant to propose (or to reject) an overnight judicial or legislative rejection of the unconscionability doctrine *given the current structure of incentives.* A transition from a legal system that upholds the unconscionability doctrine to one fully sensitive to the value of welfare and autonomy raises further empirical issues that I cannot pursue here.

III. ZOOMING IN ON THE ARGUMENT FOR THE CONVERGENCE THESIS AND THE CONTRACTARIAN THESIS

I devote this section to showing that the conceptual apparatus of welfare economics assumes propositions about property rights and autonomy that entail contractual freedom. To the extent that the propositions of welfare economics are not obvious (even though one may argue that they are analytical or tautological), their logical

---

[26] See Guido Pincione and Fernando R. Tesón, 2006, "Rational Ignorance and Political Morality," *Philosophy and Phenomenological Research*, 72, pp. 71–96.

[27] On legal contestability, see Guido Pincione, 2003, "Market Rights and the Rule of Law: A Case for Procedural Constitutionalism," *Harvard Journal of Law and Public Policy*, 16, pp. 397–454. For an economic analysis of constitutional and legal interpretation, see Robert D. Cooter, 1999, *The Strategic Constitution*, Princeton: Princeton University Press, pp. 173–174, 197–198, 225–236.

connections with contractual freedom may play justificatory roles. Such connections reveal that a commitment to both efficiency and autonomy gives us reasons to embrace a strong presumption of contractual freedom. Delving into such connections helps reinforce, then, the argument for the convergence thesis that I outlined in section I.

As we have seen, welfarism demands that resource allocation be efficient, that is, such that no reallocation will make someone better off (in terms of their preference rankings) without making others worse off. The fundamental theorems of welfare economics lay down the conditions under which efficiency obtains. The first theorem states that any competitive equilibrium (i.e., an allocation of resources that no one has an incentive to alter through voluntary exchanges) is efficient. The second theorem states the converse, that is, that any efficient allocation is a competitive equilibrium.[28] The formal system in which these theorems can be proved makes assumptions about the structure of individuals' preferences (such as transitivity). Crucially for our purposes, these are preferences ranging over *commodities*: individuals rank *spheres of control* (i.e., their ability to use, consume, and transfer certain things). In legal terminology, they rank private property rights to particular things, that is, rights to exclusive control of particular things, including legal powers to transfer them.[29] The fundamental theorems assume, then, that firms and consumers can engage in market transactions, that is, enforceable (though themselves uncoerced) contracts whereby they exchange their property titles.[30] The assumption that individuals have private property rights (including property rights over money) that determine how much they are allowed to spend is also required in indifference-curve analysis, that is, propositions stating the combinations of commodities that consumers prefer, given their budget constraints. The whole analysis focuses on the individual's choices as evidence of what they prefer, known as *revealed preferences*. Moreover, those are *free* choices – for example, uncoerced choices between quantities of apples and quantities of peas, given their prices and the consumer's budget constraints.

Why does welfarism uphold the specific structure of coercion involved in the enforcement of (uncoerced) contracts? We can provide a preliminary account of our everyday concept of coercion by means of the following:

> *P* performs action *A* under coercion if and only if *P* would not have performed *A* if another person, *Q*, had not altered *P*'s choice set (i.e., *P*'s available actions or their outcomes) in order to make *A P*'s most attractive alternative.

---

[28] For simplified proofs, see Allan M. Feldman and Roberto Serrano, 2006, *Welfare Economics and Social Choice Theory*, 2nd ed., New York: Springer, pp. 59–70.

[29] For a seminal analysis of the bundle of rights possessed by a private owner, see Tony Honoré, 1961, "Ownership," in G. A. Guest, ed., *Oxford Essays in Jurisprudence*, Oxford: Clarendon Press, pp. 107–147. Notice that the use of legal terminology in this context does not presuppose anything like a modern legal system, though it is meant to describe spheres of de facto control broadly coincident with those entailed by legal titles to full ownership. For an economic argument showing how relative threat advantages in a Hobbesian state of nature give rise to such spheres of control (a "natural distribution"), see James Buchanan, 1975, *The Limits of Liberty: Between Anarchy and Leviathan*, Chicago: University of Chicago Press, p. 23.

[30] See Barnett, "A Consent Theory of Contract," pp. 278–280 (economic analysis assumes that "market transactions" – i.e., contracts – are enforceable).

Even though A ranks highest in P's preference ranking *given Q's intervention*, Q worsened P's situation in that P could have chosen a better option had Q not changed P's choice set (e.g., by threatening P with killing him if P made the choice P was about to make as Q came into the scene).[31] Let us assume that, by coercing P, Q has in turn improved her situation. The new allocation is then Pareto-incomparable to the status quo; that is, some are better off while others are worse off. If the new allocation cannot be altered without worsening someone, then it is also efficient, though it is neither more efficient nor less efficient than that obtaining in the status quo. It does not follow, however, that a concern for efficiency should force us to suspend judgment about the general conditions under which coercion is permissible – that is, about which *legal systems* tend to generate efficient allocations. Consider a simple legal system, according to which everything is permitted, in the minimal sense that no law forbids it – the Hobbesian state of nature. Arguably, such a system leaves everyone worse off than rules that effectively protect private property rights. These rights promote the division of labor and specialization, and so enable people to exploit the gains from trade. In other words, private property takes us away from the tragedy of the commons. Efficiency calls for a move from Hobbesian anarchy to the structures of coercion embodied in a regime of private property; this much is the well-known Hobbesian case for private property.

It may be thought that some property regimes that do not allow for *private* property are also substantial efficiency improvements on the Hobbesian state of nature – substantial enough to attract ideal constitutional contractors committed, as many actual persons are,[32] to some form of egalitarianism. However, the Hobbesian case for private property is robust enough to exclude significant departures from private property. Imagine, for instance, a legal system that allows persons to use things if and only if a certain number of persons agree. In an ordinary sense of "collective owner," those persons are therefore collective owners of those resources.[33]

---

[31] This is just a first step toward a rigorous characterization of coercion, but I think it works for present purposes. Notice that I avoid moral notions; in particular, I do not require that Q have *wrongfully* altered P's choice set for A to be a coerced action. A moralized account of coercion will render circular a *defense* of the structure of coercion favored by welfarism circular. Notice, also, that on my account A would be an uncoerced action if Q persuaded P that A is P's best alternative, for persuasion does not alter an agent's available actions or their outcomes. Of course, treating persuasion as noncoercive conforms to ordinary usage. (Thanks to Mark White for helping me clarify my thoughts on these issues.) For a defense, in another context, of a moralized account of coercion, see Robert Nozick, 1974, *Anarchy, State, and Utopia*, New York: Basic Books, pp. 262–265. For a valuable discussion of the roles of descriptive and moralized concepts of coercion in the justification of classical liberalism (and so a presumption of contractual freedom as strong as the one I defend in this chapter), see Spector, *Autonomy and Rights*, pp. 14–22.

[32] Recall that my version of contractarianism is thick enough to make room for such distributive preferences.

[33] This arrangement corresponds to what G. A. Cohen calls "joint ownership," which he regards as one form of "collectivization" of external resources (as opposed to people's bodies and talent). See G. A. Cohen, 1995, "Are Freedom and Equality Compatible?," in *Self-Ownership, Freedom, and Equality*, Cambridge: Cambridge University Press, pp. 92–115. My argument need not affect Cohen's *conceptual* theses about the relationships between self-ownership, freedom, and equality (in particular, his case against Robert Nozick's defense of private property).

It can be shown that things collectively owned in the present sense will be under-utilized, because each owner has an incentive to hold out for a higher side payment by those who want to use those things. Michael Heller describes this situation as the *tragedy of the anticommons*.[34] Whereas the tragedy of the commons occurs because the absence of property rights (collective rights in another sense of "collective") gives people an incentive to deplete the commons, the tragedy of the anticommons occurs because transaction costs are so high that resources remain underutilized. A regime of private property is demonstrably more efficient not only compared to the absence of rights to exclude others from the use of resources, as in the Hobbesian state of nature, but also compared to overlapping rights to exclude others, as when the conformity of several bureaucratic agencies is required to open a store, or to sell professional services.[35] It seems reasonable to conjecture that the losses in production brought about by the two types of tragedies are large enough to increase poverty to an extent that no attractive conception of equality can condone.

Of course, I do not mean to imply that a regime that exhaustively allocates private property rights in the real world is efficient – that no alternative property system could be Pareto-superior to it. As I pointed out in section I, private markets may fail in various ways. Much ink has been spilled in debates over the sorts of legal regulations needed to overcome such failures.[36] Ideal constitutional contractors would favor those regulations, because it is of the nature of a market failure to prevent people from engaging in mutually advantageous collective action. Still, the Paretian logic that governs the reasoning of ideal constitutional contractors will ensure that the property rights allocated by such regulations are alienable through unexceptionally enforceable contracts. Thus, even if they find a reason to provide, at the constitutional level, for unemployment benefits, they would not foreclose opportunities for mutual advantage by making such benefits inalienable. We see, then, how deep-seated welfarism's commitment to contractual freedom is even in a world plagued with market failure. For, consistently with the contractarian thesis, welfarism asks legislators to establish a presumption of contractual freedom

[34] See Michael Heller, 1998, "The Tragedy of the Anticommons: Property in the Transition from Marx to Markets," *Harvard Law Review*, 111, pp. 621–668. For a formal analysis, see James M. Buchanan and Yong J. Yoon, 2000, "Symmetric Tragedies: Commons and Anticommons," *Journal of Law and Economics*, 43, pp. 1–13.

[35] A unanimity rule for the use of *particular* resources engenders the tragedy of the anticommons. However, as Buchanan and Tullock have extensively argued in *The Calculus of Consent* (1962, Ann Arbor: University of Michigan Press), when a unanimity rule governs the selection of *constitutional rules*, it yields a strong and widespread protection of private property, with allowances for collective-choice mechanisms to cope with market failure. Because the principle of efficiency is equivalent to a unanimity rule, it should not be surprising that the argument I am offering, premised on efficiency and autonomy, supports private property rights largely as strong as those yielded by Buchanan and Tullock's argument premised on "consent."

[36] Environmental control and antitrust laws are frequently defended with the market-failure argument. For an overview of efficiency arguments for regulating markets, see Allen Buchanan, 1985, *Ethics, Efficiency, and the Market*, Oxford: Clarendon Press, pp. 19–36. For an overview of market-friendly proposals to overcome market failure, see Tyler Cowen, "Public Goods and Externalities," in *The Concise Encyclopedia of Economics*, available at http://www.econlib.org/library/Enc/PublicGoodsandExternalities.html.

that yields only to those ideal (and therefore free) contracts blocked by barriers to collective action. In those cases in which this presumption is overridden, people's (redefined) property rights remain fully alienable.

We have seen that parties to an ideal constitutional contract are autonomous. They also *value* their autonomy, if only because they do not want to be subject to the forms of domination that may hinder their free pursuit of nonautonomous life plans (e.g., by freely joining an enclosed religious order).[37] Therefore, they realize that they have an interest in overcoming both the tragedy of the commons and the tragedy of the anticommons. Such tragedies prevent them from satisfying their desires (they want the objects of their desires to be available, and this often means *produced*) and thwart their successful pursuits of long-term life plans. Consequently, ideal constitutional contractors agree on a regime of private property and the contractual freedom entailed by it. Of course, they may happen to be risk-averse, just as they may have, or may assign probabilities to their developing, other more or less specific preferences. Depending on the extent of their risk aversion, they will be willing to trade off wealth prospects for minimum-income guarantees. However, under no circumstances will they give up their contractual freedom over the resources assigned to them by the constitutional contract, including their guaranteed income. For any amount of risk aversion there is a well-defined, efficient allocation of alienable property rights over particular things.

The formidable empirical difficulties involved in identifying such allocations in the real world should not distract us from seeing two momentous practical implications of a constitution that effectively guarantees contractual freedom. On the one hand, such a constitution will not generate ill-defined property rights (as under discretionary powers to redistribute resources) or inalienable rights – by leaving gains of trade unexploited, a regime of inalienable rights among consenting adults is bound to be inefficient. On the other, such a constitution would protect and promote personal autonomy: wealth is instrumental to virtually all life plans, and the total amount of wealth is a function of the specialization, division of labor, and innovation induced by contractual freedom.

It might be thought that efficiency sometimes calls for infringements on private property rights[38] for reasons unrelated to the need to overcome market failure. If true, this proposition would undermine the value of contractual freedom as a prerequisite for Pareto improvements. Consider, for example, *efficient thefts* – that is, nonconsensual transfers of property where the thief pays damages equal to the

---

[37] Recall that my ideal contractors are actual people, with their more or less autonomous, but nonetheless freely chosen, actual life plans.

[38] Just to avoid verbal disputes, let me recall that by "private property rights" I mean "alienable spheres of exclusive control of things," a notion that can in turn be spelled out by Honoré's analysis of "full ownership" (see note 29). On some understandings, private property rights would not be infringed by legal restrictions on voluntary exchanges of property. On these latter understandings, saying that A is a private owner of x is tantamount to saying that the law confers on A the exclusive use of x. Under the former understanding, but not under the latter, we can say that price regulations violate private property rights. For a philosophically rich reconstruction of the changes in the U.S. Supreme Court's conception of property rights and their impact on the Court's views about the constitutional protection of private property, see Leif Wenar, 1997, "The Concept of Property and the Takings Clause," *Columbia Law Review*, 97, pp. 1923–1946.

victim's valuation of the stolen property. Such nonvoluntary exchanges are efficient, because the thief prefers to have the stolen thing rather than the money spent
in damages, whereas the victim remains as well off as before. Ideal constitutional
contractors would nevertheless ban efficient thefts. Unlike ordinary contractors,
and even their ideal counterparts, ideal *constitutional* contractors agree on general
rules, as opposed to rules aimed at governing particular transactions. By definition,
efficient general rules maximize everyone's expected value. By consenting to such
rules, ideal constitutional contractors forfeit some efficient allocations, for they
will predict that some people will mistakenly or abusively adduce that they have
performed efficient thefts. Likewise, ideal constitutional contractors will take measures to preempt judicial mistake or abuse. For these reasons, they will in general
require consent to transfers of title to property (with the standard exceptions for
necessity, etc.).[39]

CONCLUDING REMARKS

I have argued that welfarist and autonomy-based considerations are interestingly
equivalent in their policy implications. Interest is a matter of degree, and no
doubt the argument could be further developed to display additional, nonobvious
connections. Welfarist and autonomy-based political moralities appeal in effect
to an ideal constitutional contract; this guarantees that their normative implications overlap. Still, they are distinct political moralities in that we may come to
understand why a concern for efficiency confers justificatory force to the ideal constitutional contract without realizing that such a contract is both a privileged locus
for the expression of one's autonomy, and a decision procedure for discovering the
institutional mechanisms capable of enhancing everyone's autonomy. More specifically, when welfarists argue that ideal contracts, including the ideal constitutional
contract, are decision procedures for the achievement of efficiency, they may well be
unaware of their presuppositions about property, coercion, and nondomination.
Conversely, when autonomy-based theorists regard ideal contracts as embodying
the value of personal autonomy, they may well be unaware of the efficiency of the
rules chosen in such settings, or of the rational-choice assumptions that enable us
to derive such efficiency judgments. The burden of my argument was in showing
that, despite their distinct theoretical frameworks, both welfarists and theorists of
autonomy should see each other as responding to a shared commitment to the
value of ideal consent, a commitment that should lead them to embrace a strong
presumption of contractual freedom.

[39] See Barnett, "A Consent Theory of Contract," especially pp. 281–283, 293–294.

13 Efficiency, Fairness, and the Economic Analysis of Tort Law

MARK A. GEISTFELD

Throughout its history, the economic analysis of tort law has been largely limited to one question: How should tort rules be formulated so as to minimize the social cost of accidents? Throughout its history, the economic analysis of tort law has also been controversial. The two phenomena are related. It is highly controversial whether tort law should minimize accident costs to the exclusion of fairness concerns, which in turn has fostered the belief that the economic analysis of tort law is controversial.[1]

The controversy associated with the economic analysis of tort law was initially stirred up by the provocative work of Richard Posner. Although he was not the first to apply economic analysis to tort law, Posner strongly influenced the newly developing field by forcefully propounding the claim that tort law should maximize wealth by minimizing accident costs.[2] The approach ultimately foundered as scholars, including Posner, recognized that cost–benefit analysis cannot determine initial entitlements, the basic architecture of any legal rule.[3] The specification of

---

[1] See generally Jules L. Coleman, 2003, "The Grounds of Welfare," *Yale Law Journal*, 112, pp. 1511–1544 (describing controversy surrounding the economic analysis of tort law).
[2] For example, Richard A. Posner, 1981, *The Economics of Justice*, Cambridge, MA: Harvard University Press; William M. Landes and Richard A. Posner, 1987, *The Economic Structure of Tort Law*, Cambridge, MA: Harvard University Press.
[3] Cost–benefit analysis depends on prices, which in turn depend on the initial allocation of property rights or legal entitlements. See Lewis A. Kornhauser, 1998, "Wealth Maximization," in Peter Newman, ed., *The New Palgrave Dictionary of Economics and the Law*, New York: Stockton Press, vol. 3, pp. 679–683. Posner now agrees that wealth maximization is limited in this manner; see Richard A. Posner, 1995, "Wealth Maximization and Tort Law: A Philosophical Inquiry," in David G. Owen, ed., *Philosophical Foundations of Tort Law*, Oxford: Oxford University Press, pp. 99–111.

I gratefully acknowledge the helpful comments, provided at various points throughout the evolution of this chapter from Richard Abel, Jennifer Arlen, Ronen Avraham, Oren Bar-Gill, Robert Cooter, Richard Craswell, Barry Friedman, John Goldberg, Gregory Keating, Lewis Kornhauser, Stephen Perry, Mitchell Polinsky, Eric Rasmusen, Susan Rose-Ackerman, Anthony Sebok, Catherine Sharkey, Steven Shavell, Martin Stone, and Ben Zipursky. I also received helpful comments at the 2004 annual meeting of the American Law and Economics Association, and from participants in workshops at Boalt Hall School of Law, University of California, Berkeley; New York University School of Law; Northwestern University School of Law; and Stanford Law School. The research for this chapter was supported by a grant from the Filomen D'Agostino and Max E. Greenberg Research Fund at the New York University School of Law.

initial entitlements, and thus the substantive content of any legal rule, depends on normative justification and not economic analysis.

This limitation of economic analysis was subsequently addressed by Louis Kaplow and Steven Shavell, who have constructed a proof showing that a "fair" tort rule can violate the Pareto principle by preventing the adoption of a welfare-maximizing, "unfair" tort rule.[4] By showing how a principle of fairness can prevent such a Pareto improvement, Kaplow and Shavell provide a reason for rejecting a fair tort system in favor of one that maximizes welfare. This reason also provides a justification for the conventional economic analysis of tort law. A welfare-maximizing tort system ordinarily relies on cost-minimizing liability rules, thereby reestablishing the dominant role of economic analysis. *All* issues of concern to the tort system ought to be resolved in the cost-minimizing manner, the general method for maximizing social welfare and wealth.[5]

Not surprisingly, the claim that tort law should be nothing more than an exercise of cost minimization has provoked an equally extreme response from critics. The most forceful critique has come from those who maintain that tort liability is best justified by the principle of corrective justice. This principle is based on an individual right that imposes an obligation or duty on another individual. A duty-holder who violates the correlative right has committed a wrong, creating a duty to repair or correct any wrongful losses suffered by the right-holder. This rights-based principle of justice "rules out the economic analysis of [tort] law."[6]

Such sweeping claims about the irrelevancy of economic analysis must be understood in context. If the appropriate rationale for tort liability is a rights-based principle such as corrective justice, then the justification for a liability rule does not depend on whether it is allocatively efficient. Economic analysis is ruled out as irrelevant to the rights-based justification for tort liability.

Allocative efficiency does not need to be the norm of tort liability in order to make economic analysis relevant. Economic analysis is not limited to issues of allocative efficiency and cost minimization. It is an open question whether a rights-based tort system would employ economic analysis, and if so, how.[7]

No doubt, many believe that this question does not merit serious consideration. The conventional economic analysis of tort law asks whether a liability rule would

---

[4] See Louis Kaplow and Steven Shavell, 1999, "The Conflict between Notions of Fairness and the Pareto Principle," *American Law and Economics Review*, 1, pp. 63–77; and Louis Kaplow and Steven Shavell, 2001, "Any Non-welfarist Method of Policy Assessment Violates the Pareto Principle," *Journal of Political Economy*, 109, pp. 281–286. Kaplow and Shavell have an analytic definition for "fairness," which is why I place quotation marks around the term.

[5] See Louis Kaplow and Steven Shavell, 2002, *Fairness versus Welfare*, Cambridge, MA: Harvard University Press.

[6] Ernest Weinrib, 1995, *The Idea of Private Law*, Cambridge, MA: Harvard University Press, p. 132.

[7] The issue has been explored, though not systematically. See Robert Cooter, 1987, "Torts as the Union of Liberty and Efficiency: An Essay on Causation," *Chicago-Kent Law Review*, 63, pp. 523–552; Mark Geistfeld, 2001, "Economics, Moral Philosophy, and the Positive Analysis of Tort Law," in Gerald Postema, ed., *Philosophy and the Law of Torts*, Cambridge: Cambridge University Press, pp. 250–275; Gary T. Schwartz, 1997, "Mixed Theories of Tort Law: Affirming Both Deterrence and Corrective Justice," *Texas Law Review*, 75, pp. 1801–1834. A similar, though different approach seeks to ascertain the extent to which efficiency and fairness justifications coincide or overlap. See Geistfeld, "Positive Analysis of Tort Law," pp. 265–267; Schwartz, "Mixed Theories of Tort Law," pp. 1815–1823.

minimize accident costs by deterring accidents in the future. That forward-looking inquiry seems to be utterly irrelevant to the backward-looking normative question: Is compensation in this case warranted because the defendant was responsible for violating the plaintiff's right?

Despite superficial appearances, the idea that economic analysis is incompatible with or irrelevant to a rights-based principle of justice is mistaken. A rights-based torts system can be fully compatible with the relevant requirements of welfare economics, contrary to the understanding one can easily gain from contemporary tort scholarship. The compatibility is not merely formal. Economic analysis is integral to any plausible rights-based tort system.

I. EFFICIENCY V. FAIRNESS?

The need for tort law arises because social interactions often create a conflict of individual interests resulting in physical harm. An allocatively efficient tort system mediates these interests in a fundamentally different manner than a rights-based tort system.

Consider a tort rule governing risky interactions between an automobile driver and a pedestrian. The transportation enables the driver to pursue various liberty interests, including economic interests. As an unwanted by-product of that activity, the driver exposes pedestrians to a risk of bodily injury. A pedestrian is also acting in furtherance of her liberty interests, including economic interests. In the event of a crash that physically harms the pedestrian, by definition, her interest in physical security has been injured. The pedestrian also suffers emotional harm (pain and suffering) and economic harm (such as medical expenses). If the driver were obligated to compensate any of these harms, the monetary damages would be detrimental to her economic interests. Any precautionary obligations that tort law imposes on the driver, such as a duty to drive slowly, are detrimental to her other liberty interests. Similarly, any precautionary obligations that tort law imposes on the pedestrian, such as not to jaywalk, restrict her liberty. The way in which tort law regulates the risky interaction will burden or threaten at least one party's interests: either the pedestrian's interests in liberty and physical security; the driver's liberty interests, including economic interests; or the interests of both parties. The appropriate mediation of these conflicting interests is the basic question of policy or fairness that must be addressed by tort law.

Tort law traditionally has given "peculiar importance" to the nature of individual interests.[8] The interests need to be distinguished only if there is some reason for

---

[8] American Law Institute (1965), *Restatement (Second) of Torts*, St. Paul: American Law Institute Publishers, § 77, comment i. See also W. Page Keeton et al., 1984, *Prosser and Keeton on the Law of Torts*, 5th ed., St. Paul: West Publishing, § 3, pp. 16–17 (observing that "weighing the interests [of security and liberty] is by no means peculiar to the law of torts, but it has been carried to its greatest lengths and has received its most general conscious recognition in this field"). Throughout the analysis, I will use rather simplistic notions of the relevant interests, such as "liberty" and "security" interests. The philosophical explication of these interests is much more nuanced. See Stephen Perry, 2003, "Harm, History, and Counterfactuals," *San Diego Law Review*, 40, pp. 1283–1314 (differentiating core interests from secondary or recursive interests).

prioritizing among them, and tort law does so. Most importantly, tort law gives one's interest in physical security priority over the conflicting liberty interest of another.[9]

Having prioritized the two types of interests, tort law must then specify the nature of the priority. An absolute or lexical priority of the pedestrian's security interest would justify tort rules that eliminate any risk of physical injury, effectively requiring the cessation of driving and negation of the driver's (absolutely subordinate) liberty interest in most circumstances. That outcome has been rejected by the tort system. As courts have long recognized, "Most of the rights of property, as well as of person, are not absolute but relative."[10] The right to physical security is relative to the right of liberty, giving the security interest a relative interpersonal priority over a conflicting liberty interest. Unlike an absolute priority, a relative priority allows for a trade-off of the conflicting interests, yielding liability rules that permit automobile driving while requiring drivers to act in conformance with the relative priority of the pedestrian's security interest.

Merely identifying a relative priority of the security interest over a conflicting liberty interest does not determine how the interests ought to be balanced. This issue has not been clearly resolved by tort law, creating ample room for disagreement. A relative interpersonal priority of the security interest over the liberty interest is consistent with both an allocatively efficient tort rule and a rights-based tort rule.

The economic analysis of tort law distinguishes between security and liberty interests for a fundamental reason. Costs depend on prices, which in turn depend on the initial specification of entitlements. Consistently with the priority of the security interest, economic analysis assumes that the holder of the entitlement is the party facing a threat to her physical security, such as a pedestrian who is interacting with an automobile driver.[11]

Given the set of initial entitlements, the conventional economic analysis of tort law gives no further priority to the security interest. Minimizing the social cost of accidents depends on the probability of injury, the cost of injury, the cost of safety precautions, and administrative expenses. Consequently, an individual's interest in physical security must be burdened if doing so would decrease the social cost of accidents. This feature of a cost-minimizing tort system sharply distinguishes it from a rights-based tort system.

Rights-based tort rules, including those based on the principle of corrective justice, protect morally fundamental individual interests from incurring burdens justified solely on grounds of social expediency, such as the pursuit of social welfare via the minimization of accident costs. In order for individuals to have a right to physical security, the security interest must have priority over the competing liberty and economic interests of someone else. The right-holder's physical security cannot be compromised merely because doing so would confer

---

[9] For example, Keeton et al., *Prosser and Keeton*, p. 132 ("the law has always placed a higher value upon human safety than upon mere rights in property").

[10] *Lossee v. Buchanan*, 51 N.Y. 476, 485 (1873).

[11] See Jennifer H. Arlen, 1990, "Reconsidering Efficient Tort Rules for Personal Injury: The Case of Single Activity Accidents," *William & Mary Law Review*, 32, p. 43, n. 9 (providing citations to law-and-economics analyses based on such an entitlement).

greater wealth or welfare on others. As Stephen Perry describes the position, "At least within nonconsequentialist moral theory, it makes sense to think of this [security] interest as morally fundamental, and hence as falling outside the purview of distributive justice; our physical persons belong to us from the outset, and are accordingly not subject to a social distribution of any kind."[12]

The security interest has this moral attribute for reasons of personal autonomy or self-determination. As Perry elaborates: "The main reason that personal injury constitutes harm [that may require redress as a matter of corrective justice] is that it interferes with personal autonomy. It interferes, that is to say, with the set of opportunities and options from which one is able to choose what to do in one's life."[13]

How a liability rule prioritizes the security interest accordingly distinguishes cost-minimizing tort rules from those that protect the individual right to physical security. Once the entitlement is allocated to the security interest, cost-minimizing tort rules then give equal weight to liberty and security interests, unlike rights-based tort rules. "All of the leading justice theorists by now have recognized [that] the aggregate-risk-utility test [which gives equal weight to security and liberty interests] cannot be reconciled with the principles of justice."[14] For reasons of individual autonomy, rights-based tort rules prioritize the security interest to a greater extent than do cost-minimizing rules.

Which priority should tort law adopt? The issue can only be resolved by normative judgment. A tort entitlement can be specified in various ways, including one that permits cost minimization and another that protects the individual right to physical security as a matter of autonomy. The entitlement cannot be determined by economic analysis in the first instance, making the choice of liability rules a normative question.

In an effort to guide this normative decision, Louis Kaplow and Steven Shavell have proven that a "fair" tort rule can violate the Pareto principle. For purposes of the proof, a "fair" tort rule gives evaluative weight to some factor that does not exclusively depend on individual welfare, such as rights-based tort rules that prioritize the security interest for reasons of individual autonomy. Because the principle of fairness does not solely depend on welfare considerations, the proof further assumes that the concern for fairness is continuously traded off against some component of welfare. Due to this trade-off, there will be situations in which the choice of a "fair" tort rule comes at the expense of some positive welfare gain that would be created by an "unfair," welfare-maximizing rule. If the gain

[12] Stephen R. Perry, 2000, "On the Relationship between Corrective Justice and Distributive Justice," in Jeremy Horder, ed., *Oxford Essays on Jurisprudence, Fourth Series*, Oxford: Oxford University Press, pp. 237–263.
[13] Ibid., p. 256; see also Gregory C. Keating, 2001, "A Social Contract Conception of the Law of Accidents," in Postema, *Philosophy and the Law of Torts*, p. 34 (arguing that under a Kantian conception of reasonableness, our "interest in security is entitled to more protection than our interest in liberty" for risks threatening severe physical injury, because such risks "threaten the premature end, or the severe crippling, of our agency" whereas the curtailment of liberty has less of a burden on "our capacities to pursue our ends over the course of complete lives").
[14] Richard W. Wright, 2002, "Justice and Reasonable Care in Negligence Law," *American Journal of Jurisprudence*, 47, p. 145.

produced by the welfare-maximizing rule could be costlessly redistributed to all members of society, each person would benefit from the adoption of that rule. This Pareto improvement, however, would be barred by the principle requiring the "fair" tort rule. The "fair" rule can make everyone worse off, leading Kaplow and Shavell to conclude that tort rules should only maximize social welfare – an objective that ordinarily involves the minimization of accident costs.

By assuming that fairness is continuously traded off against some component of welfare, the proof has only limited application. To illustrate, Howard Chang proposes a method for evaluating legal rules that employs a variable weight for fairness that depends on welfare considerations.[15] Because fairness has a variable weight with respect to welfare, the concern for fairness does not have to be given *any* weight for cases in which a legal rule would increase the welfare of all individuals. Such a principle would not block the adoption of a Pareto improvement, contrary to the proof of Kaplow and Shavell. Such a principle of fairness is not continuous in any component of welfare as assumed by Kaplow and Shavell – it ceases to have any weight whenever a legal rule would make everyone better off – and does not violate the Pareto principle.

In response, Kaplow and Shavell defend the continuity assumption by rejecting the type of fairness principle relied upon by Chang:

> [The continuity assumption] is one that we imagined would be endorsed by anyone who believed that a notion of fairness was worth taking seriously.... Formally, our argument only requires that the principle of fairness be continuous *in something*. (Hence, corrective justice should not be given infinitesimal weight with respect to administrative cost savings, trivial aesthetic pleasures, or the consumption of some good – in other words, to some factor that is unrelated to the notion of fairness.)[16]

Kaplow and Shavell make a compelling point. If the concern for fairness vanishes whenever the cost savings produced by an unfair rule can be distributed so as to make everyone better off, then "no matter how much unfairness is involved, it can be outweighed by the tiniest amount of administrative cost savings [shared per capita]."[17] Any theory that allows the fairness concern to become infinitesimally small under these conditions does not seem to be "worth taking seriously." Chang's conception of fairness has been criticized by others. According to the legal philosopher Leo Katz, "[t]he moral precepts that underlie our most basic legal doctrines, or at least those of criminal and tort law, are not like the 'blended' fairness theories Chang shows us how to construct by his algorithm." To avoid the conflict with the Pareto principle, "Chang is driven to construct doctrines that no longer resemble our basic moral ideas."[18]

---

[15] Howard Chang, 2000, "A Liberal Theory of Social Welfare: Fairness, Utility, and the Pareto Principle," *Yale Law Journal*, 110, pp. 173–235.

[16] Louis Kaplow and Steven Shavell, 2000, "Notions of Fairness versus the Pareto Principle: On the Role of Logical Consistency," *Yale Law Journal*, 110, p. 243.

[17] Ibid., p. 242.

[18] Leo Katz, 2006, "Choice, Consent, and Cycling: The Hidden Limitations of Consent," *Michigan Law Review*, 104, p. 666.

Chang has shown that there is no necessary conflict between the Pareto principle and fair tort rules. It is an open question, however, whether there is a set of plausible rights-based tort rules that satisfy the Pareto principle and the other tenets of welfare economics.

II. RIGHTS-BASED TORT RULES AND WELFARE ECONOMICS

According to justice theorists, the tort right protects individual autonomy, making it necessary to determine how this right protects or promotes autonomy. Under a leading formulation, individual rights are "trumps over some background justification for political decisions that states a goal for the community as a whole."[19] An individual right, more precisely, places limits or constraints on the reasons that can justify governmental actions such the enforcement of tort rules.[20] When formulated in this manner, the autonomy-based individual right excludes any justification for tort liability that is inconsistent with the concern for autonomy.

Within such a rights-based tort system, the concern for autonomy can justify liability rules formulated in terms of a relative priority of the right-holder's security interest over a conflicting liberty interest of the duty-holder. The liability rule must equally respect the autonomy of both the right-holder and duty-holder. Their conflicting interests in security and liberty are each important for purposes of autonomy or self-determination, but the interest in physical security is prior to or more fundamental than the interest in liberty. The relative priority recognizes this difference while permitting some sort of balancing of these interests in contexts where they are conflicting.

Such a relative priority of the security interest can yield a compensatory tort right. If the duty-holder's exercise of autonomy or liberty harms the right-holder's interest in physical security, tort law can burden the duty-holder's subordinate liberty interest with an obligation to compensate the harms suffered by the prioritized security interest of the right-holder. In addition to the *ex post* damages remedy, compensation can involve *ex ante* expenditures that make the right-holder whole prior to the risky interaction. This duty permits the actor to engage in risky behavior by relying on compensation to protect the security interest of the right-holder, the type of outcome required by an individual right to physical security that is relative to another individual's right to liberty.

As I have argued at length elsewhere, an autonomy-based, compensatory tort right can persuasively explain the important doctrines and practice of tort law.[21] Having specified the substantive requirements of a set of plausible rights-based tort rules, we can now evaluate this class of rules with the criteria of welfare economics.

---

[19] Ronald Dworkin, 1984, "Rights as Trumps," in Jeremy Waldron, ed., *Theories of Rights*, Oxford: Oxford University Press, pp. 153–168.

[20] See Jeremy Waldron, 2004, "Pildes on Dworkin's Theory of Rights," *Journal of Legal Studies*, 29, pp. 301–308 (explaining why this interpretation of Dworkin's formulation of rights as "trumps" is appropriate).

[21] See generally Mark A. Geistfeld, 2008, *Tort Law: The Essentials*, New York: Aspen Publishers; 2006, *Principles of Products Liability*, New York: Foundation Press; 2003, "Negligence, Compensation, and the Coherence of Tort Law," *Georgetown Law Journal*, 91, pp. 585–632.

A. Rights-Based Tort Rules and the Pareto Principle

A rights-based tort rule protects the individual interest in physical security, thereby ruling out the maximization of social welfare as the only reason for compromising the right-holder's physical security. In this important respect, the individual right constrains social welfare and can yield allocatively inefficient liability rules. The tort right, however, does not constrain social welfare in all possible states of the world. The right protects the individual interest in physical security for reasons of individual autonomy and does not bar the right-holder from exercising her autonomy. The right-holder's exercise of autonomy also promotes her welfare, eliminating any necessary conflict between the tort right and the Pareto principle.

To see why, we need to consider the circumstances in which the Kaplow–Shavell proof operates. The proof assumes a world in which "individuals understand fully how various situations affect their well-being."[22] The proof also assumes that transaction costs are sufficiently low to allow for any form of mutually advantageous redistribution.[23] Mutually advantageous redistributions can be attained by informed agreements between a right-holder and a duty-holder, such as a pedestrian and a driver. The tort right protects the pedestrian's interest in physical security, making her the seller for purposes of the exchange. The driver must purchase the right to expose the pedestrian to a risk of physical injury. In the absence of transaction costs, the parties will agree to structure the risky interaction so as to minimize costs and maximize the gains from contracting, yielding the allocatively efficient outcome. This conclusion directly follows from the Coase theorem.[24]

To illustrate, suppose an automobile accident would always kill the pedestrian. Suppose further that the amount of care exercised by the driver is continuous in the probability of accident, so that incrementally greater care incrementally reduces the probability of a fatal accident. Let B denote the total cost or burden of care incurred by the driver. For any given probability of suffering the fatal injury, the monetary cost of the risk is determined by the pedestrian's willingness to accept money in exchange for facing the risk. This amount makes the pedestrian indifferent between (1) the state of the world in which she does not face the risk and is not compensated and (2) the state of the world in which she faces the risk and receives

---

[22] Kaplow and Shavell, "Conflict," p. 65.

[23] Kaplow and Shavell have two proofs. One involves individuals who are symmetric in all relevant respects, making distributional considerations (and distributional costs) irrelevant (ibid.). The other proof allows for individual differences. For the differences to be meaningful, the welfare gain in moving from (fair) state f to (welfaristic) state w must be unequally distributed across the individuals. Some individuals may be harmed by the move to state w, so state w need not involve a Pareto improvement over state f. Kaplow and Shavell construct a new (redistributed) state r with the same total welfare as state w, in which the total welfare gain in moving from state f to state w is redistributed across all individuals so as to make each one better off in state r than in state f. Each person now prefers state r over state f, so adhering to state f for fairness reasons would violate the Pareto principle (Kaplow and Shavell, "Policy Assessment"). Clearly, state r can be compared with state f only if the redistribution of the total welfare gain in moving from state f to state w is costless (as in the proof), or more generally, if the per capita welfare cost of redistribution is less than the per capita welfare gain.

[24] Ronald H. Coase, 1960, "The Problem of Social Cost," *Journal of Law and Economics*, 3, pp. 1–44.

compensation. The amount of compensation, which is defined as the willingness-to-accept (WTA) risk measure, is the monetary benefit that exactly offsets the cost of the risk or welfare loss for the pedestrian as right-holder. If no monetary benefit could offset the certainty of death, the WTA measure would equal infinity for that particular interaction. As the interaction involves progressively lower level risks, the WTA measure decreases in magnitude. To face a 1-in-100,000 chance of dying, for example, the individual might be willing to accept around $60 (roughly the amount of increased wages required by the typical worker to face an occupational hazard of this magnitude).[25] The driver, therefore, can reduce the total WTA payment by reducing the risk. The driver's total cost – the cost of precaution (B) and the WTA payment to the pedestrian – is minimized if the driver takes precautions costing less than the associated reduction in the WTA measure. This amount of precaution, B^*, minimizes accident costs and is allocatively efficient. At the efficient level of care, the pedestrian typically faces a positive probability of being killed in an accident and requires compensation WTA* for facing that risk. By definition, the pedestrian's receipt of the WTA* compensation equalizes her welfare level to that in a world in which she does not receive the compensation and does not interact with the driver. The pedestrian is fully compensated before she has been exposed to the risk, absolving the driver of any obligation to pay compensatory damages in the event of injury. The agreement is allocatively efficient and satisfies the Pareto principle according to the first fundamental theorem of welfare economics.[26]

The compensatory tort right is justified by the concern for individual autonomy, and so the exchange must satisfy this normative principle in order to be enforceable. The pedestrian is not merely trading or waiving the right.[27] She *exercises* the compensatory right by agreeing to receive compensation for facing the risk. Any tort rule that blocked such a choice would be contrary to the right, and so an autonomy-based compensatory tort right permits the right-holder to assume the risk in this manner. Consistently with this reasoning, such an exchange would absolve the driver of liability for any damages caused by materialization of the risk under the tort doctrine of express assumption of risk.[28]

This example establishes the existence of a class of plausible, rights-based tort rules that does not violate the Pareto principle, contrary to the claim made by Kaplow and Shavell. They may have proven that all "fair" tort rules can block a

[25] See U.S. Environmental Protection Agency, 2000, *Guidelines for Preparing Economic Analyses*, Washington, DC: U.S. Government Printing Office, p. 90.
[26] This particular transaction would leave the pedestrian indifferent and only satisfies the weak form of the Pareto principle. To satisfy the strong form, the entitlement would require the duty-holder to share some of the gains of trade with the right-holder. Due to the assumption of costless redistribution, there are no strategic bargaining costs that might otherwise block such a mutually advantageous redistribution. The agreement would still induce the allocatively efficient amount of care and would necessarily satisfy both forms of the Pareto principle.
[27] Compare Allan Gibbard, 1974, "A Pareto-Consistent Libertarian Claim," *Journal of Economic Theory*, 7, pp. 388–410 (proving that the Pareto principle is not violated when individuals can trade or waive their rights), with Chang, "Liberal Theory of Social Welfare," pp. 201–202 (describing critiques of Gibbard's proof).
[28] American Law Institute, 2000, *Restatement of the Law, Torts: Apportionment of Liability*, St. Paul: American Law Institute Publishers, § 2.

Pareto improvement, but their definition of a "fair" tort rule is inapplicable to the rights-based tort rules under consideration.

Recall that the proof defines a "fair" rule as one justified by a normative principle that continuously trades off a concern for fairness against some component of welfare. This type of principle does not justify the rights-based tort rules under consideration, which instead are justified by a normative principle that constrains the tort system from maximizing social welfare at the expense of individual autonomy. The constraint is not binding when the right-holder exercises the compensatory right by assuming the risk. In these states of the world, fairness (autonomy) is not continuously traded off against welfare; there simply is no trade-off. These rights-based rules do not satisfy the continuity assumption of the Kaplow–Shavell proof, nor do they violate the Pareto principle.

Moreover, this normative principle avoids giving variable weight to autonomy in some manner that depends upon social welfare, thereby avoiding the problems created by such a principle. As Kaplow and Shavell have argued, this type of principle is problematic because "no matter how much unfairness is involved, it can be outweighed by the tiniest amount of administrative cost savings [shared per capita]" in order to satisfy the Pareto principle.[29] This problem does not exist for the compensatory tort right under consideration. The pedestrian assumes the risk because she receives adequate compensation for doing so. The compensation could be infinitesimally small to assume an infinitesimal risk. The right-holder's autonomy is not being compromised to promote social welfare, and so the constraint imposed by the individual right is not binding. In these circumstances, autonomy is not given infinitesimal weight with respect to a penny or any factor unrelated to the individual right – the type of problem generated by a decision rule that gives variable weight to justice or fairness.

The duty-holder's behavior does not affect this reasoning. A rights-based liability rule is interested in the defendant's behavior only insofar as it affects the plaintiff's tort right.[30] If the plaintiff exercises her compensatory right by accepting a penny from the defendant, the defendant's behavior is irrelevant. There is no great unfairness that has been outweighed by the one penny that induced the consent. The right-holder's well-informed, voluntary choice satisfies the concern for autonomy, eliminating the rights-based constraint that would otherwise govern the duty-holder's behavior.

B. The Pareto Principle and the Choice of Tort Rules

Although a compensatory tort right does not violate the Pareto principle under the conditions governing the Kaplow–Shavell proof, such a right might still conflict with the Pareto principle. Consider a case in which the rights-based tort rule could be replaced by a cost-minimizing tort rule in a manner that would increase the welfare of each person. Even though the change could be implemented with the consent of each right-holder, suppose that the government instead wants to

[29] Kaplow and Shavell, "Consistency," p. 242.
[30] See, for example, Weinrib, *Idea of Private Law*, p. 155.

unilaterally impose the change. Implementing the policy change in this manner would disrespect individual autonomy and could be barred by the principle of fairness, although one would need a more fully specified theory of governmental action to reach that conclusion. Assuming that the principle of fairness would bar implementation of the policy in this manner, does it follow that the Pareto principle provides a reason for rejecting these rights-based tort rules?

The answer depends on the reason why we find the Pareto principle to be normatively appealing. The relevance of the Pareto principle is determined by the social welfare function, and so the normative significance of a Pareto violation must derive from the normative rationale for the social welfare function.

To see why, suppose that the Pareto principle is satisfied by any policy change that would increase the welfare of each person, regardless of whether the affected individuals consent or otherwise have their autonomy impaired. This specification makes the Pareto principle a welfarist criterion that evaluates social policy exclusively in terms of total welfare, regardless of its source.[31] When policies are evaluated exclusively in welfarist terms, the social welfare function does not have to distribute the welfare gains of a policy change in some manner that makes each person better off. The Pareto principle no longer has any independent normative significance, nor does its violation.

For example, suppose there are 100 individuals in a community that is considering two tort rules. Rule 1 would make each person in the community better off by one unit of welfare, satisfying the Pareto principle. Rule 2 would make 99 people better off by 1.10 units of welfare, while making one person worse off by 8 units of welfare. Suppose the social welfare function is utilitarian (a form of welfarism), so that the social planner gives equal weight to each individual's welfare. The planner will choose rule 2, which has a total welfare gain of 100.9 units, exceeding the welfare gain of 100 units under rule 1. The fact that rule 1 would make everyone better off is irrelevant to the utilitarian planner, establishing the normative irrelevance of the Pareto principle within a welfarist society.

As a formal matter, a utilitarian social welfare function does not violate the Pareto principle. The Pareto principle requires a pairwise comparison of the status quo with a proposed change. The principle does not apply to a comparison of rule 1 and rule 2 when evaluated from the perspective of the status quo, as in the preceding example. The pairwise restriction of the Pareto principle makes it formally consistent with welfarism. Any Pareto improvement from the status quo, like the adoption of rule 1, necessarily increases total welfare and satisfies the requirements of utilitarianism in particular and welfarism in general.

The consistency between utilitarianism and the Pareto principle is only formal, however, leaving the Pareto principle without any independent normative content. An exclusive focus on total utility makes it irrelevant whether the policy change would make each person better off. The Pareto principle merely identifies one

---

[31] See Amartya Sen, 1982, "On Weights and Measures: Informational Constraints in Social Welfare Analysis," in *Choice, Welfare, and Measurement*, Cambridge, MA: Harvard University Press, pp. 248–251 (defining "welfarism" as the "general approach of making no use of any information about the social states other than that of the personal welfares generated in them").

set of circumstances in which the policy change would increase social utility. Other measures, such as the average increase in individual utility, have this same attribute. Like the Pareto principle, each of these measures is otherwise normatively irrelevant. For a utilitarian social welfare function, the only normative question is whether total utility would be increased by the policy change.

If the Pareto principle has no independent normative significance, then it is not relevant for evaluating tort rules. In the circumstances under consideration, a principle of justice blocks a Pareto improvement. The only violation that would occur, though, is with respect to utilitarianism itself. The autonomy-based tort right prevents the government from implementing a policy that compromises the right-holder's autonomy merely to increase social utility. The rights-based tort rule is functioning exactly as intended. Whether the right should block a policy that increases total utility is a hard normative question that depends on the respective merits of autonomy and utilitarianism, not the Pareto principle.

By contrast, the Pareto principle can have normative appeal based on unanimous consent. When a policy change would make everyone better off and each individual agrees to the change for that reason, the policy simultaneously promotes individual autonomy and social welfare.[32] When justified in this manner, the Pareto principle requires consent, eliminating any potential conflict between the Pareto principle and autonomy-based tort rights.

Indeed, the Pareto principle does not need to be justified by autonomy in order for it to require actual consent. Even if the social welfare function is utilitarian or otherwise depends only on total welfare and not its source, all affected individuals may still have to agree to a policy change in order for it to satisfy the Pareto principle. Welfare commonly refers to "individuals' actual well-being rather than to individuals' well-being as reflected in their mistaken preferences."[33] For this measure of welfare, the government's unilateral implementation of a policy could increase an individual's welfare only if the individual knows that this is the reason why her welfare has been increased. Anyone who disagreed with the unilateral nature of the change would not prefer that policy, in which case the policy change would not satisfy the Pareto principle. Each (fully informed) individual would be better off only if each one actually agrees with the change. Actual consent satisfies the autonomy-based principle of fairness, eliminating the possibility of *any* conflict between the Pareto principle and autonomy-based tort rules.[34]

Upon scrutiny, the Pareto principle provides no reason for selecting welfare-maximizing tort rules. Within a welfarist system, the Pareto principle has no independent normative significance, nor does its violation. Insofar as the normative appeal of the Pareto principle stems from unanimous consent and the associated exercise of individual autonomy, it provides support for rights-based tort rules and not welfare-maximizing rules.

---

[32] Compare Richard A. Posner, 1980, "The Ethical and Political Basis of the Efficiency Norm in Common Law Adjudication," *Hofstra Law Review*, 8, pp. 487–508 (identifying the autonomy rationale for the Pareto principle).

[33] Kaplow and Shavell, "Conflict," p. 65, n. 2 (adopting this measure).

[34] See Heidi M. Hurd, 1996, "The Moral Magic of Consent," *Legal Theory*, 2, pp. 121–146 (discussing the importance of consent for the exercise of autonomy).

This conclusion does not prove that rights-based tort rules satisfy the requirements of welfare economics. To do so, rights-based rules must also satisfy the efficiency–equity criterion.

C. The Efficiency–Equity Criterion

Any rights-based tort rule is a transfer mechanism between the right-holder and duty-holder. Under the efficiency–equity criterion, a transfer mechanism is economically optimal if it is the least costly method for satisfying a distributional need. This criterion minimizes any loss of allocative efficiency for any given distributive or equitable objective.

To determine whether rights-based tort rules satisfy the efficiency–equity criterion, we need to specify the desired distributional or equitable outcome. What is the principle of distributive justice that determines the appropriate distribution of wealth and welfare across society as a whole? Once again, the issue of whether a tort rule satisfies a criterion of welfare economics depends on the social welfare function.

To see why, consider a principle of distributive justice patterned on some simple formula like "to each in equal shares." To implement this principle, the tax system could determine the wealth of each individual in the community, much as it determines individual income, and then redistribute via individualized taxes and transfers to equalize wealth across the community. As a complement to the tax system, the tort system would minimize accident costs, thereby increasing social wealth and the total amount to be distributed by the tax system. When used in this manner, a cost-minimizing tort system can probably attain the desired distributive objective at less cost than a rights-based tort system.[35] For this type of distributive principle, the efficiency–equity criterion favors cost-minimizing tort rules over rights-based tort rules.

Rights-based rules have this property only because the principle of distributive justice is not compatible with the individual right to physical security. When the principle of distributive justice exclusively depends on the total amount of individual wealth or welfare, such as "to each in equal shares," all that matters is the fact of inequality – the source or reason for the inequality is irrelevant. Everyone is entitled to the same distribution, regardless of their behavior or any other reason for the inequality. The distributive entitlement is not affected by inequalities generated by rights violations, eliminating any reason to incur the allocative inefficiencies created by a rights-based tort system.

Other principles of distributive justice depend on the source of inequality, justifying distributive outcomes that do not solely depend on differences in individual wealth or welfare. The basic idea is that once everyone has the same, just starting point, each can pursue her conception of the good life. Different pursuits typically generate different levels of individual wealth or welfare, and so only certain types of

---

[35] See Louis Kaplow and Steven Shavell, 2000, "Should Legal Rules Favor the Poor? Clarifying the Role of Legal Rules and the Income Tax in Redistributing Income," *Journal of Legal Studies*, 29, pp. 821–835.

inequalities should be eliminated by redistribution. As Thomas Nagel puts it, "The essence of this moral conception is equality of *treatment* rather than impartial concern for well-being. It applies to inequalities generated by the social system, rather than to inequalities in general."[36] To use Ronald Dworkin's terminology, allowing for inequalities based on choice means that a distributive principle should be "endowment-insensitive" and "ambition-sensitive."[37] One's position in life should reflect ambitions and choices rather than the arbitrary circumstances of endowment beyond one's control. For this class of distributive principles, "Treating people with equal concern requires that people pay for the costs of their own choices."[38]

When operating within this class of distributive principles, cost-minimizing tort rules no longer satisfy the efficiency–equity criterion. Rights-based tort rules attain the desired overall distributive outcome at lowest cost, thereby satisfying this criterion of welfare economics.

Consider the following distribution of wealth that is deemed to be fair because the inequalities stem from individual choices and not endowments:

Fair Pre-accident Distribution of Wealth

Brad	Others	Peter
$2 million	$200,000	$110,000

Suppose that Peter negligently injures Brad while driving, causing Brad $50,000 of damages. Without a tort system, the accident would result in the following distribution of wealth:

Actual Post-accident Distribution of Wealth

Brad	Others	Peter
$1.95 million	$200,000	$110,000

The $50,000 reduction in Brad's wealth occurs only because he had the misfortune of being injured in the crash. But what if that injury is Peter's responsibility, because Peter's exercise of autonomy violated Brad's right to physical security? In that event, the principle of fairness would deem Peter to be the "owner" of the injury costs, making him responsible for the loss suffered by Brad.[39] Peter would incur a compensatory duty to Brad for the losses caused by the infringement of Brad's right. This compensatory obligation is not retributive and can be satisfied by consensual arrangements like insurance contracts.[40]

---

[36] Thomas Nagel, 1991, *Equality and Partiality*, New York: Oxford University Press. Nagel identifies five sources of inequality that can be morally distinguished: discrimination, class, talent, effort, and luck (p. 103).

[37] Ronald Dworkin, 1981, "What Is Equality? Part 2: Equality of Resources," *Philosophy and Public Affairs*, 10, p. 311.

[38] Will Kymlicka, 1990, *Contemporary Political Philosophy: An Introduction*, Oxford: Clarendon Press, p. 75.

[39] Compare Jules L. Coleman and Arthur Ripstein, 1995, "Mischief and Misfortune," *McGill Law Review*, 41, pp. 91–130 (arguing that the ownership of accident costs is a normative question).

[40] "Corrective justice goes to the nature of the obligation; it does not prescribe the mechanism by which the obligation is discharged.... Nothing about corrective justice precludes the defendant

Assuming that Peter has no insurance, the compensatory duty he owes to Brad would require the following distribution of wealth:

Fair Post-accident Distribution of Wealth

Brad	Others	Peter
$2 million	$200,000	$60,000

The movement from the actual post-accident distribution of wealth to the fair distribution requires a transfer of $50,000 from Peter to Brad. To implement this transfer, all that matters is the risky interaction between Peter and Brad; the wealth held by others is irrelevant. Peter and Brad are the two parties to the tort suit. By enforcing the rights-based tort rule, the tort system would determine that Peter violated a duty owed to Brad, giving Brad the right to receive $50,000 from Peter as compensation for the injury. *A rights-based tort rule defines the appropriate transfer rule.*

Under these conditions, it makes no sense to separate the tort inquiry from the appropriate transfer inquiry – the type of separation that would otherwise occur if tort rules were designed to minimize accident costs. A tort regime that first determined liability on grounds of cost minimization would then require the tax system to make a separate, costly inquiry regarding the appropriate tax redistribution between Peter and Brad. That tax transfer would yield the same outcome that could have been attained more directly by the rights-based tort rule requiring a transfer of $50,000 from Peter to Brad. The separate tort inquiry on cost minimization would create no social benefit, because the parties would ignore that rule and instead make their decisions by reference to the final tax-transfer rule.[41] The tort inquiry concerning cost minimization would be unnecessary and wasteful. To reduce the total costs of attaining the desired distributive outcome, the tort system could directly implement the appropriate transfer rule based on Peter's violation of Brad's right. Rights-based tort rules accordingly satisfy the efficiency–equity criterion whenever they operate within a broader system of distributive justice that depends on the source of one's wealth or welfare – the type of system that presumably is highly attractive to economists.

III. ECONOMIC ANALYSIS IN A RIGHTS-BASED TORT SYSTEM

It should come as no surprise that autonomy-based tort rules satisfy the distributional requirements of welfare economics, because the promotion of autonomy

from anticipating the possibility of liability by investing in liability insurance" (Weinrib, *Idea of Private Law*, p. 135, n. 25).

[41] The problem can be modeled as an extensive game in which the first stage involves care decisions, the second stage involves the risky interaction, the third stage involves enforcement of the cost-minimizing tort rule, and the final stage involves the tax transfers. The concept of subgame-perfect Nash equilibrium requires a strategy that is a Nash equilibrium for the entire game and for every subgame (played at each stage to the end). This concept of rationality requires each actor to consider the decision at each stage by reference to the final stage. Each actor makes the care decisions in stage one by reference to the final stage involving the tax transfers. In effect, each actor "sees through" the intermediate stage involving the cost-minimizing tort rule and instead considers the care decision in terms of the ultimate tax transfers.

is consistent with the important value judgments of contemporary welfare economics. "Put most simply, to be autonomous is to be one's own person, to be directed by considerations, desires, conditions, and characteristics that are not simply imposed externally upon one, but are part of what can somehow be considered one's authentic self."[42] Individual choice, of course, also has foundational importance for welfare economics. In addition to the Pareto principle, the "main value judgment" involved in modern welfare economics "is called *individualism*," which maintains that "social ordering ought to be based on individual orderings of alternative states, that is, on individual preferences, where it is implicitly assumed that each individual is the best judge of his or her own preferences."[43] Like autonomy, individualism rests on the normative judgment that the individual is the best person for deciding how to pursue her own life. By promoting autonomy, rights-based tort rules recognize the value of individualism embraced by welfare economics.

To be sure, the normative concern for autonomy is not ordinarily justified as a means for satisfying preferences and increasing welfare. But as Jules Coleman has persuasively argued, the concern for autonomy ultimately explains why we care about welfare:

> Of course, any plausible theory of what is valuable to a person would include the ability to act on the basis of one's preferences and desires. But that is because autonomous action is valuable to persons understood as planning agents who bear a special relationship of ownership and responsibility to how their life goes, and not because people have a taste for welfare.[44]

Due to the inherent relationship between autonomy and individual welfare, the best protection of autonomy often will involve protecting the right-holder's welfare with damages compensation and risk reduction. Consequently, a rights-based tort system will use economic analysis to formulate the substantive content of liability rules, even for a tort right that is justified exclusively by the intrinsic value of autonomy and not the welfare or any other consequence produced by the exercise of autonomy.

Consider the rights-based theory of Ernest Weinrib, who is perhaps the most resolute nonconsequentialist theorist of tort law. He argues that the tort "right is not synonymous with welfare, nor wrong with the deprivation of it."[45] "The reason that rights matter for tort law lies elsewhere."[46] Although the tort right is not justified by any concern for welfare, Weinrib also recognizes that welfare serves a critical "secondary function of concretizing rights and making them quantifiable

---

[42] John Christman, 2003, "Autonomy in Moral and Political Philosophy," in Edward N. Zalta, ed., *The Stanford Encyclopedia of Philosophy*, available online at http://plato.stanford.edu/archives/fall2003/entries/autonomy-moral/.

[43] Robin Boadway and Neil Bruce, 1984, *Welfare Economics*, New York: Basil Blackwell, p. 2.

[44] Coleman, *Grounds of Welfare*, p. 1542. See also Ronald Dworkin, 1980, "Is Wealth a Value?," *Journal of Legal Studies*, 9, pp. 191–226 (showing that the maximization of social wealth can only matter insofar as it promotes some other independent normative value).

[45] Weinrib, *Idea of Private Law*, p. 131.

[46] Ernest J. Weinrib, 2001, "Correlativity, Personality, and the Emerging Consensus on Corrective Justice," *Theoretical Inquiries in Law* (online ed.), 2, at http://www.bepress.com/til/default/Vol2/iss1/art4Weinrib, p. 14.

in particular cases."[47] In order for welfare considerations to play this functional role, the tort inquiry must rely on economic analysis.

Consider once again the tort rule governing risky interactions between drivers and pedestrians. Due to the nonconsensual nature of the interaction, tort law must first ensure that the behavior adequately respects individual autonomy. Tort law does so by objectively valuing the interests in question. Within contemporary society, automobile driving is almost essential for the exercise of autonomy, and so the tort rule cannot ban the activity merely because it might injure pedestrians. Such a ban would violate the requirement that the fair tort rule must equally respect the autonomy of the right-holder and the duty-holder. Because the fair tort rule must permit the activity despite the risk that pedestrians will be physically injured, the best protection of the pedestrian's autonomy must reside in protecting her welfare. A liability rule that adequately protects the right-holder's welfare must also equally respect the duty-holder's. The fairness inquiry, therefore, must formulate the tort rule in a manner that gives equal consideration to the welfare levels of the right-holder and duty-holder, an inquiry requiring economic analysis.

A fair resolution of this problem is difficult for reasons made apparent by economic analysis. Recall that under ideal compensatory conditions, the driver incurs total tort obligations equal to the burden of precautions (B^*) and the compensatory payment to the pedestrian for facing the residual risk (captured by the WTA* measure). The compensatory payment of the WTA* measure can take the form of a damages payment for the injury caused by the risk.[48] That form of compensation is not available in the context under consideration, because the accident would kill the pedestrian. Unless the pedestrian as right-holder is fairly compensated for the risky interaction, however, the benefits and burdens of the risky activity cannot be fairly distributed between the right-holder and duty-holder as required by the tort right. This compensatory problem is starkly posed by nonconsensual risks threatening fatal injury, although a significant problem also exists for any nonconsensual risk threatening severe physical injury.[49]

This compensatory problem can be ameliorated by negligence liability. Because the driver cannot pay the WTA* amount to the pedestrian in the form of tort

---

[47] Ibid.

[48] Consider a case in which an injury does not alter the pedestrian's utility function when the risk of injury is 1-in-100,000 and the pedestrian has a WTA risk measure of $60. The WTA measure includes the cost of risk aversion, making the pedestrian risk-neutral with respect to any decision concerning her receipt of the WTA measure. Because the injury does not alter her marginal utility of wealth, the pedestrian would be indifferent between a tort rule giving her a guaranteed receipt of the $60 WTA compensatory proceeds prior to each risky interaction and a tort rule giving her damages of $6,000,000 in the uncertain event of injury (the mathematical expectation of the uncertain damages award, $(1/100,000) \cdot \$6,000,000$, equals the $60 certainty provided by the WTA proceeds). The right-holder, therefore, can receive the WTA compensation by a damages remedy equal to the WTA measure multiplied by the reciprocal of the risk of injury ($60 \cdot 100,000$).

[49] Like premature death, severe bodily injuries can reduce the victim's marginal utility of wealth – a comatose victim being an extreme example – and so the right-holder would prefer to receive the WTA risk proceeds prior to the risky interaction rather than being provided with a damages remedy formulated in terms of the WTA measure.

damages for a fatal accident, the negligence standard of care can instead require the driver to make the WTA* payment in the form of safety precautions. A negligence standard requiring the driver to take precautions costing B^* + WTA* imposes the same total burden on the driver as she would incur under ideal compensatory conditions. As compared to the allocatively efficient standard of care B^*, the more demanding standard B^* + WTA* reduces risk.[50] The risk reduction directly protects the security interest and increases the welfare of the pedestrian by making it less likely that she will be seriously injured or killed. The increased welfare for the right-holder *partially* offsets the compensatory shortfall created by the inherent inadequacy of monetary damages in cases of premature death and serious bodily harm, a second-best compensatory outcome reflective of the nonideal compensatory conditions in which the rights-based rule must operate.[51]

When the nature of the relationship precludes the duty-holder from otherwise compensating the right-holder with other forms of *ex ante* compensation, and the nature of the injury makes it prohibitively costly or impossible for the duty-holder to fully compensate the right-holder *ex post*, then risk reduction is the only way to protect the right-holder's interest in physical security. These deterrence considerations apply correlatively to the right-holder and duty-holder, satisfying this essential requirement of corrective justice. A concern for deterrence characterizes the economic analysis of tort law, and so the importance of deterrence within a rights-based tort system further establishes the importance of economic analysis within such a system.

By quantifying, or concretizing, the tort right in welfare terms, economic analysis also produces well-defined liability rules. The preceding example shows how the standard of care for a rights-based negligence rule can be specified with the same degree of precision as the cost-minimizing rule. In a rights-based tort system, the appropriate amount of monetary damages for nonmonetary injuries can also be derived by economic methodology.[52] Overly vague tort rules create fundamental problems of fairness for duty-holders and litigants, and so any plausible rights-based tort system will use economic analysis to make the liability rules more determinate.

Indeed, the tort right is best protected by the allocatively efficient liability rule for important classes of cases, including products liability, medical malpractice, and

---

[50] One cannot choose to be negligent in exchange for paying the "price" of compensatory damages. A duty-holder who acts in this fashion is subject to punitive damages and criminal liability, creating the necessary incentive for complying with the demanding standard of reasonable care. See Mark A. Geistfeld, 2008, "Punitive Damages, Retribution, and Due Process," *Southern California Law Review*, 81, pp. 263–309.

[51] The pedestrian is still worse off than in the ideal compensatory outcome, whereas the driver's welfare is equal in the two states of the world. As a matter of equality, each party may have to suffer an equal welfare loss relative to their welfare level under ideal compensatory conditions. Such a solution will still be second best. The driver must be permitted to engage in the risky activity, and so the pedestrian will necessarily face some risk of fatal injury for which she cannot receive full compensation, either *ex ante* or *ex post*, satisfying the correlativity requirement of the right-duty nexis.

[52] The method is described in note 48. For explanation of why that method is an appropriate way to redress the violation of a tort right, see Mark A. Geistfeld, 2006, "Due Process and the Determination of Pain and Suffering Tort Damages," *DePaul Law Review*, 55, pp. 331–358.

bilateral risky interactions in which each party is simultaneously a potential injurer and victim to the same extent (like two automobile drivers). Due to the distributive nature of these interactions, the right-holder internalizes the costs and benefits of tort liability. The consumer as right-holder, for example, pays (via higher product prices) for the safety investments and injury compensation that tort law requires of the product seller as duty-holder. The internalization of costs and benefits creates an *intrapersonal* conflict of the right-holder's interests in security and liberty, and so the *interpersonal* priority of the security interest no longer governs. These safety decisions instead depend on the right-holder's willingness to pay to reduce the risk, justifying liability rules that minimize accident costs. By identifying how tort rules affect the distribution of welfare between right-holders and duty-holders, economic analysis shows why a rights-based tort system should formulate liability rules with cost–benefit analysis for important classes of cases.[53]

CONCLUSION

Just as economic analysis must be guided by a normative principle in the initial specification of legal entitlements and the ultimate specification of the social welfare function, the normative principle also depends on economic analysis at the stage of implementation. This symbiotic relationship has been almost entirely ignored in the ongoing debate about the appropriate purpose of tort law, resulting in the mistaken impression that tort law requires either a rights-based inquiry that excludes economic analysis, or an economic inquiry that excludes any concern for corrective justice or the fair redress of individual-rights violations. In addition to satisfying the distributional criteria of welfare economic, a rights-based tort system will importantly depend on economic analysis. The two modes of analysis are complements and not substitutes.

[53] See generally Geistfeld, *Tort Law; Products Liability.*

14   Retributivism in a World of Scarcity

MARK D. WHITE

In the philosophy of law, the two primary justifications and/or motivations for criminal punishment are deterrence and retributivism. Deterrence is a consequentialist concept, linking punishment to a reduction in the future crime rate through its effects on criminal behavior. Stated this way, it is easy to see why economists who study the criminal law adopt deterrence as its goal: mainstream economics is essentially consequentialist itself, emphasizing the efficiency of outcomes above all other considerations, and it also has an elaborate (though imperfect) theory of rational choice and behavior. Provided that criminal penalties are interpreted as material disincentives similar to market prices, that the harm from criminal activity can be quantified, and that current models of rational decision making are sufficiently precise and accurate – all controversial claims outside the economic approach to law – economists can, in theory, design penalties optimally to minimize the sum of harm from crime and the costs of punishment itself.[1]

On the other hand, retributivism would seem to stand in opposition to these specialized tools of the economist. Though scholars interpret the basic concept differently, at its core retributivism has a deontological component that justifies the punishment of wrongdoers as a matter of justice or right, based on desert and guilt.[2] Retributivism is usually divided into two varieties: negative, or weak,

---

[1] The seminal paper in this literature is Gary S. Becker, 1968, "Crime and Punishment: An Economic Approach," *Journal of Political Economy*, 76, pp. 169–217. Becker's economic analysis both formalizes and extends the classical work of Jeremy Bentham and Cesare Beccaria (Jeremy Bentham, 1781/1988, *The Principles of Morals and Legislation*, Buffalo: Prometheus Books; Cesare Beccaria, 1764/1986, *On Crimes and Punishments*, trans. David Young, Indianapolis: Hackett).

[2] The most influential historical retributivists are Kant and Hegel. Kant's primary writings on punishment are contained in *The Metaphysics of Morals* (1797/1996, trans. Mary Gregor, Cambridge: Cambridge University Press). (On the nature and extent of Kant's retributivism, which has recently

For helpful comments and insightful criticism on early versions of this chapter, I thank Kimberly Ferzan and Michael Cahill; participants in conference sessions on "The Methodology of Law and Economics" held at the Allied Social Science Association meetings (sponsored by the International Network for Economic Method) and the Eastern Economic Association meetings, in particular Lewis Kornhauser, Matthew Adler, Peter Huang, Tim Brennan, and David Hoffman; and participants in the Philosophy Forum at the College of Staten Island. I also thank the students in my fall 2007 Senior Seminar on Crime and Punishment, in which several of the newer ideas in this chapter were inspired and worked out. All errors and omissions remain my own.

retributivism sees wrongdoing as a necessary but not sufficient condition for punishment, whereas positive, or strong, retributivism holds wrongdoing to be both necessary and sufficient for punishment. Negative retributivism, then, emphasizes that only the guilty may be punished (and not excessively), whereas positive retributivism goes further by also *requiring* that the guilty be punished (and not too leniently). Generally, retributivism is often understood as backward looking, focusing primarily on the criminal and the crime committed, as opposed to deterrence, which looks forward to the future gains that flow from punishment (while neglecting the actual crime committed).[3] Furthermore, and most important for the purposes of the present work, retributivism does not take costs or resource constraints into account when it requires universal just punishments, so there is no room for optimization or trade-offs within its boundaries.

This chapter aims to address this problem. How can a positive retributivist system of punishment, which demands that the guilty be punished, be implemented in a world of scarcity?[4] As Michael Cahill writes, "the retributivist perspective does not lend itself to the practical compromises often necessary in the real world, where we cannot punish all wrongdoers to the full extent of their moral desert."[5] Assuming that not all guilty persons can be apprehended, prosecuted, and punished, sacrifices will have to be made – but where? I will preview this discussion with a brief summary of the economic treatments of retributivism up to now, and also the prospects for basing penalties on hybrid theories of punishment that mix deterrence and retributivism. Then I will turn to retributivist penalties for offenses and how they would compare to deterrent ones. Finally, I will confront the difficult idea of how retributivism would work in the real world, the world of scarcity, and what sacrifices would be most acceptable to achieve this.

I. ECONOMICS AND RETRIBUTIVISM

Despite their exclusive focus on deterrence as the driving force behind punishment, economists (and legal scholars adopting economic methodology) have discussed

---

become a matter of some dispute, see note 14.) For Hegel's retributivism, see *The Philosophy of Right* (1821/1952), trans. T. M. Knox, Oxford: Oxford University Press). For more recent work on retributivism, see the papers in H. B. Acton, ed., 1969, *The Philosophy of Punishment: A Collection of Papers*, New York: St. Martin's Press. Excellent critical evaluations can be found in R. A. Duff, 2001, *Punishment, Communication, and Community*, Oxford: Oxford University Press, ch. 1; C. L. Ten, 1987, *Crime, Guilt, and Punishment*, Oxford: Oxford University Press, ch. 3; and John Braithwaite and Philip Pettit, 1990, *Not Just Deserts: A Republican Theory of Criminal Justice*, Oxford: Clarendon Press, chs. 8–9.

[3] For concise summaries of retributivism and deterrence, see R. A. Duff, 2004, "Legal Punishment," in the *Stanford Encyclopedia of Philosophy* (http://plato.stanford.edu/entries/legal-punishment/); and Mark D. White, "Criminal Justice: Punishment and Retributivism" in P. A. O'Hara, ed., 2008, *International Encyclopedia of Public Policy – Governance in a Global Age*, vol. 4, GPERU: Perth, http://pohara.homestead.com/encyclopedia/volume-4.pdf, pp. 63–73.

[4] Negative retributivism poses less of a problem, and will be discussed in the next section.

[5] Michael T. Cahill, 2007, "Real Retributivism," *Washington University Law Review*, 85, pp. 815–870, 822. I only became aware of Cahill's paper late in the preparation of this chapter, but I have tried to incorporate several of its many insights (as well as others from conversations with him). I would like to think this chapter complements (and compliments) his work without excessive overlap, but readers can be the ultimate judge of that.

retributivism to some extent. However, as expected, most are dismissive, disparaging, or even mocking. Leading figure Richard Posner addressed retributivism in a 1980 article, characterizing it as "widely viewed as immoral and irrational, or at least as primitive and nonrational."[6] He does endorse its "social function" in "primitive and early societies," in which it may temper the desire of private acts of vengeance, but dismisses its usefulness in modern societies, in which the function of law enforcement is assumed by the state. He concludes (without explicitly considering arguments from justice) that "retributive theories of punishment appear to belong to particular historical circumstances rather than to have a timeless claim to be regarded as just."[7]

Much more recently, Louis Kaplow and Steven Shavell, as part of their lengthy treatise promoting an exclusively welfarist orientation to legal decision making, take aim at retributivism as an alternative to deterrence in criminal justice policy.[8] The general point of their book is that because any policy goal that deviates from welfare maximization (such as fairness or justice) will fail to maximize welfare (obviously), if welfare maximization is the goal of policymakers (for which they make no affirmative argument), then they should choose policies that maximize welfare, to the exclusion of fairness or justice.[9] They apply this thinking fairly straightforwardly to criminal law, showing that any penalties not determined purely on the basis of efficient deterrence will fail to deter efficiently. However, they do raise several intriguing arguments (and some misguided ones) against retributivism, before dismissing such thinking as based simply on intuitions, "a philosophized version of tastes for retribution," largely because "the degree of alignment between their theory . . . and tastes for retribution seems too close to be due merely to chance."[10]

[6] Richard A. Posner, 1980, "Retribution and Related Concepts of Punishment," *Journal of Legal Studies*, 9, p. 92.

[7] Ibid., p. 83. Keep in mind that Posner does (or did once) equate justice with efficiency: "A second meaning of 'justice,' and the most common I would argue, is simply 'efficiency.' When we describe as 'unjust' convicting a person without a trial, taking property without just compensation, or failing to require a negligent automobile driver to answer in damages to the victim of his carelessness, we can be interpreted as meaning simply that the conduct or practice in question wastes resources" (1975, "The Economic Approach to Law," *Texas Law Review*, 53, p. 777, quoted in Nicholas Mercuro and Steven G. Medema, 2006, *Economics and the Law: From Posner to Post-modernism and Beyond*, 2nd ed., Princeton: Princeton University Press, p. 94).

[8] Louis Kaplow and Steven Shavell, 2002, *Fairness versus Welfare*, Cambridge, MA: Harvard University Press, ch. 6.

[9] Readers prone to dizziness should sit down at this point; rarely has a question been begged this blatantly. The tautological nature of their argument has been pointed out by a number of scholars, including Jules Coleman, 2003, "The Grounds of Welfare," *Yale Law Journal*, 112, pp. 1511–1543; Kimberly Ferzan, 2004, "Some Sound and Fury from Kaplow and Shavell," *Law and Philosophy*, 23, pp. 73–102; and Mark D. White, 2004, "Preaching to the Choir: A Response to Kaplow and Shavell's Fairness versus Welfare," *Review of Political Economy*, 16, pp. 507–515. Even the authors themselves admit this (*Fairness versus Welfare*, pp. 7, 58), but nonetheless claim that this point "is not one that is well appreciated" (p. 8).

[10] Kaplow and Shavell, *Fairness versus Welfare*, p. 366. For more on the tone of this book, see White, "Preaching to the Choir," pp. 512–514. Referring to studies of determination of punitive damages, in which it is found that juries often choose damage awards that are linked more closely to blame and condemnation than to optimal deterrence, Cass R. Sunstein links such retributivist inclinations to "outrage." Although he stops short of calling such opinions "irrational," he does predict dire

However, this condescending and derogatory attitude toward retributivism is not universal among law-and-economics scholars. Donald Wittman provides the most fair and elaborate consideration of retributivism within the law-and-economics tradition, in which he models justice as a function of punishment and the number of criminals and innocent persons punished.[11] He assumes that justice is maximized at the (exogenously determined) punishment that "fits" any given crime, and declines (linearly) as punishment rises or falls from this level. He uses this model to analyze the relative injustice resulting from deviations from just punishment, from failing to punish all criminals, and from punishing the innocent, and also constructs a social utility function that would generate a societal preference for retributivist punishment. Whereas most retributivists (and deontologists in general) would be uncomfortable with the idea of even a vague "measure" of justice, Wittman's approach, if extended modestly, would enable analysis of the trade-offs involved with retributivist punishment.

More recently, Kenneth Avio has discussed the possibility of incorporating retributivist concerns into the economic analysis of criminal punishment, relying upon *hybrid* theories of punishment that combine deterrence and retributivism.[12] The most famous proponent of this idea is H. L. A. Hart, who put forth the possibility that the "general justifying aim" of the institution of punishment can be deterrence, whereas the "distribution" or assignment of specific penalties can be conducted according to retributivist principles.[13] In other words, deterrence is *why* we punish, but retributivism governs *how* and *whom* we punish; or, as in the title of Sharon Byrd's 1989 paper that casts this in Kantian terms, such a system of punishment would be "deterrence in its threat, retribution in its execution."[14]

consequences for a legal system that take them into account (2005, "On the Psychology of Punishment," in Francesco Parisi and Vernon L. Smith, eds., *The Law and Economics of Irrational Behavior*, Stanford: Stanford University Press, pp. 339–357).

[11] Donald Wittman, 1974, "Punishment as Retribution," *Theory and Decision*, 4, pp. 209–237. John R. Harris also incorporates the cost of punishing innocents into the (utilitarian) Becker model, but without mentioning retributivism (1970, "On the Economics of Law and Order," *Journal of Political Economy*, 78, pp. 165–174). On the topic of the inadvertent punishment of innocents in the economic model of crime, see also Thomas J. Miceli, 1990, "Optimal Prosecution of Defendants Whose Guilt Is Uncertain," *Journal of Law, Economics, and Organization*, 6, pp. 189–201; Louis Kaplow and Steven Shavell, 1994, "Accuracy in the Determination of Liability," *Journal of Law and Economics*, 37, pp. 1–15; and Kaplow and Shavell, *Fairness versus Welfare*, pp. 336–352.

[12] Kenneth L. Avio, 1993, "Economic, Retributive, and Contractarian Conceptions of Punishment," *Law and Philosophy*, 12, pp. 249–286.

[13] See H. L. A. Hart, 1968, *Punishment and Responsibility: Essays in the Philosophy of Law*, Oxford: Oxford University Press; precedents include W. D. Ross, 1930, *The Right and the Good*, Indianapolis: Hackett; J. D. Mabbott, 1939, "Punishment," *Mind*, 48, pp. 152–167; John Rawls, 1955, "Two Concepts of Rules," *Philosophical Review*, 64, pp. 3–32; and S. I. Benn, 1958, "An Approach to the Problems of Punishment," *Philosophy*, 33, pp. 325–341.

[14] B. Sharon Byrd, 1989, "Kant's Theory of Punishment: Deterrence in Its Threat, Retribution in Its Execution," *Law and Philosophy*, 8, pp. 151–200; Avio, "Economic, Retributive, and Contractarian Conceptions of Punishment," takes issue with the applicability of Byrd's version of the hybrid theory. For other scholars who agree that Kant espoused a hybrid theory of punishment, rather than the strict retributivism for which he is best known, see Don E. Scheid, 1983, "Kant's Retributivism," *Ethics*, 93, pp. 262–282; Jeffrie G. Murphy, 1987, "Does Kant Have a Theory of Punishment?" *Columbia Law Review*, 87, pp. 509–532; and Thomas E. Hill, 1999, "Kant on Wrongdoing, Desert, and Punishment," *Law and Philosophy*, 18, pp. 407–441. (For an application of Kant's general moral

As usually understood, this hybrid theory amounts to the standard deterrence approach constrained by negative retributivism (ruling out intentional punishment of the innocent, as well as disproportionate penalties). Some have criticized the inconsistency of such hybrid theories, contending that the ethical foundations of deterrence and retributivism are mutually exclusive, and any combination thereof will compromise them both.[15] As Avio writes, "punishments that simultaneously optimize and are deserved . . . may not exist"[16]; in fact, such penalties almost certainly will not exist, and some deterrence will have to be sacrificed for justice (or vice versa). More precisely, although few deterrence advocates would endorse deliberate punishment of innocent persons, they do recommend disproportionately high punishments to compensate for the uncertainty of apprehension and prosecution (a standard result from the economics of crime). But negative retributivists condemn excessive punishment of the guilty as well as punishment of the innocent, so they would prohibit these artificially increased penalties, as will be noted in the following.

II. COMPARING RETRIBUTIVE AND DETERRENT PENALTIES

One perpetual dilemma facing retributivists is the determination of just penalties, or how exactly to make the punishment fit the crime.[17] Deterrence theorists never confront this problem, because penalties need bear no relation to any intrinsic aspect of the crime itself, though optimal penalties are often proportional to the seriousness of the crime according to the principle of marginal deterrence.[18] But most retributivists are not concerned with determining "precisely" just penalties, seeking only to ensure that the chosen penalty is not disproportionately harsh (in negative retributivism) or light (in positive retributivism) in relation to the crime. The issue is further complicated by the ambiguity over what aspect of the crime must be matched by the penalty. Should the punishment fit the benefit to the criminal or the harm done to the victim (or society as a whole)? Each choice can be justified by retributivists arguing from different underlying presumptions. Linking penalties to benefit derives from the unfair-advantage school of retributivism, which claims that criminals deserve punishment because by violating the

theory to law and economics, see Mark D. White, 2004, "A Kantian Critique of Neoclassical Law and Economics," *Review of Political Economy*, 18, pp. 235–252.)

[15] Braithwaite and Pettit, *Not Just Deserts*, pp. 166–168; Alan H. Goldman, 1979, "The Paradox of Punishment," *Philosophy and Public Affairs*, 9, pp. 42–58.

[16] Avio, "Economic, Retributive, and Contractarian Conceptions of Punishment," p. 268.

[17] See Claudia Card, 1975, "Retributive Penal Liability," *American Philosophical Quarterly Monographs* No. 7; Andrew von Hirsch, 1976, *Doing Justice: The Choice of Punishments*, New York: Hill and Wang; and Michael Davis, 1983, "How to Make the Punishment Fit the Crime," *Ethics*, 93, pp. 726–52. For criticism of the possibility of determining retributive punishments, see Alan Wertheimer, 1975, "Should Punishment Fit the Crime?," *Social Theory and Practice*, 3, pp. 403–423; Hugo Adam Bedau, 1978, "Retribution and the Theory of Punishment," *Journal of Philosophy*, 75, pp. 601–620; and Braithwaite and Pettit, *Not Just Deserts*, pp. 166–180. Of course, the determination of optimally deterrent penalties is no simpler; see Jeffrey S. Parker, 1993, "The Economics of Mens Rea," *Virginia Law Review*, 79, pp. 754–756 (and references therein).

[18] David Friedman and William Sjostrom, 1993, "Hanged for a Sheep: The Economics of Marginal Deterrence," *Journal of Legal Studies*, 12, pp. 345–366.

laws that almost everybody else obeys, they take unfair advantage of law-abiding citizens.[19] On the other hand, linking penalties to harm has a much longer history, deriving from the *lex talionis* itself, the position that the punishment must fit the crime, punishment must represent the ideal of "an eye for an eye," and that whatever evil the criminal visits on another, he visits on himself.[20]

Without presuming to propose any new method of determining just punishments, I will assume that just punishment can be determined to be roughly equivalent to the total harm caused by the crime, both to the victim and to the surrounding community. Of course, that narrows the problem only slightly, for measuring the harm to the victim is hard enough – account must be taken of not only financial and material losses, but in some cases medical bills, emotional damage, and so on. But extending this estimation process to an entire community is exponentially more difficult, even if the concept of social harm were sufficiently understood. For instance, Lawrence Becker proposes that the nature of the social harm that ordinarily justifies the criminal category can be found in the social volatility caused by the crime, which also justifies equivalent punitive treatment of attempted and successful crimes.[21] However, rather than attempt to quantify this, I will merely note which crimes are likely to cause more or less social volatility, and adjust our harm estimates accordingly.

Of course, a more basic point, already mentioned, is that retributivism forbids disproportionately severe punishments. This is directly at odds with the standard result from the economics of crime that if punishment is uncertain, penalties must be increased to maintain deterrence. If stealing $100 is punished by a $100 fine, but there is only a 50% probability of being caught, then the criminal will face an expected penalty of $50, and will likely steal the $100 (assuming no other offsetting incentives). Deterrence would then require that the penalty be increased to at least $200, so the expected penalty is then (at least) $100 and the criminal is more likely deterred from the crime. Accordingly, then, retributivist penalties, although just, would be less harsh, and therefore less deterrent, than the optimal deterrent penalties (whereas Posner assumes they would be more harsh, resulting in "too little crime").[22]

---

[19] For a famous statement of this view, see Herbert Morris, 1968, "Persons and Punishment," reprinted in 1976, *On Guilt and Innocence*, Berkeley: University of California Press, pp. 31–58.

[20] This view is most famously attributed to Kant. Of course, on most retributivist accounts, deserved punishment must also take into account the culpability or responsibility of the offender, and adjust the harm-based punishment accordingly; see von Hirsch, *Doing Justice*, pp. 79–80; Robert Nozick, 1981, *Philosophical Explanations*, Cambridge, MA: Belknap Press, pp. 363–365; and George Fletcher, 1978, *Rethinking Criminal Law*, Boston: Little, Brown, pp. 461–463. In the interest of keeping my discussion somewhat within the realm of the economic approach to law, I will defer consideration of these alternatives to future work.

[21] Lawrence C. Becker, 1974, "Criminal Attempts and the Theory of the Law of Crimes," *Philosophy and Public Affairs*, 3, pp. 262–294. Legal economists also recommend full punishment of attempts, but for deterrent reasons; see Steven Shavell, 1990, "Deterrence and the Punishment of Attempts," *Journal of Legal Studies*, 19, pp. 435–466; and David D. Friedman, 1991, "Impossibility, Subjective Probability, and Punishment for Attempts," *Journal of Legal Studies*, 20, pp. 179–186.

[22] Posner, "Retribution," p. 82. This is part of his argument against retributivist punishment in modern times, based on "the increased concealability of criminal activity that has resulted from the greater privacy of modern life" (ibid., p. 83), which requires disproportionately high punishments in the

But the previous analysis assumes that benefit and harm are equal – after all, $100 lost is $100 gained – and this is not always the case. The thief is richer by $100, and the victim is poorer by $100, but he has also been violated, feels less secure, perhaps invests in increased security measures, forgoes activities where he feels he may be in danger, and so on. To borrow a concept from tort law (very cautiously), the harm to the victim could be equated to the amount of compensatory damages that would "make him whole," which may be much greater than $100. If these hypothetical damages are greater than $100 but less than $200, then the penalty based upon them would still be less harsh than the optimal deterrent penalty ($200). But if the harm to the victim exceeds $200 – which is easily satisfied if he has to spend just one hour with a therapist – then the retributivist penalty is more harsh than the optimal one. Furthermore, adding in harm to society in the form of social volatility would increase the retributivist penalty even more (though this aspect is unlikely to be significant in the theft of $100, unless the theft itself were very invasive and therefore seen as particularly threatening to others).

But would not deterrent penalties be based on this concept of harm as well? That depends – as Keith Hylton points out, there is still fundamental disagreement among law-and-economics scholars as to whether optimal penalties should be based on the benefit to the criminal or the harm to the victim.[23] Those who focus on harm are aiming toward optimal deterrence – only deterring crimes that represent a net loss of social well-being. In this picture, if a thief steals a vase worth $1000 to him and only $800 to its legitimate owners, this is a crime with net benefits, and should not be deterred – and an expected penalty of just $800 would achieve the preferred lack of deterrence. Of course, we have only included financial loss in the harm figure, but even if we included other aspects of personal harm, the criminal's benefit could potentially be higher (especially if vicarious thrill were included), and crimes could still be possibly "efficient." This is true even if societal harm is included, though with crimes most likely to elicit this – such as murder, kidnapping, and rape – that result becomes increasing unlikely.

But at the risk of stating the obvious, crime is not ordinarily thought of this way – aside from the standard examples of necessity, such as breaking into a deserted cabin or stealing a loaf of bread to save one's life, we do not judge crimes to be efficient or inefficient based on who places a higher value on the results of the crime. Some scholars agree, and choose not to focus on possible desirability of crime, but instead base penalties on benefit in order to deter all crime.[24] After all, it

interest of optimal deterrence. Avio makes this argument as well: "punishment that is retributive in its execution (i.e., equal in severity to the direct harm experienced by the victim) is generally not credible as an effective threat as perceived by rational prospective offenders" ("Economic, Retributive, and Contractarian Conceptions of Punishment," p. 267).

[23] Keith N. Hylton, 2005, "The Theory of Penalties and the Economics of Criminal Law," *Review of Law and Economics*, 1, pp. 175–201.

[24] On the choice between benefit- and harm-based penalties, see Hylton, "The Theory of Penalties." Becker ("Crime and Punishment") is representative of scholars advocating harm-based punishment in order to internalize the social costs of crime; the later Richard A. Posner (1985, "An Economic Theory of the Criminal Law," *Columbia Law Review*, 85, pp. 1193–1231) is representative of those supporting benefit-based penalties in order to deter crimes completely (especially those with market alternatives, such as theft). (I say "later" Posner because, as I have noted, at the time of his retribution article, he was concerned about excessively high penalties leading to too little crime.)

is the criminal's decision that the state is trying to influence, and the criminal bases
his decision on his expected benefits and costs. If expected punishment equals or
exceeds the expected benefit from crime, then the criminal will have no incentive
to continue with it, and in the ideal case, all crime will thereby be deterred.[25]

Of course, whether penalties are based on harm or benefit, deterrence requires
that they be scaled up proportionately to the probability of the offender escaping
detection. A harm-based penalty adjusted for probability is inconsistent with
retributivism, due to its excessive harshness relative to desert. But ironically, a
benefit-based penalty scaled for probability may not be, if harm is greater than
benefit to begin with. Is there any way to determine whether the benefit-based
penalty (adjusted for probability) is greater or lesser than the retributivist harm-
based one (not adjusted for probability)? This is important for determining the
impact of retributivist penalties on the criminal justice system, regardless of the
value attached to deterrence itself; for instance, if retributivist penalties were found
to be smaller, such a system would result in more crime and therefore increased
burden on the system. On the other hand, if retributivist penalties were higher,
that would have the opposite effect.[26]

If we let H represent the harm from the crime, B the benefit to the criminal, and p
the probability of being punished, we are asking under what conditions $B/p > H$
or $B/p < H$. If we assume are crimes are inefficient (especially when social harms
are considered), then $B < H$ for every crime. But the probability adjustment to
benefit may change this, especially if the probability is smaller, or benefit is closer
to harm. Both conditions are often satisfied with minor offenses, such as traffic
violations and littering: both benefit and harm are relatively small and similar, and
the probability of detection is usually set very low. (It must be recognized that p is a
discretionary policy parameter, unlike B and H, and is subject to change.) However,
for major crimes like murder, assault, rape, and kidnapping, as well as burglary
and grand larceny, harm is likely to be much larger than benefit – especially when
the impact on the community is considered – and the authorities normally devote
more resources to apprehension, implying a higher value of p. In such case, the
probability adjustment to benefit will be smaller, and the resulting benefit-based
penalty will likely remain smaller than the retributivist harm-based penalty.

If this logic is correct, then the retributivist should judge the penalties for minor
offenses to be too high. The litterbug does not deserve a fine of hundreds of dollars
based on the harm he imposes on society; the penalty is set this high solely to
economize on enforcement resources, which the retributivist does not consider a
relevant consideration in determining just punishments. On the other hand, the
retributivist would consider benefit-based penalties for major crimes like murder
to be too low, because they would be based on the benefits to the criminal, which are
normally low compared to the harm imposed on the victim (and the surrounding
community), even after allowing for the probability of punishment.

[25] In the nonideal, realistic case, criminals would have a distribution of benefits from any particular
crime, and some of them may be higher than even a very harsh penalty, which would then fail to
deter.
[26] The truth is more complicated, of course, and will be traced out in the next section.

III. RETRIBUTIVISM IN A WORLD OF SCARCITY

In the last section, we saw that if retributivist penalties were enacted in place of deterrent ones, major crimes would be punished more severely and minor offenses punished less severely. But as Braithwaite and Pettit emphasize, theories of punishment cannot be considered in isolation from the rest of the criminal justice system, or even one's theory of the state and just government.[27] Deterrence fits nicely into the utilitarian program of criminal justice and government envisioned by Bentham and his followers, but retributivism has no such natural home. Nonetheless, the changes in the penal system that the retributivist would recommend must be analyzed in the context of the entire system, for such reforms would affect not only prison operation and fine collection, but also the operations of prosecutors and police. It is in this area that economists can make their most important and appropriate contribution to the study of criminal law: their specialization in analyzing trade-offs and opportunity costs of alternative policy regimes. (It is also where they often overextend themselves by presuming to pronounce on the choice between those regimes, which economics cannot do except in terms of the much-criticized efficiency standard.)

To simplify matters, I will break the criminal justice process (somewhat arbitrarily) into three steps – apprehension (including detection), conviction (including trial and pretrial processes), and punishment. Further assume that the total resources devoted to the three stages of law enforcement are fixed, so any resources allocated to one level must come from the others. Finally, we assume that the deterrent penalties are designed to allocate resources efficiently over all three stages of the process. As a result, any retributivist penalties that differ from these will necessarily compromise efficiency in the pursuit of justice. Of course, strict retributivists would have no problem with this, but if they want their policies considered by real-world politicians and bureaucrats, as well as voters, they will need to outline and confront the precise nature of the inefficiencies created by just penalties.

A. Retributivist Punishment Only

We will start with the most limited version of (positive) retributivism,[28] and assume that only punishment of convicted persons must adhere to retributivist principles – namely, due and proportionate penalties – leaving the previous two stages, apprehension and prosecution, which influence the probability of punishment, to be optimized according to standard economic models. We must consider the two categories of crimes just analyzed. For major crimes (for which the penalty is normally imprisonment), retributivist penalties would be higher, resulting in higher prison costs per convict. However, such penalties would provide more deterrent value, which would save resources at the prosecution and apprehension stages, resulting

---

[27] Braithwaite and Pettit, *Not Just Deserts*, ch. 2.

[28] Again, I choose to deal with positive, rather than negative, retributivism because it poses a more serious challenge to the economic standard of deterrence, and also represents a more significant concern regarding resource allocation.

in lower probability of punishment. So in the case of major crimes, retributivist punishment would result in a shift of resources from police and prosecutors to the prison system. The precise nature of the severity–probability trade-off depends on many factors, such as criminals' levels of risk aversion and marginal disutility from imprisonment and the cost functions of prisons, prosecutors, and police, so we cannot predict whether the new punishment–enforcement regime would result in more or less crime. But in the simplest case of risk neutrality among criminals and increasing marginal costs at each level of the criminal justice system (a standard economic assumption), we can assume that the percentage increase in penalties demanded by retributivist principles would result in a greater percentage fall in probability (because the increase in punishment is relatively inefficient, and would draw more than the same percentage of resources from the other stages), and there-fore deterrence would fall for the risk-neutral criminal. This would result in an increase in crime and an increased burden on all levels of the system. But because penalties cannot increase to lessen the burden, due to retributivist constraints, prison costs must rise and the burden will be shifted to prosecutors and police, who will then have to lower the probability further, resulting in even less deter-rence and more crime. Whether this process would converge to an equilibrium level of probability and crime cannot be determined at this level of generality, but even if we assume it would, the increase in crime generated by this policy change represents a serious cost of a retributivist system of punishment, one that only the most strident retributivist could ignore.

With minor offenses (often punished with fines or short jail time), retributivist penalties would be less harsh than deterrent ones. The smaller penalties will lessen the burden on jails and the agencies that collect fines, but will also reduce the amount of fines collected per conviction.[29] Punishment costs per offender will fall, releasing more resources for prosecutors and police (minus the lost fine rev-enue), who can thereby increase the probability of punishment. But as before, due to increasing marginal costs, probability would not increase by as much of the penalties fall (in percentage terms), so deterrence would decrease, once again leading to an increase in the number of offenses.[30] This would again require an increase in resources throughout the system, but because punishment cannot be compromised, it would draw resources away from prosecutors and police and force the probability to fall, generating more offenses. Even if we assume, as before, that this downward spiral would converge at an equilibrium, the extra crime generated poses a dilemma for the retributivist.

Note that in both cases, whether retributivist penalties are more or less harsh than deterrent ones, the level of deterrence falls because of the adverse effect on probability. This is in stark contrast to Posner's statement that an emphasis on retribution would result in higher penalties and therefore "too little crime." Based

---

[29] Fines are considered a wash to standard measures of welfare economics, aside from collection and enforcement costs, because the loss to the payer is exactly offset by the gain to the state. However, in terms of government resources themselves, they most certainly are not (though the cost of collecting them is still minuscule compared to the costs of the prison system).

[30] This is even more likely in the case of fines, because lowering fines saves almost no resources, which are necessary to increase the probability of detection, apprehension, and prosecution.

on the preceding analysis, we see that if the scarcity of resources is acknowledged, then – regardless of their severity relative to deterrent penalties – retributivist penalties create inefficiencies in the criminal justice system that result in higher levels of crime.[31]

B. Retributivist Punishment and Prosecution

Now we expand the domain of retributivism to cover both punishment and prosecution; in other words, not only must all convicted persons be punished proportionately to their crimes, but all truly guilty persons – and no truly innocent persons – must be prosecuted. The constraints of the punishment stage remain the same, but now the prosecutors are bound to prosecute every case to the best of their ability, while at the same time doing their best to ensure that no innocent defendants are convicted. This rules out prosecutorial discretion to drop cases, as well as plea bargaining to secure pretrial convictions with lower punishments (options that we revisit in what follows).

This introduces new complications not present in the punishment stage. The type and severity of punishment is completely within the discretion of the authorities, but the likelihood of conviction of the guilty (and acquittal of the innocent) is merely *influenced* by the prosecutors – they do not wholly determine it, nor can they be held solely responsible for it. Even the best prosecutors, with the most resources, trying a case with a fair judge and impartial jury, will not always result in legal findings that correspond to true guilt or innocence.

So although outcomes cannot be assured, we will assume that this increased burden on the prosecutors to prosecute (and hopefully convict) all cases will result in higher probability of punishment, p. This simplifies things quite a bit, of course; the prosecutors must try harder to convict truly guilty defendants while not trying too hard to convict those who are (unbeknownst to them) truly innocent. We could define p_G as the probability of the truly guilty being convicted and p_I as the probability of the truly innocent being convicted; then the prosecutors would have to maximize the first and minimize the second. The difference between them represents the criminal's perceived probability of punishment from committing a crime, because he expects an increased probability $p_G - p_I$ of being punished if he chooses to commit the crime rather than not. Therefore, if we understand p to equal $p_G - p_I$, we can say that the prosecutor's goal is to maximize p, which can be done either by maximizing p_G, minimizing p_I, or some combination thereof.[32] In any case, the increased drive toward prosecutorial accuracy and effort in order to increase probability will absorb additional resources, the most important aspect for our purposes.

---

[31] Kaplow and Shavell (*Fairness versus Welfare*, ch. 6) make a similar point with a much more specific model.

[32] I acknowledge that this is a difficult task, for the two probabilities to some extent oppose each other; increased attempts to convict guilty defendants will inevitably ensnare some innocent ones, and a concerted effort to avoid conviction of innocent defendants will lose some truly guilty ones. See Harris, "On the Economics of Law and Order," for more on this trade-off.

Again we divide crimes into major crimes and minor offenses, for which retributivist penalties would be higher and lower than deterrent penalties, respectively. For major crimes, punishments would be more severe, diverting resources to the prison system away from prosecutors and police. But because the prosecutors have to increase their efforts toward conviction in the face of the reduction in resources, this squeezes the police even further, which will in part compromise the higher level of probability the prosecutors are attempting to achieve (because probability is based on the efforts of both the prosecutors and police). In the end, detection and apprehension are compromised; even though penalties are increased, and conviction of defendants brought to trial is more certain, fewer suspects will be apprehended in the first place. We have introduced yet another layer of inefficiency, leading to even lower expected penalties, less deterrence, and more crime (though those criminals that are caught are more likely convicted and punished) – assuming again that the downward spiral converges.

With minor offenses, penalties will fall in a retributivist system, freeing up resources for the prosecutors and police (minus any fine revenue lost per conviction). In the previous example, the remaining resources would be allocated optimally between the prosecutor's office and the police force, but in this one, more of those resources must be allocated to prosecutors to ensure trials and the highest probability of convictions. As before, this misallocation would hamper the police's efforts, again resulting in compounded inefficiencies: fines and jail time will be smaller though conviction more likely, but fewer suspects are caught. As with the major crimes case, crime will increase due to lower expected penalties, even though conviction rates are higher (for those actually apprehended).

Of course, if retributivist constraints were to be extended to the police as well, requiring that as many guilty suspects as possible be apprehended in order to face (certain) trial and punishment, then resources must be drawn from outside the criminal justice system to supplement the financially strapped police, because prosecution and punishment cannot be compromised. On top of this, if the police are given more resources to apprehend suspects, more will be caught, which implies that prosecutors will need even more resources to bring them to trial, and prisons will need more resources to house them.

IV. FINDING COMPROMISES IN RETRIBUTIVISM

If the preceding analysis is correct, dedication to a positive retributivist system of criminal punishment, whether restricted to punishment alone or extended further back into prosecution or apprehension, has serious implications regarding efficiency and resource allocation. Although in principle the retributivist may not be concerned with these consequences, he must at least acknowledge that such a system will be a very hard sell to politicians and administrators, who have to balance the needs of the criminal justice system with the rest of the needs of society. Critics of retributivism, who usually take aim at the justifications of the practice, have rightly pointed out the practical difficulties. For instance, Douglas Husak emphasizes three drawbacks of punishment – cost, error, and abuse – and writes that "unlike economists, philosophers have tended to theorize about punishment as though its drawbacks were unimportant to its justification."[33] He does not take issue with the position that criminals deserve punishment, but argues instead that "in light of the formidable drawbacks I have described, any prima facie rightness in repaying evil with evil may well be outweighed; it is hardly obvious that rational persons should support the luxury of actually imposing punishment simply because criminals deserve such treatment."[34]

Avio addresses the conflict between retributivism and the economic world of scarcity more directly, stating that "retributivist explanations ... fail to indicate how many resources should be devoted to criminal justice, and how to allocate these resources between apprehension and punishment."[35] If retributivist constraints were exclusively applied to punishment, then there would be little problem for economists: actually punishing convicted criminals lends credibility to threats of punishment that enhance their deterrent impact. But if retributivist ideals are extended to apprehension as well, then the scarcity of resources becomes a pressing issue. "Apprehending and punishing offenders requires the investment of real resources, resources that could be used for other socially beneficial purposes (to cure disease, etc.). Any serious theory of punishment commanding our attention must recognize and address this opportunity cost issue."[36]

Even those generally supportive of retributivist ideals recognize the problem with putting them into practice. In "Real Retributivism," Michael Cahill addresses this issue directly, concluding that strict, positive retributivism (which he terms "absolutist retributivism") is "patently unworkable, and probably affirmatively undesirable, as it leads to real-world outcomes nobody would want."[37] He also considers *threshold retributivism*, a hybrid theory of punishment in which the demands of positive retributivism are limited by particularly adverse consequences.[38] But Cahill finds this internally inconsistent and oddly discontinuous, adhering to deontological principles of justice and desert until some threshold point, at which they become irrelevant and consequentialist concerns take precedence. Instead, Cahill argues for *consequentialist retributivism*, which "sets the goal of maximizing the *total* amount of desert-based punishment, even if this means sacrificing deserved punishment in some cases for the sake of pursuing it in others."[39] Based on his belief in some

[33] Douglas N. Husak, 1992, "Why Punish the Deserving?," *Noûs*, 26, p. 451.
[34] Ibid.
[35] Avio, "Economic, Retributive, and Contractarian Conceptions of Punishment," p. 263.
[36] Ibid., pp. 264–265. See also Kenneth L. Avio, 1990, "Retribution, Wealth Maximization, and Capital Punishment: A Law and Economics Approach," *Stetson Law Review*, 19, p. 386.
[37] Cahill, "Real Retributivism," p. 857.
[38] Cahill, "Real Retributivism," pp. 830–833, 858–861. Note that this is the opposite of the hybrid theory of punishment described earlier, in which the demands of deterrence theory are constrained by (negative) retributivist concerns. The concepts of threshold deontology and retributivism are from Michael Moore, 1997, *Placing Blame: A General Theory of the Criminal Law*, Oxford: Oxford University Press.
[39] Cahill, "Real Retributivism," p. 833. As he notes in the paper, consequentialist retributivism has very few adherents, the most prominent being Michael Moore (1993, "Justifying Retributivism," *Israel Law Review*, 27, pp. 15–49); for a counterargument, see David Dolinko, 1997, "Retributivism, Consequentialism, and the Intrinsic Goodness of Punishment," *Law and Philosophy* 16, pp. 507–528. For another adherent to consequentialist retributivism, see Dan Markel, 2001, "Are Shaming Punishments Beautifully Retributive? Retributivism and the Implications for Alternative Sanctions,"

degree of desert-based punishment, and his practical concerns regarding resource constraints, Cahill concludes that consequentialist retributivism "is the only version of a retribution-oriented account of criminal justice that might accommodate the various real-world considerations necessary for a theory to work in practice,"[40] and his defense of this claim makes up a significant part of his paper.[41]

Strictly speaking, retributivism is merely a theory of punishment, and does not offer judgments or prescriptions regarding prosecution, apprehension, or any other stage of the criminal justice system.[42] But it is hard to find this satisfying, as it amounts to a certain degree of ivory-tower isolationism: if theories of punishment are meant to be put into practice, they cannot be considered apart from the rest of the criminal justice system. Nonetheless, it is difficult to discern what retributivists would have to say about the rest of the system. The constraints extrapolated to prosecution and apprehension here were simply extensions of the idea that all persons found legally guilty should be punished, to require that all legally guilty persons must be punished, which requires apprehension and prosecution to find them legally guilty.[43]

If we accept these extended constraints, along with the dire consequences of imposing them, we are led to ask: in practical terms, considering the fact of scarcity, what compromises, trade-offs, or sacrifices can a retributivist make? Certainly, some retributivists might hold firm and say "none," at which point the discussion would end. But if some retributivists believe that any amount of retributivist justice is better than none, then they would allow for compromises; the problem is determining what compromises retributivists would allow if there were to consider them. In the rest of the section, I make an effort to explore possible compromises in the criminal justice system that retributivists may endorse, but this is a project that needs and deserves much more time and attention.[44]

A. Level of Punishment

If retributivism is held to apply only to the punishment stage, "all" that is required is that all offenders found guilty of crimes must be punished accordingly. There are no

Vanderbilt Law Review, 54, pp. 2157–2242, and 2004, "Against Mercy," *Minnesota Law Review*, 88, pp. 1421–1480.

[40] Cahill, "Real Retributivism," p. 864 (pp. 861–869 contain the bulk of his argument for consequential retributivism).

[41] For related work detailing the real-world compromises made in the pursuit of desert-based justice, see Paul H. Robinson and Michael T. Cahill, 2006, *Law without Justice: Why Criminal Law Doesn't Give People What They Deserve*, Oxford: Oxford University Press, particularly ch. 4 ("Making the Most of Limited Resources").

[42] This fact is lost on Kaplow and Shavell, who fault retributivists for not pronouncing on the criminal category itself (*Fairness versus Welfare*, p. 303).

[43] Note that I am not extending retributivism to moral guilt in the absence of criminal wrongdoing; I am applying the retributivist ideal to legitimate state punishment only.

[44] As mentioned earlier, Michael Cahill's "Real Retributivism" is a significant advance in this direction. Also, I do not discuss compromises that the police could make; because the police are furthest from the determination of legal guilt that would trigger a retributivist duty to punish, I regard retributivist constraints as least binding at that level. See Cahill, "Real Retributivism," pp. 843–853, for a more thorough treatment.

related justice-based constraints on the prosecution or apprehension stages, which means that resources can be allocated efficiently at those stages without violating retributivist principles. But nonetheless, the constraints at the punishment level can have a drastic impact on the performance of the criminal justice system, especially because the probability of conviction falls, and at the same time, criminal activity increases.

What can be done to relax the retributivist constraints of punishment to reduce these negative effects? There would seem to be only two options: punish fewer convicted persons, and/or punish some convicted persons disproportionately (in either direction).[45] Deciding between these options forces us to ask: is it more important to retributivists that all guilty persons be punished to some degree, even if not in due proportion to their crimes; or rather that those punished be punished proportionately, even if not all are punished? For example, if ten persons are convicted of crimes, is it better that five are punished proportionately and five not at all, or that all ten are punished, but out of proportion to their crimes?

Of course, nonpunishment is rarely if ever considered in the economic literature on crime, except at the prosecutorial level (to which we shall turn shortly). Nonetheless, it would stand to reason that the demands of punishment in general take priority over questions of severity. In the literature on retributivism, the most heavily debated topic is the justification of retributive punishment at all, not the justification of its degree; determining the just punishment for any given crime takes on a more technical nature.[46] Although justice may not strictly be quantifiable, it may be comparable, so it may be that more justice is done if all guilty persons are punished in some degree, rather than failing to punish some in order to punish the rest more appropriately. If so, we can presume that the retributivist's priority would be making sure that all guilty persons are punished, even if the penalties would have to be adjusted away from the ideal in order to economize on resources. This would imply that the penalties would be moved closer to the economic optima: the punishments for major crimes would be reduced, and those for minor offenses would be increased. Although this would certainly represent a compromise of retributivist ideals to some extent, it would be the least bad option, and would render the criminal justice system as a whole more efficient, while reducing the crime rate.

The extent to which the retributivist would be willing to do this, however, would still be subject to debate, as would be the method by which it could be done. Would all penalties be adjusted across the board, so as to maintain the relative scaling of penalties (and their correspondence to the scale of crimes)? Or would penalties for minor offenses, or even lesser crimes in the major crimes category, be adjusted before those for the most serious crimes? For instance, would we want to reduce the penalties for grand larceny before we did the same for murder? This would alleviate the inefficiency problem to some extent, and still retain the

---

[45] Though it would seem that this can be stated more precisely as "lower punishments," we saw in the discussion of minor offenses that lowering offenses below the economic optimum creates the same problems as raising them once all the secondary effects are taken into account.

[46] See sources in note 17 on the determination of retributivist penalties.

ordinal ranking of penalties for murder and grand larceny, but would make the difference between them larger (increasing the marginal penalty for murder over grand larceny). Once again, this requires some comparability in justice: is it worth it to lessen the justice associated with punishing grand larceny in order to maintain it with regard to murder? Or second-degree murder versus first-degree murder? There are many options available to the positive retributivist open to compromise, but there is little in the literature to help us choose among them – and choose we must, if we want to avoid the negative consequences of a pure retributivist system of punishment.[47]

B. Prosecution and Apprehension

In the last subsection, we were assuming that just penalties would be imposed according to the charges of which the criminal was found guilty, and we concluded that this constraint might have to be relaxed if the ramifications for the crime rate and economic efficiency were too dire. But there is another way to achieve this flexibility in penalties: through prosecutorial discretion. Because prosecutors would not be bound by retributivist constraints, they would be free to negotiate charges and sentences, drop cases during trial or pretrial proceedings, or refuse to press charges at all. Doing so, they could relax some of the burden on the punishment system without requiring that the retributivist constraints on penalties be compromised (because penalties would still be proportionate to the charged crimes).

Although retributivism is strictly a theory of punishment, few retributivists would be comfortable with wide latitude and discretion on the part of prosecutors, and most might endorse the extension of justice-based constraints to the actions of prosecutors as well. (The meaning of "punish" in the retributivist standard would then be understood to encompass prosecution efforts as well as punishment itself.) If this were done, it would not seem to further the ideal of "punishing all guilty persons" – understanding guilt in a moral, rather than legal, sense – if prosecutors were to manipulate their case load or negotiate charges and sentences with defendants during plea bargaining. However, if retributivists accept the compromise considered – that penalties can be modified to ensure that more guilty persons are punished to some extent – then prosecutorial discretion emerges as one way to reach that compromise.[48]

Prosecutorial discretion is commonly understood to encompass decisions regarding charging offenders and the negotiation of pleas (which may involve the charges themselves). A common justification for both is efficient resource allocation: by declining to press charges, dropping cases, or negotiating pleas in cases that would otherwise impose disproportionately heavy prosecutorial burdens

---

[47] Obviously, this is one of the reasons that Cahill favors consequentialist retributivism, an alternative that I may take up in future work (but that my traditional Kantian inclinations prejudice me against for the time being).

[48] In fact, Cahill argues that only a consequentialist retributivist can endorse prosecutorial discretion ("Real Retributivism," pp. 855–856).

relative to their societal importance, more resources are freed to focus on prosecuting other, more important cases, and securing more convictions.[49] Certainly, some exercise of prosecutorial discretion also serves the cause of justice, such as the prosecutor's role in assessing evidence and probable cause before charging a suspect with a certain crime, which helps ensure that only those suspects most likely to be truly guilty are prosecuted. But absent this purpose, a purely economic rationale for choosing cases – picking "low-hanging fruit" – would clearly conflict with retributivist ideals.[50]

Whereas discretion in charging has some legitimate justice-based purpose, plea bargaining would seem to have none.[51] By its very nature, plea bargaining reflects a miscarriage of justice, resulting in punishments that are not proportionate to the charges, or charges that do not correspond with the crimes performed. As Kenneth Kipnis explains, when the prosecutor offers a reduced charge or sentence to induce the defendant to plead guilty, then, if he is truly guilty, he is punished too leniently, and if he is in fact innocent, he is punished unjustly.[52] It stands to reason that the primary rationale for plea bargaining, like prosecutorial discretion in general, is economic, which would be anathema to the steadfast retributivist, but may have relevance to a retributivist operating in a world of scarcity (or one willing to consider consequentialist variations of retributivism).[53]

Of particular note is the positive danger in plea bargaining, specifically the increased possibility of punishment of the innocent. Whereas punishing a guilty person less than he deserves is certainly a concern, but may be justified if it means

---

[49] See Robert Heller, "Selective Prosecution and the Federalization of Criminal Law: The Need for Meaningful Judicial Review of Prosecutorial Discretion," *University of Pennsylvania Law Review*, 145, p. 1323: "The commonly stated rationales for bestowing virtually unlimited discretion to prosecutors in making charging decisions . . . [include] . . . promoting prosecutorial and judicial economy and avoiding delay." See also James Vorenberg, "Decent Restraint of Prosecutorial Power," *Harvard Law Review*, 94, pp. 1548–1549: "Most of the prosecutor's work responds to the fact that there are many more offenses than there are resources to prosecute. He must drop some cases and bargain out most of the others on whatever terms are necessary to prevent the backlog from becoming intolerable. A few will be left for trial – those in which no deal could be made or the prosecutor decided to try for whatever reasons seemed sound to him."

[50] I have not mentioned another important concern with prosecutorial discretion, selective prosecution, in which persons are targeted based on class, race, or other characteristic than their culpability; on this, see Heller, "Selective Prosecution." Clearly, such a practice does not serve either deterrence or retributivism, and has no principled justification.

[51] For a critique of the justice and fairness of plea bargaining, see Kenneth Kipnis, 1976, "Criminal Justice and the Negotiated Plea," *Ethics*, 86, pp. 93–106. An extended study of plea bargaining from the viewpoint of the various legal actors in the system was undertaken by Albert W. Alschuler: 1968, "The Prosecutor's Role in Plea Bargaining," *University of Chicago Law Review*, 36, pp. 50–112; 1975, "The Defense Attorney's Role in Plea Bargaining," *Yale Law Journal*, 84, pp. 1179–1314; and 1976, "The Trial Judge's Role in Plea Bargaining," *Columbia Law Review*, 76, pp. 1059–1154.

[52] Kipnis, "Criminal Justice," p. 104.

[53] In a later article, Kipnis calls into doubt the economic basis for plea bargaining as well, based on the impact that the elimination of the practice would have on charging and sentences (Kenneth Kipnis, 1979, "Plea Bargaining: A Critic's Rejoinder," *Law and Society Review*, 13, p. 555, n. 1). For a fascinating look at the internal contradictions that plea bargaining can pose for the retributivist, see Russell L. Christopher, 2003, "The Prosecutor's Dilemma: Bargains and Punishments," *Fordham Law Review*, 72, pp. 93–168.

that more guilty persons will be punished to some degree, punishing an innocent person to any extent is widely regarded as a more pressing issue (reflected
in the popular saying that it is better to let ten guilty persons go free than punish one innocent one).[54] Concerns have been raised over the coercive nature of
prosecutorial offers and the lack of the deliberative process represented by trial
(not to mention the negotiation process itself, seen by some as antithetical to the
goal of justice normally sought in the criminal justice system).[55] Plea bargaining
may be considered less contentious and more beneficial when the defendant's guilt
is more assured, but in general, the costs of possible conviction of the innocent
may overwhelm these benefits.[56]

CONCLUSION

In this chapter, I have attempted to further discussion about the real-world implementation of (positive) retributivist systems of punishment (or criminal justice
in general). Whereas deterrence is rightly seen as a more pragmatic theory of
punishment (even with its formidable informational difficulties), retributivism
can accurately be deemed idealistic and academic, requiring unrealistic degrees of
government intelligence and tremendous allocation of scarce societal resources to
the criminal justice system. Due to their common utilitarian origins, deterrence
is perfectly suited for economic analysis based on their mutual acknowledgment
of opportunity cost.[57] In contrast, as it is commonly understood and interpreted,
retributivism spares no concern for economic constraints in its pursuit of justice.
This poses a serious problem for retributivist policies in the real world, where
scarcity of resources must be acknowledged and confronted, especially in light of
the analysis presented.

I attempted to demonstrate the implications of a retributivist system of punishment (and prosecution) on the allocation of scarce criminal justice resources,
based on the essential nonequivalence of retributivist and deterrent penalties.
It was shown that significant inefficiencies develop regardless of whether "just
deserts" imply more severe or less severe criminal penalties, an issue that real-
world policymakers who wish to implement such policies will have to confront. By
no means is this meant as an argument against retributivism – or an endorsement
of deterrence – as an abstract theory of punishment; rather it is meant as a realistic
analysis of retributivist policies within the context of resource scarcity. Although I

---

[54] Jeffrey Reiman and Ernest van den Haag, 1990, "On the Common Saying that It Is Better that Ten
Guilty Persons Escape than that One Innocent Suffer: *Pro* and *Con*," in Ellen Frankel Paul et al.,
eds., *Crime, Culpability, and Remedy*, Oxford and Cambridge, MA: Blackwell, pp. 226–248.
[55] Kipnis, "Criminal Justice."
[56] For a general consideration of the issue, outside the context of plea bargaining, see Larry Alexander,
1983, "Retributivism and the Inadvertent Punishment of the Innocent," *Law and Philosophy*, 2,
pp. 233–246.
[57] Jeremy Bentham himself cited excessive cost as an argument against certain applications of punishment: "where the mischief it would produce would be greater than what it prevented" (*Principles of
Morals and Legislation*, p. 171).

agree with those who argue that economics has little role in defining crime[58] or in understanding criminal behavior and the effects of punishment on it,[59] economists do understand, better than anybody, the process and effects of resource allocation, and by using this skill they can play an essential role in analyzing the trade-offs inherent in any system of criminal justice. But it falls to legal and moral philosophers to determine which trade-offs are least unjust, and I hope this chapter has made a modest contribution to this discussion.

[58] For instance, see Jules L. Coleman, 1985, "Crimes, Kickers, and Transaction Structures," in J. Roland Pennock and John W. Chapman, eds., *Criminal Justice: NOMOS XXVII*, New York: New York University Press, pp. 313–328 (arguing, on p. 326, that economic theory "has no place for the moral sentiments and virtues appropriate to matters of crime and punishment: guilt, shame, remorse, forgiveness, and mercy, to name a few. A purely economic theory of crime can only impoverish rather than enrich our understanding of the nature of crime").

[59] For instance, see Mark D. White, 2005, "A Social Economics of Crime (Based on Kantian Ethics)," in Margaret Oppenheimer and Nicholas Mercuro, eds., *Law and Economics: Alternative Economic Approaches to Legal and Regulatory Issues*, Armonk, NY: M.E. Sharpe, pp. 351–373 (arguing that due to its ignorance of character and the will, economic theory cannot predict criminal behavior sufficiently well to determine efficient penalties and enforcement measures), and Paul H. Robinson, 2006, "How Psychology Is Changing the Punishment Theory Debate," in Michael Freeman, ed., *Law and Psychology (Current Legal Issues Vol. 9)*, Oxford: Oxford University Press, pp. 94–104 (bringing current psychological thinking to bear on the rational-choice interpretation of deterrence).

Index

For EU product safety concerns, contact us at Calle de José Abascal, 56–1°, 28003 Madrid, Spain or eugpsr@cambridge.org.

www.ingramcontent.com/pod-product-compliance
Ingram Content Group UK Ltd.
Pitfield, Milton Keynes, MK11 3LW, UK
UKHW042316180425
457623UK00005B/22